THE GROWTH OF RELIGIOUS DIVERSITY

BRITAIN FROM 1945

J M Turner.

1995.

VOLUME I
TRADITIONS

EDITED BY
GERALD PARSONS

ROUTLEDGE

IN ASSOCIATION WITH
THE OPEN UNIVERSITY

The Open
University

A catalogue record for this book is available from the British Library.

ISBN 0 415 08326 5

Edited, designed and typeset by The Open University.
Printed and bound in the United Kingdom by the Alden Press, Oxford.

CONTENTS

PREFACE

This book is the first part of a two-volume set on the history of religion in Britain between 1945 and the early 1990s. It is published by Routledge in association with the Open University. All of the essays in both volumes were written with the needs of Open University undergraduate students primarily in mind. But the authors also hope that the essays in both volumes will be of interest and value to many other readers with an interest in the place of religion within British society in the period since the end of the Second World War.

The authors wish to acknowledge the essential contribution made to the production of both volumes by a number of other members of Open University staff: Jenny Cook (course manager), Jane Wood and Kate Clements (editors), Tony Coulson (librarian), Pam Higgins (designer), and Lyn Camborne-Paynter and Cheryl-Anne O'Toole (secretaries).

The authors also wish to thank Professor John Kent of the University of Bristol for his careful and constructive comments on first drafts of their essays. Each of the authors has benefited from Professor Kent's criticism and observations: needless to say, any inaccuracies or questionable judgements that remain are the responsibility of the authors alone.

The authors of the essays in the two volume are:
Gerald Parsons (Lecturer in Religious Studies, The Open University)
John Wolffe (Lecturer in Religious Studies, The Open University)
Terence Thomas (Staff Tutor in Religious Studies, The Open University)
David Englander (Senior Lecturer in European Humanities, The Open University)
George Chryssides (Senior Lecturer in Religious Studies, University of Wolverhampton)
Kim Knott (Senior Lecturer in Theology and Religious Studies, University of Leeds)

INTRODUCTION: PERSISTENCE, PLURALISM AND PERPLEXITY

by Gerald Parsons

Statue of the Buddha at the Community of the Many Names of God, Llanpumsaint, Dyfed. Photograph by Tom Learmonth.

Whatever else may rightly be said of it, the religious life of Britain in the period since the end of the Second World War has clearly demonstrated at least three marked qualities. First, it has displayed a profound capacity to confound those observers – both academic and popular – who have confidently predicted the steady demise of religion and the emergence of a more straightforwardly secular society and culture in late twentieth-century Britain. Secondly, it has shown a marked tendency towards diversification and variety: the religious constituency and complexion of Britain in the last decade of the twentieth century is much more variegated and multi-faceted than that of the period immediately following the end of the Second World War. Thirdly, the religious life of Britain has also become much more complicated, more puzzling and more intricately interwoven in the decades from 1945 to the early 1990s. All three characteristics are conveniently illustrated by reference to four examples of the practice of pilgrimage in recent or contemporary Britain.

On 15 April 1989, at Hillsborough football stadium, Sheffield, over ninety supporters of Liverpool Football Club, the majority of them young people, were killed when the crowd at an FA Cup semi-final was too great for the capacity of one end of the ground, and the resulting surge crushed the victims against a perimeter fence. In the days that followed, the city of Liverpool expressed its collective sense of grief in a remarkable variety of mourning rituals, formal and informal, religious and sporting, civic and personal. Such rituals, moreover, defied neat classification into one or other 'official' category: on the contrary, 'religious, civic and footballing rituals were intertwined' and defied attempts to disentangle them (Walter, 1991, p.608). One particular ritual act stood out, however.

Beginning on Sunday 16 April, the day after the Hillsborough tragedy, people began to come to Anfield, the Liverpool Football Club ground. In the week that followed over a million people visited the ground, often queuing in silence for hours to get in. Inside the ground, the Kop end, where the home supporters always gather, quickly became covered with flowers, the floral tributes then spreading towards the centre of the pitch itself, whilst the area behind the goal became a carpet of football scarves, pictures and personal messages. The local press, both secular and religious, described the phenomenon in explicitly religious terms: Anfield had become 'a shrine', Liverpool's 'third cathedral' (the official two being Anglican and Roman Catholic); the long queues of mourners became 'pilgrims'; the act of visiting the Liverpool ground became 'the Anfield pilgrimage'. Nor was it only the press that recognized the rich inter-mingling of cultures and symbols thus expressed. The Anglican bishop of Liverpool, David Sheppard, and the Roman Catholic archbishop, Derek Worlock, jointly published their own appreciation of the event, which included the following passage:

Over the goalpost and crash barriers hung red and blue scarves, with flags and banners portraying the Liver bird emblem and the inevitable assurance that 'you'll never walk alone'. On the turf below lay a field of flowers, more scarves and caps, mascots and souvenirs, and, incredibly, kneeling amidst wreaths and rattles, a plaster madonna straight from a Christmas crib.

Blasphemy, unhealthy superstition, tawdry sentimentality? Or a rich blend of personal mourning, prayerful respect and genuine faith?

(quoted in Davie, 1993, pp.206–7)

Nor was the mingling of the religious and footballing symbols limited to the Anfield pilgrimage and shrine. A similar spontaneous interaction occurred at the Requiem Mass held at Liverpool's Roman Catholic cathedral the day after the tragedy. Inside the cathedral, by the altar, hung a huge red Liverpool FC banner, made the night before by a nun on the cathedral staff. Beneath the banner the congregation left more football regalia. Outside, at an additional mass for the thousands unable to get into the cathedral, a temporary altar was covered by another Liverpool football banner which had been left by the altar before the service, and now served as an altar-cloth (Davie, 1993, p.617; Walter, 1991, p.616). Finally, it should be noted, at the official memorial service for the Hillsborough victims on 29 April 1989, the address by John Newton, the Methodist Moderator of the local Free Church Council, ended by running together in a single sentence a biblical quotation from the twenty-third Psalm and another from the unofficial 'anthem' of both the city of Liverpool and Liverpool FC: the victims of Hillsborough, he asserted, would be treasured not only in the hearts of those who loved them, but also in the heart of God, 'who has promised that, even when we walk through the valley of the shadow of death, we shall never walk alone' (quoted in Davie, 1993, p.216).

The theme of death and mourning, bereavement and remembrance links the Hillsborough tragedy and the Anfield pilgrimage with a second example of the place of pilgrimage in recent and contemporary British life. In the 1980s and 1990s, the number of people making visits to British war graves and official cemeteries dating from the two world wars rose dramatically. Personal enquiries to the Commonwealth War Graves Commission, having slumped in the 1960s to less than 1,500 a year, in 1990 numbered 28,000. In 1985, the British government initiated a scheme for subsidized pilgrimages for widows who had so far had no chance to visit the graves of husbands killed some four or seven decades earlier. And commercial tour operators had become confident enough of financial success to offer an increasing range of visits to old battlefields and their associated cemeteries (Walter, 1993a, pp.63–6). The reasons for the increase in such visits are varied: the relative ease of modern travel; changing attitudes to death, grief and bereavement which enable once suppressed emotions to receive expression; the age structure of the population and thus the fact that an increasing number of retired people have been able to visit the graves of husbands or old comrades, whilst others in their forties or fifties may now visit the graves of fathers who they hardly – or perhaps never – knew; the desire of families to honour the memories of more distant relatives and thus restore renewed meaning to once-loved faces, now rapidly becoming mere images in fading family photographs.

As with the reasons for making the visits, so too the reactions to them were varied. High among the responses appear such themes as the creation, at last, of some sense of order out of long-past experiences of chaos and loss; the sense of paying respects, of fulfilling a duty and of keeping faith with those who were killed; the affirmation that their deaths were not in vain; the sense of pilgrims to war graves somehow completing unfinished aspects of their own lives; the sense of relief or release at a process of loss and regret for shared lives that never were, perhaps long suppressed, and only now resolved (Walter, 1993a, pp.75–88). It has also been observed that, even among those who travel to battlefields and cemeteries as tourists rather than in personal pilgrimage, there is often an unexpected moment of great intensity; a discovery that 'for a few moments they have ceased to be tourists and have connected with something very deep' (Walter, 1993a, p.72); moments when, caught unawares by the sheer pathos of so many dignified memorials to long-dead people, both they and their cameras fall into silence.

For those who make such visits as pilgrims the experience, clearly, is tantamount to a rite of passage; most obviously, but not only or simply, the belated fulfilment of a funeral rite which the exigencies of war and the subsequent demands of life had not previously allowed to take place. However, for both those who visit as pilgrims, and those who go as tourists only to be surprised by the intensity of the experience, the experiences no doubt resonate with echoes of that more general celebration of 'Remembrance' which has so marked British national consciousness and identity ever since the First World War, and which is annually restated each November at the Cenotaph in Whitehall and at countless local war memorials, powerfully mingling themes of life and death, religion and remembrance, nation and community (Cannadine, 1981, especially pp.219–26 and 232–4).

Our third example of pilgrimage in modern Britain similarly – though most differently – mingles ideas of religion and community, national myths and symbols, and a rich diversity of intensely personal meanings. The small town of Glastonbury in Somerset has drawn pilgrims for centuries. The subject of a lively tradition and mythology linking it with both early Christian history and Arthurian legends of early Britain, in the pre-Reformation era Glastonbury Abbey was an important English centre of pilgrimage. In recent years it has again become a major focus of the spiritual hopes and aspirations of a remarkably wide-ranging variety of contemporary groups. Consequently, it has once again become a focus for pilgrimages – of many different kinds – and has given rise to what has been called a 'spiritual service industry' (Bowman, 1993a, p.30).

The specifically Christian tradition of pilgrimage to Glastonbury has been revived during this century and continues to flourish, drawing on the rich legacy of Christian association of Glastonbury with the figure of Joseph of Arimathea, the claim that he first brought Christianity to Britain, that he brought the Holy Grail to Glastonbury, and even that he was the uncle of Jesus and brought him, as a child, to Glastonbury (Bowman, 1993a, pp.31–2). There are now annual Anglican and Roman Catholic pilgrimages, the former having started in 1924, the latter in 1950. Since the 1960s the Anglican pilgrimage has also included participation by Orthodox Christians, and since 1986 the Anglican and Roman Catholic pilgrimages have been run over the same weekend. Each pilgrimage attracts several thousand pilgrims. There are also numerous informal pilgrimages by smaller groups of Christians and individuals, and the Anglican diocese of Bath and Wells runs a flourishing ecumenical Retreat House which receives over 2,000 visitors a year (Bowman, 1993a, pp.43–7).

It is by no means only Christians, however, who now regard Glastonbury as once again a focus of pilgrimage. Contemporary Glastonbury also attracts a vast range of other religious and spiritual groups drawn not only by its ancient Christian associations but also by a mixture of Arthurian myths, pre-Christian Druidic origins, a claimed empathy with a distinctively Celtic spirituality, and a particularly close relationship with a network of ley-lines and other symbols of esoteric or astrological significance. Not surprisingly, therefore, Glastonbury has become one of the major centres of New Age interest and concern in Britain, being perceived by a wide range of groups as a place of particularly intense spiritual significance. Consequently, a remarkable variety of New Age and alternative spiritualities, therapies and workshops are now available in and around the town and duly attract a large number of people eager to explore one or other of them (Bowman, 1993a, pp.34–41, 47–55, and 1993b). Nor do the various Christian and New Age pilgrims exhaust the range of religious options in contemporary Glastonbury. The general sense of spiritual interest and significance associated with the place has also drawn to it, for example, Sufis, Buddhists, Bahais and members of ISKCON (Bowman, 1993a).

The phenomenon of a site of ancient Christian pilgrimage now drawing pilgrims of more varied religious allegiance is also evident in our fourth example of pilgrimage in contemporary Britain. In rural mid-Wales, the village of Llanpumsaint stands on a spot traditionally associated with a community of five Welsh saints founded over a thousand years ago. Long a place of Celtic Christian pilgrimage, subsequently enriched by the culture of Welsh Nonconformity, still retaining both Nonconformist chapels and an Anglican parish church, Llanpumsaint continues to manifest a varied Christian presence. It also remains a significant place of pilgrimage, but the destination of the pilgrims is now unlikely to be an ancient Celtic Christian site. The present-day pilgrim to Llanpumsaint will almost certainly be travelling to the Community of the Many Names of God, a syncretistic Hindu-Buddhist community located just outside the village (Davies, 1990, pp.206–7).

Founded in 1973 by a Sri Lankan Guru of mixed Hindu and Buddhist descent (his father was a Buddhist, his mother a Tamil Hindu), the Community of the Many Names of God comprises two farms and includes a temple, a small community of resident members and accommodation for visitors. In the years since its foundation it has become a focus for pilgrimage attracting, in the late 1980s, as many as 15,000 visitors a year, of whom, it was estimated by the Community, about two-thirds were Hindu and one-third of more varied and eclectic religious background and belief. In addition, the Community also attracts a smaller but none the less significant number of Buddhist pilgrims, including representatives of Buddhist groups and communities in London, Milton Keynes and Chithurst in Sussex (Taylor, 1987, pp.100–7).

Although predominantly Hindu in ethos, the Community seeks to include not only Buddhist influences, but also elements of the Christian, Jewish, Sikh and Muslim traditions. In the temple, for example, the statues and pictures include Guru Nanak, Jesus, Mary and St Francis of Assisi as well as Hindu deities and saints. Similarly, the daily and annual cycles of worship include liturgical forms and symbols adapted from religions other than Hinduism. The Community's own guide for visiting devotees welcomes 'anyone wishing to worship the Lord in the Temple ... God's family is one family, and we do not recognize divisions based on differences in religion, race or background' (quoted in Taylor, 1987, pp.108–11).

These four examples of pilgrimage in recent and contemporary Britain suggest both the diversity and the continuing vitality of the religious life of the British in the closing decades of the twentieth century. Consider the number of important themes encountered in just these four cases. First, there is clear evidence of the continuing importance of traditional – and in this case Christian – religion: the role of the Anglican and Roman Catholic bishops of Liverpool in the aftermath of the Hillsborough tragedy; the contribution of the Nonconformist minister at the official Memorial Service; the sheer numbers attending the Requiem Mass the day after the tragedy; the twentieth-century resurgence of specifically Christian pilgrimage at Glastonbury; the still varied Christian presence in Llanpumsaint. Moreover, even in these few examples we see clear evidence of the major ecumenical shift within British Christianity which constitutes one of the most significant changes in British religious life in the period since 1945: at Glastonbury the Anglican and Roman Catholic pilgrimages are now held on the same weekend; in Liverpool, by history and tradition a city of intensely divided rival Catholic and Protestant identities, the two bishops and the leading Nonconformist minister act and write and work together as part of a shared ministry to their city.

Secondly, there is also abundant evidence in these four examples of the residual strength and significance of 'popular' religion, of the deeply rooted urge to respond in a ritual and religious manner to the challenges and tragedies of life and death – and perhaps especially of death – and of the stubbornly recurrent capacity of such encounters with human finitude to stimulate reflection and to surprise by awe. Both the instinctive popular response to the sudden and appallingly public deaths of almost a hundred football fans and also the steady increase in the wish to visit war graves, together with the impact upon those who do visit them, demonstrate the limitations of the 'secularization' that has occurred in British society and culture. However reduced the status and practice of 'official' religion may have become in British life, there apparently remain, not so very surprisingly, considerable reserves of instinctive, 'unofficial' religion within the British population.

Thirdly, in both the explosion of alternative spiritualities and lifestyles whose adherents are now drawn to Glastonbury, and also in the less rampantly eclectic but still determinedly syncretistic ethos of the Community of the Many Names of God at Llanpumsaint, we see compelling evidence of the remarkable diversification that has occurred in Britain's religious life in the period since the Second World War and, especially, from the 1960s. Thus Glastonbury now plays host to an enormous – indeed, bewildering – variety of spiritualities and mysticisms. To spend an afternoon browsing in the bookshops of contemporary Glastonbury is to encounter, in the space of a few shelves, a veritable universe of faiths, theologies and schemes for personal salvation and spiritual fulfilment. Books and pamphlets on most of the major religions compete in cheerful confusion with holistic, homeopathic and ecological recipes for personal and planetary redemption, with esoteric lore and arcane knowledge, and with enthusiastically undisciplined combinations of religious and spiritual ideas from here, there and almost anywhere.[1] At Llanpumsaint, meanwhile, a community with Hindu and Buddhist origins celebrates the

---

[1] The essentially diverse and highly eclectic nature of New Age ideas and beliefs is emphasized by, for example, Heelas, 1993, Lyon, 1993, and Perry, 1992.

diversity of the world's major religious faiths and annually draws to itself large numbers of pilgrims, many of them from Hindu and Buddhist communities now well established in late twentieth-century Britain.

Britain, then, at the close of the twentieth century, has by no means become a simply or straightforwardly 'secular' society. On the contrary, in the course of the last half of the twentieth century, the religious options and alternatives available within British society have become more varied and diverse than perhaps ever before. To its cluster of traditional Christian churches and denominations – themselves a markedly diverse and varied group of religious bodies – and its long and well-established Jewish community, post-Second World War Britain has now added thriving and also diverse Muslim, Hindu and Sikh communities; a fertile sub-culture of New Religious Movements and alternative and New Age spiritualities; and a number of new Christian groups, some derived from the growth of Afro-Caribbean communities and others from the growth of independent evangelical and charismatic groups. And as well as all these specifically religious groups, tendencies and communities, there continues to exist also that reservoir of unspecific residual religiosity which might find expression in occasional religious practice; in a fondness for watching *Songs of Praise* or listening to *Thought for the Day*; in a surprisingly tenacious affection for the remembered phrases of favourite hymns or the *Book of Common Prayer*; in response to moments of crisis such as the Hillsborough tragedy; in an instinctive refusal to describe oneself as definitely atheist; or simply in a nagging suspicion – often fed by very private experiences that do not fit with predominantly 'secular' modes of explanation – that there is 'more to life than meets the eye'.

If late twentieth-century Britain is thus so richly diverse in its varied religious sub-cultures, why, then, has so much attention, both scholarly and popular, tended to focus upon the alleged 'secularization' of modern Britain? Why, for at least two to three decades – from roughly the mid 1960s to the mid 1980s – was so much academic discussion of religion in modern Britain centred upon the extent to which religion was set on an apparently inexorably downward trend? Why was the increasing 'secularization' of modern Britain – its roots, its significance, its likely continuation – so central, for so long, to so much discussion of religion in contemporary Britain?

It may well be that the still widespread assumption that religion has been in steady decline in Britain in recent decades stems, in large part, from too much emphasis and attention being focused upon the statistics relating to attendance and membership in the traditional Christian churches. It is true that, in broad terms, statistics for such matters as membership and active participation, numbers of clergy, and numbers of baptisms and marriages relative to population, indicate an overall pattern of decline within Britain's traditional Christian churches in the period since 1945, and especially since the 1960s. Within that overall pattern, however, there also existed a variety of important exceptions to the predominant trend. Thus, for example, the pattern of 'decline' was not uniform across the whole of Britain: Scotland, Wales and, above all, Northern Ireland, all remained relatively more active in terms of churchgoing and church membership than England, as well as displaying further significant differences among themselves. Within the churches – in England as well as in Scotland, Wales and Northern Ireland – the evangelical and charismatic wings of the churches showed a marked tendency to growth, not decline. And, similarly, within the overall structure of the Christian community, there was a significant increase in the evangelical and charismatic presence, most notably through the growth of Black-led churches and of the House Church and Restorationist movements, and through the activities of umbrella organizations such as the Evangelical Alliance.

Quite apart from such growth against the predominant trend, however, it has also been argued that the implications and significance of even the wider general pattern of decline within the traditional Christian churches has been both exaggerated and misunderstood (Gill, 1993). It has been argued that, real though it undoubtedly is, the decline in active church membership and churchgoing is not a peculiarly twentieth-century phenomenon, nor yet a product of some inevitable process of 'secularization'. Granted that the genuine decline that has occurred is the result of a complex mixture of causes and is not reducible to one neat explanation, yet one of the important but neglected factors may well have been a quite false perception of the strength of the membership of the churches and of levels of churchgoing in the earlier decades of the twentieth century and in the late Victorian period. Nostalgia for a supposed golden age when churches were full (or at least much fuller) may have caused the 'empty' churches of more recent decades to assume a disproportionately negative significance.

Careful examination of the statistics of church building and attendance from the Victorian period onwards – and of the reactions of earlier generations of British Christians to perceived decline in their day – reveals that the Victorian period saw a serious over-provision of churches, particularly among Anglicans, Scottish Presbyterians and Methodists but also among other Nonconformist denominations. The result of competition between denominations and of an intense sense of mission, most of the churches were never full (or even nearly so), and by the beginning of the twentieth century there was already talk of decline. As the twentieth century progressed, so the cycle of the perceived emptiness of many churches leading to a sense of decline, and hence to demoralization, increased. The burdens of upkeep were further exacerbated by demographic changes: rural populations declined, urban ones shifted, and many former church members moved to suburbs. The sense of decline became steadily more oppressive and fed upon itself: declining institutions are not apt to appear attractive to outsiders – or even to those insiders who are more peripheral or marginal in their allegiance. On this interpretation of the evidence, the 'empty church' – supposedly so characteristic a symbol of the fate of religion in recent Britain – was not the product of a loss of belief in the face of a relentless and increasingly pervasive secularity. Rather, 'the empty church' was itself a significant contributory factor to the psychology of the decline in churchgoing – and the decline in churchgoing then seems to have led to a slow but steady decline in actual belief.[2]

At any rate, the decline in churchgoing – whatever its precise cause – does indeed appear to have led to a decline, perhaps not surprisingly, in the prevalence of specifically Christian belief, at least as measured by the standards of traditional Christian orthodoxy. For although a whole variety of surveys in Britain in the 1970s, 80s and early 90s revealed that large numbers of people continued to believe in God – characteristically at least 70 per cent of those surveyed – scholars who subjected the mass of survey data available to detailed examination concluded that, the closer one looked at attitudes to traditional Christian beliefs, the clearer it became that the majority were unorthodox in at least some and often in many of their religious opinions. Moreover, such scholars also noted that the evidence of unorthodoxy increased particularly markedly among the young, even to the point of suggesting that, in this period, a significant generational shift may have been occurring within religious belief and knowledge in Britain (Davie, 1990a and b; Gill, 1993, pp.202–7; Osmond, 1993).

---

[2] For a full statement of this argument see Gill, 1993. Two further details of his argument should be noted. The first is the telling contrast which he draws between the ratios of church buildings to potential church members for Roman Catholics and other major Christian denominations. Despite their substantial efforts in church building, Roman Catholics, Gill points out, did not 'over-provide' church accommodation for their communities. By contrast, the other denominations had too many places for their actual memberships, and yet still went on building more churches. The result, in general terms, was increasingly 'empty' Protestant churches (and in due course closures and an associated sense of 'failure'), but still 'full' Catholic ones. A further consequence was the steady emergence of a Protestant sense of decline and a Catholic sense of growth. The second point concerns the significance of the growth of charismatic, evangelical and Black-led churches in the last two or three decades. Whilst acknowledging their genuine growth, Gill nevertheless urges caution in three important respects. First, he suggests that a significant part of their expansion may be at the expense of other churches – thus adding to the sense of decline elsewhere. Secondly, that current predictions of their likely future growth may be over-optimistic and their large initial growth better understood as conforming to earlier examples of periodic surges in evangelical Christianity in Britain. And thirdly, that in often sub-dividing congregations and taking over large 'redundant' churches, the burgeoning Afro-Caribbean churches may be in danger of repeating the errors of the older denominations, acquiring increasing costs of upkeep whilst reducing overall numbers per single church.

In the period before the Second World War, and even to a large extent in the late 1940s and 50s, most people in Britain still had some direct contact with the churches and with traditional Christian belief – if not from churchgoing itself then at least from Sunday school, from still stoutly Christian religious education at school, or from the BBC religious broadcasting on radio and early television. In the period since the 1960s, however, generations have grown up with an increasingly tenuous link with the churches and traditional Christianity. Not only did churchgoing itself diminish, but in addition Sunday schools underwent a particularly severe decline amounting to a virtual collapse; religious education and the practice of worship in school assemblies became much less overtly Christian; and religious broadcasting similarly became less traditionally and monolithically Christian in tone and content. In such a context, it is hardly surprising that one commentator should conclude that, as religious practice and religious knowledge have both declined, so 'orthodox Christianity and popular belief have, inevitably, been drifting apart' (Davie, 1990b, p.460).

Such a drifting apart of 'orthodox Christianity' and 'popular belief' in Britain in the last twenty-five to thirty years was not, in fact, a new phenomenon. A Mass Observation survey in 1947 – entitled, significantly, *Puzzled People* – had reached conclusions that were not all that different, although they were expressed in a rather different way and on the basis of less extensive survey evidence. It too found widespread belief in God, but in the majority of cases only, at best, a tenuous link between such belief and a full range of traditional Christian beliefs (Mass Observation, 1947).[3] What may perhaps be new in the last quarter of the twentieth century, however, is the degree of sheer ignorance of traditional Christian beliefs; the extent not simply of disbelief in particular doctrines but also of clear knowledge of what those doctrines are in the first place. Increasingly, it seems, there may have been already a substantial loss of contact with a wide range of ideas and concepts, words and phrases, which once constituted a significant part of the Christian background and context of British society and culture (Brown, 1987, p.255; Davie, 1990b, pp.457–62; Osmond, 1993, ch.2).

It cannot be emphasized too often, however, that such a decline in familiarity with traditional Christian beliefs does not at all imply a drastic decline in religious beliefs and ideas in general – or indeed in the incidence

---

[3] And in turn *Puzzled People* itself represented, in many respects, not a new departure but rather a further development of trends clearly identified some thirty years earlier in *The Army and Religion*, a survey of religious attitudes and beliefs among soldiers in France during the First World War. For a brief account of the earlier survey, of the similarities and differences between it and *Puzzled People* and of their shared place within a much longer sequence of surveys and reports, see Gill, 1993, pp.179–82, 187–8 and 201–6.

of religious experience. On the contrary, recent studies of the frequency and nature of religious experience in Britain suggest that such experiences are in fact widespread but often kept secret. Between half and two-thirds of the adult population, it has been suggested, at least once or twice in their lives, may have had an experience of a transcendent kind which, under certain circumstances, they would describe as religious. The experiences described are of varied kinds and include, for example: a profound sense of purpose or patterning in life; a sense of divine presence, sometimes described as 'God', sometimes not; a sense of response to prayer; intense premonitions; experiences connected with death and mourning; a sense of a sacred presence in nature. The special circumstances required for such experiences to be disclosed are often no more than the confidence that disclosure will be treated with seriousness and respect; that it will not prompt dismissal, incredulity or, worse still, ridicule; or that it will not be subjected to rejection or attack. If the perceived taboos surrounding such experiences can be overcome, then it seems there may be a great deal of suppressed and repressed religious experience which might find expression (Hay, 1987 and 1990; Maxwell and Tschudin, 1990).

Among the young, also – who in general, it is agreed, are least likely to accept or even to be familiar with traditional Christian belief – there is no lack of interest in religion as such. Again, on the contrary, some surveys suggest that, as the twentieth century nears its end, many young people who may be antipathetic towards traditional religious doctrines may yet be profoundly 'religious' in the seriousness with which they treat ecological, moral and ethical questions about the purpose of human existence and its relationship to the earth itself (Davie, 1990b, p.462). Similarly, it has been observed of students of religion and religious studies that, whilst not much interested in denominational Christianity, rigorous theology or dogmatics, they are fascinated by religion itself, by spirituality and by mysticism. For such students, talk of 'holiness' may cause unease, but a freewheeling and diffuse religiosity, emphasizing 'wholeness' and 'holistic' approaches, will characteristically find a ready response (Walker, 1992, p.51).

In the British context, moreover, the possibilities for thus exploring religion in a freewheeling, diffuse, eclectic way have never been richer than in the last decades of the twentieth century. In the four decades from the mid 1940s, the variety of major religious traditions present in Britain underwent an immense expansion. Asked to characterize the religious 'identity' of Britain in 1945, it would have been relatively easy and unproblematic to reply that Britain was a Christian culture and society. There was, of course, already a well-established Jewish community, and there were also other groups outside the Christian 'mainstream', as well as a few fairly isolated representatives of other major faiths such as Buddhism, Hinduism, Sikhism and Islam. But in 1945 these were peripheral, marginalized – in many cases one might say almost 'invisible' – minorities.

Forty years later the situation was quite different. The end of empire brought with it substantial migration to Britain from a variety of former colonies. And that in turn brought the religious diversity of the former empire back to Britain's shores. By the 1980s, Britain might still reasonably be called a Christian country in terms of its *majority* religious tradition. But by then it was increasingly impossible to deny that it was also now a fundamentally religiously plural society as well. The well-established Jewish community had been joined by well-established Muslim, Hindu and Sikh communities. Other religious groups and traditions also flourished in increasing profusion, including Buddhism, although in that particular case more by the attraction and conversion of increasing numbers of Britons to one or other variety of Buddhist teaching and practice than as a result of migration to Britain by Buddhists from elsewhere. Although Christianity remained by far the biggest single religious tradition in Britain (though itself sub-divided into various groups), 'religion in Britain' in the 1980s and 90s was, inescapably, a matter of many religions not one. Britain had become a multi-religious society, with all the challenges and opportunities, tensions and dilemmas that that involved.

It is true that even in the early 1990s the multi-religious character of late twentieth-century Britain remained much clearer in some areas than in others. Certainly in most cities – and increasingly even in most towns of any size – the reality of religious pluralism was indeed inescapable. The sheer presence of mosques, gurdwaras and temples alongside synagogues and churches (and sometimes, indeed, occupying now redundant churches) was eloquent testimony in itself. In small towns and rural areas, by contrast, the multi-religious nature of late twentieth-century Britain might still appear a somewhat distant and abstract matter rather than a pressing reality. Such considerations have led to the suggestion that 'a limited pluralism is probably the best way to describe the religious life of Britain' (Davie, 1990a, p.400).

The note of caution is appropriate. But as the examples of both Glastonbury and Llanpumsaint show, even rural areas are by no means exempt from the changing patterns of British religious life. Moreover, the attention of the press and broadcast media ensured that many of the issues raised by increasing religious pluralism were brought firmly – if often sensationally – into the arena of public and popular debate. Thus in the 1980s and 90s increasing numbers of articles and documentaries began to appear about Judaism, Islam, Hinduism and Sikhism, as well as about Afro-Caribbean religious groups, New Religious Movements and New Age spiritualities. Heated debates took place over religious education and the educational needs and rights of minority religious groups. And, of course, the Rushdie affair provided perhaps the single most dramatic symbol of the continuing (indeed, resurgent) significance of religion in public life and debate in late twentieth-century Britain, raising as it did a whole host of other issues about the meaning of 'religious pluralism' or a 'plural society', 'blasphemy', 'free speech', the religious rights of minorities (of several kinds), and so forth.

The religious life of Britain in the final decade of the twentieth century thus exhibited great variety and much intensity. To the traditional Christian churches of Britain (themselves more resilient than many of their critics recognized) and to the Jewish community had been added several thriving religious traditions relatively new to Britain. And beyond the ranks of those formally committed to one of the major world faiths now present in Britain, there stretched two further and much broader strands of religious interest. On the one hand, there remained the many residual believers, many of them probably recalling and valuing occasional experiences of great intensity, yet saying little or nothing about them, and engaging in no regular religious practice. And on the other hand there were the newer brand of religious seekers, happy to be living in a multi-religious society where they might shop around in the supermarket of faiths and combine the ingredients which they found in a seemingly endless variety of interesting ways.[4]

The essays in this volume examine the development of eight of the principal religious traditions of Britain during the period since the end of the Second World War. In so doing, the essays seek, both individually and collectively, to illuminate the processes that led to the religious diversity characteristic of Britain in the late 1980s and early 1990s which is described here. The eight religious traditions are: the traditional Christian churches, Judaism, Islam, Hinduism, Sikhism, Afro-Caribbean religion, New Religious Movements, and 'the religions of the silent majority'. The longest of the essays is the first, on the traditional Christian churches. The substantially greater amount of space allocated to this tradition reflects both its historical significance within British life and culture, and also the continuing numerical predominance of the churches concerned within the structure and texture of recent and contemporary British religious life. The relative strength and prominence of the Christian tradition as a whole within British religious life between 1945 and the early 1990s is also reflected in the allocation of essays to the 'religions of the silent majority' and to Afro-Caribbean religion. The former, although not only concerned

---

[4] To take but one example: several of the surveys which revealed that, characteristically, something over 70 per cent of the population claimed to believe in God, also revealed that roughly 25 per cent of the population claimed to believe in reincarnation (Gill, 1993, p.206; Perry, 1992, p.96; Walter, 1993b, pp.133 and 144). Since reincarnation is not part of the Judaeo-Christian tradition, this constitutes a striking illustration of the extent to which a popular 'pick-and-mix' pluralism is at work in late twentieth-century Britain.

with the continuing strength and influence of residual Christian belief, takes such diffused Christian allegiance and opinion as a central theme. The essay on Afro-Caribbean religion, meanwhile, focuses predominantly, though again not exclusively, upon the way in which Afro-Caribbean migration to Britain from the late 1940s to the 1960s gave rise to a flourishing and vibrant new strand within British Christianity.

The essay on Afro-Caribbean religion also demonstrates a further principle in the construction and organization of the volume as a whole. The essays on Judaism, Islam, Hinduism and Sikhism, together with that on Afro-Caribbean religion, all focus upon religious traditions which, in a British context, are predominantly sustained by, and representative of, ethnic minority communities. It is for this reason that the essays in this volume do not include a separate treatment of Buddhism, the development of Buddhism in a British context being distinctive precisely by not being so closely linked to the history and development of a particular ethnic community. The essay on New Religious Movements, however, includes some discussion of Buddhism – a reflection of the similar pattern of development among both Buddhist groups and New Religious Movements in Britain. (The second essay in this volume's companion, *Issues*, includes a more extensive discussion of Buddhism and its adaptation to a specifically British context.)

In the companion volume, a further seven essays explore key issues that engaged the attention of the various religious traditions present in Britain since 1945. It is the authors' collective hope that the essays in both volumes will contribute to the emergence of a clearer understanding of the origins and implications of the religious diversity of contemporary Britain, the growth of which they chart.

Bibliography

BOWMAN, M. (1993a) 'Drawn to Glastonbury' in Reader, I. and Walter, T. (eds).

(1993b) 'Reinventing the Celts', *Religion*, 23, pp.147–56.

BROWN, C. (1987) *The Social History of Religion in Scotland since 1730*, Methuen, London.

CANNADINE, D. (1981) 'War and death, grief and mourning in modern Britain' in Whaley, J. (ed.) *Mirrors of Mortality*, Europa, London.

DAVIE, G. (1990a) '"An Ordinary God": the paradox of religion in contemporary Britain', *The British Journal of Sociology*, 41, pp.395-421.

(1990b) 'Believing without Belonging: is this the future of religion in Britain?', *Social Compass*, 37, pp.455-69.

(1993) '"You'll Never Walk Alone": the Anfield pilgrimage' in Reader, I. and Walter, T. (eds).

DAVIES, D. (1990) 'A Time of Paradox Among the Faiths' in Cole, D. (ed.) *The New Wales*, University of Wales Press, Cardiff.

GILL, R. (1993) *The Myth of the Empty Church*, SPCK, London.

HAY, D. (1987) *Exploring Inner Space*, Mowbray, London.

(1990) *Religious Experience Today: studying the facts*, Mowbray, London.

HEELAS, P. (1993) 'The New Age in Cultural Context: the Premodern, the Modern and the Postmodern', *Religion*, 23, pp.103–16.

LYON, D. (1993) 'A Bit of a Circus: notes on Postmodernity and New Age', *Religion*, 23, pp.117–26.

MASS OBSERVATION (1947) *Puzzled People: a study in popular attitudes to religion, ethics, progress and politics in a London borough*, Victor Gollancz, London.

MAXWELL, M. and TSCHUDIN, V. (1990) *Seeing the Invisible: modern religious and other transcendent experiences*, Arkana, London.

OSMOND, R. (1993) *Changing Perspectives: Christian culture and morals in England today*, Darton, Longman and Todd, London.

PERRY, M. (1992) *Gods Within: a critical guide to the New Age*, SPCK, London.

READER, I. and WALTER, T. (eds) (1993) *Pilgrimage in Popular Culture*, Macmillan, London.

TAYLOR, D. (1987) 'The Community of the Many Names of God: a Saivite ashram in rural Wales' in Burghart, R. (ed.) *Hinduism in Great Britain: the perpetuation of religion in an alien cultural milieu*, Tavistock Publications, London.

WALKER, A. (1992) 'Sectarian Reactions: pluralism and the privatization of religion' in Willmer, H. (ed.) *20/20 Visions: the futures of Christianity in Britain*, SPCK, London.

WALTER, T. (1991) 'The mourning after Hillsborough', *The Sociological Review*, 39, pp.599–625.

(1993a) 'War Grave Pilgrimage' in Reader, I. and Walter, T. (eds).

(1993b) 'Death in the New Age', *Religion*, 23, pp.127–45.

1

CONTRASTS AND CONTINUITIES: THE TRADITIONAL CHRISTIAN CHURCHES IN BRITAIN SINCE 1945

by Gerald Parsons

Inauguration of the Council of Churches of Britain and Ireland in Liverpool, 9 September 1990. From the left: Archbishop Worlock, Bishop Sheppard and John Newton. Photograph by Carlos Reyes-Manzo, Andes Press Agency.

> William Temple's *The Church Looks Forward* (1944) makes a convenient starting point. There Temple, looking to the post-war situation, advocated as the ideal an integrated society on a coherent Christian pattern. He argued that 'the Church' – for him essentially the Church of England – had the right to lay down the principles which should govern the ordering of human society…
>
> (Kent, 1980, p.73)

> Whether in the global scale or just within the confines of these islands off the shore of Western Europe, Christians have to live with religious pluralism … Like most of the other countries of the old Christian 'heartlands' Britain is now a 'multi-faith' society.
>
> (Cracknell, 1990, p.129)

The subject of this essay is the changing nature, position and experience of the traditional Christian churches of Britain between the late 1940s and the early 1990s. As the two quotations above suggest, central to that experience was the transition from a social and cultural context in which it could still make considerable sense to speak of Britain as 'a Christian society' to one in which Christianity was simply the largest religious tradition within a thoroughly religiously plural society. This essay will focus on the group of Christian churches – Anglican, Presbyterian, Methodist, Baptist, Congregational and Roman Catholic – which primarily constituted that tradition in the latter decades of the twentieth century.

This is not to deny that there were also other well-established groups in Britain during this period representative of the Christian tradition, broadly defined. Thus, for example, such diverse groups as the Salvation Army, the Pentecostalists, the Brethren, the Seventh Day Adventists, the Quakers, and the Unitarians were also significant elements in the overall Christian presence. Such groups, however, as well as having to some extent distinctive or unorthodox beliefs or forms of organization, were also numerically considerably smaller than the major denominations noted in the opening paragraph. Thus, in 1970, just over half-way through the period under review, whilst the total membership of the Anglican, Presbyterian, Methodist, Baptist, Congregational and Roman Catholic churches in England, Scotland, Wales and Northern Ireland was calculated as 8,058,697, the total membership of all the other Christian denominations together was only 723,158 – a figure that included not only the groups listed above but also the various Eastern Orthodox churches present in Britain and the rapidly growing community of Black-led churches (Davie, 1990a, p.398). On both grounds therefore – the combination of relatively small size and the tendency to distinctiveness of belief or organization of such groups – the present essay will focus upon the numerically predominant Christian churches of post-war Britain. In so doing it will address what may reasonably be called the 'mainstream' of traditional British Christianity.[1]

As the title of the essay implies, a study of the post-war history of the major Christian denominations of modern Britain reveals *both* the emergence of significant contrasts *and* the maintenance of marked continuities. Indeed, so crucial is this tension between change and continuity that it is appropriate to begin with two very broad characterizations of the churches' positions in, respectively, the late 1940s and the early 1990s.

In the late 1940s the religious life of Britain was still principally defined by the traditional denominational structures and identities – Anglican, Presbyterian, Methodist, Baptist, Congregationalist and Roman Catholic – of modern British Christianity. The presence within British society of other religious groups notwithstanding, in the context of the late 1940s discussion of the place and status of 'religion in Britain' would still characteristically have assumed that this meant, for all practical purposes, discussion of Christianity as represented by these major denominations. They provided the dominant features of the religious landscape; their presence and influence constituted the overwhelming bulk of the religious life and the religious activity of immediately post-war Britain. Moreover, the status of such 'traditional' or 'mainstream' Christianity was endorsed implicitly and maintained by the religious aspects of the 1944 Education Act. True, that Act, even as it required that the school day should begin with a collective act of worship and that religious instruction according to an Agreed Syllabus be given regularly to all pupils, did not actually specify *what* religion was thus to be presented. But in practice the conferences which defined each Agreed Syllabus did not make provision for the representation of faiths other than Christianity, and it is clear that it was assumed tacitly that a generalized form of Christianity – non-denominational, but definitely 'mainstream' – was what the Act envisaged. It was also what it produced (Cox and Cairns, 1989, pp.2–4).

It is possible to argue that, because the religious education thus provided was so unspecific and undoctrinal, in the long run it weakened the position of traditional Christianity in British society (Hastings, 1991, p.421), but the assumption of the Act was quite the opposite. As well as recognizing pragmatically that undenominational teaching was necessary if inter-denominational rivalry over the Education Act was to be avoided, the Act also assumed that the presentation of an undenominational Christianity in schools would make sense to children against the background of

---

[1] In the present context, this definition, of course, implies no value judgement concerning either the beliefs or organization of the groups outside the traditional denominational 'mainstream' of British Christianity. It merely explains the reasons for the focus of the present essay, at the end of which we shall return, briefly, to some of the ambiguities implicit in this distinction.

the more specific teachings provided by the churches. In fact, this assumption was already inaccurate and unrealistic (Cox and Cairns, 1989, pp.3–4), but in the present context it is the general confidence in the validity of the assumption in the mid to late 1940s that is significant.

Religious broadcasting in the immediately post-war period offers another pertinent illustration of the position of mainstream Christianity. In the late 1940s the religious output of the BBC was firmly Christian – and indeed predominantly Anglican, though not exclusively so. It is true that by the close of that decade this religious 'monopoly' was beginning to encounter steadily mounting pressure for wider religious representation in BBC broadcasting, but in the late 1940s, unorthodox or non-believing opinion was still strictly limited and controlled in broadcasts. The traditional mainstream Christian position was carefully shown in a consistently good light, opposition to it being held within what were deemed respectable and safe limits (Wolfe, 1984, chs 25, 26). Now it can be verificated.

The social and cultural position of the churches was thus protected. The principal challenges then perceived were the decline in numbers of active church members; the secular assumptions of an intellectual establishment, many (but by no means all) of whose members were self-consciously and often overtly unbelieving; and, perhaps most significantly, the recognition of widespread indifference or at best benevolent neutrality towards religion and especially towards the specifically doctrinal or theological dimensions of belief. As a Mass Observation survey of a London borough concluded in 1947, whilst actual hostility towards religion was not widespread and 'an attitude of "goodwill" towards the *idea* of religion and religious faith' was apparent, this frequently co-existed with a 'hostile attitude towards the Church, and a personal religious faith of an exceedingly vague and unorthodox kind'.

> To very many religion has come to mean little more than being kind and neighbourly, doing good when opportunity arises. Belief in the Golden Rule, common factor of numerous religious and ethical systems, persists, but without the sanction of faith, or any other sanction than habit and vague memories of childhood teaching.
>
> (Mass Observation, 1947, p.157)

This was not a new situation. The roots of just such a widespread but diffusive pattern of belief can be traced at least to the later decades of the nineteenth and early decades of the twentieth century – as the churches themselves had long been aware (Parsons, 1988a). In the late 1940s, however, the churches could confront such challenges in good heart, confident that their traditional denominational structures remained adequate to address the post-war situation. The founding of the British Council of

Churches in 1942 had already signalled the beginning of an ecumenical co-operation between the churches which would become increasingly prominent in the post-war period, but in the late 1940s British Christianity remained firmly denominational. Denominational identities were still clearly, even fiercely, defined, especially in the case of Roman Catholicism which fostered a self-consciously separate sub-culture. The various denominations worshipped in distinctive ways. The ethos of the various churches remained distinct and definable, and denominational loyalties strong.

Comparison of this state of affairs with that which pertained in the early 1990s is revealing – of both continuities and contrasts. Denominational structures still remained important. For all the intense ecumenical efforts of the intervening half-century, and despite an immense growth in inter-denominational co-operation, most of the schemes for actual union had failed. And yet, if denominational structures and identities thus survived, for the most part at least they did so in a quite different overall context. By the late 1980s the traditional denominations had become something like partners – some more prominent, some less – in an unofficial 'ecumenical establishment'. Increasingly, in seeking to speak to society (as opposed to addressing their own members), the churches spoke less as individual denominations and more as a community of traditional Christian churches. Similarly, their worship and their theologies, though still retaining individual emphases, had moved much closer together and now looked more like one another than ever would have been imaginable in 1945.

Indeed, by the late 1980s – and for some time before that – the most important differences within the community of traditional Christian churches in Britain appeared to lie not *between* denominations but *across* them. They lay, for example, between those with evangelical, 'born-again' and charismatic 'spirit-filled' spiritualities and those who remained more conventional and less effusive in their faith and worship. Or again, they lay in the contrast between those whose faith and theology were conservative and whose beliefs were traditional, and those whose faith, theology and beliefs were, in one way or another, liberal, radical or politicized – be it by, for example, a critical and liberal attitude to the Bible and the Christian tradition, by feminism, or by a conviction that radical political action was an essential element of Christian faith. Or, again, there were divisions between those for whom issues of personal, and especially sexual, morality were resolved on strict and traditional lines by an appeal to the biblical text or the traditional teaching of the church, and those for whom such issues were more ambiguous, more open to personal choice, more susceptible to 'modern' and 'permissive' solutions.

All these issues cut decisively *across* the traditional denominational divisions of British Christianity. By the early 1990s it was no longer possible, as it would have been forty years earlier, to give even a tolerably clear definition of the nature of each traditional denomination. Whilst each retained important elements of its traditional ethos, each had also moved closer to an ecumenical middle ground and at the same time had tended to become increasingly internally diverse as radical, evangelical, traditionalist, charismatic, feminist, liberal and ecumenical emphases and interest groups competed for attention and influence. Increasingly, charismatics, feminists or theological liberals (or any other sub-group one might choose) might find more in common with fellow charismatics, feminists or liberals in another denomination than with other members of their own denomination who did not share their particular charismatic, feminist or liberal orientation.

And whilst all this went on *within* the traditional Christian churches, their overall context within British society and culture had also changed. On the one hand there had been a significant decline in numbers of churchgoers, clergy and churches. For example, membership of the major denominations fell from just over 8 million in 1970 to just over 6 million in 1987. The total for other denominations had, meanwhile, risen from some 723,000 to 835,528 (Davie, 1990a, p.398). Moreover, there had also been a decline in the churches' status within society. They remained significant in national life, and conventional institutional religion remained one of the most popular voluntary activities. But that whole cultural context, in which to discuss 'religion in Britain' was essentially to discuss the major Christian denominations, was now quite gone.

By the early 1990s informed discussion of 'religion in Britain' would still include the traditional churches, but now as only one element in a much wider variety of religious groups and traditions. Religion in Britain in the early 1990s included well-established Jewish, Muslim, Sikh and Hindu communities; an assortment of New Religious Movements and New Age philosophies and spiritualities; and, within the Christian tradition itself, both new and expanding Black-led churches and local and independent evangelical churches, which stood outside the structures of conventional British Christianity and seemed to possess a marked capacity for growth in notable contrast to the decline evident in most of the traditional denominations. Religion in Britain in the early 1990s was a much more complex and richly diversified phenomenon than it had been in the late 1940s – and even if the Christian churches, taken together, continued to constitute by far the largest single religious tradition in British society, such diversification inevitably transformed their position within the overall pattern and structure of British religious life.

The changed circumstances were reflected in the religious broadcasting of the BBC and attitudes towards religious education. Religious broadcasting by the BBC was no longer exclusively Christian, nor geared to the promotion of an exclusively favourable view of Christianity. Indeed, from as early as 1977, the official objective of BBC religious broadcasting had been redefined as: 'to seek to reflect the worship, thought and action of the principal religious traditions represented in Britain, recognizing that those traditions are mainly, but not exclusively Christian' (Annan, 1977, p.319). The position concerning religious education was more ambiguous but no less revealing. The 1988 Education Reform Act sought to clarify and make more specific the clauses of the 1944 Education Act concerning religious education. The 1988 Act required that the religious education provided in state schools should 'reflect the fact that the religious traditions in Great Britain are in the main Christian, whilst taking into account the teaching and practices of the other principal religions represented in Great Britain'. It also reiterated the requirement for a daily act of worship and stipulated that this worship should be 'wholly or mainly of a broadly Christian character' (Cox and Cairns, 1989, pp.27, 33). There are two significant points here. Firstly, unlike the 1944 Act, even as it asserts the priority of Christianity, the 1988 Act explicitly requires recognition of other religious traditions as well. Secondly, despite such recognition, the passing of the Act caused considerable controversy because of the prominence it gave to Christianity. It was, indeed, a far cry from the easy 'Christian' assumptions of the 1944 Act.[2]

Such thumbnail sketches of the position of the traditional Christian churches at the beginning and end of the period under review are, inevitably, impressionistic and incomplete. Nevertheless, they convey something of the tension between change and continuity within the principal British churches during the post-war period and thus also provide a starting point for closer study. It is impossible in a single essay to trace in detail the processes of change and continuity within each of the individual Christian denominations of post-war Britain. Instead, in the present essay we will examine the post-war history and experience of the traditional Christian churches in Britain in three main stages.

Firstly, we will examine the case of the Roman Catholic church in post-war Britain and will suggest that the transformations that occurred in this tradition, though particularly striking and profound, were in fact indicative of much wider patterns of change which affected most of the traditional Christian churches in this period. Secondly, we will examine developments in the other main churches of post-war Britain. Third and finally, we will identify a number of key trends which have affected the traditional churches in general during this period, and in so doing will return to the question of the contrasts between and the continuities within the situations in which the traditional British churches found themselves in the late 1940s and the early 1990s.

[2] For a more detailed discussion of the 1944 and 1988 Education Acts and their significance for religious education, see Volume II, Essay 5.

1 'Into the mainstream': Roman Catholicism in post-war Britain

At first sight, it would seem improbable that the history of the Roman Catholic church in post-war Britain might provide a viable and helpful framework for the interpretation of the history of the traditional British churches in general in this period. After all, England, Scotland, Wales and Northern Ireland are traditionally 'Protestant' countries – not, of course, exclusively, but predominantly so, and by very clear majorities in each case. Thus, English Protestantism is traditionally distrustful of Roman Catholicism, which historically conditioned notions of Englishness have long associated with 'foreignness', 'disloyalty' and 'oddity'. Moreover, despite the fact that for much of the post-war era the Catholic Church continued to make notable gains in numbers of members (whilst the other traditional English churches suffered decline in membership for most of the years in question), yet the 'informal' or 'residual' religious allegiance of the English remained unquestionably and firmly, if also often very vaguely and confusedly, with the Church of England, or one or other of the Protestant Nonconformist churches (Hastings, 1991, p.605). Similarly, Scotland and 'Scottishness' are proverbially, if often ambiguously and confusedly, associated with the Scottish Presbyterian tradition (Brown, 1987, pp.6–14; Hunter, 1991, pp.78–84; Walker and Gallagher, 1990, pp.1–7). Wales, also, is traditionally no less strongly associated with Protestant Nonconformity (Davies, 1990, p.211; Jenkins, 1975, pp.44–8). And, moreover, as with the English case, quite apart from the question of regular religious practice, the residual penumbra of religious allegiance within Scotland and Wales in the post-war period remained overwhelmingly Presbyterian or Nonconformist, not Roman Catholic. In Northern Ireland, meanwhile, the ascendancy of Protestantism continued to be not only a religious but also a political reality of ongoing and frequently tragic significance (Badham, 1990; Bruce, 1986; McSweeney, 1989).[3]

Nevertheless, there remain good grounds for concentrating initially in this essay on Roman Catholicism. If regular church attendance figures are used as the criterion (as opposed to general statements of religious allegience, regardless of actual practice), then by the 1980s the Roman Catholic church had a serious claim to be the largest denomination in Britain (Hornsby-Smith, 1989b, p.85). This, of course, is only part of the picture – as already suggested, *residual* religious allegiance cannot be

---

[3] For a fuller discussion of the relationship between denominational allegiances and concepts of national identity, and especially the significance of the Catholic–Protestant division, see Volume II, Essay 3.

ignored if the subtleties of the position and influence of the various traditional denominations in modern Britain are to be properly understood. But it remains important, none the less, that Roman Catholicism had thus become so statistically significant an element within the overall pattern of *regular* religious practice within the Christian community. Moreover, there is also the question of how Roman Catholicism in Britain changed in the post-war period, both in respect of the ethos and nature of the Roman Catholic community itself and in respect of the Roman Catholic church's position within British life in general and amongst the traditional Christian churches in particular – two processes that were inextricably bound together.

In 1945 British Roman Catholicism remained what it had deliberately sought to be for almost a century, namely, a distinctive sub-culture with clearly, even aggressively, demarcated boundaries between itself and the surrounding non-Catholic culture. Catholics were different. And the differences were not merely noted by others but were proudly owned by Catholics themselves and upheld and sustained as symbols of their distinctive religious identity and commitment. Since the mid-nineteenth century, the Roman Catholic church in Britain had aimed to create a Catholic community that was, as far as possible, not only religiously but also socially and educationally self-sufficient. Thus, even as Roman Catholicism ceased – in general – to be actively discriminated against and became accepted as a minority tradition within British life, so the Catholic church itself set about creating and maintaining a religiously self-disciplined sub-culture (Parsons, 1988b).

The specifically religious expression of this distinctive sub-culture was to be found in the structure of the church, in the nature of Catholic belief and devotional life, and in Catholic moral teaching. Thus, the Catholic church was a disciplined and centralized hierarchy. Clerically dominated, the Catholic faith was set out for the laity in the Catechism, taught to them by the clergy, and was clear, certain and authoritative. The individual Catholic's duty was to fit obediently into the scheme. In devotional terms the heart of Catholic faith lay in regular attendance at mass (which was celebrated in Latin and at which the priest was the centre of attention within the ceremonial, the celebrant on behalf of the people, and the congregation was largely reduced to being a passive audience), in regular confession to a priest, and in a variety of distinctively Catholic devotional practices such as Benediction, the saying of the Rosary, the Stations of the Cross and devotions to the Virgin Mary. Fasting before communion and abstaining from meat on Fridays were similarly distinctive Catholic activities. In terms of moral teaching, meanwhile, Roman Catholicism was distinguished by a particularly strict and severe stance in matters of marriage and sexual morality. Marriage was held to be indissoluble: consequently divorce was (religiously speaking) impossible. Artificial contraception was also contrary to the church's teaching, and a matter of particularly grave sin since its use required deliberate and premeditated decision, and thus could not be regarded as a momentary lapse. This strictness in matters of sexual morality was part of a Catholic worldview – theological, devotional and moral – commonly recognized by historians (Coman, 1977, pp.4–5 and ch.2; Coventry, 1982; Hastings, 1991, ch.31), but probably nowhere better evoked than in the opening chapter of David Lodge's novel of post-war Catholic life, *How Far Can You Go?* (Lodge, 1980a, pp.1–29).

The bans on contraception and divorce and regulations such as the Friday abstinence from meat distinguished Roman Catholics from the rest of society. Such sub-cultural distinctiveness was further consolidated by the attempt to sustain a separate system of Catholic schools, by the discouragement of mixed marriages between Catholics and non-Catholics, and by Catholics being encouraged to focus their social lives within a Catholic context, joining Catholic societies and forming Catholic friendships. In the immediately post-war period, moreover, the typical Catholic parish in England and Scotland remained urban, working class and, in many cases, had a sense of identity as not only Catholic but Irish as well. In such ways the Catholic church of the late 1940s and the 1950s remained, as Adrian Hastings has put it, 'a law unto itself' (Hastings, 1991, p.473). It was a confident church: confident in itself and its achievements in the last century; confident of its ability to continue to attract converts; confident in its organization and discipline; confident in its certainties and order. And yet, beneath the surface of this apparently resolute and monolithic church, important changes were already, slowly, under way. Thus, in the 1950s there were modest initiatives in Catholic worship, as for example in the use of the 'Dialogue Mass' which introduced some lay participation (albeit still in Latin), in permission for evening celebrations of mass, and in reforms of the liturgy for Easter Week (Crichton, Winstone and Ainslie, 1979, ch.4). By the end of the 1950s permission had also been given for the Lord's Prayer to be used on occasion with non-Roman Catholic Christians (whereas in the immediately post-war years even this modest exercise in ecumenical contact had been forbidden).

Of equal significance, however, was the process of social change that began to affect British Catholicism in the post-war period. Divided – in England and Scotland at least – principally between an old aristocratically and 'county'-based Catholic community that had survived from pre-Reformation days, and a new working-class Catholicism largely resulting from Irish immigration, British Catholicism had historically lacked a strong middle class, such middle-class support as it had being predominantly the result of conversions (Coventry, 1982, pp.10–11). Post-war social developments began rapidly to change this situation. The coming of the welfare state; the rise in the number of Catholic grammar schools in the wake of the 1944 Education Act (which enabled the Catholic church to extend its educational provision); a consequently rapid rise in the number of Catholics who went on to higher education; and the general increase in social and geographical mobility of the post-war era; all of these factors set in motion a social transformation within British Roman Catholicism. By the end of the 1950s, British Catholicism had begun to develop a new, university-educated, geographically mobile, professional middle class. It had also begun to expand noticeably beyond its traditional urban and inner-city areas of strength, and to develop a new suburban – and, again, significantly middle-class – style of parish.

Such developments were soon to transform the life of the Roman Catholic community in Britain, but in the late 1950s this was not yet clear. Certainly, it is important not to allow nostalgic versions of Roman Catholic history to portray the 1940s and 1950s as a kind of golden age in which a disciplined and ordered church was blissfully free of the turmoils and divisions which it subsequently experienced. There were undoubtedly already significant tensions and discontent within the Catholic community, not least over the traditional teaching on contraception and the perceived authoritarianism of some priests (Hornsby-Smith, 1987, pp.26–31). Nevertheless, the Roman Catholic church in Britain at the close of the 1950s gave the appearance of being monolithic and disciplined, confident and successful. Probably more respected in British society than ever before; with numbers increasing and converts in England alone in 1959 at 13,735; with a school system stronger and more extensive than ever; and with a new upwardly mobile middle class – it must, indeed, have been a good time to be a Catholic bishop (Hastings, 1991, p.561).

Then came the 1960s. The 1960s, as we shall see, were to prove a challenging and tumultuous decade for the traditional Christian churches of Britain in general – and indeed, in retrospect, a watershed for the religious life of post-war Britain as a whole. For Roman Catholicism, however, the impact of the 1960s was particularly dramatic. The general social and cultural ferment of the 1960s – the sudden sense of broadened horizons and increased prosperity, the pervasive and often rebellious challenge to established authorities, the emergence of increasingly informal and permissive lifestyles and moral values – coincided with two crucial developments *within* the Roman Catholic community itself.

Firstly it coincided with the coming to maturity of that post-war, grammar school and university-educated generation of Catholics noted above. The older, relatively small pre-war Catholic middle class had shared both the traditional distinctiveness and the tradition of lay obedience to authority of pre-war and immediately post-war British Catholicism.

Indeed, since so many, proportionally, of them were converts this was only to be expected: converts in any tradition tend to adopt the more traditional and even extreme versions of their faith precisely because of the significance of their conversion experience. By contrast, the new – and numerically much more significant[4] – post-war, grammar school and tertiary educated middle-class Catholic generation was very definitely not dominated by converts opting out of the cultural mainstream and into a self-consciously defined sub-culture. On the contrary, they constituted a group who, Catholic by birth and nurtured within the sub-culture, had then ventured decisively beyond it through their education – developing in the process a tendency to form ideas and opinions shaped not only by Catholicism but also by the wider cultural influences to which their education had introduced them. Such Catholics tended to be unwilling to accept the traditional 'massive authority of the parish priest' (Coventry, 1982, pp.11–12). *Melton: similar — particularly :– e/Hilt E, Avick.*

The other significant development was the Second Vatican Council. Summoned by Pope John XXIII – who had been elected in 1958 as an elderly and, it was supposed, safely conservative figure – the Council met in Rome for four annual sessions between 1962 and 1965. It proved to be a genuinely momentous event. The Roman Catholic church, for so long officially monolithic, authoritarian, theologically conservative and opposed to ecumenism, suddenly officially embarked upon a process of renewal, reform and dialogue. Vatican II, as the Council became known, set in motion a process of debate and change from within, which transformed the Roman Catholic church. In place of the old clerically dominated and hierarchical model of the church came one in which the key concept was the church as 'the people of God' and in which the laity were called to participate fully with the clergy in the life of the church. Ecumenical contacts and dialogue with other Christians became not merely permissible but desirable. The liturgy was to be celebrated not in Latin but in the vernacular language. Worship was to become more participatory, with preaching taking a more prominent place and the laity becoming more involved in the services. And a whole variety of theological issues previously regarded as closed became open to discussion. Even the traditional teaching on contraception came under review: in 1962 a Pontifical Commission was set up to study the family, population and birth control, and when Pope John died in 1963 his successor, Pope Paul VI, enlarged the

---

[4]   The significance of the numbers involved here may be gauged from the estimate that, in the case of English Catholicism alone, there were only a few hundred Roman Catholic university graduates a year before the Second World War, whereas by the mid 1960s there were as many as 5,000, and another 4,000 completing courses at Colleges of Education (Sharratt, 1977, p.132).

Very similar idea Ifd.

Commission and specifically called for a re-examination of the church's traditional teaching on contraception in the light of the arrival of the contraceptive pill.[5]

At first the impact of Vatican II on British Roman Catholicism was moderate enough. British Catholicism, intent on maintaining its identity and confident of its progress on the basis of that strategy, had not shared in even the modest questioning and calls for change that had already emerged in French, Belgian, Dutch and German Catholicism prior to the calling of Vatican II. For most British Catholics the first – and for some time probably the only – significant effect of the Council came in 1964 with the introduction of English to major sections of the liturgy. Initially, only specific minorities within the Catholic community were particularly exercised by the Council. For a small minority of both priests and laity the Council was a cause of intense optimism, the dawn of an opportunity to initiate a new and radical Catholicism. By the mid 1960s a variety of radical initiatives had been started. Thus, for example, in 1962, when edged out of his job as editor of the *Catholic Herald* newspaper for being too progressive, Michael de la Bedoyere founded *Search*, an informal newsletter which acted as a focus for radical Catholic opinion. In 1964 another periodical, *Slant*, was founded with the explicitly radical aim of articulating a Catholic faith informed by Marxism. The Dominican journal, *New Blackfriars*, meanwhile, under the editorship of Herbert McCabe, mediated critical and left-wing thought to the Catholic middle class. One might also note that a short volume of essays entitled *Objections to Roman Catholicism*, published in 1964 by a group of critical but would-be loyal Catholics, became a bestseller; and, indeed, that the cheap paperback edition of the actual *Documents of Vatican II* also became a minor bestseller; and that in the early and mid 1960s there was an upsurge of letters to both the Catholic and national press from an increasingly prominent, articulate and critical Catholic graduate middle class (Coventry, 1982, p.16; de la Bedoyere, 1964; Hastings, 1991, pp.565–6, 571–2; Sharratt, 1977, pp.131–3). At the other extreme, meanwhile, there were clergy and laity for whom the changes initiated by Vatican II inevitably constituted a retrograde or even threatening step; a betrayal of the Catholicism in which they deeply believed (and to which some of them had converted), and tantamount to a 'Protestantization' of the Catholic church and faith. They included such prominent figures as

---

[5] It should not be thought, however, that Vatican II was simply and unambiguously 'liberal'. Although the Council represented a massive liberalization in comparison with the strict conservatism and rigidity of the Roman Catholic church prior to the Council, it was also a compromise between liberal and conservative elements in the church. The documents and pronouncements of the Council reflected this and thus contributed to the debates within post-Vatican II Catholicism about just how far the changes were intended to go.

Frank Sheed, one of the most successful lay Catholic apologists of the post-war era; Dom David Knowles, the widely esteemed historian of the monastic and religious orders in England; and the novelist and convert Evelyn Waugh (Hastings, 1991, pp.483–4, 565, 567–8).

It was not until the second half of the 1960s that the impact and implications of Vatican II began to be felt widely within British Catholicism. The most obvious impact was in the area of worship and liturgy. The fully vernacular mass was introduced in 1967 and quickly became the new norm. Increasingly, also, temporary altars were introduced to enable the priest to celebrate mass facing the people, and the laity were encouraged to participate in the liturgy in a variety of ways, including reading from scripture and leading the prayers. The central act of Roman Catholic worship thus became, in general, less formal and ceremonial and more communal. Other aspects of Catholic devotional and spiritual life were similarly transformed. Traditional devotional practices such as the Rosary, Benediction, Stations of the Cross or Devotions to the Sacred Heart declined in popularity whilst parish prayer groups, bible study and discussion groups were introduced. The practices of confession, fasting and abstinence from meat on Fridays were reinterpreted so as to reduce the emphasis on simple obedience to rules and encourage instead conscientious reflection on the importance of personal responsibility and commitment in Christian life. Theological emphases changed too: the traditional emphasis on passive and obedient reception of a package of doctrines to be believed was replaced by an approach that was at once more exploratory, more experiential, more tentative, and also more biblical in style. Among the new Catholic middle class especially, discussion of belief became common and a new genre of paperback theology – often by theologically informed and articulate lay Catholics – flourished (Coventry, 1982, p.22; Sharratt, 1977, pp.131–2).

The changes did not occur everywhere with uniform speed, nor were they everywhere welcome, nor did the older traditions simply disappear. Different parishes moved at different paces (the newer suburban middle-class parishes often moving much faster than the older working-class parishes) and often the same parish might contain different emphases side by side, effectively having different sets of worshippers at masses at different times, celebrated in more or less modern style (Hornsby-Smith, 1975 and 1989a, ch.5). Such variations notwithstanding, however, the overall change that had occurred by the 1970s was remarkable. The extent of the transformation, it has been observed, may be measured by consideration of two striking contrasts. Thus, on the one hand, it is clear that no Roman Catholic in the 1950s could have imagined the scale of the changes in Catholic worship and devotion that were to occur by the early 1970s, whilst young Catholics in the 1970s similarly could not easily imagine what the worship and devotional ethos of their church had been two decades earlier. And on the other hand, there is the question of the relationship between Catholic worship and devotional life and that of other major Christian denominations. In the 1950s the differences between them were glaring; by the 1970s, the overwhelming differences between Roman Catholic worship and that of other major Christian denominations had gone – indeed, modern Roman Catholic and modern Anglican worship in particular might on occasion appear almost identical (Hastings, 1991, pp.526, 567).

The greater similarity in matters of worship, moreover, was not the only example of the impact of Vatican II upon relationships between Catholicism and the other major Christian denominations. It had been one of the aims of the Council to foster a new and closer relationship with other churches – thus, the presence of observers from other churches at the four sessions of the Council was a major innovation. The subsequent transformation of relations between Catholics and non-Catholics was as dramatic as the internal transformation of Catholic worship and devotional life. At the official level in Britain it resulted at once in the participation of Roman Catholics in ecumenical meetings and activities. Thus, in 1964 Roman Catholics were for the first time *active* observers at the Faith and Order Conference of the British Council of Churches at Nottingham. Also in that year, Cardinal Heenan accepted, as head of the English Catholic community, an invitation from the Archbishop of Canterbury and the Chief Rabbi to become a joint chairman with them of the Council of Christians and Jews. In 1966 the Archbishop of Canterbury, Michael Ramsey, paid an official visit to Pope Paul VI in Rome. It was not the first such visit – Ramsey's predecessor Geoffrey Fisher had visited Pope John XXIII in 1960 – but the symbolic significance of Vatican II can be seen in the different moods of the two visits. On the insistence of the pre-conciliar Vatican bureaucracy, Fisher's visit had been strenuously low key, almost clandestine, lest it should seem to afford official recognition to Anglicanism. Ramsey's visit was not merely open but highly publicized and celebratory in tone – and from it came directly the setting up of a joint Roman Catholic–Anglican Commission to study doctrinal differences between the two churches. At the local level, meanwhile – and equally importantly, especially in the long run – inter-parish and inter-denominational contacts and co-operation between Catholics and non-Catholics began to flourish in many areas (Chadwick, 1990, pp.316–23; Coventry, 1982, pp.28–30; Hastings, 1991, pp.522–3, 568–9).

Finally, and no less importantly, along with changes in worship, devotional life, theological style and attitudes to ecumenism went a fundamental change in the relationship between clergy and laity. Vatican II called for the replacement of the clerical and hierarchical model of the church in which the clergy led and the laity followed obediently, by a consultative, participatory, 'collegial' model in which clergy and laity co-operated as the whole 'People of God' in taking responsibility and making decisions in the church. As with the changes in liturgy, so also here the change of style was welcome in varying degrees in different parishes and it was notable that it was the new tertiary educated post-war Catholic middle class that enthusiastically embraced the new participatory model of the church – which was not entirely surprising since the active, vocal, critical, consultative outlook required precisely the skills and attitudes with which their higher education had equipped them. By the 1970s, however, parish and diocesan councils and consultative commissions on a wide variety of aspects of church life had already become widespread.

The change in ethos between pre-Vatican II and post-Vatican II Roman Catholicism in Britain has been well defined in terms of two vocabularies reflecting, respectively, the persistence of pre-Vatican II attitudes and the presence of post-Vatican II attitudes within the post-conciliar church. The vocabulary of pre-Vatican II attitudes includes, characteristically: hierarchy, uniformity, segregation, coercion, non-participation, obedience, certainty, authority, passivity, dependence, and uncritical loyalty. The vocabulary of post-Vatican II attitudes, by contrast, characteristically includes: 'People of God', pluralism, ecumenism, collaboration, participation, co-operation, questioning, democracy, activity, independence, and critical loyalty (Hornsby-Smith, 1989a, p.204).

The foregoing description of the changes in British Catholicism as a result of the Second Vatican Council, though not without hints of tensions within the process, on the whole appears to imply that the transition was a smooth one. It was not. Between the pre-conciliar Catholicism of the 1950s and the post-conciliar Catholicism of the 1970s and 1980s there lay a period of intense controversy in the late 1960s. Nor was the post-conciliar church of the 1970s simply a neat replacement of the old pre-conciliar church. On the contrary, another of the striking contrasts between the pre- and post-conciliar churches was the extent to which the old clearly definable British Catholicism of the 1950s had been replaced by a much more varied, complex, contested phenomenon.

The issue of birth control and the traditional Roman Catholic prohibition of the use of contraception provided the crisis point. In the early and mid 1960s the general atmosphere of reform at the Second Vatican Council, together with the appointment of the Pontifical Commission to consider the family, population and birth control (including, specifically, the Pill), had prompted a widespread hope that the church's traditional teaching on contraception would be revised. The issue was increasingly debated by informed lay Catholics. In 1966 and 1967 it became known that the Commission was moving towards a recommendation for change: contraception was to be a matter for individual Catholic consciences. Many laity, especially middle-class laity, now anticipated the Commission and practised artificial contraception in good faith. Not a few of the more liberal clergy similarly counselled parishioners to the effect that a conscientious decision on their part was morally acceptable.

In 1966, matters took a dramatic turn with the very public resignation of a leading English Catholic priest and theologian, Father Charles Davis. A prominent English Catholic theologian, editor of the prestigious journal the *Clergy Review*, and a well-known speaker, Davis had concluded that the Pope was being fundamentally dishonest over the birth control issue. (The Pope was by then publicly stalling on the issue whilst insisting that the traditional teaching remained strictly in force until a future pronouncement was made.) Davis left both the priesthood and the church and denounced the entire system. The furore that ensued was considerable and revealed that, just one year after the end of Vatican II, there were profound tensions within the church. On the one hand, the suddenness and totality of Davis's action seemed extreme and exaggerated, even if many of his specific criticisms of the church were well founded. On the other hand, the ferocity of much of the official reaction – especially from the Bishops – towards those who expressed any sympathy with Davis suggested that, whatever Vatican II might have said, traditional authoritarianism was alive and well in the church (Clements and Lawlor, 1967; Davis, 1967; Hastings, 1991, pp.573–5).

The conservative instincts and outlook of many of the Bishops had already become evident in other, earlier pronouncements concerning aspects of Vatican II – a tendency that was particularly notable among the bishops of the Scottish Catholic church (Cooney, 1982, pp.96–7). The Davis controversy sharpened the sense of tension within the church. The publication of the Papal Encyclical on birth control, *Humanae Vitae*, in 1968 then finally ignited controversy in earnest. The Encyclical reaffirmed the traditional teaching, despite the known recommendation for change of the Pope's own Commission. It was a moment of crisis. The clash was not merely over contraception but over authority and the reality (or not) of the post-conciliar model of the church as participatory not authoritarian. The Commission – which had symbolized participation in having a majority of lay experts – had reported for change. Papal authority had pronounced otherwise. There was an explosion of opposition from both laity and clergy. The more conservative bishops took a hard line against priests who dissented publicly from the Encyclical. A lay-led group, the Catholic Renewal Movement, was set up to assist such priests. In Scotland a similar group emerged, the Scottish Lay Action Movement (renamed the Scottish Catholic Renewal Movement in 1969).

Arguably, the two most significant results of the furore over *Humanae Vitae* were the decisive independence of mind shown by the laity and the disappointment and demoralization that ensued in the church as a whole and among the clergy in particular. The laity – and especially the new, critical middle-class laity – took the Vatican II rhetoric of participation at face value and simply declined to take any notice of the Pope. Regarding birth control as a matter of personal conscience, they continued to practise contraception and to regard themselves as good Catholics. For the clergy matters were more difficult. Privately – in the context of confession, for example – liberal clergy might continue to advise that contraception was a personal matter. But they faced discipline from the bishops if they dissented publicly. It was a demoralizing situation and a deep and lasting decline in ecclesiatical morale duly set in.

Thus, despite the genuine transformation that had occurred in British Catholicism as a result of Vatican II, the Roman Catholic Church in Britain in the first half of the 1970s seemed curiously indecisive and dejected. Some of the early radical initiatives had by then ended altogether – *Search*, for example, had ceased publication in 1968, and *Slant* had folded in 1970. A crisis had also set in among the clergy and the religious orders. The combination of radical re-thinking of traditional roles in the light of Vatican II and yet reassertion of traditional style authority in *Humanae Vitae* (and also in the matter of clerical celibacy, which had been reaffirmed as essential in 1967) led to an increasing number of clergy leaving the priesthood and an even sharper decline in the religious orders. The losses from the priesthood, moreover, included many of the most academically and intellectually able among the clergy – a trend that continued steadily into the 1980s, thus causing concern that the overall intellectual quality of the priesthood was declining as well as its numbers (Hastings, 1991, p. xxiv).[6] Figures for converts and for regular mass attendance and confession also began to decline in the late 1960s and early 1970s – and for British Catholics the experience of such decline was the more shocking because it stood in marked contrast to the steady statistical advance which had for so long been characteristic of British Roman Catholicism (Hastings, 1991, pp.580, 631–4).

For conservative and traditionally minded Catholics this crisis and decline demonstrated how mistaken the reforms of Vatican II had been, or at the very least proved that the liberals and radicals had taken things altogether too far, too fast. By the end of the 1960s and the beginning of the 1970s conservative pressure groups were emerging to defend traditional Catholic practices and beliefs and oppose changes in the church. In 1968, for example, the Catholic Priests Association was set up by a group of Catholic clergy opposed to what they saw as the lax theological liberalism

[6] For two instructive personal accounts of the process of leaving the Roman Catholic priesthood see, Hastings, 1978 and Kenny, 1986.

of Vatican II; in 1970 a similar lay movement, *Pro Fide*, was founded; and the Latin Mass Society, meanwhile, promoted the continued celebration of the mass in Latin wherever possible. The late 1960s and early 1970s also brought the emergence of another significant group. In 1967 in America a Catholic Charismatic Movement had begun. It duly crossed the Atlantic and established itself within British Catholicism. Its influence was neither straightforwardly conservative, nor straightforwardly radical. On the one hand, it was very biblical, personal, informal and ecumenical – characteristics that might seem to locate it on the liberal post-conciliar wing of the church. On the other hand, it was also theologically conservative and uncritical, centred upon intense personal spirituality, and impatient with the debates over structural reform of the church that followed Vatican II (Hastings, 1991, pp.639–40).

The active membership of these various groups – including the Catholic Renewal Movement – was numerically relatively small. But their significance lay in the way in which they spoke for much wider constituencies and trends within the Roman Catholic community. They were significant also in both demonstrating and contributing to the sense of conflict and dissatisfaction in the Roman Catholic church in the 1970s. The leadership of the church was caught between various groups of post-conciliar radicals eager for more change, and varieties of traditionalists who wanted a halt to change and reconsolidation. It was at once a recipe for widespread frustration and a symbol of how far the church had changed since the 1950s.

Just as the opening chapter of David Lodge's novel *How Far Can You Go?* provides an effective evocation of the ethos of the pre-conciliar Catholicism of the 1950s, so also the later chapters provide a telling portrayal of the ferment and excitement of Vatican II and the early 1960s: the crisis of *Humanae Vitae*; the emergence of the pressing question of just 'how far you can go' in dismantling traditional belief without throwing out something essential; and the confusion and conflict within Catholic life by the mid 1970s (Lodge, 1980a, chs 3–7; Parsons, 1992). As Lodge observed in an essay published in the same year as *How Far Can You Go?*, the Catholic church which had emerged out of the upheaval of Vatican II was at once a more decent, humane and open-minded Christian community than it had been, yet also arguably blander, duller and more amorphous. It was also now 'a pluralistic kind of church' which looked much more like Anglicanism than would have been imaginable before Vatican II and in which radicals, conservatives and charismatics could 'all find a corner to do their thing with like-minded people' (Lodge, 1980b, p.187). And yet – a point also noted by Lodge at the end of both his novel and his essay – in 1978 an extremely conservative Pope, John Paul II, had been elected and was clearly intent on reasserting traditional discipline in the Catholic church worldwide. What then was the future of British Catholicism? In the 1980s, Pope John Paul II did indeed set out to halt the process of change in the Roman Catholic Church and reassert traditional teaching and authority. His conservatism encouraged the traditionalists in the church and frustrated the radicals. But by the end of the 1980s it was clear that, the Pope notwithstanding, British Catholics were, on the whole, determined to retain and consolidate the fundamental changes initiated by Vatican II.

At the beginning of the 1980s two events indicated the difficulty the Pope was likely to face in reversing the post-conciliar trends within British Catholicism. In May 1980, after some two years of preparation, the Catholic Church in England and Wales held a National Pastoral Congress in Liverpool. There were over 2,000 delegates, the vast majority of them lay and selected at local level to represent their churches and dioceses. The aim was the renewal of the church in the spirit of the teaching of Vatican II. The reports that emerged showed the influence not just of Vatican II but also of the new Catholic graduate middle class within the post-conciliar church. The reports called for a range of initiatives for which the Catholic Renewal Movement had also been calling for years: Catholic entry into the British Council of Churches; acceptance of the use of contraception; acceptance of inter-communion with Christians of other denominations, especially within mixed marriages; a review of the possibility of ordaining both women and married men. The bishops, caught between a determinedly post-conciliar laity and an equally adamantly conservative Pope, subsequently published a response which welcomed the ethos of the Pastoral Congress but stalled on or rejected the specific calls for change. This caused disappointment; but significantly the bishops also subsequently represented the views of the laity to Rome and stoutly defended the post-conciliar ethos of the English and Welsh church (Hastings, 1991, pp.644–7; Hornsby-Smith, 1987, pp.36–41; Stanford, 1993, pp.20–22, 55, 67–9). The Pope's visit to Britain in 1982 similarly demonstrated the extent of the shift in outlook that had taken place in British Catholicism since Vatican II. There were fears among 'progressive' Catholics that the presence of a deeply conservative but personally highly popular Pope might initiate a renewed conservatism within British Catholicism. The reaction of the laity to the visit, however, showed that independence of mind was firmly established: they liked the Pope as a man, but continued to insist on deciding for themselves on moral and social issues (Hornsby-Smith, 1987, pp.41–2; 1991, ch.6).

The attitudes revealed by the National Pastoral Congress and the Pope's visit to Britain were confirmed in the later 1980s by the publication of the results of over fifteen years of sociological research by Michael Hornsby-Smith into changes in Roman Catholicism and Roman Catholic belief in post-war Britain, especially since Vatican II. Hornsby-Smith examined the social structure of post-war Catholicism; the changing nature of parishes, priests and parishioners, and Catholic beliefs (Hornsby-Smith, 1987; 1988; 1989(a) and (b); 1991; 1992). By the mid 1980s, he concluded, Catholics in Britain had ceased to be the distinctive sub-culture they had been in the 1950s. They had moved 'into the mainstream' of British society; or put more pejoratively, they had become 'just like everyone else'. Although still characterized by a distinctive stance on some issues – their tendency to be prominent in opposition to abortion for example, though even there Catholic opinion was far from uniform – British Catholics tended, by the 1980s, to share much more markedly the moral and social values of British society in general than had been the case twenty-five years earlier. More and more Catholics were seeing issues of personal morality, including divorce, but most especially contraception, as areas of personal decision in which the advice of the clergy and the teaching of the church would be valued but not definitive. Moreover, the Catholics who took this view included many of those who were highly articulate and committed within the church.[7] By the mid 1980s Catholics were also much more likely to marry non-Catholics and to form circles of friends which were not predominantly Catholic. They also increasingly showed signs of deciding for themselves in matters not only of morality but of belief – thus many lay Catholics would practise inter-communion with other Christians whatever the official line of their church. And, significantly, such independence appeared particularly marked among younger Catholics.

What, then, was the balance-sheet of gains and losses, strengths and weaknesses in British Roman Catholicism by the late 1980s and early 1990s? The situation was, above all, ambiguous. On the one hand, despite both the widespread disillusionment after the high hopes of Vatican II and the 1960s, and the restraining influence of a highly conservative Pope, there had nevertheless been a steady consolidation of many aspects of the legacy of Vatican II. The laity were increasingly involved in the active life and mission of the church – although the more radical continued to protest at the restrictions that remained (Hastings, 1992, pp.23–4). The integration of Roman Catholicism with both British society and the overall Christian community of Britain was more thorough than at any time since the

---

[7] This transformation in lay Catholic attitudes was, once again, noted by David Lodge in one of his subsequent novels. Just as *How Far Can You Go?* portrayed the generation which actually struggled with *Humanae Vitae*, so in his later novel, *Paradise News*, the central character, Bernard Walsh, reflecting on his experience as a Roman Catholic parish priest in the 1980s, observes: 'Perhaps fortunately for me, the great row about birth control and *Humanae Vitae*, which dominated Catholic pastoral life in the sixties and seventies, had died down by the time I came onto the parochial scene. Most of my parishioners had settled the question in their own consciences, and tactfully avoided raising it with me' (Lodge, 1991, p.151; see also Parsons, 1992, p.190).

Reformation. Lay Catholics, as we have noted, freely mixed with and married into the mainstream of British life. And at the 'official' level, the later 1980s saw the re-organization of the formal structures of ecumenical co-operation in Britain and the full integration of the Roman Catholic church into the new arrangements which came into force in 1990. Indeed, the recognition that it was essential to include Roman Catholicism fully within the 'ecumenical mainstream' of British Christianity was one of the principal causes of the decision to replace the British Council of Churches with a new Council of Churches for Britain and Ireland and local councils in England, Scotland, Wales and Ireland (Palmer, 1990).

On the other hand, British Roman Catholicism also remained deeply troubled and beset with difficulties. The attempt to reassert papal authority in the 1980s exacerbated the dissatisfactions and conflicts which had been initiated back in 1968 by *Humanae Vitae*. Despite the willingness to 'choose for themselves', significant numbers of young middle-class Catholics left the church, frustrated by the continuing limitations of the post-conciliar church. Others stayed, but were demoralized by having to exist in ongoing 'conscientious disobedience' to the official teaching of the church in a variety of areas, both moral and theological. The decline in rates of attendance at mass and also in the number of clergy continued, leading to a shortage of priests and an emerging crisis of pastoral provision in many dioceses (Hastings, 1991, pp.xxii–xxv; 1992, pp.22–4; Powling, 1991, pp.153–8; Stanford, 1993, p.19). Moreover, in addition to problems of demoralization and decline there also remained at least two sets of important tensions within the Catholic community. First there was the ongoing tension between 'progressives', who wished to press on with the post-conciliar model of the church, and 'conservatives', who wished, like the Pope, to call a halt to change. Secondly – and perhaps in the long run even more seriously – there was the tension between the mainly middle-class graduate and professional activists and progressives and the relatively passive majority in the pews. The extent to which the enthusiastic, post-Vatican II, lay-participating church favoured by the new middle class at once both discriminated against and left untouched many 'ordinary' Catholics of a less vocal and self-confident variety remained a pressing and unresolved issue.[8]

The British Roman Catholic experience in the post-war decades – and especially the encounter with the social and cultural turmoil of the 1960s – was thus a particularly intense one. Indeed, this very intensity in one sense marks Roman Catholicism out from the other traditional Christian churches in this period precisely because it was so dramatic. Yet in other

[8] For a passionate attack on the 'oppression' of the older working-class Catholicism by the new post-Vatican II middle-class Catholicism, see Archer, 1986.

ways, the Roman Catholic case can be seen not as simply unique and different, but rather as an extreme example of a set of experiences common to most of the traditional British churches in this period.

For example, there is the basic move from separateness into the mainstream: the Roman Catholic entry into the cultural and ecumenical mainstreams was paralleled by a more general shift away from denominational distinctiveness and towards an ecumenical middle ground. Or again, there is the process of grappling with liturgical and theological change *within* a particular tradition: Anglicans, Presbyterians, Methodists, Congregationalists and Baptists also confronted such questions in these decades. Or yet again, there is the encounter with the 1960s – and in particular the challenging of established authority and the rise of a more 'permissive' sexual ethic – and the subsequent reactions to and controversies over these matters in the 1970s and 1980s. And running through all of these issues, for non-Catholics as well as for Catholics, is the underlying question, 'how far can you go?' Indeed, David Lodge's novel of that title may arguably be read as a paradigm not only of Roman Catholic but also of non-Roman Catholic religious life in Britain since 1945 (Parsons, 1992) – a theme to which we will return later.

2 Recovery and consensus: the Protestant churches in the 1950s

In retrospect, it is the quiet and essentially conservative confidence of the major non-Roman Catholic churches of Britain in the late 1940s and 1950s that is most striking. That is not to suggest that there were no controversial issues, nor to ignore the presence of genuinely innovative projects and initiatives. But the controversies and the innovations within these churches in the late 1940s and 1950s were modest when compared with what followed subsequently.

In the decade and a half before the outbreak of war in 1939 the predominant trend within the principal Protestant churches in Britain was one of numerical decline. Initially, the impact of war itself increased the rate of decline, but from the middle of the war onwards this trend began to show signs of being reversed (Brown, 1992, pp.42–7). Confronted with both the background of widespread pre-war decline and the apparent upturn in their fortunes during the later stages of the war, the Protestant churches of Britain seized the coming of peace in 1945 as an opportunity to recover lost ground and reassert their position and relevance within British society. Evangelistic initiatives duly abounded. Thus, in 1945, a Church of England report, *Towards the Conversion of England*, briefly became a minor bestseller.

Although many of its formal recommendations were not implemented the report nevertheless stimulated local activity including, for example, many diocesan, deanery and parochial missions (Welsby, 1984, pp.44–9). In Scotland, similarly, the immediately post-war years brought a series of initiatives in mission and evangelism, characteristically based upon intensive local preparation and visits to all the homes in the target area. The leading figures in the movement were two Church of Scotland ministers, D.P. Thomson and Tom Allen. In the early and mid 1950s Thomson and Allen became the principal organizers of the 'Tell Scotland' campaign of evangelism, which sought to develop such initiatives on a nationwide scale and did so, moreover, on an interdenominational basis, not merely as a Church of Scotland project (Highet, 1960, ch.3).

There were also other initiatives which illustrate both the determination of the churches to seize the opportunity presented by the coming of peace and the ethos of the projects that they initiated. Thus, the Baptist Union launched a 'Baptist Advance' in 1949, and the Congregational Union a 'Forward Movement' in 1950 (Thompson, 1982, p.93). The Methodist Church, meanwhile, organized a series of 'Christian Commando Campaigns', in which evangelists (ministers, deaconesses and laity) concentrated on a particular town and sought entrance to factories, schools, colleges, or indeed any work or leisure venue where they might present their message to substantial numbers of people (Brake, 1984, pp.390–1). Evangelistic initiatives in Edinburgh and Glasgow in 1947 and 1950 were similarly styled as 'Christian Commando Campaigns' – a use of the language and associations of wartime to describe the peacetime strategies of the churches which, if entirely understandable, was also somewhat ironic (Highet, 1960, pp.82–3). *(Robert Wolfe the style in 1967)*

In 1954 and 1955 the American evangelist Billy Graham conducted the first of his mass crusades in Britain. Both in London in 1954 – where it was estimated that in three months his audiences totalled over 1.3 million – and in Scotland in 1955, where he conducted an equally successful six-week long 'All Scotland Crusade' at the invitation of the 'Tell Scotland' movement, he made a remarkable impact. Reactions to Graham varied. As well as enthusiasm for his uncompromising message, his deeply conservative and evangelical theology and his call for decision and conversion, there were also those who criticized him either for his dramatic and emotive style or for the theological and intellectual crudity of the doctrine he presented – or for both. Thus, when Graham was also invited by evangelical students to conduct a mission to Cambridge University in 1955, an Anglican clergyman, H.K. Luce, sparked a substantial correspondence in *The Times* by asking on what basis, since universities existed for the advancement of learning, Graham's attitude to the Bible (which Luce described as 'fundamentalist') could claim a hearing in Cambridge. Similarly, Michael Ramsey, Bishop of Durham (and subsequently Archbishop of Canterbury during the turbulent 1960s), suggested that Graham's theology and his demand for immediate decision might have the effect of stifling the mind (Welsby, 1984, pp.59–60). Others questioned just how effective Graham and his mass crusades were. How enduring and permanent were the effects of his preaching and the 'decisions for Christ' that he prompted at the climax of his meetings? Was the major effect of such campaigns really to be seen in new converts, or was the principal influence, rather, to be found in the raising of the morale of those already in the churches and in the conversion into enthusiasm and greater commitment of those already on the periphery of church life? Such questions were voiced about both Graham in particular and the post-war evangelistic campaigns in general by informed (and not overtly hostile) observers in both England and Scotland (Highet, 1960, ch.4; Thompson, 1982, p.93).

Whatever conclusions are drawn, however – and it is also possible to cite evidence for both the long-term effect of Graham's crusades and his ability to reach those completely outside the churches (Bebbington, 1989, p.259; Calver, 1987, pp.26–7) – in retrospect it is clear that Graham's 1954–55 visits were important events in the post-war history of the Protestant churches in Britain. Arguably, they marked a decisive point in the resurgence of an interdenominational evangelicalism which continued to gain in strength and influence throughout our period – a theme to which we will return. In the context of the late 1940s and the 1950s, however, it is possible to see Graham's 1954–55 crusade not only as an important beginning within the post-war history of British evangelicalism but also as the climax and conclusion to the various immediately post-war initiatives in evangelism. Viewed from this perspective, Graham's visit and the response which it evoked was a suitably encouraging symbol of the Protestant churches' apparently successful reversal, during the first post-war decade, of the predominant pre-war pattern of decline. For by the mid 1950s the steady decline of the preceding two decades had been halted.

The precise relationship between the reversal of the process of decline and the various evangelistic campaigns of the post-war years remains, however, elusive and unclear. How far the various initiatives were actually the cause of a modest revival of religion, or conversely how far they were themselves a symptom and reflection of a much more general and broadly based resurgence of interest in religion and the churches is a good – and also a difficult – question. Whatever the verdict, however, it is clear that they were, at the very least, part of what has been described as a 'general feeling of religious revival or, perhaps better, of restoration' within the Protestant churches of Britain in the 1950s. This mood of restored confidence lasted for a dozen or so years and fitted well with the prevalent political and cultural mood of the 1950s – optimistic, idealistic, determined

This is clearly it enabled
the call 48 planned and to offer for the
ordained ministry.

to build a better post-war world, and yet also rather conservative (Hastings, 1991, pp.443–4). But what – evangelism and mission aside – were the other principal concerns of the churches thus encouraged by the post-war upturn in their fortunes?

In common with the nation as a whole, the post-war era presented the Protestant churches of Britain with the problem of reconstruction and the making good of wartime damage. Many destroyed and damaged churches and other church property, especially in the cities, had to be rebuilt, and as new housing was provided and new towns created so new churches were also required for these. At the same time as they confronted the challenge of reconstruction, however, the churches also had to address the possibility that their traditional pastoral and administrative arrangements were in need of reform. Not only had the war disrupted the supply of ordinands and candidates for the ministry in the various churches but, in addition, the demands of both rural and urban post-war ministry suggested the need for new initiatives and greater flexibility in pastoral provision. In rural areas the lack of clergy and of resources to support them was already leading to increasing dependence upon lay leadership and the grouping of several churches under one minister. Thus, for example, in 1949, in South Ormsby, Lincolnshire, several Anglican parishes were grouped into one pastoral unit, moving away from the traditional Church of England ideal of a resident priest in every parish and adopting something nearer to the traditional Methodist pattern of ministry (Welsby, 1984, p.40). Nor was it only the Church of England that thus addressed the challenges of rural ministry. The issue was also addressed, for example, in the Church of Scotland and in the Methodist and Congregationalist churches (Brake, 1984, pp.412–21; Highet, 1960, pp.174–5; Thompson, 1982, pp.89–90).

In the urban context, meanwhile, the churches continued to struggle – as they had for decades already – with the challenge of largely 'unchurched' populations. To this long established dilemma, however, there were now added the steady increase in suburbanization (a process that not only necessitated the building of new churches but also frequently removed key members of existing urban churches); the decline and redevelopment of many town and city centres with a consequent destruction of traditional communities; and the general rise of a more mobile society in which social or family allegiances to particular local churches were loosened or even broken altogether as individuals and families moved to new areas and often failed to re-establish links with a church in their new environment. Such challenges were met in various ways. On the one hand, various denominations (including the Church of England, the Church of Scotland, and the Methodist, Baptist and Congregationalist churches) reviewed their pastoral arrangements and sought to improve both their efficiency and flexibility (Brake, 1984, pp.386–407; Forrester, 1984, pp.161–2; Hastings,

Wickham
Gowland).

1991, pp.438, 462; Thompson, 1982, pp.95–6; Welsby, 1984, p.28). On the other hand, there were also more specific initiatives such as the foundation of 'Industrial Missions' and the appointment of industrial chaplains (Highet, 1960, pp.136–9; Welsby, 1984, pp.35–8). Or again, there were initiatives stemming from the concern of particular groups within the churches, such as the Anglican 'Parish and People Movement', which set out to revitalize parish life by making worship more free and participatory, and by focusing on the parish communion as the main weekly service and the centre to which the rest of parish life related (Hastings, 1991, pp.441–2; Jagger, 1978, chs 2–4). Such concern with worship and liturgy and with the attempt to make them more obviously relevant to contemporary parish life led to calls for revision of the Church of England's *Book of Common Prayer* in order to make its language less archaic and to render it more flexible and adaptable for the needs of particular congregations and occasions. Official recognition of these concerns came in 1955 with the establishment of a Church of England Liturgical Commission (Jasper, 1989, ch.9). And again, the Anglican case was not the only one: pastoral and liturgical rethinking was similarly a feature of other Protestant churches in post-war Britain (Brake, 1984, pp.356–8, 386–407; Hastings, 1991, pp.441–3, 462–3; McIlhagga, 1982, pp.161–4; Thompson, 1982, p.105; Walker, 1983, pp.23–4).

Theologically, the principal Protestant churches of post-war Britain were concerned predominantly with a very 'churchly' set of issues. The nature of the church itself and of the ordained ministry; the meaning of baptism, confirmation and church membership; the nature and meaning of the sacraments – such were the subjects of many of the most important theological works of the late 1940s and 1950s. The various denominations – and the different parties within the denominations – characteristically explored the history of Christianity in general and of their own denomination in particular in order to explicate the meaning of such concepts and ideas. The titles of many of the most significant books demonstrate the ethos of such theological work. Thus from the Church of England came, for example, *The Shape of the Liturgy* (1945); *The Apostolic Ministry* (1946) and *The Ministry of the Church* (1947); *Catholicity* (1947); *The Seal of the Spirit* on baptism and confirmation (1951); and *The Historic Episcopate* (1954). From the Free Church tradition, meanwhile, wartime publications such as *The Nature of Catholicity* (1942), *The Baptist View of Church and Ministry* (1944) and *The Fellowship of Believers* (1944) were followed in the post-war years by works such as *The Catholicity of Protestantism* (a Free Church reply to the Anglican volume *Catholicity*) (1950) and *An Approach to the Theology of the Sacraments* (1956).[9]

[9] For further details concerning these works and for brief accounts of their main arguments, see Brake, 1984, pp.347–51; Hastings, 1991, pp.446 , 462–3; Thompson, 1982, pp.102–3; Welsby, 1984, pp.60–4.

For
many
to discover
the
Church!

If in one sense, however, the theological concerns of the Protestant churches of Britain in these years appear terribly safe, inward-looking, and preoccupied with 'domestic' issues, in another sense, concern with these very issues was anything but inward-looking. Thus it was significant that many of these works, despite an often combative tone, were also attempts to bridge long-standing theological divisions and discern greater common resources within the Christian tradition than had commonly been assumed. To see only narrowness and introspection, therefore, would be to overlook the still predominantly denominational structure of British Christianity in the late 1940s and the 1950s and the still limited parameters of ecumenism. Viewed within that context, explorations of the meaning of concepts of ministry, church membership and church order could be highly innovative, especially when they questioned the rigidity and validity of conventional denominational understandings and divisions on such matters.

The other major strand in the theology of the traditional Protestant churches in this period was emphatically biblical in nature. A generation of Old and New Testament scholars from across the various denominations shared an approach to the Bible which was known as 'Biblical Theology'. It was an approach that insisted on the essential unity of the Bible beyond its various parts. The Bible, according to this theological perspective, was unified by its consistent witness to a number of key theological ideas within the Christian tradition. The Bible – which was therefore very much the church's book – was thus properly interpreted only within the context of the church's preaching. Within that context, moreover, it had a theological authority over and above critical and historical questions about different aspects of the text and its contents. Rightly understood critical and historical questions – about, say, the historical accuracy of a particular passage in the Bible – were part of the preparation for interpreting the biblical text, but the interpretation was properly undertaken only within the context of the church's faith and proclamation. Thus the theological interest in such matters as the nature of the church and its ministry was complemented by an equally church-centred approach to the Bible and its meaning.

Such theological concern for matters of ministry and the nature of the church and the emphasis on the unity of the Bible within the context of the church's preaching were also at once a product of, and a further encouragement to, greater ecumenism. The ideal of greater co-operation, fellowship and unity between the various denominations had steadily gained ground in the inter-war period (Davies, 1979, ch.2; Hastings, 1991, ch.18; Payne, 1972, ch.1). The demands and exigencies of the Second World War then provided further ecumenical contacts, opportunities and challenges. In 1942 the British Council of Churches was founded with official representatives from all of the major Protestant denominations – and also many of the smaller denominations – of England, Scotland, Ireland and Wales (Payne, 1972, pp.5–8, 37–9). It was a key moment, for the Council was to emerge as one of the central organizations within British Christianity in the ensuing decades, not least by virtue of its various departments for issues such as education, evangelism, social responsibility and international affairs. The Council rapidly began to function as a means of enabling the various churches to act together on subjects of national importance and in discussion with government.

In 1946 another important ecumenical moment occurred when Geoffrey Fisher, then Archbishop of Canterbury, preached a sermon in Great St Mary's Church, Cambridge, in which he appealed to the non-episcopal churches to 'take episcopacy into their own system' and thereby open the way to full communion between the churches, whilst not actually uniting them into one church. Despite the fact that this amounted to the Anglicans asking the other churches to change whilst Anglicanism itself changed nothing, the sermon proved to be the beginning of a number of further initiatives. A Joint Conference of representatives of the Church of England and the English Free Churches met for three years and produced a report entitled *Church Relations in England* (1950), which set out the principles upon which negotiations leading to inter-communion might be conducted between the Church of England and other individual Free Churches. In 1955, the Church of England and the Methodist Church began official 'Conversations' to this end, and in 1958 both accepted an *Interim Report* recommending a two-stage scheme whereby the two churches would first unify their ministries and enter into full communion with each other and then proceed to complete union as one church (Davies, 1979, pp.55–8; Welsby, 1984, pp.80–2).

Ecumenical 'conversations' also took place in the 1950s between the Church of Scotland and the Church of England. Out of these came a proposal, in 1957, for the introduction of bishops into the Presbyterian system of the Church of Scotland, and for the introduction of a more conciliar style of episcopacy and a form of lay eldership within the Church of England. In this instance, however, the response to the report of official ecumenical 'conversations' was a negative one. After a fierce campaign in the pages of the *Scottish Daily Express*, the 1959 General Assembly of the Church of Scotland rejected 'The Bishops' Report' (as the 1957 proposal had become known). Official conversations between the churches continued, but the incident revealed the depth of feeling which ecumenical discussions could arouse when historic denominational identities were involved – especially when, as in this case, aspects of national identity were also felt to be at stake and the Church of England could be seen as insensitive to Scottish religious sensibilities and traditions (Gallagher,

1990; Highet, 1960, pp.153–9). The controversy over 'The Bishops' Report' was thus a salutary reminder of the limits of post-war ecumenism. Yet by the end of the 1950s ecumenical activity had become an established feature of the life of the British churches – at both national and local level. The annual calendar of British church life now included an annual Week of Prayer for Christian Unity each January and an annual ecumenically organized appeal for Christian Aid. At the local level, meanwhile, the 119 local Councils of Churches of 1950 had risen to 300 by 1960. Thus despite the many continuing rigidities in inter-church relations, the 1950s witnessed the steady advance of the notion of an overall Christian community in British life, above and beyond denominational differences.

If the ecumenical implications of the predominant theological trends of these years were thus innovatory, however, the overall ethos of the theology of the post-war British churches was not. The decade and a half from 1945 was not an era noted for the radicalism of its theology. Indeed, it has been well observed of the theology of the 1950s that, on the whole, the basic content and substance of Christian belief and doctrine were barely questioned by the churches. There was discussion of how the message might best be presented in a more 'relevant' and 'modern' style, but there was little or no debate about what the message actually was (Clements, 1988, p.146). Thus, even in the pages of the influential journal *Theology* – in which virtually all the theological issues of the day were discussed (and which was edited throughout this period by an Anglican priest, Alec Vidler, who was to figure prominently in the theological upheaval of the 1960s) – the underlying bases of Christian doctrine were seldom debated. There was a confident assumption that the theological foundations were secure and did not require re-examination, and that the interpretation of traditional doctrine to the contemporary world was not in itself problematic. The truth of traditional Christianity was largely taken for granted, whilst in the concern with such matters as ministry, church order and sacraments, efforts were made to tidy up the life of the Christian community (Clements, 1988, pp.152–3; Edwards, 1989, pp.13–15; Welsby, 1984, p.67).

It was, it has been pointed out, the era in which C.S. Lewis – layman, Professor of English Literature and convert from atheism – became firmly established as the most popular and influential contemporary apologist for Christianity. And the keynote of Lewis's theology was a 'no-nonsense' version of Christianity which emphasized God and Christ, angels and devils, sin and redemption, and the authority of scripture, and which – ironically in view of the interests of professional theologians – had little to say about the doctrines of the church, ministry or sacraments (Hastings, 1991, pp. 493–5, 537). But if he thus eschewed many of the preoccupations of contemporary professional theologians, yet in the robust confidence of his version of Christian faith Lewis reflected the prevailing mood of the Protestant churches of Britain in the post-war era. The characteristic mood of Britain's principal Protestant churches at the close of the 1950s was one of solid confidence in the relevance and truth of their traditional teaching combined with enthusiasm for modest initiatives and innovations (in worship or in ecumenical co-operation for example) in the way that teaching was presented. The publication of the *New English Bible* (or at least the New Testament thereof) in March 1961 may serve as a fitting symbol of this mood.

The origin of the *New English Bible* lay in a resolution passed by the General Assembly of the Church of Scotland in May 1946 recommending a new translation of the Bible in contemporary language. Subsequently, representatives of the Church of Scotland, the Church of England and the Methodist, Baptist and Congregationalist churches agreed that such a translation should be undertaken. A Joint Committee on the New Translation of the Bible was set up by these churches, and representatives of the Presbyterian Church of England, the Society of Friends, the Church in Wales and the Church of Ireland were invited to join it – as were representatives of the British and Foreign Bible Society and the National Bible Society of Scotland. The Joint Committee was chaired, successively, by three Anglican bishops (J.W. Hunkin, A.T.P. Williams and Donald Coggan). But the vice-chairman, chairman of the New Testament panel of translators, General Director of the project, and – by general consent – the outstanding influence upon it was the eminent Congregationalist scholar, C.H. Dodd.

The aim was to produce a translation of the Bible that would not only be as accurate a version of the ancient texts as modern scholarship allowed, but would also be dignified enough for public use in worship and modern enough in its language to make the biblical text more accessible – especially to those for whom the traditional language of the existing Authorized and Revised Versions was either opaque, alienatingly old fashioned, or so familiar as to have ceased to have any real impact (Dillistone, 1977, p.204). When the *New English Bible* New Testament was published in March 1961 it aroused much attention. There were queries on details in the translation and some protests that the modern language represented a decline in the standard of English – a theme that would be heard much more strongly in subsequent years about both new translations of the Bible and new liturgical texts. But the general reaction was enthusiastic. The secular press and the broadcast media gave the new translation much attention. The popular reaction was favourable. The book became a bestseller.

A genuinely ecumenical project – innovative in its attempt to make the medium in which the message was delivered more relevant – and a popular bestseller: it was a fitting climax to the Protestant churches' optimism in the 1950s and seemed to suggest a bright future in the 1960s.

But by the time the Old Testament section of the *New English Bible* came out a decade later in 1970 a new translation of the Bible was no longer a symbol of exciting innovation and optimism. By then the mood of the churches had been transformed by the social and cultural upheavals of the 1960s, and what had seemed so innovative in 1961 now appeared rather tamely conventional. For good or ill – and with considerable ambiguity – the intervening decade had transformed both the context and the internal ethos of the traditional Protestant churches of Britain.

3 From confidence to crisis: the impact of the sixties

In the same year that the *New English Bible* became a bestseller, an obscure verse of the traditional version of the Old Testament (Genesis 27:11, 'My brother Esau is an hairy man, but I am a smooth man') became famous as the opening line of a sketch by Alan Bennett in the revue *Beyond the Fringe*. Bennett satirized both the conventional sermon and its unquestioning platitudes, and the would-be trendy clergyman and his attempts to be contemporary in speech and idiom. *Beyond the Fringe* and Bennett's lampooning of the contemporary image of the churches were, it has been observed, part of that wider upsurge of essentially irreverent humour in the early 1960s of which the magazine, *Private Eye,* and the television programme, *That Was The Week That Was,* were other examples. And such calculated irreverence was, moreover, not merely a challenge to traditional religious decorum and convention but was also, in turn, one element within the emergence of a restlessly and relentlessly critical and self-critical spirit during the 1960s (Clements, 1988, p.143). The traditional Protestant churches of post-war Britain were not immune to this ethos. Indeed, the churches contributed their full share to the intellectual and cultural turmoil and turbulence of 'the sixties'. Three incidents in 1962 indicated the change in mood that was to come in contrast to the comfortable confidence of the 1950s. *I was in Sheffield & it was all here (see My Halloween 1932 - 1965)*

From the Nonconformist perspective, 1962 brought the publication of Christopher Driver's *A Future for the Free Churches?*, a frankly critical survey of the recent past and likely future prospects of the Methodist, Baptist, Congregationalist and Presbyterian churches. Driver was not sanguine about the future of the major Nonconformist churches and, indeed, concluded that the extent of their decline relative to their former strength was so severe that they had little chance of recovery as independent entities: their best hope was for union with Anglicanism, albeit over a considerable period of time. Events in the Church of England, meanwhile, supplied further evidence of an emerging challenge to the hitherto prevalent mood within the churches. They also provided both a telling example of the increasing influence and significance of the media – and especially television – in the creation of the churches' public image, and a curtain-raiser to what was to become the symbolic moment in the British Protestant churches' encounter with the changing mores and ethos of the 1960s. In the 4th November edition of the Sunday evening BBC religious discussion programme, *Meeting Point*, the Dean of King's College, Cambridge, Alec Vidler, engaged in discussion with Paul Ferris, an agnostic who had recently published a book about the Church of England. It was Vidler, however, who aroused controversy. The church, he said, should not concentrate narrowly on religion but should seek to help people in the whole of their lives; the church would gain from the presence within it of more questioners since it was too complacent and conformist and suppressed doubt and intellectual integrity; and in questions of morality, including sexual morality, he suggested, there was too much dependence on moral rules as fixed and rigid codes to be obeyed.

The programme caused a furore. Traditionally minded members of the Church of England protested vigorously – although often in ways that suggested that Vidler's criticisms were not without foundation (Clements, 1988, pp.162–8). The programme also provided excellent publicity for the publication of a volume of essays which were the product of several years of informal discussion between a group of Anglican theologians at Cambridge. Edited by Vidler, *Soundings: essays concerning Christian understanding* challenged the theological consensus of the 1950s in which the fundamental beliefs and doctrines of Christianity were taken for granted and raised critical questions about Christian doctrine, the study of the Bible, Christian ethics, and the relationship between religion and both philosophy and science. In the following year Vidler and three other Anglican members of the Cambridge Divinity Faculty published a further and more popular example of theological questioning entitled *Objections to Christian Belief* (Clements, 1988, pp.152–62, 168–71; Vidler, 1962 and 1963).

The controversy sparked by Vidler's *Meeting Point* appearance and fuelled by the publication of both *Soundings* and *Objections to Christian Belief* in turn provided both the prelude and the context for a much more dramatic theological furore in 1963. On the front page of *The Observer* of Sunday 17 March 1963 there appeared the banner headline: 'Our Image of God Must Go'. The article was by John Robinson, the Bishop of Woolwich, and in it he summarized the ideas in his book entitled *Honest to God*, which was to be published the following week. The book – a short volume of only 143 pages, written by Robinson whilst he recovered from a slipped disc – in due course became a bestseller. It also initiated the most widespread and intense theological controversy in post-war British Christianity; became both the symbol and catalyst of Christian radicalism in the 1960s; and arguably marked a watershed in the life of the churches in post-war Britain. However one evaluates the contribution of *Honest to God* – as a basically positive or negative influence upon the churches' life – it is difficult to escape the conclusion that its publication marked decisively the 'end of the 1950s' and the opening, for good or ill, of a new phase in the history of the British churches.

Robinson set out to address the gulf which he was convinced existed between 'the traditional orthodox supernaturalism in which our faith has been framed and the categories which the "lay" world ... finds meaningful today' (Robinson, 1963, p.8). In so doing he argued, for example, that God should not be thought of as 'up there' or 'out there', but rather as 'within the depth of our being'. He took a critical view of the Bible and of much traditional belief – but did so precisely because he believed that by so doing the meaning of Christian faith could be made real for contemporary men and women. His theology was thus optimistic and humanistic, exploratory not dogmatic, flexible not fixed. Responses varied. Inevitably, Robinson aroused a great deal of opposition, much of it intense. Traditional believers – lay and clerical – saw his work as a betrayal and his beliefs as tantamount to atheism. Other theologians, themselves critical of aspects of orthodox belief, nevertheless criticized *Honest to God* as lacking in rigour and merely rehashing the ideas of a number of radical German theologians. And yet others found the book a breath of fresh air, a liberation from anxiety over their own questionings of traditional Christian beliefs and attitudes, and a stimulus to a radical rethinking of the churches' engagement with society (Clements, 1988, ch.7; Edwards and Robinson, 1963).

Perhaps without the publicity of *The Observer* article *Honest To God* would have remained no more than another relatively minor contribution to a flurry of theological questionings within the Church of England in the early 1960s. In fact it became the landmark and symbol of the change of mood which overtook the life of the traditional churches in Britain in that decade. Theologically it opened the floodgates on a new era of questioning and exploration. Whereas the theology of the 1950s had probed questions of ministry, worship and church order but taken the underlying foundations of Christian belief to be secure, the more liberal and radical theologians of the 1960s questioned even the most fundamental of traditional doctrines. Many of the most characteristic theological questions and catchphrases of the radical theology of the mid and late sixties were already present in *Honest to God*, either as the titles of chapters or as sub-headings within chapters. 'The end of theism'; 'the man for others'; 'worldly holiness'; 'the new morality'; 'must Christianity be super-naturalist?'; 'must Christianity be religious?'; 'depth at the centre of life'; 'non-religious understanding of prayer'; 'nothing prescribed – except love'; all these were phrases from *Honest to God* which became part of the radically fashionable theological jargon of the mid and late sixties, either in the specific form noted above or in such related concepts as 'the new reformation', 'religionless Christianity'; 'secular Christianity'; 'man come of age' and so forth.[10]

The titles of three of John Robinson's subsequent books similarly caught the mood of the radical theology of the period. *The New Reformation?* (1965) consisting of a series of lectures in North America developing the ideas expressed in *Honest to God*, caught the contemporary radical sense of both the need and the opportunities of the moment for reform in the churches' life and thought. *But that I can't believe!* (1967) was a collection of short pieces written mostly for the popular press on various aspects of Christian belief as conventionally and popularly understood. It aimed to make Christian belief possible for people who found particular aspects of Christianity as conventionally presented a barrier to Christian faith, but in its calculatedly provocative title it also conveyed the sheer bravado of much of the radical theology of the decade. Finally, *Christian Freedom in a Permissive Society* (1970) (which was a re-presentation of ideas on the nature of Christian morality which Robinson had first explored in a series of lectures on 'Christian Morals Today' in 1963) reflected the concern of the radical theologians of the sixties to move away from an understanding of Christian morality as based essentially on rules and fixed moral codes, and towards one based upon the absolute priority of the command to love and wide flexibility as to how this imperative was to be concretely expressed in specific situations.

There was of course much more to the upsurge of theological radicalism in the 1960s than the controversial views of one particularly turbulent bishop and the controversies that his views generated. In the field of biblical interpretation, for example, the 'biblical theology' of the 1950s, with its emphasis on the unity of the Bible and the need to read it primarily in the context of the church's preaching and proclamation, was confronted by renewed interest in questions of historicity. Confidence in the unity of the Bible was once more challenged by recognition of its ambiguities and of the fact that it was a complex text from a variety of cultures, different from each other and all of them far removed from the twentieth century. In

---

[10] Robinson, it should be noted, did not invent such phrases and concepts. Most of the specific phrases and the ideas behind them were derived either from recent or contemporary German theologians such as Paul Tillich, Rudolf Bultmann and, in particular, Dietrich Bonhoeffer, or, especially in the area of moral theology and ethics, from contemporary American theologians such as Joseph Fletcher. Robinson's great significance, however, was to mediate such ideas to the British public in a popular and accessible form.

Christian ethics, meanwhile, no less a figure than Ian Ramsey – a widely respected Bishop of Durham then tipped to be a future Archbishop of Canterbury – edited an important symposium, *Christian Ethics and Contemporary Philosophy* (1966), in which he endorsed the view that Christian morality was not simply a matter of rules and slavish obedience to commands but involved the application of moral principles in countless particular, empirical situations. And all the while, it should be recalled, the wider context of such moral theologizing was the post-Lady Chatterley trial, post-Pill Britain of the mid to late sixties, in which the liberalization of the laws governing capital punishment, divorce, abortion, the availability of contraceptive advice under the National Health Service, theatre censorship, and homosexuality was high on the political agenda.[11]

In addition to such home-grown experiments in theological questioning, the mid 1960s also witnessed a rush of interest in a wave of American radical theological works such as Harvey Cox's *The Secular City*, Paul Van Buren's *The Secular Meaning of the Gospel*, Joseph Fletcher's *Situation Ethics* and, perhaps most controversially, the 'Death of God theology' associated with William Hamilton and Thomas Altizer. Such transatlantic influences were generally far more overtly and determinedly radical than the ideas of Robinson or any other British theological radicals of this period. Nevertheless, they contributed greatly to the creation of a general sense of theological crisis and turmoil – and in retrospect also contributed a good deal to the widespread disillusionment with the radical theology of the sixties which subsequently quickly set in. In a British context, however, it is John Robinson who remains the most effective representative and symbol of the radical turn in theology in the 1960s, not least because, as Adrian Hastings has observed, just as C.S. Lewis was adept at the popular presentation of traditional Christian belief, so from the radical side 'nobody else in Britain [other than Robinson] could express these things so aptly, so attractively for the mass media, so infuriatingly for the conservative' (Hastings, 1991, pp.537–8). How well one remembers it All .

The engagement of Britain's Protestant churches with the critical and innovative spirit of the 1960s was not, however, only a matter of theology, belief and morality. A sense of urgency and questioning also emerged in matters of ecumenism, pastoral organization and worship, and frequently led to a merging of initiatives in these three areas of the life of the traditional churches. In the ecumenical sphere, the Anglican–Methodist unity talks, which had begun in 1955 and produced an interim report in 1958, resulted in a further report in 1963 which recommended that, ongoing theological differences notwithstanding, the two churches should now commit them-

---

[11] For a more detailed discussion of both the moral debates and their social context, see Volume II, Essay 7.

selves to a two-stage scheme leading to full union. In 1965 the official bodies of both churches approved this in principle and detailed discussions began. By this time, however, the Anglican–Methodist discussions had been joined by a much broader and more ambitious ecumenical initiative.

Internationally, the early 1960s were a period of great ecumenical activity and dynamism. The World Council of Churches was highly active; in developing countries, churches previously constrained by colonialism were becoming more prominent; reunion schemes were advancing in various parts of the world; and there were seemingly endless ecumenical conferences. The British churches shared in this sense of ecumenical optimism. Accordingly, the British Council of Churches Faith and Order Conference at Nottingham in 1964 issued two challenges to the British churches. Firstly, it urged them 'to covenant together to work and pray for the inauguration of a union by a date agreed amongst them', and expressed the hope that the date would be not later than Easter Day 1980. Secondly, it called on the churches to set up areas of ecumenical experiment in new towns and housing estates, or where local congregations wanted them. Although most churches subsequently declined to make such a covenant, local ecumenical initiatives began to develop and by the early 1970s Local Ecumenical Projects and shared churches were becoming increasingly common.[12] Within the Nonconformist community, meanwhile, discussions on union between the Congregationalists and English Presbyterians in the 1960s resulted in the formation of the United Reformed Church in 1972. And on the Protestant–Roman Catholic front, 1966 – as we noted earlier – saw the ground-breaking visit of the Archbishop of Canterbury, Michael Ramsey, to Pope Paul VI. One observer thought the difference in mood between Ramsey's visit and that of Archbishop Fisher in 1960 was more like a distance of five centuries than five years (Chadwick, 1990, pp.316–23).

The emergence of Local Ecumenical Projects was also closely related to widespread rethinking and new initiatives in both worship and pastoral provision during the 1960s. A significant number of new liturgies and orders of service were produced; and in the Church of England, the Liturgical Commission that had been set up in 1955 issued a steady stream of proposals, revisions and new texts, culminating (at this stage, at least) with the publication in 1967 of 'Series II' – a new version of the communion service. Significantly, however, liturgical revision in the Church of England

---

[12] By 1974 there were 46 designated LEPs in Britain, rising to 289 by 1977 (Welsby, 1984, p.176). As Welsby points out, it is clear that, despite some difficulties, such local ecumenical activity did quite as much as (and probably much more than) large-scale national or denominational schemes to bring about greater Christian unity, a point endorsed by Palmer (1990, pp.16–21).

did not end with the production of this new service: even as the Series II service was accepted for 'experimental use', the Liturgical Commission began work on further revisions, including a thorough-going 'translation' of the church's services into modern language and idiom. As well as addressing all the church's services and rites (including, for example, Morning and Evening Prayer and the orders of service for baptism, confirmation, marriage and burial), the work of the Liturgical Commission also furthered the trend towards making the celebration of the Eucharist the main weekly service and the centre of the worshipping life of the ordinary Anglican parish (Jasper, 1989, chs 10–12).

The liturgical movement which had already made such an impact on both Anglican and Roman Catholic worship also increasingly made its influence felt within the Methodist, Presbyterian and Baptist traditions. Indeed, the ecumenical dimensions and implications of developments in worship and liturgy received striking expression. In 1963, at the instigation of the Archbishop of Canterbury, Michael Ramsey, the Joint Liturgical Group was formed with official representatives from the Churches of England and Scotland, the Methodists, Baptists, Congregationalists, Presbyterians and Churches of Christ. The group produced a number of agreed texts including a Lectionary, a Daily Office, Holy Week services and a collection of prayers common to all the denominations (Jasper, 1989, pp.227–9, 268–74; McIlhagga, 1982, pp. 165–6; Welsby, 1984, pp.154–5). Within the Nonconformist churches, there was also a continuing increase in the importance attached to the celebration of Communion as a central moment in the church's spiritual life; a trend towards the use of more liturgically structured forms of service (with, for example, more congregational responses than was customary in these denominations); and a similar trend towards a more structured observance of the Christian year and its cycle of seasons (Advent, Christmas, Epiphany, Lent, Easter, Pentecost, and so forth). And there was a growing emphasis upon the idea of 'Family Services' and 'Family Church' – the conviction that adults and children should worship together rather than be separated (the latter going to Sunday School or Junior Church). Such initiatives led – as in the Church of England – to the call for changes in the language of worship. In the Nonconformist churches too, the sixties saw the beginning of a deliberate effort to translate services into modern idiom (McIlhagga, 1982, pp.165–73; Walker, 1983, pp.25–7).

Across the various denominations, the call for the use of self-consciously modern language in worship – epitomized by the use of 'you' and 'your' rather than 'thee' and 'thy' in the Lord's Prayer – was complemented by increasing enthusiasm for new and linguistically modern translations of the Bible, and calls for new collections of contemporary prayers and new hymns. The process began of compiling both new hymn books and supplements to existing ones, and anthologies of prayers, written deliberately in contemporary style. In many cases the results did not appear until the 1970s, but the initial impetus from which they originated was firmly located in the experimentation of the mid and late 1960s (McIlhagga, 1982, pp.163, 169–70; Welsby, 1984, pp.158–60).

The overall thrust of such changes was towards greater lay involvement in worship and greater informality – albeit in retrospect an often rather structured and controlled, even artificial, 'liturgical informality', though at the time it undoubtedly represented a major break with conventional formality in worship. And beyond such licensed yet still liturgical informalities there lay a further range of experimentation involving 'youth services', 'folk services', eucharists and communions in informal house groups, discussion groups, and an enthusiasm for radically contemporary spirituality such as that represented in the briefly phenomenally popular *Prayers of Life* by the Roman Catholic Michel Quoist (an excellent example of informal ecumenism, in that his collection of contemporary meditations became popular right across denominational boundaries). The ethos of the more extreme varieties of devotional informality of these and subsequent years – in the non-Roman Catholic as well as the Roman Catholic contexts – is perhaps nowhere better conveyed than in David Lodge's fictional accounts of the informal 'agapes' celebrated by his eagerly radical characters and the liturgical arrangements in a radically minded college chapel in *How Far Can You Go?*:

> Each week the students chose their own readings, bearing on some topical theme, and sometimes these were not taken from Scripture at all, but might be articles from *The Guardian* about racial discrimination or poems by the Liverpool poets about teenage promiscuity or some blank-verse effusion of their own composition. The music at mass was similarly eclectic … They sang negro spirituals and gospel songs, Sidney Carter's modern folk hymns, the calypso setting of the 'Our Father', Protestant favourites like 'Amazing Grace' and 'Onward Christian Soldiers', and pop classics like Simon and Garfunkel's 'Mrs Robinson' … or the Beatles' 'All You Need Is Love'. At the bidding prayers anyone was free to chip in with a petition, and the congregation might find itself praying for the success of the Viet Cong, or for the recovery of someone's missing tortoise, as well as for more conventional intentions.
>
> (Lodge, 1980a, p.133; see also pp.141–4)

Innovations in worship and devotional style were accompanied by a growing sense that traditional pastoral arrangements and church structures were inadequate and in need of reform and, perhaps, even replacement. Thus in the Church of England, for example, the 'Parish and People' movement became more radical than it had been in the 1950s, and began to campaign for the development of a new style of parish life, theologically and liturgically self-conscious and contemporary, with a flexible approach to patterns of pastoral ministry, a greater role for the laity and a commitment to social action. It was, in many ways, an attempt to respond pastorally and liturgically as well as theologically to the kind of ideas presented in *Honest To God*. Significantly, some of the most radical pastoral experiments took place in Woolwich, where Robinson was bishop (Hastings, 1991, pp.538–9; Jagger, 1978, chs 6–8). Nor were such pastorally oriented initiatives limited to the Church of England. Similar groups also arose within other churches and denominations. The leaders of such initiatives, moreover, were apt to be ecumenically minded: thus the enthusiasm of the various denominational 'reform' groups contributed significantly to the emergence of an ethos in which local ecumenical experiments could develop. And alongside these initiatives were other examples of Christian commitment of a more social – and often socially radical – kind such as the remarkable growth of Christian Aid during the 1960s; the important contribution of Christians to the emergence of a whole range of new voluntary social welfare agencies (for example, Shelter, the Cyrenians and Amnesty International); and the emergence of a particular concern within the churches over issues of race and racism. In the latter case, although the churches were themselves subsequently obliged to face a painful recognition of their own early failures in relation to the issues raised by the development of a multi-racial society, yet the 1960s saw the beginnings of what was to become, in the 1970s and 1980s, an increasingly determined official stand against racism and racial prejudice and in support of a multi-racial society[13] (Chadwick, 1990, pp.165–76; Ecclestone, 1985; Leech, 1985, 1988).

At one level this kaleidoscope of radicalism, self-criticism and innovation within the life of the principal Protestant churches of Britain in the 1960s was exciting, vibrant and exhilarating; suggestive of vitality and new initiative within the various denominations. Inevitably, however, it also produced much controversy, disquiet and resistance. To those within the churches – both lay and clergy – for whom traditional beliefs, structures and styles were not merely adequate but deeply valued, the radical turmoil of the sixties was threatening, distressing and indicative not of vitality and innovation but, rather, of trendiness, capitulation to the prevalent secular mood, and sheer loss of nerve. By the later 1960s, moreover, the heady optimism of the various strands of radicalism and innovation within

[13] For this issue, see also Essay 6 in this volume, and Essays 3 and 4 in Volume II.

Britain's Protestant churches was already beginning to give way to a mixture of self-doubt, disillusionment and a sense of crisis and sudden decline. By the early 1970s such doubts about the long-term effects of the distinctly intoxicating euphoria of the early and mid sixties had resulted in a discernibly hungover mood.

It was not merely that the radicalism of the early and mid 1960s pushed and pulled the churches very rapidly in a variety of different and not always compatible directions. Nor was it simply the fact that many of the initiatives were either over-ambitious and over-optimistic or insufficiently thought through. Such factors, though relevant (Hastings, 1991, pp.544, 549, 582), were by no means the whole story. The sense of crisis – and then, in many cases, of despondency – that followed the upheavals of the early and mid sixties was also the product of, on the one hand, the sheer intractability of many of the issues addressed and, on the other hand, the fact that the broader social and cultural revolution of the 1960s deprived the churches of the seemingly secure social and cultural location which they had appeared to enjoy in the immediately post-war world and through the 1950s. The turmoil of the 1960s finally removed a good many illusions of security and essential well-being which the churches of the 1950s had tended to accept at face value.

For an example of the sheer intractability of many of the problems with which the churches wrestled in these years, one need look no further than the fate of the Anglican–Methodist unity scheme. No scheme of these years was prepared with more care, effort and thought than this one. The 'Conversations' on union had proceeded steadily through the 1960s, culminating in 1968 in a final scheme for reunification preceded by a Service of Reconciliation. And yet, in two successive votes, the first in 1969 and the second in 1972, the scheme failed to secure the 75 per cent majority required for approval from the Church of England (Hastings, 1991, pp.549–52). It was a depressing moment for the ecumenically minded. But for ecumenical radicals one of the hardest lessons of the 1960s was that, whatever might be achieved locally, institutional union and the actual ending of denominational barriers was rarely possible. The formation of the United Reformed Church in 1972 was a rare example of success at the institutional level, but significantly it was a union between churches whose traditions were relatively close already. The wider picture was less promising. When Kenneth Slack, an ecumenical enthusiast and General Secretary of the British Council of Churches, rewrote in 1969 a brief survey of *The British Churches Today* which he had first written some nine years earlier in 1960, he found that he had to excise much of the earlier text as 'strangely optimistic' (cited in Hastings, 1991, p.548).

Other problems also became apparent. By the end of the 1960s the temporary halt to decline which had been achieved during the 1950s had been replaced by a renewed and much more drastic phase of decline. By the early 1970s it was clear that the 1960s had seen a dramatic fall in some statistical indicators of church life – in membership figures and in numbers of ordinands and ordinations for example – accompanied by equally dramatic rises in certain other statistics such as those for the closure of churches and of theological colleges. A depressing number of other church institutions, societies and publications also either closed or faced deep crises (Davies, 1979, pp.101–7; Hastings, 1991, pp.548–9 and 610), including many of the most optimistic initiatives of the 1960s. The Parish and People movement, for example, came to a sudden end, merging with other denominational reform groups to form a new group, 'One for Christian Renewal' – but the new group, despite its ecumenical basis, was in reality less influential than Parish and People had actually managed to be in its heyday in the 1950s and early 60s, or had hoped to be as the cutting edge of Christian radicalism in the later 1960s (Jagger, 1978, ch.9). By the early 1970s the keynote of radical and would-be reforming Christians within the principal Protestant churches of Britain was no longer, as in the early and mid sixties, the hoped-for dawn of a 'new reformation'; instead, the characteristic note was that of the 'church in crisis'.[14]

And at the same time that the sense of crisis became clear in the late 1960s and early 1970s, so also other trends that had been present within the overall turmoil and ferment of the 1960s began to emerge more clearly than hitherto. Along with the flourishing of radical Christian ideas and groups, and a sudden explosion of a variety of 'new religious movements' and alternative spiritualities within the general ferment of sixties pop culture and experimentation (Leech, 1976), the 1960s also witnessed the emergence of important trends of an essentially conservative kind within the Protestant churches of Britain – trends, moreover, that were to become increasingly significant in the 1970s and 1980s. At least three such trends should be noted, although in practice there was considerable overlap and interconnection between them.

First, it is important to note that within the Protestant churches of Britain, although a dramatic decline in overall numbers of committed members and regular worshippers occurred in the 1960s, the evangelical wings of the major denominations resisted the predominant trend and actually showed signs of growth. In retrospect, we may recall, it is possible to identify a steady growth in evangelical strength within the British

---

[14] For two examples of this changed tone, different in style but similar in reflection of a general tendency, see *The Church of England in Crisis* by Trevor Beeson (1973) and *Who Cares?* by Nicholas Stacey (1971). Beeson had been secretary of Parish and People and editor of its journal during its headiest mid sixties days; Stacey had been the pastorally radical Vicar of St Mary's Parish Church, Woolwich, when his bishop, John Robinson, wrote *Honest to God*.

churches from at least the first national crusades by Billy Graham in 1954–55. In the 1960s, however, the sense of growth and strength became more marked. Two areas in particular merit note. In denominational terms the growth of Anglican evangelicalism was particularly striking. Of particular importance was the National Evangelical Anglican Congress held at Keele in 1967. At this event, attended by over 1,000 people, Anglican Evangelicalism tried to break free of the essentially negative and narrow image it had inherited from its recent history. Thus, whilst remaining firmly conservative in their attitude to the Bible and to the central doctrines of Protestant Christianity – and thereby maintaining a stand against the liberal and secular theologies of the 1960s – the Keele Conference signalled an evangelical acceptance of ecumenism, of the desirability of the celebration of communion as the central corporate act in the church's life, and of the necessity of addressing social issues as a key element of evangelical action and witness. Anglican Evangelicalism thus appeared both sure of its traditional beliefs and yet also open to new ideas in ecumenical, liturgical and social matters, and duly left the 1960s and entered the 1970s in good heart (Bebbington, 1989, pp.249–50; Hastings, 1991, pp.552–4; Manwaring, 1985, ch.14). The other area in which evangelicals, across the various denominations, thrived in the 1960s was in universities and colleges. Local Christian Unions, consolidated by the nationally organized Universities and Colleges Christian Fellowship, established themselves as the largest student Christian presence within most institutions. Moreover, the growth of the Christian Unions – already rooted in steadily increasing work by evangelicals among students in the 1950s and destined to continue during the 1970s and 1980s – was rendered the more significant because of the drastic decline in the previously influential and theologically liberal Student Christian Movement (Hastings, 1991, pp.453–4, 542–3, 549; Preston, 1986).

A second strand of resistance to the theological liberalism and questioning of the 1960s was to be found in the development of the charismatic movement with its emphasis upon 'baptism in the Holy Spirit'; upon 'spiritual gifts' such as 'speaking in tongues', prophecy, healing and exorcism; and upon informality, intensity, spontaneity and unrestrained emotion in worship. The charismatic movement within the 'mainstream' churches in Britain dates from the early 1960s and, in particular, from the experiences and influence of an evangelical Anglican curate, Michael Harper, in 1962–63. After contact with a visiting Californian charismatic, Harper experienced 'baptism in the spirit' and 'speaking in tongues'. He subsequently resigned his post as a curate in 1964 and founded the Fountain Trust, an organization that sought to spread and establish the charismatic movement within the various major denominations – an aim in which it had largely succeeded by the end of the decade. The charismatic movement was highly antithetical to the radical theological ideas of the sixties: where radical theology was anti-supernatural and demythologized heaven and hell, miracles, angels, devils and prayer, charismatics were intensely supernaturalist, believed in miracles and demons and regarded intercessory prayer as a vital element of their faith. Yet at the same time, the charismatic movement was also curiously appropriate to the general ethos of the decade with its celebration of feeling and rejection of conventional inhibitions – it was, it has appropriately been observed, very much a Christian version of 'doing your own thing' (Bebbington, 1989, pp.240–8; Hastings, 1991, pp.556–8; Hocken, 1986; Manwaring, 1985, pp.167–71; Perman, 1977, ch.5).

Finally, a third strand of renewed conservatism stemming from the 1960s was to be found in the emergence of organizations such as the National Viewers and Listeners Association (founded in 1965 by Mary Whitehouse to defend and promote 'traditional' moral values, especially in relation to sexual morality) and the Nationwide Festival of Light (founded in 1971 to combat 'moral pollution' in society with Lord Longford, Malcomb Muggeridge and Mary Whitehouse as leading supporters). By the close of the decade, the changes in attitudes to sexual morality, both in society in general and among liberal Christians who advocated a more contextual and less 'rules-based' approach in such matters, had produced a significant body of opinion within the churches willing to support renewed protests against 'permissiveness' and to campaign for a reassertion of traditional moral attitudes and precepts in matters of personal – and especially sexual – morality (Chadwick, 1990, pp.162–4; Leech, 1976, pp.128–31; Perman, 1977, ch.11; Thompson, 1992).[15]

What, then, may be said of the significance of the 1960s for the Protestant churches of Britain? For some it has always been clear that the root of the decline which began to afflict the churches in the 1960s lay in the liberal, radical and permissive theologies of that decade: the ferment and questioning was at best confusing and suggestive of a loss of nerve; at worst it was betrayal. For those who see matters thus, the subsequent growth of the evangelical and charismatic parties are their reward for having resisted the liberal, radical and secular theological trends of the post-*Honest to God* years. For others, however, it has been equally clear that the tragedy of the 1960s was that the radical initiatives and the questioning and reconstruction were not taken far enough; that the resistance to change was too great for the 'new reformation' to occur; and that the subsequent resurgence of evangelical and charismatic religion is both a flight from and a denial of the challenge of articulating a version of Christianity which is both fully honest and fully modern. Which side of the argument one

[15]   Again, for fuller discussion of this development, see Volume II, Essay 7.

prefers will probably turn as much upon one's assumptions about the nature of Christianity as about the nature of the historical evidence.

There are, however, other judgements which may be made on historical rather than theological grounds. Here it is instructive to recall once more David Lodge's literary portrayal and interpretation of Roman Catholic religious life during this period. In *How Far Can You Go?* Lodge portrayed a Catholicism which, in the 1960s, left behind a confident and safe existence in the 1950s; embarked upon a process of self-questioning, reform and innovation; passed through a period of optimism and excitement; and ended up wondering whether things had gone too far, in a state of both crisis and disillusionment – and yet the change that had occurred was fundamental, and after the 1960s Roman Catholicism was different. The experience of the major Protestant churches was, in broad terms, very similar. They too found the safety and confidence of the 1950s challenged by radical self-questioning and experiment in various aspects of their life. They too passed rapidly from optimism and excitement into crisis and disillusionment and into wondering how far things could go. And they too had conservatives who were sure that things had gone far enough or, indeed, too far. But, as the next two decades were to show, the Protestant churches, like Roman Catholicism, had also been fundamentally changed by the 1960s. The clarity and definedness of the 1950s had gone for good. The Protestant churches of Britain in the 1970s and 1980s were to be much more complex and complicated institutions than they had been twenty or thirty years earlier, before the watershed of the sixties.

4   The seventies and eighties: cross-currents and complexities

If the predominant characteristic of the principal Protestant churches of Britain during the later 1940s and 1950s was a quiet, even complacent confidence, and if their predominant characteristic during the 1960s was radical criticism and turmoil giving way to uncertainty and a loss of morale, what then was the predominant characteristic of these churches in the 1970s and the 1980s?

The cycle of decline that began in the 1960s continued during the 1970s and 1980s. The all-too-familiar combination of churches declared redundant and closed or demolished, of falling numbers of members and regular attenders, and of declining numbers of ordinands, and closing of theological colleges continued, demoralizingly. Between 1970 and 1985, it has been estimated, the total active membership of the Christian churches of Britain fell by about 1.5 million to a total of just under 7 million. By the mid 1980s the proportion of the population which claimed actual membership of a Christian church was only 15 per cent – although by this time, the rate of decline had slowed significantly (Davie, 1990a, p.397; Hastings, 1991, pp.602–3; Thompson, 1988, pp.216–27). Moreover, the statistics of decline obscured at least three other important aspects of the position of the principal Protestant churches during these decades.

Firstly, they obscured the marked regional and national differences between levels of active participation in the life of the churches in, respectively, England, Wales, Scotland and Northern Ireland. Thus, whilst in England actual church membership was as low as 13 per cent of the population, in Wales it was 23 per cent, in Scotland 37 per cent and in Northern Ireland 80 per cent (Thompson, 1988, p.216). Secondly, the figures also obscured the fact that whilst the overall pattern was one of decline, yet both the evangelical and charismatic wings of the churches continued to grow. Thus, by the late 1980s, both evangelicalism and the charismatic movement were proportionately much stronger and more influential within the life of Britain's main Protestant denominations than they had been twenty years earlier (Bebbington, 1989, p.270; Hastings, 1991, p.615). Thirdly, figures for active membership of the main Protestant churches of Britain exclude substantial numbers of people on the periphery of active church life who retained nominal or residual sympathy or affiliation. There is considerable evidence that many of those who are not active church members nevertheless continue to believe in a rather vague and unspecific but nevertheless 'mainstream' version of Christianity, derived from the ministry and life of the traditional churches, though no longer very actively integrated with them. It is clear that in the 1970s and 1980s such 'believing without belonging' still represented a substantial penumbra to the active strength of the traditional churches – and especially to the still 'national' Churches of Scotland and England. What is less clear, however, is whether or not such residual 'believing without belonging' was itself already undergoing a profound generational shift whereby the majority of the younger generation was ceasing either to belong or to believe in even a residual version of Christianity (Davie, 1990a and b).

Apart from the anxieties and ambiguities of continued statistical decline, however, what were the other predominant characteristics of the main Protestant churches in this period? It is difficult to provide a clear answer to this question. In part, this reflects the lack of perspective with which the historian is confronted in addressing the recent past. But it may also be that the lack of clarity is itself an important element of the answer. It is at least plausible to argue that the distinguishing feature of the principal British Protestant churches in the 1970s and 1980s was precisely their lack of a clear, predominant and defining characteristic or direction. The churches, it has been observed, have seemed, since the 1960s, to have tried every conceivable movement, gone through each of them, and emerged not being at all clear about where to go next (Hastings, 1992, p.20).

In one sense, this all constituted a continuation of developments in the 1960s. In the sixties, as we have seen, the Protestant churches were suddenly subjected to radical pressure to move rapidly in a number of (not always compatible) directions at once. In the subsequent two decades, this continued to be the case: but increasingly the pressure groups and directions became more and more varied and, at the same time, often less and less compatible. Thus, in the seventies and eighties, it was not only liberal and radical pressure groups within these churches that urged change; increasingly pressure for change also came from groups concerned with promoting a return to 'conservative' Christian teaching, both theological and moral.

Although the liberalism and radicalism of the 1960s had ended rather abruptly in a sense of crisis, the seventies and eighties nevertheless saw the continuation of a variety of liberal and radical challenges within the Protestant churches of Britain. Theological liberals and radicals continued to challenge traditional beliefs and formulations of doctrine and to urge the case for a thoroughly critical approach to both the Bible and to the churches' creeds, confessions and traditional teachings. Advocates of such an approach characteristically urged the churches to recognize both the historicity of all theology and belief (the fact that any particular statement of belief was necessarily influenced and limited by its historical context), and the need for a provisional, questioning, and exploratory tone in articulating belief in the modern context. The traditional doctrines of the Trinity and the Incarnation in particular were subjected to liberal and radical criticism and challenge. Many theological liberals also became increasingly aware of the challenges posed to traditional Christian doctrine by the rise of an overtly religiously pluralist society and urged the churches to reconsider traditional Christian claims in the light of this.[16] Particularly fierce controversies were aroused in 1977 with the publication of a collection of essays entitled *The Myth of God Incarnate* (Hick, 1977) and again in 1984 when, in a television interview, the newly appointed Bishop of Durham, David Jenkins, questioned traditional and literal understandings of the resurrection and virgin birth (Clements, 1988, ch.8; Harrison 1985). Behind such high-profile controversies, however, most denominations were obliged to continue to address the question of the legitimacy and limits of liberal and radical theological criticism and reinterpretation of traditional Christian belief. (See, for example, Brake, 1984, pp.367–70; Clements, 1988, pp.219–20; Herron, 1982; Parsons, 1989.)

---

[16] For a fuller discussion of this theme, see Volume II, Essay 1.

In general, at this institutional level, liberal theology continued to be tolerated but was not welcomed. Denominational leaders and official bodies were aware that the issues that liberal theologians raised were both real and intractable, and thus generally avoided outright rejection of their contribution. But such leaders were also aware that articulate theological liberalism was a minority view, deeply opposed by many in the churches, and especially by those within the growing evangelical and charismatic wings. Thus, whilst seldom *officially* rejected, theological liberalism was characteristically and consistently criticized for being 'parasitic' upon traditional Christian belief, too 'negative' and too 'individualistic', too little conscious of the Christian community as the context of theology and belief, too embued with both the rational spirit of the post-Enlightenment era and the 'permissiveness' of the 1960s.

Such a position – tolerating theological liberalism, yet simultaneously disparaging it – was itself less than wholly coherent. It also left largely unaddressed at least three interesting questions. Firstly, how far were the positive elements in what the theological liberals said never really heard because of the hostile furore which always greeted their work? Theological liberals and radicals were repeatedly confronted, on the one hand, by sustained, militant and vociferous opposition from conservative believers within the churches; and on the other hand, by the tendency of the media to sensationalize and caricature both the issues involved and the positions taken by the liberals and radicals. Nor were these two factors independent of each other. Whilst the media were apt to reduce often complex theological controversies to convenient 'sound-bytes' and sensationally eye-catching headlines, theological conservatives were only too willing to supply apparently clear, straightforward and starkly polarized accounts of what the issues involved, usually emphasizing the allegedly 'negative' character of the liberal or radical position and the 'positive' nature of their own beliefs. In media terms, therefore, the liberals and radicals were apt to be placed consistently at a disadvantage: liberal theology tended to be inclusive of a wide range of views and approaches to Christian life, conscious of the ambiguity and complexity of the Christian tradition and its expression in the modern context, and not, therefore, either simply defined or conveniently and convincingly reducible to a thirty-second media moment (Bruce, 1990, pp.131–2, 137–8; Jenkins, 1991, ch.9).

Conservative theology, by contrast, frequently appeared reducible to clear and straightforward statements, although whether conservative positions were really so simple remains an important question. Thus, for example, it has been pointed out that the apparently simple and traditional phrase 'biblical Christianity' – which was frequently used in the media, especially by those for whom it was a convenient way of summarizing everything they stood for and a shorthand way of denigrating those who held different viewpoints – is in fact both an extremely vague and emotive, and also a distinctly contemporary and highly politicized, concept (Carroll, 1991, ch.3; see also, Maitland, 1992). Conversely, a less sensational and more informed analysis of a figure such as the controversial Bishop of Durham, David Jenkins, would reveal that, far from being radically unorthodox, he was in fact deeply – though critically – orthodox in many aspects of his attempt to express the pastoral implications of Christian faith and theology in a contemporary context (Hastings, 1991, p.xxvi; Jenkins, 1991, p.33). Indeed, something similar might even be said about many aspects of the theology and pastoral concern of John Robinson, despite his role as the symbol of sixties radicalism. He too remained, in many ways, much more conservative than his reputation would imply (Bowden, 1988, pp.44–5; Edwards, 1988, pp.93–5). This, moreover, provides a salutary caution against supposing that 'liberal' and 'radical' theology was itself monolithic. The liberalism of David Jenkins, for example, and even the sixties radicalism of John Robinson, remained much more 'orthodox' and 'traditional' than the overtly unorthodox and determinedly radical theologies proposed by figures such as John Hick and Don Cupitt during the 1970s and 1980s.[17]

The second question left unaddressed by the widespread toleration yet disparagement of liberal theology concerned how far there was, in fact, a considerable but largely silent constituency within the churches for whom a 'liberal' and exploratory approach to contemporary Christian faith might have proved liberating – if only it had been able to be presented clearly and without the repeatedly negative and sensationalizing controversy. Although only impressionistic, there was substantial evidence that such a constituency existed and was by no means negligible. Thus, for example, as well as protests and distress, analyses of the letters received by both John Robinson and David Jenkins revealed numerous expressions of gratitude for the views they had expressed (Harrison, 1985, pp.86–7; Jenkins, 1991, pp.27–8; Towler, 1984, especially chs 2 and 4). Similar evidence of the existence of such a constituency is revealed by clergy willing to recognize and welcome such questioning among their congregations (Baker, 1988, pp.4–5; Dawes, 1988, 1990); by the experience of religious broadcasters (Priestland, 1986, pp.271, 276); and by surveys of the range and nature of lay belief in rural churches (Davies, Watkins and Winter, 1991, pp.269–81). Perhaps most notable of all, a Gallup Poll commissioned in 1984 by the theologically conservative Church Society in the wake of the controversy over David Jenkins' views, suggested that 47 per cent of the

---

[17] For a brief introduction to Hick and Cupitt and their context, see Clements, 1988, pp.220–30. For a discussion of Hick's particular significance for the development in Britain of Christian attitudes to other religions, see Volume II, Essay 1.

churchgoing Anglican laity were unorthodox or unsure in their beliefs concerning the resurrection and the virgin birth, whilst 69 per cent did not believe that the miracle stories in the gospels were historical events. Among churchgoing Nonconformists the figures for unorthodoxy or uncertainty on these points were even higher (*The Times*, 10 December, 1984).

Thirdly, the ambiguous 'official' attitude towards liberal theology raised the question of how far many of those in the middle ground within the churches (not self-conscious 'liberals', but also not self-consciously 'conservative' in theology either) were in fact implicitly closer to the 'liberals' than they would probably have cared to acknowledge, precisely because they themselves questioned and reinterpreted at least some aspects of their faith in terms derived from the 'liberal' approach and perspective. A comparison of two volumes of essays both published in 1988 illustrates the point. *God's Truth* was a collection of 'liberal' essays published for the 25th anniversary of *Honest to God* (James, 1988). *Different Gospels* was a collection of essays designed to defend orthodoxy against corrosive theological liberalism (Walker, 1988). The overall clash of styles and attitudes is clear; the absoluteness of the division is not. In effect, it was yet another variation of Lodge's question, 'how far can you go?'

Indeed, the latter question was pertinent within the evangelical movement as well. If evangelicals were, as a whole, the most consistent opponents of theological liberalism in the 1970s and 1980s, yet they too included a variety of positions within their ranks. Conventionally stereotyped as uniformly anti-intellectual and 'fundamentalist', in the 1970s and 1980s evangelicalism in Britain not only grew in strength but also developed a greater range of internal opinion. Thus, by the 1980s British evangelicalism ranged, theologically, from the cautiously and moderately critical, through a middle ground probably still best characterized by the ever popular writings of C.S. Lewis, to the fiercely conservative, uncritical and indeed near 'fundamentalist'. At the moderate end of the spectrum individuals might in practice be closer in spirit to the middle ground in the churches than to their fellow evangelicals at the extreme conservative end. Similarly, at the conservative end of the spectrum, individuals might in reality be closer in spirit to the staunchly and uncompromisingly conservative and anti-critical stance towards theology and the Bible of the rapidly expanding 'Restorationist' or House Church movement than to the ethos of the traditional Protestant denomination to which they belonged.[18] Thus the essential theological conservatism of evangelicalism – which evangelicals proudly owned as a virtue – did not prevent the emergence of debate

[18] For the Restorationist/House Church Movement, see Bebbington, 1989, pp.230–2; Calver, 1987, pp.55–7, 78–9; Hastings, 1991, pp.619–20; Walker, 1987, 1988 and 1992.

over 'how far you could go' within the evangelical tradition itself. Indeed, as the evangelicalism of the 1970s and 1980s both grew in strength and developed greater diversity, complex and varied internal tensions became increasingly evident. Thus, for example, whilst some evangelicals developed increasingly socially and politically radical versions of evangelicalism, challenged traditional evangelical attitudes towards questions of gender and the respective roles of men and women, or revised traditional evangelical opposition to Roman Catholicism, others maintained stalwartly traditional and conservative evangelical stances on such matters and called for a halt to the broadening and, in their view, dissolution of the authentic evangelical witness. Or again, whilst many evangelicals enthusiastically embraced the charismatic movement, others insisted that it represented a potentially dangerous drift into an emotionally and experientially centred spirituality which neglected the discipline and rigour of a genuinely evangelical regard for the Bible and its authority (Bebbington, 1989, pp.247–8, 267–70; Hastings, 1991, pp.617–18; Manwaring, 1985, ch.15; Powling, 1991, pp.66–9; Tinker, 1990).

It is important, therefore, to recognize that both the evangelical and the liberal/radical strands within the Protestant churches of Britain in the 1970s and 1980s were themselves internally varied and not reducible to simple stereotypes. It certainly remained true that, looking at British Christianity in the 1970s and 1980s as a whole, a fundamental theological fault-line could be discerned between 'liberals and radicals' on one side and 'conservatives and traditionalists' on the other. Indeed, the avowedly theologically radical John Hick went so far as to characterize the division as one between two different Christianities – and duly argued for the desirability of the 'second' and thoroughly radical one (Hick, 1983). Similarly, in an interpretation of the recent history and current position of evangelicalism in Britain in the late 1980s, the General Director of the Evangelical Alliance, Clive Calver, equally starkly polarized a staunchly theologically conservative evangelicalism against a sceptical theological liberalism symbolized for him above all by David Jenkins (Calver, 1987). At their respective extremes, the conservatives and radicals were indeed so polarized as to appear to constitute two different Christian religions. At their more moderate ends, however, the distinction was less clear: once again, the 'liberal evangelical' and the 'conservative liberal' might well find more in common than either felt with the more extreme representatives of their own 'side' of the liberal–conservative divide.

In matters of personal morality, and in particular sexual morality, meanwhile, there was inevitably a continuation of the debates initiated in the 1960s by the liberalization of the laws concerning divorce, abortion and homosexuality, by the impact upon sexual morality of the contraceptive pill, and by the emergence within the churches of 'situation ethics' and 'the new morality'. The underlying issue within debates over such issues as divorce and the remarriage of divorcees, abortion, the nature of human sexuality in general and the issue of homosexuality in particular, continued to be the tension between a flexible situation-based approach to Christian ethics and a more traditional appeal to fixed rules. The dramatic rise in the divorce rate in Britain during the 1970s and 1980s, the consequent concern over the status and stability of the traditional ideal of the family, the rise of the Gay Liberation Movement and of a Gay Christian Movement, and in the 1980s the arrival of AIDS, all served to sharpen the overall debate on personal morality within Britain's principal Protestant churches. As with matters of theology, so also in matters of personal and sexual morality. In the 1970s and 1980s the 'liberals' managed to secure widespread recognition by church leaders and representative bodies of the principle that a simple appeal to infallible rules in Christian ethics was unsatisfactory, whilst the 'conservatives' increasingly urged their churches and leaders to reassert 'traditional moral values', often pointing to the increasing number of abortions, the soaring divorce rate and, from the mid 1980s, to AIDS, as evidence of the need to do so. In general the result, at the official level, was an uneasy compromise between the two approaches.[19]

Whilst the debate over personal morality thus tended to divide along liberal–conservative lines similar to those at work in matters of doctrine and theology, the debates over both social morality and feminism were less clear cut. The 1970s and 1980s witnessed the emergence within Britain's main Protestant churches of a variety of groups concerned to make the social and political application of the Christian faith a priority. Such groups insisted that the moral imperatives of the Christian gospel were such that the churches should side decisively in social issues with the poor and the socially under-privileged. Often borrowing directly from the politically radical and left-wing Roman Catholic tradition of 'Liberation Theology' (but also including ideas derived from specifically evangelical and theologically radical sources as well), such groups called for action on poverty and social deprivation and for active opposition to racism to become central and integral elements of the contemporary life and witness of the churches.

The impact and advocacy of such ideas was to be found both at the level of church leadership – among leading clergy, in synods, assemblies and annual conferences, and in official reports from denominational agencies and boards – and also, importantly, at the local level in attempts to express such commitment in concrete terms within the local community (see for example, Dunn, 1986; Vincent, 1992). The significance of these developments within the churches was made clear in the 1980s when the

---

[19]   Again, for a fuller discussion of this issue, see Volume II, Essay 7.

social consequences of the policies pursued by the successive Thatcher governments during that decade led to a series of conflicts between the government and the churches over social policy and the legitimate role of the churches in political life. Two of the more spectacular moments of controversy centred upon the government's anger over the Church of England's 1985 report *Faith in the City*, and the reactions to Thatcher's own interpretation of the social implications of Christianity in an address to the General Assembly of the Church of Scotland in May 1988. Nevertheless, the social policies of the Thatcher governments also had their supporters within the churches. Thus, the 1980s also saw both the emergence of determined protests from other church members who saw the currently predominant social and political stance of the churches variously as ill-conceived, secularized, or a sell-out to left-wing opinion, and the emergence of a new 'radical Christian right' which sought to mobilize conservative Christian opinion in a manner sometimes reminiscent of the 'moral majority' in the USA. There was thus a complexity and plurality in Christian social attitudes as well as in matters of doctrine and personal morality during the 1970s and 1980s. Moreover, the complexity was increased in this case by the fact that, in social matters, it is likely that the majority of church members, even if they were not self-consciously on the right politically, were none the less significantly more conservative than the leadership within the various churches.[20]

Of equal importance during the 1970s and 1980s – and increasingly so as the two decades passed – was the impact on the churches of the general social, cultural and political debates over feminism and the place of women in society, and the steady development of a specifically Christian feminism within the churches. The particular issue of women's ordination (or the absence of it) and the protracted controversy over this within the Church of England was apt to dominate public perceptions of this whole area of debate (Field-Bibb, 1991; Langley, 1989, pp.301–8). In reality, however, the questions and challenges posed to the traditional Christian churches by both feminism in general and Christian feminism in particular were far more extensive than the single issue of whether women should be ordained as clergy. The implications of a feminist critique of traditional Christianity potentially extended over every aspect of the church's life, practice and belief (Elwes, 1992; Langley, 1989, pp.309–11). Indeed, in its most rigorous form, a feminist critique not only challenged the specific historical and contemporary practices and beliefs of particular churches and theological positions, but asked whether the Christian tradition and its structures and

[20] This issue is discussed in more detail in Volume II, Essay 4. For an overview, however, see Bradley, 1992, ch.5.

beliefs were, in fact, as a whole inherently and inescapably patriarchal (Hampson, 1990).[21]

In the whole area of worship and liturgy, meanwhile, yet another set of traditionalist/radical variables became increasingly evident during the 1970s and 1980s. The processes of liturgical revision continued and issued in yet more new services and revisions of the traditional liturgies and orders of service of most major Protestant denominations (Brake, 1984, pp.358–9, 376; Cuming, 1982, pp.127–30; Forrester, 1984, pp.163–5; Jasper, 1989, chs 13–15; McIlhagga, 1982, pp.170–2). Such changes sometimes excited considerable opposition from those who perceived the passing of the traditional liturgies and styles of service to be a loss not a gain – and such opposition itself embraced different groups, including, for example, both those who were deeply and articulately committed to the traditional worship and ethos of a particular denomination and saw liturgical revision as the dilution of cherished expressions of belief, and also those on the periphery of the churches who attended church irregularly and believed imprecisely but experienced loss when old familiar forms were changed. The most spectacular example of such opposition concerned the protests over the introduction of the Alternative Service Book in the Church of England in 1980 (Martin, 1979; Martin and Mullen, 1982), but the issue was by no means confined to the Church of England and its particular liturgical controversies. (See, for example, Bradley, 1992, ch.4; Forrester, 1984, p.164.) Even the most enthusiastic revisions of traditional liturgies, however, were not notable for their theological liberalism. On the contrary, it was observed that the new texts and services tended to be conservative in their use of the Bible and in their implications for the understanding of traditional Christian doctrine. Theological liberals and enthusiasts for new liturgies – although both responsible for exciting controversy and initiating change within their churches – were by no means to be lumped together as representatives of a single movement (Baker, 1988, especially pp.5–7, and 1990; Barton, 1988; Houlden, 1978, ch.7 and 1991, ch.9).

In matters of worship, moreover, the seventies and eighties also witnessed the emergence of a further area of change, innovation and controversy within the life of Britain's main Protestant churches. The charismatic movement – which, we have seen, was itself another development from the 1960s – made an increasingly widespread impact upon the worship of the various denominations during this period. The general tendency of charismatic worship was overwhelmingly in the direction not only of greater intensity and emotional fervour but also of even greater informality and physicality in worship. And it frequently involved a disregard for the constraints of formal liturgy – both old style and new

---

[21] For more detailed discussion of this issue see Volume II, Essay 6.

(Bebbington, 1989, p.241; Martin and Mullen, 1984, pp.107–26). But the theology of charismatic worship was resolutely conservative in its attitude both to the Bible and to traditional doctrine. Again, radicalism in worship and radicalism in theology were demonstrably not merely different but potentially in marked conflict with each other. Moreover, although officially welcomed by the majority of the Protestant churches, charismatic informality and demonstrativeness in worship could arouse the opposition not only of liberals and middle-of-the-road liturgical traditionalists but also of otherwise theologically conservative believers (Walker, 1983, pp.27–9; and more generally for a range of opinions on the charismatic movement, Martin and Mullen, 1984).

Ecumenism in the 1970s and 1980s was a similarly complex and often paradoxical affair. On the one hand, formal initiatives for closer union between various churches met with repeated setbacks and failures. In England the second Anglican rejection of the Anglican–Methodist unity scheme in 1972 was followed by a decade of exploration by various churches of the notion of 'Covenanting for Union' on the basis of agreed propositions. The discussions proceeded uncertainly within many of the individual churches and finally met with formal rejection from the Church of England in 1982, ten years after the final demise of the Anglican–Methodist scheme. By then, 1980 was already past, and thus the target date for unity so boldly and optimistically set out at the Nottingham Faith and Order Conference of the British Council of Churches in 1964 had come and gone and unity was not in sight. In Scotland, also, discussion between the largest Protestant denominations failed to reach agreement on recognition of each other's ministries. Only in Wales did it prove possible to complete a formal Covenant to work towards eventual full union – and even then not all of the major Protestant denominations felt able to join in (Bradley, 1992, p.45; Davies, 1979, pp.118–22; Davies, 1990, p.215; Hastings, 1991, pp.626–7).

However, it has also been observed that, by the early and mid 1980s, despite the failure of so many official schemes, the ecumenical spirit had never before been so widely diffused or so pragmatically and flexibly structured. Inter-church commissions discussed theological issues; collaboration increased in ministerial training; ecumenical approaches became the norm in higher education. Local Ecumenical Projects and intiatives were increasingly common, especially in areas of new housing but also in old and established communities – by 1989 the total number of such initiatives had risen to 1,138. Local councils of churches and joint activities for Christian Aid, for Christmas, Lent or Easter, or for local evangelism or social action were becoming the norm rather than the exception. Moreover, ecumenical activity of this kind involved increasingly not only the various Protestant churches of Britain but also Roman Catholics. Thus, although at the institutional level it might seem that ecumenism had simply run out of steam by the 1980s, yet at the same time there had also by then emerged nothing less than an awareness, beyond the continued existence of the various denominations, of a common Christian community with a common mission and a common faith (Brierley, 1991, p.17; Hastings, 1991, pp.626–8).

There were symbolic moments and relationships which particularly well illustrated this state of affairs. Thus increasing contacts were built up between the General Assembly of the Church of Scotland and the Scottish Roman Catholic bishops, ending a long established official silence between the churches. So also the traditional Catholic–Protestant rivalry in Liverpool was steadily replaced by warm co-operation between the Anglican bishop, David Sheppard, and the Roman Catholic archbishop, Derek Worlock – a collaboration that also included the local Nonconformist leadership. In 1982, meanwhile, the Papal visit to Britain included both a visit by the Pope to Canterbury Cathedral and a televised ecumenical service in which he participated, and a no less symbolic public meeting between the Pope and the Moderator of the Church of Scotland (Bradley, 1992, p.45; Palmer, 1990, pp.7–9). Similarly, in issues of national life, such as the clashes between government and the churches in the 1980s, it became more and more common for representatives of various churches, including Roman Catholics, to combine in their public statements. Or again, in 1989 the Revised English Bible (a reworking of the New English Bible) was published having been prepared by a committee which included, as full members not just observers, Roman Catholics from England, Ireland, Scotland and Wales as well as representatives of the other major denominations of these countries – a significant advance, ecumenically speaking, on the committee which had prepared the New English Bible in the 1950s, 60s and 70s (Powling, 1991, pp.333–6).

Indeed, by the mid 1980s it had become clear that a thorough reorientation of the formal structures of ecumenism in Britain was widely desired. Whilst the British Council of Churches – by now over forty years old – had achieved much, yet the continued failure of specific schemes of union suggested that a new initiative was needed. In addition, it was widely recognized that the future success and development of ecumenism in Britain required both the full integration of the Roman Catholic church into the formal ecumenical framework and also the extension of that framework to include other Christian groups not previously involved in the mainstream of British ecumenical activity – including in particular the thriving and expanding community of Black-led churches. Consequently, in 1985, the leaders of thirty-nine British churches initiated an 'Inter-Church Process' of 'prayer, reflection and debate together on the nature and purpose of the Church in the light of its mission'.

Entitled 'Not Strangers but Pilgrims', the process aimed to combine both discussion between church leaders and hierarchies and local, grass-roots opinion, thereby tapping the reserves of local ecumenical activity and experience which had developed over several decades even as more grandiose schemes failed. The Inter-Church Process shifted the ecumenical emphasis away from the achievement of 'unity' as such and towards 'pilgrimage together'. In due course a conference at Swanwick, Derbyshire, in 1987 initiated the replacement of the British Council of Churches by a new structure of four separate Councils of Churches for, respectively, England, Scotland, Wales and Ireland, and an overall Council of Churches for Britain and Ireland (Palmer, 1990). The new structure came into force in September 1990. With much looser constitutions and much wider memberships than the old British Council of Churches, the new structures were both an explicit recognition of the need for new flexibility and breadth in ecumenical relationships, yet also an implicit recognition of the continuing importance of existing denominational structures. Thus, whilst the new ecumenical structures were genuinely innovative, yet it was also possible to interpret them as evidence that the denominations had 'tamed' the ecumenical movement (Willmer, 1992, pp.140–2).

In the 1970s and 1980s, therefore, the principal Protestant churches of Britain, like the post-Vatican II Roman Catholic church, contained a rich and sometimes bewildering mixture of sub-groups and parties, tendencies and trends, jostling and competing with each other to influence the future shape of particular denominations as well as the cross-denominational 'mainstream' of British Protestantism. Moreover, the various sub-groups were not easily classifiable into simple categories of 'liberal' and 'conservative', 'radical' or 'traditionalist'. Whilst some might combine conservatism on all fronts (say, tending to the right in politics, against liberalism in theology, opposed to liturgical change, and against the ordination of women); and whilst others might be consistently liberal on all issues (say, pro-women's ordination, supportive of theological liberalism and a 'situationist' view of morality, enthusiastic about liturgical innovation and tending to the left in politics), such consistency was generally the exception. Much more common was an imprecise mixture of 'conservative' and 'liberal' attitudes on different issues.

Of course, this situation was by no means wholly new. The various major denominations of British Christianity had long contained within themselves a variety of strands and emphases – and from the Victorian period onwards such 'internal pluralism' had tended to become steadily more pronounced. By the 1970s and 1980s, however, the sheer diversity within the various denominations had increased to such a point that it began itself to look like one of the essential and defining features of both individual churches and of 'mainstream' Christianity in Britain as a whole.

Increasingly, late twentieth-century British Christianity came to resemble not so much a rich and intricate patchwork, complex in construction yet possessed of an underlying pattern and stability, but rather an unpredictable kaleidoscope of apparently endlessly shifting and realigning groups and trends. Such diversity might plausibly be read either as a sign of continuing vitality despite the statistics of decline, or as a sign of catastrophic confusion and loss of direction. Either way, to the outside observer, casual or scholarly, it also rendered the churches in question both increasingly complex and increasingly untidy phenomena – but not, consequently, either less interesting or less significant.[22]

5 Contrasts and continuities once more

This essay began by contrasting, in broad terms, the position of the traditional Christian churches in Britain in the late 1940s and their position in the late 1980s and early 1990s. In conclusion, it now returns to this theme and attempts to identify the more salient features of the churches' position in Britain at the close of the period under review. Four themes in particular stand out.

First, as noted at the beginning of the essay, by the late 1980s there had been a decisive shift away from a predominantly denominational ethos within British Christianity and towards a predominantly ecumenical one. From a situation in the late 1940s in which, although ecumenical contacts and relationships were increasing, the prevailing assumptions and outlook nevertheless remained denominational in style, the mainstream of British Christianity by the 1980s had become essentially ecumenical – although the majority of formal schemes of union had failed and most of the conventional denominational structures not only still survived but were to be incorporated in the new ecumenical structures replacing the British Council of Churches.

In the late 1980s and early 1990s, therefore, denominations and denominational identities still mattered and were still different. Thus, for example, both the Church of England and the Church of Scotland, although thoroughly immersed in the ecumenical mainstream of British

---

[22] For a vivid sense of both the range and variety of the untidy complexity and the continuing significance of the traditional churches in Britain at the close of the 1980s and beginning of the 1990s, see the anthology of articles from 1988–90 by *The Times'* Religious Affairs Correspondent, Clifford Longley (in Powling, ed., 1991) and the survey of the recent history, current position and likely future of the churches by Ian Bradley (1992).

Christianity and quite clear that in practice they represented two more denominations along with the rest, yet retained a particular significance and salience within their respective national contexts. In part this was a consequence of their 'nationwide' parochial systems and the fact that they thus retained an official presence even in areas of weakness. It was also a result of a long tradition of these churches being the 'national' churches of their respective countries, and of thus being the churches to which most people who were not regular churchgoers went if they felt a need for religious counselling, advice or rites. The residual strength and significance of these churches thus remained much greater than a mere calculation of numbers of active members would suggest (Bradley, 1992, pp.22, 28–9, 31–5, 215–16; Davie, 1990a, p.399).

The residual strength of other denominations also should not be overlooked. Thus, the penumbra of adherents of, say, the Methodist, Baptist or United Reformed Churches – people but loosely connected and by no means regular attenders, yet whose instinctive choice in time of need was one of these churches – was also significantly larger than the simple counting of active church members would suggest. On the other hand, however, it has also been pointed out that this penumbra of adherents had itself shrunk in relation to its size in the earlier twentieth or late nineteenth century. And even more problematically, as churches made the best of their various statistics, the question increasingly arose as to how far even some of those still counted as active church members might in fact be more realistically regarded as part of the penumbra of only loosely affiliated adherents (Royle, 1987, p.337).

Other denominational characteristics also continued. Thus, for example, Methodism – especially in its leadership and among its most active members – was apt to be particularly prominent in its espousal of social issues, whilst the Baptists, as a body, were in general much more conservative and evangelical than other denominations taken as a whole. But such distinctions were strictly relative, not absolute, and as we have seen were increasingly to be located within a much wider and predominantly ecumenical mainstream and consensus. By the early 1990s, what David Lodge had earlier observed of the post-Vatican II Catholic church was increasingly true of the other traditional churches of Britain as well, and also of the ecumenical consensus of which they were all a part: they were much more pluralistic than they had once been and allowed all kinds of groups (radical, conservative, charismatic, feminist, and so on) to express their particular version of Christian faith often with like-minded believers from another denomination (Lodge, 1980b, p.187).

If the shift from the priority of denominationalism to the priority of ecumenism is the first overarching theme that we may note, the second is the striking increase in prominence and influence of, respectively, Roman

Catholicism, Protestant evangelicalism and the charismatic movement. Despite the dilemmas and demoralization within Roman Catholicism in Britain as the Catholic church and community struggled to assimilate the transformations of Vatican II and simultaneously remain loyal to a deeply conservative Pope, by the late 1980s Catholicism in Britain was both one of the principal Christian denominations (rivalled in influence only by the Churches of England and Scotland) and also more integrated and central to the ecumenical mainstream than ever before. And it was all the more significant that this was so in Britain as a whole given the continuing tragedy of Northern Ireland and the crucial significance of the Protestant–Catholic divide there.

No less striking was the growth in Protestant evangelicalism. Whilst most individual churches experienced significant numerical decline during the period from 1945 to the 1990s, the evangelical wings within the Protestant churches experienced steady growth, thus becoming proportionately much stronger within both individual denominations and within British Christianity as a whole. Similarly striking was the rise of the charismatic movement. From a small presence in the 1960s, the charismatic movement had become a significant and steadily growing presence within all the traditional churches of post-war Britain – including, importantly, the Roman Catholic church. And, again like Protestant evangelicalism, the charismatic movement was growing against the overall trend of decline.

The evangelical and charismatic movements were not synonymous with each other: a point clearly demonstrated by the fact that the charismatic movement included Roman Catholics as well as Protestants. Even within the Protestant context, however, the simple equation of evangelicals and charismatics was not accurate. There were differences and sometimes tensions between the two movements (Bebbington, 1989, pp.247–8). That said, however, it was certainly the case that the overlap between them was substantial (and increased during the 1970s and 1980s) and that it was their combined impact upon the traditional churches in Britain that was so significant by the late 1980s and early 1990s. Nor was the significance of evangelicals and charismatics within British Christianity limited to their impact within individual denominations. By the 1980s their significance was equally to be found in an extensive range of cross-denominational organizations, networks and publications. Such organizations, moreover, did not only draw together evangelicals and charismatics from the principal traditional denominations of British Protestantism. They also linked evangelicals and charismatics from these churches with the wider evangelical and charismatic upsurge among, for example, older evangelical denominations such as the Brethren and the Pentecostalists, and newer groups such as the Restorationist and House Churches and the Fellowship of Independent Evangelical Churches (Bebbington, 1989, pp.240–7; Bradley, 1992, pp.52–8, 142–50; Calver, 1987, pp.27–9, 34–7 and ch.7).

By the late 1980s and early 1990s the extent and apparent vitality of such cross-denominational evangelical and charismatic Christianity was sufficient to prompt sympathetic historians and observers to speculate that the future of Protestant Christianity in Britain might lie, essentially, with this movement and that it might be the basis for a significant renewal of the Protestant churches and a revival of Christianity in Britain (Bebbington, 1989, p.247; Calver, 1987). Such hopes and predictions might or might not prove correct, but even in the early 1990s it was already clear that such an outcome was neither a straightforward nor a forgone conclusion. The vitality and growth in evangelical and charismatic Christianity in the 1970s and 80s had indeed been statistically impressive, but it was not without ambiguity. Indeed, the very scale and intensity of its growth was already posing new questions and dilemmas for evangelicals and charismatics themselves and for the churches in general.

Thus, as we noted earlier, the growth in evangelical and charismatic numbers was accompanied by an evangelical and charismatic version – or rather several versions – of the question 'how far can you go?' Were evangelicals and charismatics to co-operate with other Christians, including theological liberals and Roman Catholics? Or were they to oppose them, insisting on the need for a distinctive, unecumenical, resolutely uncompromising version of evangelicalism? Such questions, moreover, were sharpened by the fact that within the evangelical and charismatic *milieu* itself it was often the most avowedly and staunchly uncompromising groups which apparently displayed the greatest capacity for growth. Such groups were apt to be dogmatic, authoritarian, patriarchal, and actively – often intolerantly – opposed to other versions of Christianity, other faiths, and indeed social groups in general which did not share their particular social and moral values (Bradley, 1992, p.211; Maitland, 1992, pp.29, 36–40; Walker, 1987, pp.200–8). And there were also other questions about the nature and scale of evangelical and charismatic growth and, therefore, about its likely future prospects. Much of the growth within the House Church, Restorationist and Independent Evangelical sector, it was noted, was the result of evangelicals and charismatics leaving 'traditional' churches and denominations with which they had become dissatisfied (Gill, 1993, pp.218–20; Walker, 1988, pp.263–73, and 1992, p.61). Similarly, it was again observed – as it had been of Billy Graham's first British visits in the mid 1950s – that much of the appeal and 'success' of evangelical and charismatic religion lay in the increase in intensity which it brought to the already converted and in the 'conversion' of people already on the periphery of church life and in any case predisposed to the certainties and self-confidence of evangelical or charismatic Christianity (Bruce, 1984, pp.102–4 and 1990, p.138).

Others again acknowledged the vitality of evangelical and charismatic Christianity but doubted whether it had the same ability to reach 'the great unchurched majority' as did the principal historic denominations with their 'capacity to be broad, inclusive churches'. Such churches, it was argued, both could and should still witness to a different kind of Christianity which positively valued 'understatement and reserve, genuineness and honest doubt, gentleness and humility', and which accepted that – this side of eternity – hesitancy, pilgrimage, puzzlement and uncertainty might also be equally authentic Christian experiences (Bradley, 1992, pp.211–21). At this point, however, the plea for the continuance of more tentative Christian spiritualities alongside the assertive certainties of evangelical and charismatic faith blends into a third, key theme in the history of the principal Christian churches in Britain since 1945. The balance and ethos of the various churches and denominations was affected during these decades not only by the evangelical and charismatic movements but by the impact of 'reforming' and 'activist' movements in general. In another notable parallel between the experience of the Roman Catholic church and the experience of the other major British denominations, it is clear that a whole range of initiatives within the churches served to sharpen the distinction between the 'activists' – of various types – and the 'passive majorities' in the pews or on the periphery.

It was not only evangelicals and charismatics who sought to make the ethos and the membership of the traditional churches more 'committed', more 'involved' and more 'participatory' in the post-war – and especially the post-1960s – era. This characteristic was one shared, albeit with different emphases, by other movements in the life of the churches in this period. Thus the movements for liturgical revision, for ecumenical dialogue and co-operation, for greater lay participation, and for making the church increasingly 'communal' in ethos, and 'active' within the local community, all shared (both with each other and with evangelicalism and the charismatic movement) a desire to make the churches and their members more self-conscious, more articulate and more active and participatory in the practice of their faith. Conversely, they all militated, in different ways, against passive or diffuse belief and membership (Baker, 1988, pp.4–6; Bradley, 1992, pp.96–124).

It may well be objected that it is only natural that the committed – whatever their particular version of Christian faith – should seek to foster such qualities within the churches or that, indeed, to be true to itself Christianity must demand such a level of commitment. In a British context, however, such commitment to activism cut decisively across a widespread and quite different understanding of Christianity. For many 'ordinary believers' in Britain, Christian faith was not a matter of active participation, self-conscious commitment, and passionate involvement. Rather, it was a matter of passive belief (of a more or less 'orthodox', more or less 'unorthodox' kind); of more or less regular participation in worship; and of attachment and affection for particular expressions of Christian faith held dear by virtue of family tradition or some personal contact. The vehicles of such piety might be the Authorized Version of the Bible, the Book of Common Prayer, the ethos of a traditional Methodist, Baptist or Presbyterian service, or simply traditional hymns as offered on the average BBC *Songs of Praise* broadcast. In its own more active version such passive faith would have expressed itself in regular but private, unobtrusive, rather uninvolved church attendance. In its more diffuse versions it would have varied from occasional attendance, through 'believing without belonging', to an identifiably Christian, yet definitely 'implicit' or 'folk', religion.[23]

Much more varied . (handwritten marginalia)

For the activists, of whatever variety, such passive belief was apt to be frustrating, inauthentic and inadequate; an obstacle to the church and the faith becoming the committed realities they were intended to be. Conversely, for those whose faith was of this passive, less overtly committed kind, many of the changes in the churches in the 1960s and afterwards were alienating and confusing. New versions of the Bible; new liturgies; new types of service; discussion groups and informality; the insistence on involvement and participation; the pressure to be informed and articulate about one's faith: such trends seemed both to threaten the privacy and remove the fixed points and bases of many a passive believer's faith. And there is no doubt that the churches of the late 1980s were much more attuned to the ethos and the spirituality of the various competing groups of 'activists' than they were to the ethos and spirituality of the 'passive believers'. For the latter, the old familiar landmarks had vanished steadily from the 1960s onwards. It is likely that, apart from that minority of 'passive believers' who were converted to one or other variety of post-60s activism, the majority of such passive and peripheral believers were more alienated than attracted by the competing Christian activisms of the 1960s, 70s and 80s (Bradley, 1992, ch.4; Hastings, 1991, pp.665–7). If they continued 'to believe', they probably 'belonged' even less.

The underlying issue is an important one. To the extent that the traditional Christian churches both wish to maintain and succeed in maintaining their links with such 'passive belief', they will continue collectively to represent not only the largest body of active religious believers in modern Britain, but also the principal religious outlook within British society as a whole. If, however, the churches continue to advance steadily along the 'activist' paths of the 1960s, 70s and 80s, paying less and less attention to the sensibilities and intuitions of those within the substantial

[23] For examples of the complex ways in which 'believing without belonging' might vary according to denominational and social context, see Bailey, 1986 and 1989; Bradley, 1992, ch.4; Ahern and Davie, 1987, pp.71-4.

86

periphery of Christian 'believing without belonging', they may find themselves no longer the representatives of the principal religious outlook of modern Britain, but only the largest committed religious group. The 'implicit' or 'passive' religion of Britain, by contrast, may drift slowly but steadily away from 'traditional Christianity', and become increasingly eclectically derived from the diversity of religious faiths and movements which have become a part of modern British life and society – an outcome that may be more likely if, as has been suggested, the traditional pattern of British 'believing without belonging' may itself be undergoing a significant generational shift (Davie, 1990b, pp.457–62).[24]

It is precisely the rise of religious pluralism in post-war Britain, meanwhile, that constitutes the fourth salient characteristic of the position of the traditional Christian churches by the late 1980s and early 1990s. We noted at the outset of this essay that, in 1945, to speak of religion in Britain was to speak, overwhelmingly, of the mainstream Christian churches. By the late 1980s such a way of speaking was, for the informed observer, quite impossible. On the one hand, whilst the traditional churches remained by far the largest representatives of the Christian tradition in Britain, the four and a half decades after 1945 also saw the emergence and rapid growth of a number of other significant (but not in a British context 'traditional') Christian groups. Thus the period saw the growth not only of the House Church, Restorationist and Independent Evangelical churches at the evangelical–charismatic end of Christianity, but also the emergence of a numerically significant Eastern Orthodox presence within British Christianity (Hastings, 1991, pp.605–6) and of a rapidly expanding group of Black-led churches.[25] The shape of the Christian community in Britain had thus changed significantly in the four and a half decades since the end of the Second World War – a fact reflected not least in the replacement of the British Council of Churches by the looser yet wider ecumenical structures initiated in 1990. A consideration of the Christian churches in Britain which *began* in 1990, rather than 1945, could thus not focus so centrally as this essay has done upon the 'traditional' British churches. To begin from 1990 would require inclusion from the outset of a now much wider Christian 'mainstream' which included at least the Eastern Orthodox and Black-led churches, and perhaps also independent evangelical and House churches.

At the same time, however, the wider religious context and landscape had also changed. The Britain which emerged from the Second World War was still a predominantly Christian culture: pluralist in the sense that other

[24] For further discussion of the significance of the encounter between 'passive belief' and the sheer religious diversity of modern Britain, see Essay 7 in this volume and Volume II, Essay 1.

[25] For the particular significance of which see Essay 6 in this volume.

religious groups were free to worship and practise their faith, but Christian in the sense that such groups were firmly on the periphery of the religious life of the nation as a whole. The Britain that entered the 1990s was pluralist in quite another sense. Still a Christian society in the sense that Christianity remained the majority religious tradition, by 1990 Britain had also become an obviously, inescapably religiously plural society. Alongside new versions of the Christian faith, Britain – and in particular British cities – had become increasingly familiar with the presence, the buildings, the worship and the witness to their faith of a variety of Jews, Muslims, Hindus, Sikhs and others. And around all of these groups there was a further increasingly diffuse but apparently widespread enthusiasm for a mass of new religious movements and alternative spiritualities, philosophies and lifestyles.

Where did this leave the traditional Christian churches? It certainly left them still by far the largest overall religious tradition in Britain, despite the significant decline they had suffered in the previous decades. And it left them as well with a still substantial residual periphery of adherents and passive believers more or less closely connected with the ongoing life of the traditional churches. But it left them also with a range of difficult choices. Should they continue to promote the various activist models of church membership, without regard for the possible alienation of the peripheral believer, seeing the potential for conversion into active participation as the only value in such peripheral belief? Or should they deliberately seek to preserve and cultivate the contacts with the peripheral and passive believers, at the cost of sacrificing some of the ardour and fervour of the activist approach? And what were the theological implications of these options? Would a decision to opt for the highly committed style inevitably imply an increasingly sectarian outlook, an increasing detachment from the mainstream of British life and culture and an acceptance of existence as just one more (albeit the biggest) atypically committed religious minority in a basically secular culture? And conversely, would a decision self-consciously to maintain and foster links with the residual Christian culture of Britain in fact amount to an acceptance of a slow but steady accommodation to an already only vaguely Christian ethos?

Such were the underlying issues facing the traditional churches of Britain as they entered the last decade of the twentieth century. Things had indeed changed since 1945 when the end of the Second World War had initiated a decade of reconstruction in which the churches, no less than the nation, were quietly confident that the traditional order was essentially secure.

Bibliography

AHERN, G. and DAVIE, G. (1987) *Inner City of God: the nature of belief in the inner city,* Hodder and Stoughton, London.

ANNAN, N. (1977) *Report of the Committee on the Future of Broadcasting,* HMSO, London.

ARCHER, A. (1986) *The Two Catholic Churches: a study in oppression,* SCM, London.

BADHAM, P. (ed.) (1989) *Religion, State, and Society in Modern Britain,* Edwin Mellen Press, Lampeter.

(1990) 'The Contribution of Religion to the Conflict in Northern Ireland' in Cohn-Sherbok (ed.).

BAILEY, E. (1986) 'The Religion of the People' in Moss, T. (ed.) *In Search of Christianity,* Firethorn Press, London.

(1989) 'The Folk Religion of the English People' in Badham (ed.).

BAKER, T. (1988) 'Is Liturgy in Good Shape?' in James (ed.).

(1990) 'This is the Word of the Lord', *Theology,* 93, pp.266–73.

BARTON, J. (1988) *People of the Book?,* SPCK, London.

BEBBINGTON, D. (1989) *Evangelicalism in Modern Britain: a history from the 1730s to the 1980s,* Unwin Hyman, London.

BEESON, T. (1973) *The Church of England in Crisis,* Davis-Poynter, London.

BOWDEN, J. (1988) 'Honesty is Not Enough' in James (ed.).

BRADLEY, I. (1992) *Marching to the Promised Land: has the Church a future?,* John Murray, London.

BRAKE, G. (1984) *Policy and Politics in British Methodism 1932–1982,* Edsall, London.

BRIERLEY, I. (1991) *Prospects for the Nineties,* MARC Europe, London.

BROWN, C. (1987) *The Social History of Religion in Scotland Since 1730,* Methuen, London.

(1992) 'A Revisionist Approach to Religious Change' in Bruce, S. (ed.) *Religion and Modernization: sociologists and historians debate the Secularization Thesis,* Oxford University Press, Oxford.

BRUCE, S. (1984) *Firm in the Faith,* Gower, Aldershot

(1986) *God Save Ulster: the religion and politics of Paisleyism,* Oxford University Press, Oxford.

(1990) *A House Divided: Protestantism, schism and secularization,* Routledge, London.

CALVER, C. (1987) *He Brings Us Together,* Hodder, London.

CARROLL, R. (1991) *Wolf in the Sheepfold: the Bible as a problem for Christianity,* SPCK, London.

CHADWICK, O. (1990) *Michael Ramsey: a life,* Oxford University Press, Oxford.

CLEMENTS, K. (1988) *Lovers of Discord: twentieth-century theological controversies in England,* SPCK, London.

CLEMENTS, S. and LAWLOR, M. (1967) *The McCabe Affair,* Sheed and Ward, London.

COHN-SHERBOK, D. (ed.) (1990) *The Canterbury Papers: essays on religion and society,* Bellew, London.

COMAN, P. (1977) *Catholics and the Welfare State*, Longman, London.

COONEY, J. (1982) *Scotland and the Papacy: Pope John Paul II's visit in perspective*, Paul Harris Publishing, Edinburgh.

COVENTRY, J. (1982) 'Roman Catholicism' in Davies (ed.).

COX, H. (1965) *The Secular City*, SCM, London.

COX, E. and CAIRNS, J. (1989) *Reforming Religious Education: the religious clauses of the 1988 Education Reform Act*, Kogan Page, London.

CRACKNELL, K. (1990) 'Christianity and Religious Pluralism: the ethics of interfaith relations' in Cohn-Sherbok (ed.).

CRICHTON, J., WINSTONE H. and AINSLIE, J. (1979) *English Catholic Worship: liturgical renewal in England since 1900*, Geoffrey Chapman, London.

CUMING, G. (1982) 'Liturgical Change in the Church of England and the Roman Catholic Church' in Davies (ed.).

DAVIE, G. (1990a) '"An Ordinary God": the paradox of religion in contemporary Britain', *British Journal of Sociology*, 41, pp.395–421.

(1990b) 'Believing without Belonging: is this the future of religion in Britain?', *Social Compass*, 37, pp.455–69.

DAVIES, D. (1990) 'A Time of Paradox Among the Faiths' in Cole, D. (ed.) *The New Wales*, University of Wales Press, Cardiff.

DAVIES, D., WATKINS C. and WINTER, M. (1991) *Church and Religion in Rural England*, T & T Clark, Edinburgh.

DAVIES, R. (1979) *The Church in Our Times: an ecumenical history from a British perspective*, Epworth, London.

(ed.) (1982) *The Testing of the Churches 1932–1982*, Epworth, London.

DAVIS, C. (1967) *A Question of Conscience*, Hodder and Stoughton, London.

DAWES, H. (1988) 'In the Pulpit' in Eaton, P. (ed.) *The Trial of Faith: theology and the church today*, Churchman, London.

(1990) 'Liberal Theology in the Parish: a lost cause?', *Theology*, 93, pp.117–24.

DE LA BEDOYERE, M. (1964) *Objections to Roman Catholicism*, Constable, London.

DILLISTONE, F. (1977) *C.H. Dodd: interpreter of the New Testament*, Hodder and Stoughton, London.

DRIVER, C. (1962) *A Future for the Free Churches?*, SCM, London.

DUNN, J. (ed.) (1986) *The Kingdom of God and North-East England*, SCM, London.

ECCLESTONE, G. (1985) 'Church Influence on Public Policy Today', *The Modern Churchman* (New Series) 28, pp.36–47.

EDWARDS, D. (1988) 'Why the Conservative Backlash' in James (ed.).

(1989) *Tradition and Truth: a critical examination of England's radical theologians*, Hodder and Stoughton, London.

EDWARDS, D. and ROBINSON, J. (eds) (1963) *The Honest to God Debate*, SCM, London.

ELWES, T. (ed.) (1992) *Women's Voices: essays in contemporary feminist theology*, Marshall Pickering, London.

FIELD-BIBB, J. (1991) *Women Towards Priesthood: ministerial politics and feminist praxis*, Cambridge University Press, Cambridge.

FLETCHER, J. (1966) *Situation Ethics: the new morality*, SCM, London.

FORRESTER, D. (1984) 'Worship since 1929' in Forrester, D. and Murray, D. (eds) *Studies in the History of Worship in Scotland*, T & T Clark, Edinburgh.

GALLAGHER, T. (1990) 'The Press and Protestant Popular Culture: a case-study of the *Scottish Daily Express*' in Walker and Gallagher (eds).

GILL, R. (1993) *The Myth of the Empty Church*, SPCK, London.

HAMPSON, D. (1990) *Theology and Feminism*, Blackwell, Oxford.

HARRISON, T. (1985) *The Durham Phenomenon*, Darton, Longman and Todd, London.

HASTINGS, A. (1978) *In Filial Disobedience*, Mayhew-McCrimmon, Great Wakering.

—— (1991) *A History of English Christianity 1920–1990*, Collins, London.

—— (1992) 'All Change: the presence of the past in British Christianity' in Willmer (ed.).

HERRON, A. (ed.) (1982) *The Westminster Confession in the Church Today: papers prepared for the Church of Scotland panel on doctrine*, The Saint Andrew Press, Edinburgh.

HICK, J. (ed.) (1977) *The Myth of God Incarnate*, SCM, London.

—— (1983) *The Second Christianity*, SCM, London.

HIGHET, J. (1960) *The Scottish Churches: a review of their state 400 years after the Reformation*, Skeffington, London.

HOCKEN, P. (1986) *Streams of Renewal: the origins and early development of the Charismatic Movement in Great Britain*, Paternoster Press, Exeter.

HORNSBY-SMITH, M. (1975) 'Plural Parish Liturgies', *Clergy Review*, 60, pp.518–24.

—— (1987) *Roman Catholics in England: studies in social structure since the Second World War*, Cambridge University Press, Cambridge.

—— (1988) 'Into the Mainstream: recent transformations in British Catholicism' in Gannon, T. (ed.) *World Catholicism in Transition*, Collier Macmillan, London.

—— (1989a) *The Changing Parish: a study of parishes, priests and parishioners after Vatican II*, Routledge, London.

—— (1989b) 'The Roman Catholic Church in Britain since the Second World War' in Badham (ed.).

—— (1991) *Roman Catholic Beliefs in England: customary Catholicism and transformations of religious authority*, Cambridge University Press, Cambridge.

—— (1992) 'Recent Transformations in English Catholicism: evidence of secularization?' in Bruce, S. (ed.) *Religion and Modernization: sociologists and historians debate the secularization thesis*, Oxford University Press, Oxford.

HOULDEN, J. (1978) *Explorations in Theology 3*, SCM, London.

—— (1991) *Bible and Belief*, SPCK, London.

HUNTER, A. (1991) 'Watching From a Distance: a Scottish perspective on multi-cultural Britain' in Hooker, R. and Sargent, J. (eds) *Belonging to Britain: Christian perspectives on a plural society*, CCBI Publications, London.

JAGGER, P. (1978) *A History of the Parish and People Movement*, The Faith Press, Leighton Buzzard.

JAMES, E. (ed.) (1988) *God's Truth: essays to celebrate the twenty-fifth anniversary of 'Honest to God'*, SCM, London.

JASPER, R (1989) *The Development of the Anglican Liturgy 1662–1980*, SPCK, London.

JENKINS, D. (1975) *The British: their identity and their religion*, SCM, London.

JENKINS, D. and R. (1991) *Free to Believe*, BBC, London.

KENNY, A. (1986) *A Path From Rome: an autobiography*, Oxford University Press, Oxford.

KENT, J. (1980) 'From Temple to *Slant* (Aspects of English Theology 1945–70)' in Ambler, R. and Haslam, D. (eds) *Agenda For Prophets: towards a political theology for Britain*, The Bowerdean Press, London.

LANGLEY, M. (1989) 'Attitudes to Women in British Churches' in Badham (ed.).

LEECH, K. (1976) *Youthquake: spirituality and the growth of a counter-culture*, Abacus, London.

(1985) 'The Church and Immigration and Race Relations Policy' in Moyser, G. (ed.) *Church and Politics Today: the role of the Church of England in contemporary politics*, T & T Clark, Edinburgh.

(1988) *Struggle in Babylon : racism in the cities and churches of Britain*, Sheldon Press, London.

LODGE, D. (1980a) *How Far Can You Go?*, Penguin, Harmondsworth.

(1980b) 'The Church and Cultural Life' in Cumming, J. and Burns, P. (eds) *The Church Now*, Gill and Macmillan, Dublin.

(1991) *Paradise News*, Secker and Warburg, London.

MAITLAND, S. (1992) 'Biblicism: a radical rhetoric' in Sahgal, G. and Yuval-Davis, N. (eds) *Refusing Holy Orders: women and fundamentalism in Britain*, Virago Press, London.

MANWARING, R. (1985) *From Controversy to Co-Existence: evangelicals in the Church of England 1914–1980*, Cambridge University Press, Cambridge.

MARTIN, D. (ed.) (1979) 'Crisis For Cranmer and King James', *PN Review*, 13.

MARTIN, D. and MULLEN, P. (eds) (1982) *No Alternative: the prayer book controversy*, Blackwell, Oxford.

(1984) *Strange Gifts? A guide to charismatic renewal*, Blackwell, Oxford.

MASS OBSERVATION (1947) *Puzzled People: a study in popular attitudes to religion, ethics, progress and politics in a London borough*, Victor Gollancz, London.

MCILHAGGA, D. (1982) 'Liturgical Change in the Free Churches' in Davies (ed.).

MCSWEENEY, B. (1989) 'The religious dimension of the "Troubles" in Northern Ireland' in Badham (ed.).

PALMER, D. (1990) *Strangers No Longer*, Hodder and Stoughton, London.

PARSONS, G. (1988a) 'A question of meaning: religion and working-class life' in Parsons, G. (ed.) *Religion in Victorian Britain, Volume II: controversies*, Manchester University Press, Manchester.

(1988b) 'Victorian Roman Catholicism: emancipation, expansion and achievement' in Parsons, G. (ed.) *Religion in Victorian Britain, Volume I: traditions*, Manchester University Press, Manchester.

(1989) 'The rise of religious pluralism in the Church of England' in Badham (ed.).

(1992) 'Paradigm or Period Piece? David Lodge's *How Far Can you Go?* in perspective', *Journal of Literature and Theology*, 6, pp.171–90.

PAYNE, E. (1972) *Thirty Years of the British Council of Churches 1942–1972*, British Council of Churches, London.

PERMAN, D. (1977) *Change and the Churches: an anatomy of religion in Britain*, Bodley Head, London.

POWLING, S. (ed.) (1991) *The Times Book of Clifford Longley*, HarperCollins Religious, London.

PRESTON, R. (1986) 'The Collapse of the SCM', *Theology*, 89, pp.431–40.

PRIESTLAND, G. (1986) *Something Understood: an autobiography*, André Deutsch, London.

RAMSEY, I. (1966) *Christian Ethics and Contemporary Philosophy*, SCM, London.

ROBINSON, J. (1963) *Honest to God*, SCM, London.

(1965) *The New Reformation*, SCM, London.

(1967) *But that I can't believe!*, Collins, London.

(1970) *Christian Freedom in a Permissive Society*, SCM, London.

ROYLE, E. (1987) *Modern Britain: a social history 1750–1985*, Arnold, London.

SHARRATT, D. (1977) 'English Roman Catholicism in the 1960s' in Hastings, A. (ed.) *Bishops and Writers*, Anthony Clarke, Wheathampstead.

STACEY, D. (1971) *Who Cares?*, Hodder and Stoughton, London.

STANFORD, P. (1993) *Cardinal Hume and the Changing Face of English Catholicism*, Geoffrey Chapman, London.

THOMPSON, D. (1982) 'The Older Free Churches' in Davies (ed.).

THOMPSON, K. (1988) 'How Religious are the British?' in Thomas, T. (ed.) *The British: their religious beliefs and practices 1800–1986*, Routledge, London.

THOMPSON, W. (1992) 'Britain's Moral Majority' in Wilson, B. (ed.) *Religion: contemporary issues (the All Souls seminars in the sociology of religion)*, Bellew Publishing, London.

TINKER, M. (ed.) (1990) *Restoring the Vision: Anglican Evangelicals speak out*, MARC, Eastbourne.

TOWLER, R. (1984) *The Need For Certainty: a sociological study of conventional religion*, Routledge and Kegan Paul, London.

VAN BUREN, P. (1963) *The Secular Meaning of the Gospel*, SCM, London.

VIDLER, A. (ed.) (1962) *Soundings: essays concerning Christian understanding*, Cambridge University Press, Cambridge.

(ed.) (1963) *Objections to Christian Belief*, Constable, London.

VINCENT, J. (1992) 'Christianity as a Movement of the Poor' in Willmer (ed.).

WALKER, A. (1987) 'Fundamentalism and Modernity: the Restoration Movement in Britain', in Caplan, L. (ed.) *Studies in Religious Fundamentalism*, State University of New York Press, New York.

(1988) *Restoring the Kingdom: the radical Christianity of the House Church Movement*, Hodder and Stoughton, London.

(ed.) (1988) *Different Gospels*, Hodder and Stoughton, London.

(1992) 'Sectarian Reactions: pluralism and the privatization of religion' in Willmer (ed.).

WALKER, G. and GALLAGHER, T. (eds) (1990) *Sermons and Battle Hymns: Protestant popular culture in modern Scotland*, Edinburgh University Press, Edinburgh.

WALKER, M. (1983) 'Baptist Worship in the Twentieth Century' in Clements, K. (ed.) *Baptists in the Twentieth Century*, Baptist Historical Society, London.

✓ WILLMER, H. (ed.) (1992) *20/20 Visions: the futures of Christianity in Britain*, SPCK, London.

WELSBY, P. (1984) *A History of the Church of England 1945–1980*, Oxford University Press, Oxford.

WOLFE, K.M. (1984) *The Churches and the British Broadcasting Corporation 1922–1956*, SCM Press, London.

2

INTEGRATED BUT INSECURE: A PORTRAIT OF ANGLO-JEWRY AT THE CLOSE OF THE TWENTIETH CENTURY

by David Englander

Lucy Mahler, a Batmitzvah girl, with Rabbi Francis Berry at the Bristol and West Progressive Synagogue. From the exhibition 'One City – Many Faiths'. Photograph © Mark Simmons.

Fifty years after the destruction of German fascism, the scale of anti-semitism and the level of neo-Nazi activity in these islands remained a matter of concern to British Jews. Beadles, fearing vandalism and worse, patrolled their synagogues like security guards. Woburn House, head-quarters of the United Synagogue, was barred and bolted and in a perma-nent state of siege. The young pressed for the formation of self-defence groups, their elders for improved police protection. By the summer of 1990 fears of racial violence had become acute. Since the beginning of the year synagogues and cemeteries had been desecrated and Jews beaten and stoned. Senior police officers at Scotland Yard were said to be alarmed at the increase in anti-semitic attacks; the Home Secretary expressed concern (*Daily Telegraph*, 29 August 1990; *JC*, 31 August 1990).

Internally, too, the Jewish community felt threatened. In the years since 1945 Anglo-Jewry had suffered a massive haemorrhage of the faith-ful. The Jewish population, which peaked in 1951 at an estimated 430,000, declined by about 25 per cent in the next thirty years (Waterman and Kosmin, 1986, pp.6–7). In 1988 Anglo-Jewry numbered 300,000 compared with 330,000 in 1985, and the true figure may well have been lower (*JC*, 6 September 1991). The defection of the young, as measured by the slump in synagogue marriages, was particularly disturbing. At the close of the eighties it was reported that up to two thirds of young Jews did not marry in synagogues. The trend was worrying, 'because synagogue marriage shows ritual commitment to Judaism and is, in effect, a method of recruit-ing the future generations of the community' (*JC*, 23 June 1989).

By the beginning of the sixties, Jewish continuity was no longer assured. Pundits gathered at the graveside. The Board of Deputies in desperation turned to social science. A Statistical and Demographic Research Unit, created in 1965, monitored the collapse. Its publications made anguished reading. Secularism, some said, was succeeding where the Holocaust had failed. Others argued that Judaism, a non-missionary faith, should abandon tradition and seek converts as replacements for those lost through indifference or intermarriage (Cohn-Sherbok, 1991, p.51).

Jewish decline was in no small part a function of an ageing population with a high death-rate and low birth-rate. The minority population at the close of the century included a larger proportion of the middle aged and elderly than the general population as well as a deficit in the younger age groups. Particularly alarming was the long-term decline in the Jewish marriage rate. Investigation showed that, statistically speaking, only half of those Jews born in the later 1950s and early 1960s who were expected to marry in synagogues in the early 1980s actually did so. As one analyst put it, 'more Jews are dying Jewish than are marrying Jewish' (Moonman, 1980, p.13).

Although the discrepancy between the expected and the actual number of Jewish marriages was more easily described than explained, intermarriage was thought to pose the most serious threat to Jewish survival. Those who married out of the faith, said the Chief Rabbi, should be mourned as dead. 'A sense of grief should be cultivated ... tantamount to bereavement' (*JH*, September/October 1987). No reliable figures existed, but it was estimated that one in three Jews married out.

'The practice of religion at home', said one post-war commentator, '... is now dying fast' (Henriques, 1949). In 1949 the observation was controversial; forty years later it was a commonplace. By then the Jewish family, the very citadel of the faith, seemed on the verge of collapse. Although the Jewish divorce rate was not as high as that of the general population, it rose steadily from the fifties in the same direction. In 1974 the Office of Population, Census and Surveys found that 6.3 per cent of those marrying in synagogues were divorcees. By 1979 the proportion had risen to 9.4 per cent and only 82.4 per cent of synagogue marriages were first marriages for both partners (*JH*, August/September 1987).

The break-up of traditional Jewish communities aggravated the crisis. Jews who can't stay together can't pray together. Without an adequate population base the infrastructure of worship, education and dietary observance is unsustainable. The population movements that accompanied the post-war changes in the socio-economic distribution of Jewry intensified uncertainties. Was it the case that Jews who had 'got on' were also the most likely to get out? Scholars most certainly thought so. J.D. Gay, author of a pioneering study of the geography of religion, presented the most gloomy forecast. 'All the signs', he concluded, 'point towards an accelerating disintegration of the distinctive Jewish settlement pattern. Slowly but inevitably the Jews are being absorbed into the prevailing national culture and in time there will be little left in England which is distinctively Jewish in character. Eventually English Judaism is likely to become the concern of the historical geographer' (Gay, 1971, p.220).

And yet there is a paradox in all this. At the time when Judaism was on its knees, the Jewish community had never been more highly regarded. Chief Rabbi Jacobovits, ennobled by Mrs Thatcher, was thought to be more popular with the prime minister than the Primate himself (Young, 1989, pp.423–5). Being Jewish, once considered a burden, was now considered chic. Columnist and author Julie Burchill, for example, told readers that her greatest regret was not being born Jewish. 'Once you've been around Jews', she explained, 'gentiles seem like shadow people, undead, zombies. Whatever a gentile man's got, a Jewish man's always got more of, whether it's money, a sense of humour or schlong' (*Sunday Correspondent Magazine*, 15 April 1990, p.54). Jacobovits himself was voted 'Man of the Year' in 1991, along with Nottingham Forest's Brian Clough (*JC*, 8 November 1991)!

How was it that Jewish observances were at an all-time low when Anglo-Jewry was at an all-time high? And was it not curious that *fin de siècle* Jewry should have been upheld as a model of pluralist integration, when Jews themselves felt so uncertain of the future of their faith? How was it that Jews, the oldest and best integrated non-Christian minority in Britain, were also one of the most unsettled and threatened of religious communities?

1   Anglo-Jewry in profile

British Jews, like other minorities, were not an undifferentiated mass. Anglo-Jewry, though small, displayed extraordinary diversity. The majority of British Jews were the descendants of the Russian and Polish immigrants who settled before the First World War. The foreign-born element, though steadily diminishing in number, was still significant at the beginning of our period. Distinctions of rank, for example, were in part related to place of origin. Litvaks (Lithuanian Jews), who regarded them-selves as superior sorts, thought the Romanians wild, the Galizianers (Galician Jews) sharp and the Hungarians shiftless. 'It was most natural for Litvaks to believe that the dream of every Hungarian woman was a Litvak husband', wrote one observer at the close of the forties. Dutch Jews, never in high regard, were considered sound in character but deficient in appear-ance – '*Mieskeits* from *mieskeit* land! Such *ponim*!'[1] And there was tension between first generation immigrant Jews and the native élite. The latter, said to be more English than Jewish, were polite, distant, reserved and all too formal for the likes of their less Anglicized co-religionists (Brotz, 1955, pp.153–65).

The exodus of refugees from Nazi persecution – 50,000 in all – brought a significant increment. In the post-war period German and Austrian Jews accounted for 10 per cent of the community. Numbers were also boosted by the arrival of immigrants from the hard-pressed Jewish communities of the Orient. Two thousand 'Baghdadi' Jews came from India following independence, a substantial contingent of Egyptian Jews arrived in the aftermath of the Suez affair and there were small settlements of Yemeni, Morrocan, Adeni and Libyan Jews.

The differences between native and immigrant Jews were wide. Some Orientals, indeed, felt that they were to the English Jews as the Blacks to the

---

[1]   *Mieskeit* is a Yiddish term to describe one with a face like the back of a bus; *ponim* is the plural of 'face'. Information on Dutch Jews is based on memories of exchanges among customers in the East End family butcher shop in which the author spent much of his early life.

goyim (Holmes, 1988, p.245). The differences between German Jews and English Jews were no less significant. Anglo-Jewry was said to be too loud, too materialistic, deficient in education and in culture. 'You never see them at lectures'; 'There are no books in their houses', and they preferred business to the professions (Berghahn, 1988, pp.217–20, 231–4, 246–9). Spiritual differences were also pronounced. Immigrants from the Middle East gravitated towards the Sephardim (Jews of Spanish descent), but resisted total assimilation and loss of identity. In addition to the Persian *minyan* (quorum of ten adult males required for public religious service) that met at Finchley Synagogue and a mixed congregation at Jews' College, there were substantial Adeni and Persian synagogues at Stamford Hill as well as the 1,000-strong Oriental *shtiebl* (small conventicle for worship) at Golders Green. The formation of the Eastern Jewry Community in 1955 and the Iraqi Jewish Centre in 1989 were all part of the as yet unstudied attempt to give shape to an Oriental *kehilla* (community) (*JC*, 24 July 1989; 27 September 1990). German immigrants, from a more polarized religious environment, were a considerable influence upon the post-war fragmentation of Anglo-Jewry.

The newcomers, whatever their origins, shared certain characteristics. Neither group consisted of penniless people without skills or resources. The Orientals were mercantile types used to the world of business; the Germans were overwhelmingly middle class with backgrounds in business, the professions and the arts. Neither group, moreover, settled in the East End of London, the traditional reception centre of immigrant Jewry. The Germans made for Hampstead; the Orientals for north-east and north-west London. The net effect was to accentuate the tilt of Anglo-Jewry towards the professional, managerial and skilled non-manual occupational classes.

The process of embourgeoisement, which had been almost continuous since the 1880s, advanced rapidly in the post-war years. By the close of the seventies the Jewish sweated trades were a thing of the past; the pressers and cutters, cabinet-makers and *sleppes* had acquired careers, skills and self-employment. 'The key to this mobility', wrote Waterman and Kosmin, 'has been education which has transformed the sons of Jewish labourers into professionals and small businessmen' (Waterman and Kosmin, 1986, pp.44–6). The social class composition of Anglo-Jewry reflected these changes. The bulk of the Jewish population was comfortably middle class or situated on the boundaries thereof; the number of Jews at the bottom end of the social hierarchy was negligible.

These shifts in the socio-economic profile of Anglo-Jewry have resulted in equally significant changes in the spatial distribution of the community. Most striking of all was the abandonment of the Whitechapel ghetto. The post-war years were the years in which the East End of London ceased to be the economic, cultural and religious centre of Anglo-Jewry. Its decline, evident before the close of the 1930s, was much accelerated by the destruction of the environment and dispersal of the community during the Second World War. By 1949 the East End accounted for less than a tenth of London's Jewish population. Numbers dwindled rapidly thereafter. The *mikvahs* (ritual baths) closed, the *shuls* relocated, kosher butchers retired and cultural life collapsed. The *Jewish Times*, the once vibrant Yiddish-language daily, went into terminal decline. 'Circulation for 1946 is still considerably below the 1937 level', its accountants told the Royal Commission on the Press in 1948. Four years later it ceased publication (HO 251/30; Sharot, 1976, p.146). Apart from the elderly, those who remained were the failures, that small unskilled element that 'couldn't even get out of the East End' and the *grob Yidn*, the rough sorts, who ate their meals with unwashed hands, dropped their aitches, and generally lacked the social graces of the upwardly mobile folk of north-east and north-west London (Brotz, 1955, pp.142–3).

The pattern of Jewish settlement had, then, shifted. The Greater London area, with two-thirds of the minority population, remained the biggest concentration of Jews in the United Kingdom. Hackney, with some 20,000 Jews, was the only inner-city community of substance. The largest number of Jews lived in an arc extending from St John's Wood, across Edgware, Stanmore and into Hertfordshire. In the borough of Barnet, which took in Hendon, Golders Green and Finchley, Jews constituted nearly 17 per cent of the total population. In the north east, Redbridge represented a smaller but sizeable settlement that spilled into south-west Essex. Whitechapel was a memory visited by tourists, middle-aged children and the handful of social workers who provided for their aged parents (Caudrey, 1987, pp.22–5).

Jewish migration from the centre to the periphery was by no means only a metropolitan phenomenon. Provincial Jewry, too, moved on up. An estimate of the Anglo-Jewish population in 1985, showed that 129,000 lived outwith Greater London spread throughout some eighty communities. At that point, Manchester, with a population of around 30,000, was the largest provincial community followed by Leeds (population 14,000) and Glasgow (population 11,000). In the course of the previous forty years the ghetto areas of Chapeltown in Leeds, Cheetham in Manchester and the Gorbals in Glasgow had been abandoned in favour of suburban settlement in Moortown, Prestwich and Newton Mearns.

For the rest, Jews were thinly scattered across the country. Only 15 centres had a Jewish population that could be counted in four figures; and with few exceptions the inland settlements were in decline. Communities were left without synagogues, synagogues without ministers and individuals without company or comfort. In the fifty years since 1945 the Jewish population of Liverpool fell from 7,500 to 4,500; of Sheffield from 2,175 to 800 and Birmingham from 6,000 to 5,500. Darlington had a synagogue but only thirty families; Grimsby had lost its rabbi in 1965 and could not support another; and since 1986, when their synagogue closed its doors, the Jews of Derby had prayed in Nottingham (Brook, 1989, p.292; *JYB*, 1989, pp.183–4). Expansion was confined to popular coastal resorts. Blackpool, Bournemouth, Southend and Southport were the principal growth points. Brighton, with a Jewish population of around 10,000, became the fourth largest community outside London and Glasgow.

These changes, we shall see, have affected the faith, the politics and the relationship of the Jewish minority with the wider society.

2 The Anglo-Jewish establishment

In the three hundred and fifty years following the Cromwellian Resettle-ment of the mid-seventeenth century, Britain's Jews developed a dense organizational network to service the needs of the community. The diver-sity was extraordinary. There were leagues of this and friends of that; there were councils and committees, boards and trusts, clubs and circles, guilds and societies – all devoted to the advancement of persons and causes. The *Jewish Yearbook* for 1989 listed more than 300 voluntary associations. Included were representative organizations, religious organizations, edu-cational and cultural organizations, youth organizations, organizations concerned with Israel and a bewildering array of international organiza-tions. Some were very old. The Jewish Initiation Society, founded in 1745, supplied trained *mohelin* to perform the rite of circumcision. The Polish Jewish Ex-Servicemen's Association (est. 1945), a comparative newcomer, nevertheless seemed decidedly middle-aged when set alongside the Jew-ish Feminist Group, a collective formed in 1979 to satisfy a new kind of minority need. Seldom had so few people been so well organized!

The growth of effective community-wide organization was, however, a product of the Victorian era. Three institutions were of primary import-ance – the Chief Rabbinate, the United Synagogue and the Board of Deputies. Together they gave Anglo-Jewry its distinctive centralized hier-archical character. In these years the hitherto autonomous rabbinate was replaced by an ecclesiastical establishment under the supervision of a primate in whose hands great powers were concentrated. Attempts to limit the authority of the Chief Rabbi were few and easily evaded. Apart from a self-denying ordinance on the excommunication of heretics and the intro-duction of a retiring age in place of a life appointment, Chief Rabbi Brodie, who took office in 1948, enjoyed the same rights and privileges as his predecessors. The form of worship and religious observances, and all matters of religious administration of synagogues within his jurisdiction were under his supervision and control. No person could preach or officiate in the service of the synagogue without his approval; candidates for the ministry likewise required his certification as to their religious and moral fitness.

In 1953 the Chief Rabbi's official designation was changed. The 'British Empire', hitherto a descriptor of his jurisdiction, was omitted. He has since been known as 'Chief Rabbi of the United Hebrew Congregations of the British Commonwealth of Nations'. The 'United Hebrew Congregations' included those bodies which contributed to the Chief Rabbinate Fund by which his office was sustained. The chief contributor was the United Synagogue, which also bore the financial responsibility for the *Beth Din* (the Court of the Chief Rabbi), the body which, apart from the determination of civil disputes, supervised *Kashrut* (dietary law), the licensing of *Shochetim* (slaughterers of meat and poultry) and the granting of Jewish religious divorce.

Easy-going, dignified, tolerant, sometimes likened to 'the Anglican Establishment (Jewish Branch)', the United Synagogue provided religious facilities for 38,000 families (approximately 100,000 people), was the largest synagogal body in Britain – possibly the largest in the world – and was the representative of mainstream Orthodox Judaism. Established in 1870 under authority of an act of Parliament, it brought a hitherto loose union of metropolitan Ashkenazi synagogues within the jurisdiction of the Chief Rabbi. Uniformity within the United Synagogue was secured by the provision whereby the Chief Rabbi assumed sole responsibility for the form of worship and all matters connected with the religious administration of that body and its subsidiary charities (Bermant, 1969, p.186).

The Chief Rabbinate and the United Synagogue were essentially creatures of that cousinhood of bankers and brokers who, until the beginning of our period, provided Anglo-Jewry with its leaders. The same aristocracy of finance also dominated the Board of Deputies, which was formed in the eighteenth century, but came into its own in the struggles for emancipation of the 1830s. The transfer of power from a prosperous and highly acculturated élite to the descendants of the East European immigrants, began during World War I and was completed by the end of World War II. Zionism was central to the struggle for communal control. The new regime was not only more democratic than its predecessor, it was also more responsive to the idea of a Jewish national home. To the grandees, the idea appeared dangerous and divisive and inconsistent with their self-image as Englishmen of the Jewish persuasion; to those of Russo-Polish parentage, by contrast, Zionism seemed like the saviour of Jews threatened with destruction. Memories of pogroms and pillage, and later the evidence of

Nazi violence, made anything short of total commitment seem incomprehensible if not irresponsible. The State of Israel, its security, progress and development, became for the Jews of Britain almost a surrogate religion in its own right.

The Board of Deputies constituted the lay leadership of Anglo-Jewry and was the recognized intermediary between the Jewish community and the state. Its remit in broad terms was to safeguard the civil rights and essential interests of the minority, to ensure that no Jews should suffer disability by reason of their religion. The basis of representation on the Board was primarily synagogal: 80 per cent of its representatives were elected by congregations in London and the provinces; the remainder came from secular organizations such as the Association of Jewish Ex-Servicemen, the Union of Jewish Students and the Federation of Women Zionists. Commonwealth communities, too, were represented. The deputies met monthly to receive, discuss and vote upon the reports and submissions prepared by the Board's executive officers and specialist standing committees who together managed its day-to-day affairs.

The Board was concerned with the external interests of the minority; matters of faith were not its province. Thus the right of Jews to slaughter animals according to their beliefs, rites and rituals had to be defended while the precise form and regulation was for the rabbis to determine. Likewise, it was the right to observe the Sabbath rather than a commitment to Sabbatarianism, that provoked a challenge to certain alleged anti-Jewish employment practices within the Metropolitan Police in 1990.

The Board, though politically non-partisan, was very much involved in the political process. It monitored new and proposed legislation pertaining to the rights of citizens of the Jewish faith, and any discriminatory measures, legal or social, that could affect them. It watched over the interests of its co-religionists overseas, and intervened, where possible, to improve their condition. Its preference was for behind-the-scenes activity with departments of state, police authorities, local administrators and relevant public bodies.

The work of the Board was well regarded. The state, though not directly involved in the management of the Jewish community, had long been supportive. Its confidence found statutory recognition in the special role assigned to the Board in the marriage registration process and in the enforcement of Sunday trading legislation. In 1836 the Marriage and Registration Acts in effect entrusted the appointment of registrars of Jewish marriages to the President of the Board of Deputies. One hundred years later recognition was again accorded to it under the Shops (Sunday Trading Restrictions) Act, in which the Board of Deputies was designated as the body to set up a Jewish Tribunal for cases of religious conscience arising out of the Act.

The Board's performance nevertheless excited controversy within the community. Its effectiveness was said to be more apparent than real. Its deputies, claimed the critics, were vain, loud-mouthed mediocrities, its policies timid and ill-considered, its successes illusory. The Board's standing was probably higher outside the community where it was sometimes perceived as a paradigm parliament for ethnic or religious minorities. The parliamentary analogy, though, was misleading. The Board of Deputies had no legislative or statutory power and could only make its influence felt by representations to the authorities on the same basis as any other interest group. And it is on this basis that it ought to be appraised. The Board, alas, still awaits its historian, and so it is prudent to reserve judgement. A provisional assessment might, without denying its defects, note its positive contribution to the maintenance of a Jewish identity. The Board provided synagogues and secular institutions with a platform and ensured that Jewish opinion and interests were well represented within the political process. It could no doubt have done more. But its resources were slender, and its constituents by no means consensus-minded.

3   Orthodox Judaism

The Jews of Britain, if well organized, were not united. The Orthodox Establishment, which accounted for 65 per cent of Jews, was a declining force (*JC*, 11 October 1991). Its losses were in part a reflection of the wider changes that affected religion, but might also have owed something to certain specific features of the United Synagogue.

The typical British Jew, ran the summary report of one of the national dailies, 'Belongs Orthodox; Thinks Reform; Practices Liberal' (*The Guardian*, 20 January 1988). The first statement was correct, the second dubious and the third erroneous. Survey research in the sixties and seventies showed significant differences in the level of religious practices performed by Orthodox and Progressive Jews. Pollsters reported in 1971 that only 19 per cent of Reform and Liberal Jews kept a kosher home compared with 82 per cent of United Synagogue members. Although the latter were no more regular in attendance than their counterparts in the Church of England, and although few performed the full range of prescribed ritual observances, the standards of the United Synagogue were accepted as right and proper even if they were not always attainable (Sharot, 1976, p.162).

The battle against decline and drift, though waged with vigour and imagination by the United Synagogue, was conducted upon an inadequate knowledge-base. Its priorities too often rested on opinion rather than research. The reconstruction of Jewish religious life after the Second World

War, for example, seems to have been driven by a topsy-like dynamism of its own. The secularization of the synagogue thus advanced rapidly in the post-war period. The United Synagogue and its affiliates sought to make the *shul* the centre of a wide range of educational, cultural and recreational activities. Communal halls, meeting rooms and club rooms were built and programmes developed to make the synagogue more meaningful. A specially-created Youth and Community Services Department sought to co-ordinate policies and resources. Education was accorded priority.

Until the end of the sixties Jewish religious education was received at the *cheder,* the traditional school attached to the synagogue. Classes were held on Sunday morning and twice weekly after school hours. Children were drilled in the elements of prayer-book Hebrew, in Bible translation and in rabbical texts and commentaries. The boys, and they were overwhelmingly boys, were also coached in preparation for their *bar mitzvah*. Standards were low, methods primitive. Instructors were untrained and ill-paid. Questions were unwelcome, discipline severe. There was yelling and thumping and little enlightenment. In short, the *chedarim* teachers were to education as the Dave Clark Five were to music.

With the installation of Chief Rabbi Jacobovits in 1967 all this changed. In his inaugural sermon he proclaimed an emergency and called for the mobilization and shift of resources into the classroom to combat the slide into indifference and infidelity. 'Jewish education', he declared, 'represents our defence budget in the communal economy, and it must be given the highest priority over every other Jewish effort'. His greatest achievement, indeed, lay in the planned expansion of Jewish schools in London and the provinces. A Jewish Educational Development Trust was formed in 1971 to develop a programme. Apart from additional places at both primary and secondary level, plans were laid for the creation of several Jewish sixth-form colleges and the provision of bursaries for the training of new teachers (Bermant, 1990, pp.192–204). In the years that followed activity was intense. Existing schools were refurbished or relocated, new ones built and enrolment and exposure to Jewish education raised substantially. The *cheder* system was upgraded but diminished in significance. In 1967 part-time supplementary education accounted for more than two-thirds of the total enrolment; fifteen years later less than half the student population was *cheder*-educated. Of the 30,248 children who were then enrolled in Jewish schools, 80 per cent received their education under the agency of the Orthodox (Waterman and Kosmin, 1986, p.39). By the close of the eighties the United Synagogue was spending more than 25 per cent of its annual budget on education.

For all that, the United Synagogue continued to lose numbers. Women, in particular, were thought to be alienated. Orthodox Judaism in relation to women was said to be discriminatory, insensitive and, indeed, hostile. Women, it was noted, were excluded from much of the ritual life of the synagogue: they were exempted from the requirement to pray three times a day, debarred from the priesthood or the judiciary and condemned as a source of impurity in their person and presence. Their inferior position in relation to Jewish family law was a cause of personal distress and communal controversy. The rabbinate could neither change the law nor moderate its excessive severity. In consequence estranged wives who remarried without having secured a *get*, or bill of divorcement from their former partners, were deemed to have committed adultery. The children of adulterous unions were bastards without claim to Jewish status.

The pain and the frustration that arose from this particular interpretation of the law broke the surface towards the close of our period as victims became more vocal and gender issues more prominent within the community. Jewish women, influenced by the growth of the women's movement, became more conscious of the unfairness of the traditional roles assigned them, and more prone to contest them.

The United Synagogue presented a large target. It was not always the big issues that hurt most. *Notes for the Guidance of Mourners*, for example, stated bluntly that women were not welcome at Orthodox funerals, and reminded the bereaved that *kaddish*, the prayer for the dead, should be recited by the sons of the deceased (Burial Society of the United Synagogue, 1986, pp.2, 5). Women, cold-shouldered at the graveside of their nearest and dearest, could draw but little comfort from a summary service that was sometimes read with unseemly haste and little feeling. Given that access to burial rites was a principal incentive for synagogue membership, this negative encounter provided few reasons for further contact. The synagogue itself was in any case scarcely more welcoming.

Thrust upstairs into the ladies' gallery, or screened off behind a *mechitzah* (partition), lest they distract the men from their devotions, women watched the service but took no part. Women were debarred the making of a *minyan*; denied the right to a prayer-shawl and excluded from the prestigious and ceremonial parts of the proceedings. Within the laity, too, their position was negligible. The belated enfranchisement of women seatholders in 1954, for example, left them ineligible for election to Boards of Management, without a say in rabbinical appointments and thus largely confined to fund-raising and social activities (Newman, 1976, pp.194–7). 'They have their guilds and organized events', said one rabbi, and that, he implied, ought to have been sufficient (Brook, 1989, p.184). The establishment of the home, bearing of children and management of the family – these were the true concerns of the Jewish women. Arrangements which took women beyond their proper sphere, said Chief Rabbi Jacobovits in December 1986, were detrimental to the faith. 'If by opening up our institutional leadership ranks to women', he told officers of the United Synagogue, we would lose or weaken their primary commitment to securing stable marriages, building happy homes and raising intensely Jewish children, the sacrifice of further eroding the strength of Jewish family life would not be worth the gain in improving the management of communal affairs ... Once the primacy of the Jewish home and education is safeguarded, by all means we should mobilize for community service the enormous resources of our women.

(Brook, 1989, p.186)

His hostility to any enlargement of women's roles was a matter partly of tradition and partly of numbers. At a time when Jewish survival was threatened by the non-replacement of an aged and increasingly assimilated population, feminism was a luxury that the community could ill afford (Bermant, 1990, p.140).

The practical importance of all this in relation to the falling membership of the United Synagogue was difficult to establish. There was a common-sense connection, but in the absence of significant historical research or empirical inquiry there was little to suggest a coherent policy initiative. The same lack of knowledge characterized United Synagogue response to the perceived defects in the traditional way of worship.

The want of reverence remained a standing complaint. As in the first half of the twentieth century, so in the second: prayer punctuated by shop talk and idle gossip resisted eradication. The most observant were often the worst offenders, *davening* (praying) at break-neck speed to catch up with the congregation. Then there were those who turned up for a holy service as though dressed for a disco. The old dockside *shul*, which prohibited the attendance of services in sea-boots, wrote one irate correspondent, set a standard in respect of formal attire which others might usefully reflect upon. Problems of prayer and presentation, bad enough among men, were just as serious among women worshippers. The want of spiritual uplift in the synagogue and the minimal role performed by women created a catwalk consciousness and irreverent environment that was truly shocking. One maid of Kent, who attended Catford and Bromley Synagogue on *Rosh Hashana* (New Year) was scandalized. 'The decorum in the women's section', she wrote, 'was appalling, mainly due to the fact that nothing could be heard of the actual service and so the women talked constantly throughout – loudly' (*JC*, 23 October 1987). One of the principal attractions of Bushey, the fastest growing of suburban congregations, was that it was more like the House of God than the House of Dior. 'You can wear what you like', said one woman worshipper; 'there's no competition here' (*JC Magazine*, 25 September 1987, p.14).

Experiments to accommodate growing demands for variety in its services pleased some but offended others. The alternative *minyan*, which was meant to provide for the most strictly Orthodox members, in some cases denuded the established congregation of its most faithful members. Attempts to widen the scope of lay participation were described as a 'communal tragedy' by a spokesman for the almost defunct *chazanut* (cantors). 'In the so called alternative *minyanim* and in synagogues where no properly trained person acts regularly as *chazan*, almost anyone who can read Hebrew and can more or less carry a tune is invited to lead the prayers. As a result the services are uninspiring, unattractive, and boring' (*JC*, 2 August 1991). It may well be that the widening of choice has diminished the outflow of the most Jewishly committed of United Synagogue members to the independent ultra-Orthodox congregations. Innovation might just as easily have weakened the attachment of regular worshippers. We do not know. Indeed, towards the close of our period the United Synagogue authorities concluded that they too were insufficiently informed. An in-depth review of the structure and organization of the United Synagogue, announced at the close of 1991, promised to apply market research to discover how members felt about the institution and what they wanted of it.

4 Progressive (Reform and Liberal) Judaism

Reform Judaism, a product of the Enlightenment, was historically the most significant response to the disintegration of the autonomous corporate structure of traditional Jewry. It represented a means of adjustment whereby the desire for social integration and acceptance could be satisfied without resort to the baptismal font. Orthodox Judaism was thus to be modified, and a living Judaism created in line with modern conditions. By process of constructive change and careful revision it was hoped to maintain a high standard of Jewish religious life.

Apart from certain liturgical changes and revisions in ritual designed to make the service of the synagogue more intelligible to the laity, Reform Judaism was distinguished by an insistence upon the superiority of scripture over the oral law. Rabbinical Judaism, with its emphasis upon election, exile, expiation and restoration encased the faith within a nationalist framework that privileged Jews and served to perpetuate their social and cultural isolation. All this was unacceptable to a Reform Movement that presented Judaism as a universal faith and a source of reconciliation and enlightenment. In Britain, where social acceptance preceded emancipation, pressures to modernize the faith were slight. Moreover, mass immigration from Eastern Europe, the heartland of Orthodox Judaism, meant that the space for modernization was limited. Until the beginning of our period, then, Reform Judaism was a marginal concern.

Hitler's war changed all that. For the Reform Movement in Anglo-Jewry the take-off into self-sustaining growth came from the stimulus supplied by the Nazis. Refugees from Central Europe, and above all Germany, provided Albion's reformers with human and material resources, a distinct ideology and a theological potential. The newcomers, bearers of a rational religion with an established tradition, found Judaism in Britain lacking in reason, decorum and dignity. *Shuls* with a 'German' character were much preferred. As one of them explained: 'It is much nicer in our synagogue, much quieter. The English Jews are so restless and noisy' (Berghahn, 1988, p.234). Some founded their own communities. Alyth Gardens Reform Synagogue in north-west London and Belsize Park Liberal[2] Synagogue were largely German Jewish congregations.

The Nazis supplied more than just the laity. German Reform refugees included a cadre of rabbis, many of them graduates of the Berlin Hoch-schule, the famous centre of Reform Jewish learning, whose training and knowledge did much to improve the standards and status of the backward British. Distinguished scholars and teachers such as Werner Van Zyl, Ignaz Maybaum, Ellen Littmann and Aryeh Dorfler were essential to the forma-tion of a Reform ministry capable of meeting post-war requirements.

Infrastructural growth was rapid. The 1940s saw the formation of the Association of Synagogues in Great Britain to co-ordinate the expansion followed by the creation of a Rabbinic Assembly and a Reform Beth Din to guide the movement, settle marital disputes and determine questions of status. The Leo Baeck College, a seminary to train recruits for the ministry and provide rabbinic leadership, was opened in 1956. The Reform Syna-gogues of Great Britain (RSGB), the present name of the Reform Move-ment, was adopted in 1958.

Reform Judaism in Britain in the course of the past half century established itself as a significant part of Anglo-Jewry. Its headquarters, at the Sternberg Centre for Judaism in London, formed part of the largest non-orthodox community outside North America. Apart from the purely spiritual, it had cultural, education and welfare facilities, a youth move-ment and made special provision for women. Its rabbis were media person-alities and its influence was considerable. Its 40 congregations were concentrated in the Greater London region, but were also to be found in the provinces and in new communities such as Milton Keynes. All in all the movement by the last decade of the twentieth century accounted for 15 per cent of Jews and the proportion was rising.

The growth of the British Reform Movement was largely a post-war phenomenon. Only five of its congregations existed before 1945 (Bermant,

---

[2] 'Liberal' in a German context is the equivalent of 'Reform' in English.

1969, p.237). Liberal Judaism, by contrast, was growing even before the impact of German immigration. By the close of World War I there was a Liberal Jewish Synagogue. By the close of World War II there was a Liberal Jewish Movement (Kershen, 1990, p.24). The Union of Liberal and Progressive Synagogues (ULPS), formed in 1944, was kept busy organizing congregations, groups and attendant facilities. In 1949 there were eleven congregations recognized by the ULPS; the Liberal Progressive population, its president told a parliamentary inquiry, probably accounted for 10 per cent of British Jews (Gluckstein, 1949, qq.34, 64–5). New machinery to provide guidance on religious questions was subsequently developed. The Rabbinic Conference came into being in 1964 and there followed a Rabbinic Board which does for the Liberals what their ecclesiastical courts, *botei din*, do for the Orthodox and Reform communities.

Differences between traditionalists and progressives were deep. Orthodox and Reform-Liberal institutions were dissimilar in organization and ethos as well as in theology, practices, customs and ceremonies. The non-Orthodox communities were congregationalist in sentiment and more democratic in their arrangements. The RSGB and the ULPS were essentially federations of autonomous congregations with little of the top-down management that characterized the United Synagogue and Chief Rabbinate. Progressive rabbis, though not submissive like their Orthodox compeers, were more directly accountable to their congregations. Those who offended synagogal sensibilities, or otherwise proved unworthy, placed pulpit and salary at risk.

The gender base of the progressive rabbinate was equally distinctive. Like the Church of England, the United Synagogue was resistant to the claims of women. The scope for participation was narrower in respect of leadership positions in the laity and non-existent in the ecclesiastical sphere. Reform and Liberal Judaism were markedly more egalitarian in the recruitment of the ministry, in their religious practices and in the administration of the synagogue. Women became accepted as rabbis, wardens and senior office holders in the RSGB and ULPS. Progressive synagogues, moreover, had no women's gallery. Neither the service of the synagogue nor the liturgy were gender-specific. Women sat with the men, prayed with the men, and performed an equal part in the ritual observances.

Equality was not the only innovation encountered among the non-traditionalists. Equally striking was the latitude permitted in the act of worship. The wearing of prayer-shawls and head-coverings, *de rigueur* in the Orthodox synagogue, were optional. The didacticism of the service, much of it recited in English, was another source of differentiation. The Progressive service sought to instruct the faithful, the Orthodox to inspire them. The RSGB's prayer books, which included extensive study anthologies for home reading, were in spirit closer to the Open University than to Zion. Liberal Judaism was, if anything, even more cerebral. Stephen Brook, a kind of Jewish Defoe, who made a tour of the whole community in the late eighties, found Liberal worship distant, rational and austere, with all the spontaneity of a military tattoo. Joining the Sabbath service at the South London Liberal Synagogue was like praying in a cold store (Brook, 1989, pp.133–4).

In personal and domestic observances, particularly in relation to the dietary laws, there was equal diversity. *Kashrut*, condemned as a source of Jewish separatism, was abandoned by the Liberals and frowned upon by Reform Jews. A more divisive move could scarcely be imagined. Progressive homes and synagogues became suspect; social interaction with the Orthodox ceased; relations were restricted to the public and the formal. For Jewish traditionalists this was proof sufficient that the un-Orthodox were no better than *goyim* (gentiles). Confirmation, if at all required, was in any case supplied by the Progressive approach to marriage and conversion.

Out-marriage, it was noted earlier, presents Anglo-Jewry with its greatest challenge. Traditionalist attempts to fortify the faithful, centred upon improved educational provision and measures to make the United Synagogue more attractive, stopped short of radical innovation in respect of mixed marriages and the admission of converts arising from such unions. The steady refusal to countenance conversions of convenience on the part of the Orthodox authorities, and their denial of the patrilineal progeny of such marriages, stood in marked contrast with the much more flexible position adopted by the Progressive rabbinate. On the basis that a new Jew is better than a non-Jew and a half-Jew is better than none, the Liberal and Reform authorities were altogether more accommodating towards those who wished to marry into the faith and raise their children accordingly. Such conversions were not recognized by the Chief Rabbi who in this respect was even more demanding than his counterpart in Jerusalem.

The gap between Orthodox and Progressive supplied the most obvious, but by no means the sole, source of cleavage within Anglo-Jewry. The distance separating Reform Judaism from Liberal Judaism was narrower but nonetheless significant. The Liberals, who in some respects were to Judaism as the Unitarians to Christianity, were much more radical in their theological formation. Judaism, in their hands, became a form of ethical monotheism. In dealing with the Bible, its laws, stories and prophecies, the 'critical' position was adopted. The opening of the Red Sea and the suspension of sunset became man-made miracle stories; festivals, holy days and ceremonies mere props. Sabbath observance was said to be a rabbinical creation, ritual circumcision a form of barbarism, the prohibition on cremation outdated and ritual mourning one of the many antiquated customs that served to crush the true spirit of religion (Lazarus, 1937). All in all,

Orthodox Judaism was said to be too mechanical, legalistic and unthinking. The Torah was cast aside and the Sinaitic Revelation replaced by a Progressive Revelation based upon the higher dictates of individual conscience and reason. Liberal Judaism became a religion of the Prophets who, according to one exponent, 'helped to lift Judaism out of the rut of a narrow nationalism and of a rigid ceremonialism and make it a living force in the everyday life of the individual. They broke down every barrier which would act as a check on its universalism'. And, she concluded: 'It is not too much to assert that if Judaism is to survive, it must be based upon the Judaism of the Hebrew Prophets' (Lazarus, 1937, p.46).

In the third quarter of the twentieth century it became clear that Progressive Judaism in Britain was too far in advance of the laity. The Holocaust, the establishment of the state of Israel and the wars which followed had strengthened Jewish identity and made some progressive tenents questionable. Universalism and optimism, in particular, had been badly shaken by World War II. There was evidence, too, that attachment to tradition was more solid than might have been expected. The Jacobs Affair, the great disruption of the late fifties and early sixties (see below, pp.119–25) seemed, if anything, to show that there was little demand for the reconstruction of Orthodox Judaism.

The repositioning of the RSGB during the seventies and eighties found expression in a more positive attitude towards questions of self-identity and religious tradition. Its about-turn on Jewish nationalism was particularly striking. Zionism, once viewed as the very worst form of Jewish particularism, was now seen as fulfilling essential spiritual and security requirements. The RSGB joined the World Zionist Organization and took its place alongside the Orthodox establishment as cheer leaders for the state of Israel. The establishment of a Reform Jewish Day School was also symptomatic of a more accommodative stance towards separatist sentiments. The process of realignment was equally marked in the spiritual sphere. The Talmud, formerly deemed to be an inferior source, was more quoted than the Prophets. Hasidic texts were revalued upwards and rabbinic commentaries made part of the scholar's curriculum. Kosher food alone was served on synagogue premises. The restoration of particularist prayers to the Reform liturgy, the reinstatement of Hebrew in the service of the synagogue, the enthusiasm for Jewish ceremonial and the general attempt to move divorce and conversion procedures closer to the Orthodox mainstream, were all part of the reappraisal of tradition and search for acceptance within a conservative community in which Reform Judaism had yet to establish its credentials (Romain, 1990, pp.44–8).

Having moved furthest from tradition, the ULPS had more ground to recover. The RSGB, in shifting its safety-net closer to encourage would-be Orthodox defectors, compelled the Liberals to move in the same direction.

The weakened market position of Liberal Judaism also suggested a new orientation. Liberal synagogue membership increase in London, so rapid in the post-war period, seems to have slowed down by the mid sixties and grown slightly, if at all, thereafter (Prais and Schmool, 1968). The Reform synagogues, by contrast, increased their market share by more than a third between 1970 and 1983 (Waterman and Kosmin, 1986, p.31). Merging, the most obvious solution, was mooted but rejected. Institutional inertia, personal rivalries and differences in ideology and outlook served to frustrate unification. Instead, the Reform and Liberal movements preferred to work within a special relationship. In education and the training of *mohalim* (circumcisors), co-operation was particularly close, but it was in the conjoint management of the Leo Baeck College that it was most significant. The training of ministers in the same seminary was expected to diminish the differences between Reform and Liberal Jews. The transition phase, though, seems to have been more protracted than was once thought likely (Sharot, 1976, p.161). Certainly, the return to tradition among Liberals encountered continuing resistance. Rabbi Julia Neuberger, for example, who found the idea of *Succoth* (harvest festival) celebrations in Streatham ridiculous and considered circumcision uncivilized, harked back to the utilitarian priorities of Claude Montefiore and Lily Montague, the founders of Liberal Judaism. For people such as these, the claims of *Halacha* (Jewish Law) had to be established rather than assumed. Apart from their greater scepticism of tradition, Liberal and Reform Jews remained divided by their differing approach to sensitive status issues. Unlike the RSGB which upheld a matrilineal conception of Jewish descent, Liberal Judaism in the last quarter of the twentieth century continued to accept the children of a non-Jewish mother provided they had been brought up as Jewish and undergone confirmation (Brook, 1989, pp.136–8).

5 The ultra-Orthodox

Orthodox Judaism was equally divided. The United Synagogue and Federation of Synagogues provided for a membership which was not in general observant outside the *shul*. Those who wished to carry their religion into their everyday life looked towards the ultra-Orthodox communities of north-east and north-west London. In the last quarter of the twentieth century these expanded dramatically. Between 1970 and 1983 the ultra-Orthodox congregations more than doubled their proportion of the synagogue-affiliated population of London. As Anglo-Jewry approached the year 2000, its most vigorous growth point was located in certain exotic subcultural groups who in speech and appearance seemed strangely out of place in Stamford Hill and Clapton. The Yiddish-speaking Hasidim, with uncut beards and sidelocks, black hat or furry *shtreimel*, and with their long dark coats, numerous progeny and bewigged wives have, in the past forty years or so, replaced the upwardly mobile East-enders as the dominant Jewish population in the area. Variously estimated at between 10,000 and 15,000, the Hasidim were sufficient both in number and resources to sustain a self-segregating community with a dense network of synagogues, schools and attendant support systems. An assortment of sub-sects – Vishnitz, Satmar, Bobov, Lubavitch, Gur – each with its own *rebbe* or spiritual leader, and each with a special dress code, Hasidic groups traced their roots to a particular town or village East of the Elbe. 'But whereas there were hundreds of miles between one town and another before the war', said one of them, 'now you can walk down the street and go from Hungary to Romania to Poland to Germany to White Russia, all within a few hundred yards' (*Radio Times*, 2–8 November 1991). The proliferation of *stieblach*, tiny synagogues, often just rooms in houses, was striking. In Cazenove Road alone there were four: number 78 housed the Beth Talmund Centre; the Mesifta Synagogue occupied numbers 82–4; Kehillah Chasidim Synagogue was at number 85 and Beth Hamedrash Yetiv Lev next door at number 86 (*JYB*, 1989, pp.97–8). In all, Stamford Hill possessed 35 such synagogues.

Contact with the outside world was minimal. Television did not invade Hasidic homes; newspapers neither. News and information was relayed through the medium of the *Jewish Tribune*, a part-Yiddish, part-English weekly. Marriage partners were also recruited from within. In the event that the local supply of eligible Hasidim proved inadequate, then a match might be arranged with a suitable partner from one of the comparable communities in Antwerp, Gateshead, Manchester, New York or Israel. There was little interaction with the Anglo-Jewish mainstream. 'Many of them', a contemporary reported, 'regard the Chief Rabbinate itself as a vaguely goyish institution which has no place in Jewish life' (*The Observer*, 1 September 1991).

State schools, too, were shunned. The Hasidim maintained 25 primary and secondary schools, six *yeshivot* (academies of higher learning) and two seminaries for girls. There was hardly a sect that did not have its own private school. In these, strict segregation of the sexes was enforced. The language of instruction was Yiddish. The curriculum, designed for a life of Torah study and prayer, was said to be narrow-minded and oppressive, but was probably more effective and fulfilling than the critics sometimes allowed. The boys were preoccupied with religious studies; the girls exposed to some secular learning. At 15, they left school. Girls might attend a seminary; boys transferred to a *yeshiva* to continue their studies. A few underwent vocational training in law and accountancy. Universities, deemed dangerous and subversive, were ignored.

The Hasidim lived a life of simple piety regulated by the Torah and its requirements. These found joyful expression in their daily observances, in the celebration of the Sabbath and festivals and in the dancing and feastings associated with weddings and similar occasions. More striking still was their extraordinary charity, and willingness to succour the sick and the needy. In an age in which conscience was satisfied by a donation and the employment of professional care workers, the Hasidim practised an active charity, bringing unfortunate people into their homes and treating them as members of the household. It was all the more remarkable since their large families, special educational requirements and want of housing meant that Hasidim were themselves often poor, homeless and in need of assistance (*JC*, 13 April 1990). In late twentieth-century Britain there were few other communities in which doors and hearts were opened – as well as wallets.

In politics, too, Stamford Hill was different. Israel, for example, was regarded as a nuisance, if not a positive source of evil, rather than the civil religion worshipped by Anglo-Jewry. The Lubavitch and Gur Hasidim were politically non-Zionist; the 300-strong Satmar Hasidim were Zionist while the handful of non-Hasidic militant anti-Zionist *Neturei Karta* (Guardians of the City) displayed Yiddish posters in their windows condemning Israel's very existence as a blasphemy (*The Independent*, 28 May 1990).

The cohesion of the community, dependent as it was upon voluntary association, was sustained by the close proximity in which its members lived. Kept up to the mark by glances, gossip and subtle social pressures, the Hasidism lived like inmates in a spiritual panopticon. Covert coercion was the norm. Overt sanctions, though, were not unknown. Surprisingly pragmatic in their response to the state and its servants – the Hasidim elected a Labour representative to Hackney Borough Council, negotiated public assistance in housing and education, and police assistance in clearing the Amherst Park district of its prostitutes – the ultra-Orthodox reserved their sternest sanctions for those who would resolve internal differences outwith the community. In the summer of 1991, for example, the mobbing of a family who, contrary to custom, had taken complaints of child abuse to the civil authorities, required a strong police presence to preserve public order (*The Independent*, 11 August 1991). Communal sanctions of this nature were used sparingly. In general the strong commitment to a distinctive religio-culture made them superfluous.

Less outlandish than the Hasidim of north-east London, but equally *frum* (observant) were the ultra-Orthodox communities of Hendon and Golders Green. These traced their lineage to the Central European immigrants of the 1880s. Inspired by the example of Samson Raphael Hirsch of Frankfurt-am-Main, these German and Austro-Hungarain settlers sought to replace the tainted Anglo-Jewish establishment with their own *autritts-gemeinde* (alternative community). Following the Frankfurt tradition, synagogue membership was confined to those of strict orthodox observance, *kashruth* and educational facilities were developed, a burial society created and the banner of orthodoxy hoisted high. The Union of Orthodox Hebrew Congregations, a loose association of like-minded synagogues established in 1926, laid the foundations for the rapid expansion of the late thirties that followed upon the arrival of large numbers of Orthodox refugees from fascism.

The newcomers, concentrated in the Golders Green and Hendon district, developed during the post-war period to become a coherent community with about a dozen constituent congregations, a network of thriving day-schools, primary and secondary, and a very lively cultural life. Although certain judicial, dietary and *mikvah* (ritual bath) facilities were shared with the Hasidim of Stoke Newington and Stamford Hill, the two ultra-Orthodox communities differed in several respects. Sober in appearance, the German immigrants and their descendants were subdued in manner and meticulous in prayer. There was little of the gaiety or revivalist fervour of the Hasidim. Louis Jacobs, who in the early fifties was assistant rabbi in the Golders Green Beth Hamedrash, the largest and most influential of ultra-Orthodox synagogues, was struck by the precision of the proceedings:

> The 'congregation' was very German … strictly observant … [with] a neo-Prussian emphasis on doing this or that exactly right. The service was conducted with the utmost decorum. No one dared to engage in conversation during the services and not a line of the most insignificant liturgical poem was ever skipped. Many of the congregants were Frankfurtians, bringing Hirschian ideals to Britain. A favourite word in the congregation was 'discipline'. Whenever I was questioned as to why they were expected to do one thing and refrain from another, all I had to do was to murmur something about it being part of the Jewish discipline, and that was the end of the matter.
>
> (Jacobs, 1989, p.70)

The Hirschians were also more worldly than the Hasidim. S.R. Hirch's belief that there was no essential incompatibility between secular culture and authentic Judaism was reflected in their rather dissimilar lifestyles. Observers agreed that the Hirschians were drawn from a professional, literary and artistic background. Rabbi Eli Munk, founder of the Golders Green Beth Hamedrash, had obtained his doctorate in Germany for a dissertation on Wordsworth. The community, it was noted, 'includes, among others, university professors, eminent barristers, solicitors, scientists, men who have been through the great public schools and the ancient universities, who have been exposed to the full blast of Western enlightenment … whose whole life is nevertheless guided by the minutiae of Jewish observance' (Bermant, 1969, p.225). The material base of Hasidism is unknown. As yet we have no studies comparable with those of Satmar Hasidism in Williamsburg, New York (Kranzler, 1964; Poll, 1962). The impression, though, is that the ultra-Orthodox of Clapton and Stoke Newington were occupationally narrower and less cultivated than their co-religionists in the north west.

There was, however, a consensus, among contemporaries and scholars, that the success of ultra-Orthodoxy derived in no small part from its educational strategy and the consequent absence of the generational conflict common elsewhere in Anglo-Jewry (Sharot, 1976, p.155). Apart from burial facilities, Hirschians and Hasidim both gave priority to religious instruction. A Jewish Secondary Schools Movement, established in the 1920s by the Union of Orthodox Hebrew Congregations, had by our period transformed itself into a network of preparatory, primary and secondary schools, some private and some voluntary-aided. With the 'yeshiva stream', started in 1961, the Hasmonean High School for Boys created a link with the Gateshead yeshiva, the largest and most prestigious Talmudical college in Britain.

The Gateshead yeshiva, founded in 1927 to perpetuate the highest standards of rabbinical learning and scholarship, was East European in spirit but German in organization. Growth was slow and unspectacular until the persecution of German Jewry brought the transfer of students, teachers and financial security. By the 1960s the yeshiva stood at the centre of a vast educational complex which included a nursery school, with primary and secondary provision (Carlebach, 1991, pp.421–2). It was one of five yeshivot, where ultra-Orthodoxy created its cadres of learned leaders with whom the future rested. Staffed with yeshiva-trained graduates, the Jewish day schools did much to nullify the problem of second generation commitment.

The strictly Orthodox communities, however, did more than retain numbers. By natural increase and missionary means, they grew appreciably. The demography of ultra-Orthodoxy remains to be investigated, but it seems likely that the prohibition on birth control and positive valuation of large families made a significant contribution to the expansion of the population. Families of ten and more children, however, were more than an expression of a Biblical imperative. They were also a replacement population for those destroyed in the Holocaust and an affirmation of the Jewish commitment of the survivors. As one Hasid put it, 'If Jews stop being Jews today, fifty years after the war, Hitler will have won' (Radio Times, 2–8 November 1991). Newborn Jews were not the only source of population growth. Born-again Jews, too, were significant in the expansion of ultra-Orthodoxy, though it is difficult to say by how much. The revival of Orthodox Judaism, widespread within contemporary Jewry, has been well documented in the United States but as yet is little studied in Britain. The social composition of returnees to Judiasm, their age, occupation, gender and number, the possible reasons for their return and the stability of their commitment, all require investigation. More is known about the organizational aspects of the phenomenon and the outreach programmes that were developed to assist the recruitment of returnees. In both the United States and Britain this was the special province of the Lubavitch Hasidim.

Lubavitch, an international outreach movement to uncommitted Jews, arrived in Brooklyn in 1940 and crossed the Atlantic twenty years later. Well funded, and well organized, it created a string of schools, seminaries and community centres in London and the provinces and applied the repertoire of television and street evangelism to encourage the return of wayward Jews. Whereas most ultra-Orthodox preferred disengagement from a polluted secular society, Lubavitch tried to beat the hell out of it. Its methods, as well as its message, provoked continuous controversy. For the mainstream Orthodox, the Lubavitchers were vulgar but valid. Progressives thought them closer to the Moonies than to Moses. The resultant polemics generated more heat than light but testified to a new and formidable missionary presence within Anglo-Jewry. Even if claims to have brought tens of thousands of British Jews back from the brink of assimilation to a strictly Orthodox observance were exaggerated, Lubavitch played a significant role in presenting Orthodox Judaism as the embodiment of an authentic faith and a way of life that valued family, stability and a sense of direction.

6 The Jacobs Affair

Conflict between Orthodox and Progressive Jews became endemic in the second half of the twentieth century. The status of the Board of Deputies and the substance of its work were compromised by the fragmentation of the faith. The privileged position occupied by the Chief Rabbi in its counsels reflected the Victorian origins of its Constitution. Framed in the interests of an Orthodox establishment, its provisions were singularly ill-adapted to the requirements of an increasingly heterodox community. Amendment created controversy and conflict. Questions concerning marriage preliminaries and registration were particularly contentious.

The arrested development of Reform and Liberal Judaism in Britain owed something to its unequal status. Disabilities arising from the marriage registration process sustained the impression that variant forms of Judaism were inauthentic and invalid. The veto exercised by the Chief Rabbi on the marriage-making capacities of dissident congregations thus served as a stamp of inferiority in the eyes of a status-conscious community influenced, as it was, by the ethos and social predominance of the Anglican establishment. The rapid growth in the Liberal Jewish Movement during the 1940s made the Chief Rabbi's role as the Board's religious adviser challengeable as well as intolerable.

The refusal of the President of the Board to extend statutory recognition to the form of marriage in three new Liberal congregations provoked the first post-war religious crisis within the minority. Attempts to obtain an amendment to the Constitution of the Board of Deputies so as to exclude the Chief Rabbi from the certification process in respect of Liberal Jewish applicants, were defeated following the intervention of Dr Israel Brodie, the newly-installed Chief Rabbi. Defeated but defiant, the dissidents withdrew in protest against the intolerance and injustice of their Orthodox opponents. On 1st June 1949 the London *Evening Standard* reported the widening split within the community as the oldest Reform Synagogue and the oldest Sephardie Synagogue joined the Liberals in refusing to elect representatives to the Board of Deputies. Ultimately, special legislation was required to obtain facilities for the certification and registration of marriages in Progressive synagogues (Gluckstein, 1949; 'Liberal Jewish Congregations' HO 45/24303/922198/5). The Marriage Act of 1959, however, did much for Liberal self-esteem but little for communal solidarity, as the Clause 43 controversy was to show.

Pressure to amend the Board's constitution provoked further controversy when, shortly after Lord Jacobovits took office, the Progressives renewed their demands for parity with the Chief Rabbi in respect of the guidance required by the Board in religious matters. To this end Clause 43 of the Board's Constitution was to be amended. This was simply too much for the ultra-Orthodox elements who refused to acknowledge the dissidents as proper Jews, let alone seek their advice on religious issues! Rather than extend consultative status to the Reform and Progressive rabbinates, they walked out (Bermant, 1990, pp.92–3). The basis of representation was widened, but the constituency diminished. The Jacobs Affair, however, was easily the most damaging of post-war conflicts, and to this we must now turn.

We Have Reason to Believe was hardly the literary event of 1957. *Jewish Values*, published three years later, was also quietly received. And why not? Both volumes were thought to be little more than simple restatements of traditional Judaism in the light of modern thought and scholarship. The methods and implications of Biblical higher criticism were recognized, the literal inspiration of the Pentateuch denied and a human role in the composition of the Bible acknowledged. The flames of controversy once kindled by such issues had long since cooled. Orthodox Judaism, though hostile to the new learning, was defensive in spirit and concerned more with consolidation than with confrontation. Differences between literalism and liberalism were left to the rabbis to ponder; communal wisdom held that it was better to do than to think. And so the aforementioned texts made little stir. Anything else would, indeed, have been surprising given that the author, Dr Louis Jacobs, was a pillar of the Establishment and generally deemed to be sound in faith, sensible in judgement and impeccable in credentials.

A poor *yeshiva*-boy from Manchester, Louis Jacobs had spent long years in advanced study at the semi-monastic Gateshead *kolel*, taken *Semichah* (rabbinical ordination) and obtained a doctorate from University College, London. Jacobs was equally impressive as both preacher and teacher. Occupant of the most prestigious pulpit in the United Synagogue – that of the New West End Synagogue in St Petersburg Place, Bayswater – and tutor and lecturer at Jews' College, he was also the *Jewish Chronicle's* anonymous 'religious consultant', pronouncing on this and that aspect of Jewish observance and belief. An unusually gifted man, with a warm and engaging personality, Jacobs seemed destined for the highest office. By some he was spoken of as the natural successor for the principalship of Jews' College; others tipped him as the next Chief Rabbi.

Dr Jacobs shared similar expectations. In 1959 he abandoned the premier pulpit at St Petersburg Place for a comparatively lowly position at Jews' College on the understanding that he would be appointed principal on the retirement of the aged incumbent, Dr Isidore Epstein. The latter reluctantly stood down three years later. But the expected call never came. Chief Rabbi Brodie, notwithstanding his initial encouragement, had had second thoughts about Dr Jacobs' candidature. Indeed, he had become convinced that the would-be heir apparent was unorthodox in belief and quite unfitted for a position of authority within the ecclesiastical hierarchy. Not only would he not countenance Dr Jacobs' elevation to the headship of Jews' College, he also declined to sanction his reinstatement in his old pulpit without a public recantation and an assurance by the theologian that his errant views would not be repeated. Dr Jacobs refused to submit. When his old congregation became as intransigent as its former minister and chose to reappoint him in defiance of the Chief Rabbi, the community was in crisis.

The war of words was unusually sharp. Dr Jacobs, supported by a secessionist congregation of the well connected and the wealthy, was sustained in his defiance by the *Jewish Chronicle*, which favoured a rational and orderly religion and feared the rising tide of extremism within the community. The Chief Rabbi and the dark forces behind him were described as bigotted, unenlightened, medieval, intolerant, irrational, illiberal, imprudent, fanatical, reactionary and so on. The votaries of establishment Orthodoxy were no less generous in the use of pejoratives. Dr Jacobs and his supporters were spoken of as dangerous schismatics and enemies of the faith. The *Jewish Chronicle*, said Dr Brodie, was an abuse and a tyranny. The non-establishment ultra-Orthodox were rather less restrained:

> When he [Jacobs] professes to call himself a Jew ... and to stay within our fold with the sole aim of seducing people to blaspheme our Holiness, defaming our religion, of uprooting the foundation, of corrupting the mind, of defiling the soul, and of being paid for it with fame and honour, then our only answer must be the Torah itself – 'Bring forth him that has cursed beyond the Camp and let all the congregation overwhelm him with stones'.
>
> (Jacobs, 1989, pp.175–6)

The disruption made excellent copy: an obscure minister of a minority faith was suddenly on everyone's lips, the subject of conversation on trains and buses and of amused comment in pubs and clubs. As if from nowhere the Anglo-Jewish establishment had produced the greatest heretic since Martin Luther. 'In the early weeks of 1964', the journalist Chaim Bermant recalled, 'one could hardly open a paper, daily, evening or Sunday, without encountering the familiar bearded visage, the heavy eye-brows and the pensive eyes' of Louis Jacobs (Bermant, 1969, p.250).

How had such things come to pass? Contemporaries were perplexed. Some emphasized the clash of personalities. The Chief Rabbi, a courteous, dignified and once liberal-minded English gentleman, had, it was said, been intimidated by his intolerant obscurantist advisors on the Beth Din. These Talmudic traditionalists, recruited from Russia and Germany, often spoke little English and were quite out of tune with the undemanding and somewhat invertebrate religion practised by the majority of British Jews. Others blamed the victim. Dr Jacobs, by his bombastic and ill-founded claims, had aggravated matters and prolonged the dispute, said Emmanuel Jacobovits, soon to be appointed Brodie's successor as Chief Rabbi. The personal element was undoubtedly pronounced. As Jacobs wistfully recalled: 'Practically every one of my supporters rallied round me, not because of any theological issue but because they believed I had been treated unjustly. I wish it had been otherwise' (Jacobs, 1989, p.171).

An outraged sense of fair play is not, however, a sufficient explanation. The theological content of the crisis, though to some extent drowned in the din of battle, should not be minimized. To Jacobs' opponents it was anything but marginal. Their position requires analysis; and there are other issues. The timing of the conflict, for example, was as startling as the substance. To some, Jacobs seemed to be acting as a Jewish John Robinson. To others, the whole affair seemed curiously reminiscent of the furore unleashed by the publication of *Essays and Reviews* in the 1860s. Why, we may wonder, did Anglo-Jewry have to wait until the 1960s to experience a comparable crisis? And what have been the consequences? To understand the true significance, we must try to set this extraordinary *brouhaha* within its specific historical and sociological context.

Anglo-Jewry was little affected by the controversies associated with nineteenth-century modernism. Bishop Colenso's attack on the historical accuracy of the Pentateuch in the 1860s did, it is true, provoke a serialized book-length refutation in the *Jewish Chronicle*, and there were intermittent interventions into the debate on science and belief. But these were exceptional. In general, the issues raised by biblical criticism, so disruptive of German Jewry, seemed less urgent in the liberal democratic environment inhabited by British Jews. Mass immigration from Eastern Europe, in any case, meant that there was no space for the development of a home-grown *Wissenschaft des Judentums* (Science of Judaism). The implications of historical and scientific advances were remitted to that sorry group, the Anglo-Jewish intelligentsia, a handful of scholars and writers who struggled for an audience and found none.

Conflict, though it might be delayed, could not be postponed indefinitely. Jewish acculturation was relentless. Second and third generation Jews increasingly bumped up against the 'critical' perspectives and diffusive Darwinism of the dominant society. Parents and teachers, confronted by youthful sceptics, were left anxious and confused. Inquiring minds, though easily fobbed off, were rarely satisfied with their elders' performance. The inner history of the *chederim*, should it ever come to be written, would, I suspect, show ill-equipped teachers stumbling around the demography of the Exodus or trying desperately to convince their puzzled charges that Jonah was swallowed by an unknown species of big fish.

Generational change, social mobility and geographical dispersal were not the sole factors making for confrontation. War-related change, above all immigration from central Europe, also contributed to the conflict in the making. Progressive Judaism, we have seen, found itself supplied with troops and the theological hardware necessary for combat. Orthodox battle-preparedness was likewise boosted by the refugee rabbis who were appointed to congregations in London and the provinces, and in due course replaced the native incumbents on the Court of the Chief Rabbi. Strict traditionalists, and acutely aware of the heightened importance of the London Beth Din in the aftermath of Nazi destruction, these men determined upon a rigorous application of religious law (Lipman, 1990, p.220). The post-war Progressive take-off, which confirmed their worst fears, placed the Orthodox rabbinate under pressure. Louis Jacobs was as much a symptom as a cause of the resultant explosion.

His argument, that the Torah was not of divine origin as transmitted to Moses on Sinai, subverted the foundations of classical Judaism. Its implication was that Jews must alter the concept of revelation and, without denying the supernatural idea of God at work in history, must acknowledge the human element in the development of Jewish thought and practice. The argument that revelation was best understood in spiritual rather than literal or historical terms had possibilities, but these, if made, were not heard. What struck the Orthodox rabbis most forcefully was its rampant individualism, and it was this that made Dr Jacobs, an otherwise very conservative figure, seem as radical as any Liberal. How, it was asked, could individual Jews who had discovered their own religious salvation generalize the application? Reliance upon the enlightened conscience was, it was feared, destructive of the traditions that had preserved the Jewish people for so long (Brodie, 1969, pp.343–60). Pluralism was not possible within Judaism simply because it was impossible to legitimate that which denied the constitutive element of the faith, the binding authority of the Law. From this perspective there was little difference between the Progressive Conservatism of Dr Jacobs and the variant deviant forms institutionalized in the RSGB and the ULPS.

That the dissidents were the gravediggers of Judaism was a charge easily rebutted. Other claims, though, were more effective. The dismissal of Progressive Judaism as an inauthentic expression of the faith damaged the reformers' self-esteem and diminished their public standing. Time and again British Jews were reminded that in the state of Israel the Orthodox rabbinate exercised a monopoly of Jewish religious authority. The secessionists, it was implied, were not so much wayward Jews, as not Jews at all. Their rabbis were denied recognition, their rites and practices deemed invalid and every effort made to freeze them out of the religious life of the community. Social intercourse was restricted and children of halachically doubtful Jewish status excluded from schools under Orthodox supervision.

Within the United Synagogue itself occurred a comparable reassertion of traditional standards. The anglicizing influences introduced in the period up to the First World War were deemed inappropriate by a generation that found in non-Jewish models of worship a less useful frame of reference than had their grandparents. Mixed choirs were thus removed, the *mechitzah* reintroduced, canonicals abandoned and the traditional rabbinate reinstated as the proper model for the Jewish ministry. Cantorial music and the *chazanim* who performed it also became casualties of the return to a rather more austere and less labour-intensive tradition of prayer (*JC*, 17 February 1989; 26 July 1991; Sharot, 1976, pp.158–9).

The outcome of these changes confounded both observers and participants. Divisive and painful, the return to tradition exerted a profound effect upon the character of Anglo-Jewry. Reform and Liberal Judaism were not crushed in the Orthodox offensive; nor did Progressive Conservatives succumb. Indeed, the formation of the Masorti Assembly of Synagogues in

1985 brought together five congregations under their Presiding Rabbi, Dr Jacobs, to promote an interpretation of Orthodoxy in line with modern scholarship. Nevertheless the centre of gravity had shifted. Progressive Judaism, like the post-Thatcherite Labour Party, looked very different at the close of the Orthodox attack than at the beginning. Its transformation was such that Dr Jonathan Sacks, who succeeded Lord Jacobovits as Chief Rabbi in 1990, felt able to look beyond the rhetoric towards a process, albeit a very protracted one, of reconciliation (Sacks, 1989, pp.221–5). Godless marxists were by no means alone in their faith in the dialectic!

7 Interfaith relations

The Jewish community, with a continuous presence in Britain for some 350 years, was, at the close of the twentieth century, the oldest non-Christian minority. Its apparent success in revising its rituals and religious practices to accommodate the laws and norms of the wider society has been upheld as a vindication of British tolerance and decency and also as an example for other immigrant minorities who continue to struggle for a new identity in a multi-faith society (Holmes, 1991, p.99; Patterson, 1971, p.48). Both assumptions are questionable. Intolerance, it has recently been argued, so far from a marginal feature of 'the British tradition', forms part of its political and cultural mainstream (Kushner, 1989). And whether the evolution of the Jewish community represents possible lines of development for more recent immigrant groups depends on the latter's actual rather than prescribed wants. Particularly noteworthy in the process of Jewish acculturation was the positive valuation placed upon the Anglican establishment. Once religious tests and other disabilities had been removed, Jews found much to applaud in the position occupied by the National Church. Before the First World War neither Jews nor Christians were disposed to question a church–state relationship that hardly seemed detrimental to the Orthodox minority.

The destruction of European Jewry changed all that. The awful recognition that the death camps were an outcome of a specifically Christian civilization made a redefinition of the relations between the peoples of the covenant urgent. For the churches, revision posed theological problems of exceptional complexity. Apart from repentance and reconciliation, there was a need to purge the liturgies of their anti-Judaism; to confront Christian teaching and practice and to reconsider the significance of the State of Israel in relation to the Land of Israel. No systematic revision took place. The inherent difficulties in such a project proved too great. Steps towards dialogue and encounter relied instead upon piecemeal pronouncements and personal initiatives.

Progress was inevitably slow. The central tenets of a world religion, nearly two thousand years old, resisted rapid adjustment. Church leaders, conscious of the heavy responsibilities laid upon them by faith and history, inched forward. The connection between deicide and genocide, though not formally acknowledged by the Second Vatican Council, was implicit in the decree *Nostra Aetate* (1965) by which Jews were absolved of responsibility for the Crucifixion. The tenth and twentieth anniversaries of the decree underscored the Church's opposition to anti-Semitism in any form, its commitment to a deeper understanding of Judaism and its recognition of the continuing role of the Jewish people in God's purpose.

The Protestant churches, too, were keen to make amends. In 1954, the World Council of Churches, which represented Anglican and other denominations, spoke of the need to redress the 'grievous guilt of Christian people towards the Jews throughout the history of the Church'. Statements issued from its various assemblies and commissions during the next thirty years or so reminded Christians that Jews must not be blamed for the passion of Jesus and urged them to abandon the stereotype image of Judaism as a museum piece, and to view rabbinic Judaism as a creative and dynamic faith. Christians were also asked to consider coercive proselytism a violation of human rights; to recognize the place of Israel in Jewish self-understanding and to accept that the covenant of God with the Jewish people remained valid (Braybrooke, 1990).

British Jews made a positive response. Eschewing inter-faith services and theological dialogue, successive Chief Rabbis nevertheless showed themselves ready to work for a better understanding between church and synagogue. The Council of Christians and Jews, founded in 1942 by Archbishop Temple and Chief Rabbi Hertz, gave concrete expression to a new determination to combat prejudice, discrimination and intolerance among people of different ethnic and religious origins. Apart from the Archbishop of Canterbury and the Chief Rabbi, its ex officio presidents in due course included the Cardinal Archbishop of Westminster, the Moderator of the Free Church Federal Council, the Moderator of the Church of Scotland and the head of the Greek Orthodox Church in Britain. Chief Rabbi Jacobovits, the most ecumenical of incumbents, hoped that the CCJ might collectively function as a moral beacon for the nation, presenting a sense of direction in an uncertain age. In this he was disappointed. Christians were not united in their attitudes towards personal conduct, duty and responsibility, and neither were Jews.

The point was brought home forcibly by the Chief Rabbi's contribution to the *Faith in the City* controversy. *From Doom to Hope*, a sixteen page pamphlet written at the request of Archbishop Runcie, presented a vigorous 'they pulled themselves up by their bootstraps' interpretation of the Jewish immigrant experience in Britain. *Halacha* and history were enlisted in support of an enterprise culture and work ethic which Conservative Central Office could scarcely have improved upon. Its extreme voluntarism, censorious tone and strong Thatcherite sympathies offended some and pleased others. Reform and Progressive Jews were outraged and there were many Orthodox Jews who blanched at the content. Contemporary comment, however, was more than an argument about urban deprivation and the politics of poverty; it also raised new and disturbing questions about Jewish identity.

The emergence of a multi-faith society affected the situation and status of the Jewish minority. The Jewish immigrant experience differed from that of non-Christian New Commonwealth immigrants in several respects. The newcomers from Eastern Europe were received into an established community that was well organized, well heeled and well regarded. In the two and one-quarter centuries that separated the Cromwellian Readmission from the passage of the May Laws in 1882, the Jews had prospered, acquired civil rights and created an institutional framework for the regulation of majority-minority relations and the socialization of their co-religionists from the Pale. The process of adjustment, which made for integration without loss of identity, was accomplished without fundamental changes in the nature of the state. The space required for Jewish worship and observances – the keeping of the Sabbath, the ritual slaughter of meat, religious marriages, and so on – was small and easily accommodated within the existing pattern of church–state relations. The Church of England, indeed, supplied the role-model for the United Synagogue and was a major influence upon the shape and temper of Anglo-Jewry (Englander, 1988, pp.233–5).

The weakening of the Church of England since 1945 has undermined the nineteenth century settlement and deprived Anglo-Jewry of its bearings. With the legitimacy of the national church no longer assured, and disestablishment a real possibility, the Jewish community in the late twentieth century faced the prospect of negotiating a post-Christian order with ethnic and religious minorities to whom it was sometimes difficult to relate. The anguished debates about ethnic affiliation and the census and the hesitant support for race relations legislation were symptomatic of these difficulties. In its opposition to the ethnic representation of Anglo-Jewry in the census, the Board accurately reflected the sentiments of a highly acculturated community which felt ill at ease with the concept of minorities defined in non-religious terms. Its preoccupation with anti-Semitism and comparative neglect of colour prejudice in the race relations sphere were likewise indicative of a certain resistance to programmes of affirmative social action and other radical initiatives associated with Blacks and others. Politically, too, immigrant minorities tended to be located within an anti-Zionist pro-Palestinian politics that, in London at any rate, found vocal expression in a Livingstonian Labour Party with whom suburban Jews found little in common (Alderman, 1989, pp.118–41).

Opportunities for co-operation on religious issues were also circumscribed. Chief Rabbi Jacobovits, who was keen to include British Muslims within the inter-faith community, startled both his own constituents and the nation at large by his unreserved condemnation of Salman Rushdie's *Satanic Verses* in 1989. The book, readers of *The Times* were informed, was an abuse of freedom of speech, a travesty and act of blasphemy which ought to be prohibited. The Chief Rabbi's intervention should not, however, be understood as an ongoing initiative to promote mutual understanding. Lord Jacobovits, though undoubtedly sympathetic to Muslim grievances, was primarily concerned to secure greater recognition of the place of religion in the life of the nation. Judaism was diminished and immorality made rampant when religion, be it Christianity or Islam, was mocked and marginalized. An insult to one was an offence to all. And for this reason, he remained a steadfast supporter of the Anglican Establishment, often seemingly more enthusiastic than the Primate himself! Chief Rabbi Sacks, his successor, who had attended a Church of England school where the Jewish children had a separate assembly, explained the bracing effects of such an environment. 'It made us, of course, acutely aware that we were different, but because those around us were taking their religion seriously, it made us consider our Judaism seriously too … From living with those who valued their tradition, I learnt to cherish my own'. Or, in the words of Jacobovits' biographer, 'it was easier for Jews to preserve their identity in a country which was conscious of its own' (Bermant, 1990, pp.179–81). Anglo-Jewry, then, considered the separation of Church and State and dethronement of Christianity as neither necessary nor desirable. A niche within the Christian polity having proved sufficient, British Jews hesitated to disturb existing arrangements (Sacks, 1991, pp.67–8).

8 Conclusion

Is Judaism in Britain in terminal decline? The prognosis, we have seen, is not good. Population shrinkage, a rising rate of intermarriage, increased divorce and family instability and empty synagogues all signalled the end was nigh. Information gathered by the Statistical and Demographic Research Unit of the Board of Deputies showed that, unless he came quickly, the Messiah might as well not come at all, as on present trends there would soon be no Jews in Britain to redeem.

It also showed that the need for accurate data was never more pressing. Shortly before the Second World War, the *Jewish Chronicle*, with remarkable prescience, called for the formation of a high-powered fact-gathering agency to provide a rational basis for policy formation (*JC*, 3 December 1937). The belated creation of an excellent but under-resourced community research unit in 1965 meant that, for much our period, policy was still grounded in guesswork rather than research. The education-led survival strategy pursued by the United Synagogue under Lord Jacobovits, for example, may well prove to have been a less efficient use of resources than once seemed likely. Studies undertaken towards the close of the twentieth century showed little evidence to justify the enormous investment in Jewish day schools. Sampling a large number of children at Jewish and non-Jewish schools, one investigator found that those at Jewish schools scored higher in terms of ritual practice. But once home background was taken into account there was virtually no difference between the two groups in attitudes towards *mitzvot*, or feelings of Jewish peoplehood. More disturbing still was the finding that those at Jewish schools displayed a weaker religious belief and sense of Jewish ethics. No less damning was the Redbridge Survey which concluded that Jewish secondary schooling had a negative impact upon religious practices and behaviour and that teenage synagogue classes and adult education were at least as effective in their outcomes as Jewish day schools (Kosmin and Levy, 1983).

Optimistic forecasts generalized from American experience may likewise prove to have been misplaced. The thesis recently advanced by Dr Jonathan Sacks, that the forward march of Orthodoxy has been resumed, and that Anglo-Jewry is experiencing a religious revival comparable with that of American Jewry, is based on opinion, not research (Sacks, 1989; 1991). Even if true, it would not follow that the apparent success of the ultra-Orthodox provides a model for the United Synagogue. Adjustment in that direction must entail major changes in organization and orientation with no guarantee that the expected improvement in recruitment and retention would exceed the outflow through intermarriage and social erosion. Progressive Judaism might in the short-run gain from the resultant disruption.

Reform and Liberal movements, it has been seen, have charted a careful course, persistently trailing the Orthodox, varying their distance, but always remaining close enough to encourage and receive those who for personal and theological reasons were alienated from the United Synagogue. Progressive Judaism was, indeed, frequently said to act as a break-fall for those who were pinned on the slopes of uncertainty. As a Liberal spokesman, at the beginning of our period, put it: 'A great number of Jews … who would not otherwise practise religion at all and would fall into irreligion or something worse, come to us and we are, therefore, I feel, fulfilling a most important need in the Jewish community' (Gluckstein,

1949, q. 66). The principal defect of this safety-net strategy was that it redistributed a diminishing synagogue-affiliated population but did little to increase it.

The Orthodox–Progressive split, however, was a symptom rather than a cause of Jewish decline. Unity was less important than strategy, and in this respect neither camp had much to offer. Both preferred to rely on faith rather than facts, and on hunches, common sense and short-term expedients in lieu of policies based on empirically-grounded research. 'It is time', the *Jewish Chronicle* declared, 'that we ... realised that facts and figures are the eyes and ears of a community bent on dealing with the present and safeguarding the future ... Otherwise we may one day find that too big a price – far too big – has been paid for the luxury of lethargy and stonewall indifference'. Those words were written on 3 December 1937. The price is now being exacted.

Bibliography

The following abbreviations have been used in the text:

HO   Home Office Papers (Public Record Office)

JC   *Jewish Chronicle*

JH   *Jewish Herald*

JYB   *Jewish Year Book*

RSGB   Reform Synagogues of Great Britain

ULPS   Union of Liberal and Progressive Synagogues

ALDERMAN, G. (1989) *London Jewry and London Politics 1889–1986*, Routledge, London.

BERGHAHN, M. (1988) *Continental Britons: German-Jewish refugees from Nazi Germany*, Berg, Oxford.

BERMANT, C. (1969) *Troubled Eden: an anatomy of British Jewry*, Vallentine Mitchell, London.
(1990) *Lord Jacobovits: the authorised biography of the Chief Rabbi*, Weidenfeld and Nicolson, London.

BRAYBROOKE, M. (1990) *Time to Meet: towards a deeper relationship between Christians and Jews*, SCM Press, London.

BRODIE, I. (1969) *The Strength of My Heart*, G.J. George and Co., London.

BROOK, S. (1989 edn) *The Club: the Jews of Modern Britain*, Pan Books, London.

BROTZ, H. (1955) 'The Outlines of Jewish Society in London' in Freedman, M. (ed.) *A Minority in Britain*, Vallentine Mitchell, London.

B.S. ROWNTREE PAPERS, unpublished typescript of aide-mémoire of meeting with B. Henriques on 28 October 1949, Leisure Time Enquiry 63, Borthwick Institute, York.

BURIAL SOCIETY OF THE UNITED SYNAGOGUE (1986) *Notes for the Guidance of Mourners*, United Synagogue, London.

CARLEBACH, J. (1991) 'The Impact of German Jews on Anglo-Jewry – Orthodoxy, 1850–1950' in Mosse, W.E. (ed.) *Second Chance: two centuries of German-speaking Jews in the United Kingdom*, J.C.B. Mohr, Tübingen.

CAUDREY, A. 'The Vanishing Jews', *New Society*, 2 October 1987, pp.23–5.

COHN-SHERBOK, D. (1991) *Issues in Contemporary Judaism*, Macmillan, London.

ENGLANDER, D. (1988) 'Anglicized not Anglican: Jews and Judaism in Victorian Britain' in Parsons, G. (ed.) *Religion in Victorian Britain: Traditions*, Manchester University Press, Manchester.

GAY, J.D. (1971) *The Geography of Religion in England*, Duckworth, London.

GLUCKSTEIN, L. (1948–9) Evidence submitted to Joint Select Committee on Consolidation Bills – Marriage Bill [H.L.] [232] Parliamentary Papers vi.

HOLMES, C. (1988) *John Bull's Island: immigration and British society 1871–1971*, Macmillan, London.

HOLMES, C. (1991) *A Tolerant Country?: immigration, refugees and minorities in Britain*, Faber, London.

JACOBS, L. (1989) *Helping with Enquiries: an autobiography*, Vallentine Mitchell, London.

KERSHAN, A.J. (ed.) (1990) *150 Years of Progressive Judaism in Britain*, London Museum of Jewish Life, London.

KOSMIN, B. and LEVY, C. (1983) *Jewish Identity in an Anglo-Jewish Community*, Board of British Jews, London.

KRANZLER, G. (1964) *Williamsberg: a Jewish community in transition*, Philipp Feldheim, New York.

KUSHNER, T. (1989) *The Persistence of Prejudice: anti-semitism in British society during the Second World War*, Manchester University Press, Manchester.

LAZARUS, O. (1937) *Liberal Judaism and its Standpoint*, Macmillan, London.

LIPMAN, V.D. (1990) *A History of the Jews in Britain since 1858*, Leicester University Press, Leicester.

MOONMAN, J. (1980) *Anglo-Jewry – An Analysis*, Joint Israel Appeal, London.

NEWMAN, A. (1976) *The United Synagogue 1870–1970*, Routledge and Kegan Paul, London.

PATTERSON, S. (1971) 'Immigrants and minority groups in British society' in Abbott, S. (ed.) *The Prevention of Racial Discrimination in Britain*, Oxford University Press for the United Nations Institute for Training and Research and the Institute of Race Relations, London.

POLL, S. (1962) *The Hasidic Community of Williamsberg: a study in the sociology of religion*, Free Press of Glencoe, New York.

PRAIS, S.J. and SCHMOOL, M. (1968) 'The size and structure of the Anglo-Jewish population 1960–1965', *Jewish Journal of Sociology*, pp.5–34.

ROMAIN, J. (1990) 'The Changing Face of British Reform', in Kershen (ed.).

SACKS, J. (1989) *Traditional Alternatives: orthodoxy and the future of the Jewish people*, Jews' College Publications, London.
(1991) *The Persistence of Faith: religion, morality and society in a secular age*, Weidenfeld and Nicolson, London.

SHAROT, S. (1976) *Judaism: a sociology*, David and Charles, Newton Abbot.

WATERMAN, S. and KOSMIN, B. (1986) *British Jewry in the Eighties: a statistical and geographical guide*, Board of Deputies of British Jews, London.

YOUNG, H. (1989) *One of Us: a biography of Mrs Thatcher*, Macmillan, London.

3

FRAGMENTED UNIVERSALITY: ISLAM AND MUSLIMS

by John Wolffe

Bristol Jamia Mosque. From the exhibition 'One City – Many Faiths'. Photograph ©
Mark Simmons.

In 1889 one of the first mosques in Britain was built at Woking in Surrey with funds provided by the Begum Shah Jehan of Bhopal in India. In 1989 Muslims became prominent as a result of their outrage at Salman Rushdie's novel, *The Satanic Verses*, and the intervention of an Iranian spiritual leader, the Ayatollah Khomeini. The century had seen many changes, both in British society and culture, and among Muslims themselves, but the events of 1989 dramatically demonstrated that substantial issues remained.

The 'Rushdie affair' and the media's crude misrepresentations and over-simplifications had a profound impact on the consciousness of Muslims and non-Muslims alike. We shall discuss its significance at the end of the essay. At the outset, however, the reader must be warned of the danger of viewing the history of Islam in Britain over the last half-century through 'post-Rushdie' spectacles and is urged to identify and suspend any preconceptions. The impact of *The Satanic Verses* was substantial but undue concentration upon it would distort the overall picture. It is accordingly essential to begin with a description of the historic development of Islam, before considering the development of Muslim communities in Britain since the Second World War. The essay will conclude with a consideration of how Islam has related to the British situation.

1 The historical and global context[1]

The founder of Islam as an organized religion was the prophet Muhammad (570–632). Although emphatically not accorded by Muslims the divine status attributed to Christ by Christians, he has still been the focus of tremendous reverence, as the vehicle for the divine revelation of the Qur'an and as a role-model for the performance of Islam. To the ordinary Muslim believer, the Qur'an is quite simply and literally the Word of God, in the Arabic text as originally given. Throughout the world Arabic, as the language of Muhammad and the Qur'an, is the language of Muslim devotion.[2]

The institutional history of Islam dates from the last decade of the life of Muhammad. Following an initial period during which the revelation of the Qur'an had commenced and the Prophet had begun to preach in

---

[1] This section is in no way intended as an overall introduction to Islam, but is designed to highlight those of its characteristics most relevant to understanding the position of Muslims in Britain. See Cragg (1987), El-Droubie (1991), Esposito (1988) and Welch (1984) for further information on the general development of Islam as a world religion.

[2] It is thus impossible to study Islam without using the original Arabic terms. For the sake of simplicity these have been transliterated without diacritical marks.

Mecca, in 622 he and his followers set up the first Muslim community at Medina. Mecca submitted in 630 and, within a few decades of Muhammad's death, the Islamic state that he had founded ruled over much of the Middle East and north Africa. During the eighth century, Muslim political power extended into Spain and the Indian subcontinent.

The early history of Islam thus differs from that of Christianity in the important respect that from the outset political and religious authority were intertwined. It was only with the conversion of the Roman emperor Constantine, three centuries after Christ, that the Christian church became linked with the state, and relations between the two entities have been a major issue ever since; but any concept of religion distinct from the state and of separated 'secular' and 'sacred' spheres is alien to historic mainstream Islam. An important corollary of this is the Islamic ideal of the *umma*, the universal community of all Muslims united in obedience to the teachings of the Qur'an and following the *sunnah*, the normative example of Muhammad as recorded in the *ahadith* (singular, *hadith*), records of his sayings and doings. The working out of specific applications was a complex process of reasoning by analogy and identifying the consensus of the Muslim community. This generated four main schools of law among Sunni Muslims: the Hanafi, Maliki, Shafii and Hanbali.[3] The Hanafi predominates in the Middle East and the Indian subcontinent and hence among Muslims in Britain, but the other schools are also represented in the United Kingdom.

The solidarity of Muslims is derived from their relationship with God, the nature of which is encapsulated in the Arabic concept of *islam*, best rendered into English by linking the two words 'peace' and 'commitment'. This can be further illustrated by quoting the opening *surah* (chapter) of the Qur'an:

> Praise belongs to God, the Lord of all Being,
> the All-merciful, the All-compassionate,
> the Master of the Day of Doom.
> Thee only we serve; to Thee alone we pray for succour.
> Guide us in the straight path,
> the path of those whom Thou hast blessed,
> not of those against whom Thou art wrathful,
> nor of those who are astray.[4]

---

[3] There are also four *Shi'ite* schools.

[4] Quotations from the Qur'an are from the translation by Arberry (1964). It must be stressed that for Muslims there can be no substitute for the original Arabic text.

Believers are united in their sense of submission to God which overrides all other authority, and in their shared claim to follow the 'straight path'.

The so-called 'five pillars of Islam' all reinforce this submission to God and the sense of being part of the world-wide Muslim community.

1   *Shahadah* (witness) is the public enunciation of the fundamental statement of Muslim belief: 'There is no god but God; Muhammad is the messenger of God'. It is the second clause that unequivocally distinguishes Muslims from Christians and Jews.

2   *Salat* (ritual prayer) is required at dawn, midday, afternoon, sunset and at night. It consists of a prescribed sequence of prostrations and recitations. It must be preceded by ablutions of the exposed parts of the body. In the performance of the salat the communal dimension of Islam is strikingly apparent: all face Mecca and (with the sexes segregated) line up shoulder to shoulder. Although it is preferable to perform the salat in a mosque whenever possible, there is no requirement to do this except for men at midday prayers on a Friday.

3   *Zakat* (alms-giving) is simultaneously a purification to justify the holding of property, an expression of the sincerity of the individual's commitment to Islam, and a means of practical social welfare in the Muslim community.

4   *Siyam* (fasting) is the obligation of able-bodied Muslims over twelve years of age to abstain from food, drink and sexual intercourse between dawn and sunset throughout the month of Ramadan. This shared expression of commitment and self-control serves further to strengthen solidarity.

5   *Hajj* (pilgrimage) is the duty of all Muslims (unless prevented by physical or financial circumstances) to travel to Mecca once in their lifetime to participate in the rites celebrated from the eighth to the thirteenth day of the month of Dhu'l Hijja. The convergence of believers from all points of the compass graphically illustrates the universality of Islam and the importance of its central focus on the city where Muhammad lived fourteen centuries ago.

The subsequent history of Islam has resulted in the formation of numerous different groups and ways of believing within the basic structure outlined above. The earliest major division was that which occurred in the late seventh century between the Sunnis, now about 90 per cent of all Muslims in the world, and the Shiahs, now around 10 per cent of the total (proportions from Watt, 1988, p.125). The divergence originated in political dispute over the leadership of the Muslim community. Whereas the Sunnis accepted the authority of the Ummayad and later the Abbasid caliphs, the Shiahs rejected the authority of the caliphs and followed rather the succession of *imams* descended from the Prophet himself through his daughter Fatima and his son-in-law Ali, the first imam – 'Shi'ite' means 'party of Ali'. The word 'Sunni' denotes the 'people of the Sunnah', implying specific adherence to the example and teaching of Muhammad, as mediated in practice through the *shari'a* (divine law) reached over generations through the *ijma* (consensus) of scholars. Shi'ites, for their part, attribute infallible authority to the imams.[5] However since the succession of imams ended in the ninth century, and pending the anticipated return of the last imam at the end of history, the *ayatollahs* (meaning 'signs of God') serve as the spiritual guides of Shi'ites. Shi'ite devotion differs from that of Sunnis in the veneration of imams and saints and in a more elaborate ritual calendar. It is itself divided: disputes over the succession of the later imams led to the emergence of the Ismailis, whose most important subsection is led by the Aga Khan. This group was especially strong among Indians who had migrated to east Africa and who subsequently came to Britain in the 1960s and 1970s. The Ismaili community is particularly wealthy and well-organized and has become a significant force in the London business world (Hallam, 1972; *The Times*, 18 August 1987).

A further major source of conflict in early Islam was Sufism, a mystical movement which resisted the legalism and austerity of Sunni orthodoxy in favour of the cultivation of inward spiritual experience, the veneration of saints, and the use of music and ritual in public worship. The synthesizing genius of Abu Hamid al-Ghazzali (1058–1111) produced a framework in which a controlled Sufism was integrated into the Sunni mainstream in a brilliant combination of mysticism, law and theology (Esposito, 1988, pp.105–7). However the tension between outward legalism and inward spiritual experience continued to have both a creative and a divisive impact. It was represented personally and institutionally by the presence of two kinds of religious élite: *ulama*, experts in Islamic law theology, and Sufi *pirs* (also known as *sheikhs* and *derveshes*), guides to their disciples on the mystical path (Metcalf, 1982, p.17). The two categories could overlap but could also potentially become polarized.

An awareness of these ancient divisions is important for understanding the varieties of outlook among Muslims in modern Britain, but the more immediately relevant context is the development of Islam since the eighteenth century on the Indian subcontinent, where the majority of settlers in Britain originated. In numerical terms Muslims have always been a minority overall in India,[6] and thus faced particular problems in the

---

[5] The special significance attributed to the word 'imam' by Shi'ites should not be confused with its more general use to denote the leader of the prayers in any mosque.

[6] The word 'India' when used here with reference to the period before 1947 refers to the whole subcontinent, including present-day Pakistan and Bangladesh.

light of the presumption of classical Islam that Muslims live in an Islamic state. Their position, however, was eased by the fact that regionally, notably in the north and north west and in Bengal, they were a majority. During the sixteenth and seventeenth centuries, moreover, under the rule of the Mogul emperors, Muslims were dominant politically over much of India. During the eighteenth and nineteenth centuries the decline of the Mogul empire and the growth of British power in the subcontinent presented a real dilemma for Muslims of how they were to live with a Hindu numerical majority under Christian rule. The difficulty was heightened when after the so-called 'Indian Mutiny' in 1857 the last nominal Mogul emperor was deposed by the British, and all semblance of general Muslim rule thus ended (Hardy, 1972, pp.2–11, 23–30, 61).

The later nineteenth and twentieth centuries were an important period of readjustment and revival among Indian Sunni Muslims, from which emerged a number of movements now represented among settlers in Britain. The Deobandis took their name from the *madrasa* (school) founded in 1867 in the town of Deoband ninety miles north east of Delhi. This became the effective headquarters of the movement. The Deobandis have sought to promote a revival of Islamic observance, spirituality and culture while accepting that they would not be assisted by the state, let alone be able to control it. Their theological standpoint has been in some respects a revival of the classical synthesis of al-Ghazzali, with the acceptance of some limited aspects of the strong Sufist tendency of popular Indian Islam controlled by a strong emphasis on the obligation to study and observe the shari'a (Metcalf, 1982, pp.138–97).

The Ahl-i-Hadith movement, which also emerged in the aftermath of the 'Indian Mutiny', went much further in the desire to purify the faith. Its adherents condemned Sufism and rejected the established structure of shari'a in favour of a return to the rigorous application of the Qur'an and the ahadith, hence their name. This led them to a puritanical style of life and variations in the form of prayer which were disruptive of worship in the mosques. Like the Deobandis they accepted the reality of a non-Islamic state in India (Metcalf, 1982, pp.268–96; Robinson, 1988, pp.6–8). They are less numerous in Britain than the Deobandis, but still have branches in most major cities and are particularly strong in Birmingham (Raza, 1991, p.15). They have an agenda for the purification of Islam in Britain from what they consider to be a range of accretions and superstitions (Mirpuri, 1987, p.10). In the late nineteenth century the Ahl-i-Hadith split, and the Ahl-i-Qur'an emerged. They insisted that only the Qur'an provided authentic authority. Otherwise known as the Pervaizi, after one of their leaders, they have a small presence in Britain (Raza, 1991, p.16; Robinson, 1988, pp.7–8).

The Barelwis, so called after their founding figure Ahmad Riza Khan Barelwi (1856–1921), represent a converse tendency to the Ahl-i-Hadith.

Whereas these latter have sought a return to a perceived early Islam, and the Deobandis have endeavoured to restore the classical medieval forms of the religion, the Barelwis found their inspiration in their own environment of nineteenth-century India and particularly in Sufi devotion. This meant in practice the veneration of saints and the endorsement of other customs (Robinson, 1988, pp.8–9). In particular Ahmad Riza had an intense devotion to the Prophet and held strongly to the Sufi doctrine of *nur-i muhammadi*, that there was a pre-existent and eternal 'light of Muhammad'. Accordingly considerable importance was given to celebration of *mawlid*, the anniversary of the prophet, variously interpreted as commemorating his birth or his death (Barton, 1986, pp.97–8; Metcalf, 1982, pp.300–2). Like the Deobandi and the Ahl-i-Hadith, the Barelwis initially saw the colonial state as irrelevant, an attitude which has in general been replicated in their attitude to government and politics in Britain. Ahmad Riza's acceptance of much of the practice of popular Islam gained an extensive following in those parts of rural India which were subsequently to be major sources of migration to Britain. Accordingly the Barelwis probably constitute the largest group among British Muslims.

These three movements in different ways reflected a concern to reassert Islamic identity in an unfavourable political and cultural environment. This implied the development of strong structures of belief and community which resulted in antagonism towards other Muslims as much as, if not more than, towards Christians and Hindus. One scholar has explained this process as follows:

> It was, it seems, crucial to define oneself against other Muslims, to distinguish sheep from goats among those with whom one could communicate. Simply to validate one's worth on the grounds of being Muslim was too theoretical: debates with Christians and Hindus offered an opportunity to consolidate one's position, but offered no meaningful exchange. Among Muslims, however, there were shared symbols of controversy…

> (Metcalf, 1982, p.358)

Thus the leaders of the various groups spent considerable time denouncing the teachings of the others. Tensions between the Barelwis on one side and the Ahl-i-Hadith and the Deobandis on the other tended to be reinforced by the social distinction between the former, generally poorly educated rural people, and the other two groups which appealed to more sophisticated urban Muslims (Metcalf, 1982, p.313). The move to Britain heightened, if anything, the need to define Muslim identity and thus strengthened the sectarian divisions of Indian Islam (Raza, 1991, pp.23–4).

The Ahmadiyya, founded by Mirza Ghulam Ahmad (1839–1908), have been particularly subject to the hostility of other groups, which usually deny their claim to be Muslims at all. Ahmad proclaimed himself a *Mahdi* (expected one) who would regenerate Islam, as well as believing that he was both a representative of the Hindu god Krishna and the resurrected Jesus, who, he maintained, had been buried in Srinagar in Kashmir. The movement has been characterized by an emphasis on vigorous proselytization, and as a result of persecution in Pakistan, recently moved its world headquarters to London, thus giving it a prominence in Britain out of proportion to its relatively small number of supporters in the country (Robinson, 1982, pp.12–14). It is further divided into two groups, the Qadianis and the Lahoris; the latter having had a long association with the mosque in Woking (Johnstone, 1981, p.179).

The tendency of all the movements considered so far to reject Western government and culture in the Indian subcontinent was contested by the very different approach of Saiyid Ahmad Khan (1817–98). He argued that there was nothing intrinsically unislamic in Western thought, stressed the common ground between Islam and Christianity and maintained that the future for Muslims in India lay in coming to terms with the British. With a view to schooling the next generation of leaders in this vision, he founded during the 1870s the Anglo-Muhammadan Oriental College at Aligarh (Esposito, 1988, pp.136–40; Hardy, 1972, pp.94–104). Muhammad Iqbal (1875–1938) resembled Ahmad Khan in his readiness to draw on both Islamic and Western intellectual sources but differed from him in seeking not accommodation with the British but the creation of an independent Muslim state. During the inter-war period his thought became the major ideological source of the Muslim League and eventually provided the rationale for the formation of the state of Pakistan in 1947 (Esposito, 1988, pp.140–5). The intellectual tendencies represented by Ahmad Khan and Iqbal became influential among well-educated Muslim élites seeking to link the practice of their religion to a strategy which permitted the exercise of genuine political power. Their impact can be discerned among the corresponding elements of the Muslim community in Britain (Robinson, 1988, pp.11–12).

The continuing political and religious ferment of the Indian subcontinent in the twentieth century led to the emergence of two further movements which represent strongly contrasting responses to the problem of how to live as a Muslim in the modern world. The Tablighi Jamaat, which developed in the Delhi area from the 1920s, evolved from the Deobandi tradition, sharing its political quietism but eschewing its introverted religious controversialism. Their emphasis, reflecting the Sufi inheritance, has been on the spiritual renewal of faith and a gently energetic missionary endeavour. Readily recognizable by their distinctive male dress, a cap, beard and long shirt, they have a visible presence in Britain centred on Dewsbury (Raza, 1991, pp.14–15; Robinson, 1988, pp.14–16). The Jamaat-i-Islami, on the other hand, was founded in 1941 by Abul Ala Maududi

(1903–79) to promote Islam as a total system for human life and hence to create an Islamic state which practised the principles of the religion. Since 1947 they have been a significant political force in Pakistan, resisting perceived secular tendencies (Esposito, 1988, pp.153–60; Robinson, 1988, pp.16–19). Their importance in Britain lies not in any substantial body of committed support, but in their external links, their organizational capacity and their potentially radical programme which would tend to have a natural appeal to a community in a state of insecurity and transition. The UK Islamic Mission and the Islamic Foundation reflect their influence (Johnstone, 1981, p.177; Raza, 1991, pp.19–20; Robinson, 1988, p.20).

The reader perplexed by the complexity of the varieties of Islam originating in India should not become obsessed with detail, but rather ponder the general significance of these movements and the divisions between them for understanding the situation of Muslims in Britain. The community has been an internally divided one, especially as few of its members are more than one generation removed from their south Asian origins and many maintain close links with families still living in the Indian subcontinent. Imams often came directly from similar posts in Pakistan and Bangladesh. Accordingly, historic disputes continued to cast their shadow even when they were imperfectly understood. Moreover a further range of internal tensions arose from cultural and linguistic differences between communities drawn from different ethnic groups; and from the engagement of Muslims in the turbulent politics of their countries of origin, most notably in the Pakistani civil war of 1971, in which Indian inter- vention led to the formation of the state of Bangladesh. Such issues may have had little directly to do with religion, but they still tended to preclude united organization for Islamic purposes (Barton, 1986, p.68). At the same time, however, south Asian Islam has provided Muslims in Britain with potential answers to the problem of preserving Muslim integrity under non-Muslim government; means to a constructive resolution of the historic tension between Sufism and legalism; and the stimulus of a number of revivalist movements. This is an inheritance of considerable religious vitality, even if its application to a new social and cultural environment has presented a considerable challenge.

Although the formative influences on the majority of Muslims in Britain have been drawn from the Indian subcontinent, developments in the Arab world and Iran have also, particularly during the second half of our period, had an important impact. This is partly attributable to the presence of significant minorities of Arabs and Iranians among Muslims in this country and to the readiness of oil-rich countries to support Islamic organizations in Britain. It also arises from what seemed to be a dramatic resurgence of Islam in that part of the globe during the 1970s and 1980s which attracted the attention of Muslims everywhere. The defeat of Egypt, Syria and Jordan in the Six-Day War with Israel in 1967 was perceived as a low point in Muslim fortunes, and led to soul-searching, a yearning for truly Islamic civilization, and an increasing rejection of the perceived values of the West. In October 1973 another war against Israel coincided with Ramadan and was conducted in a mood of notable Islamic fervour. An Arab embargo on oil supplies demonstrated a new-found potential to coerce the West and was a further important boost to morale. Above all the Iranian Revolution of 1978–9 served as an inspiration to recover the vision of a truly Islamic social order. Although the Iranian Shiahs were viewed with a certain coolness by Sunni Muslims in Britain and elsewhere their achievements still stirred admiration. The result has been to stimulate further a revivalist mood, the rejection of perceived Western cultural and social values (though not technology) and the assertion of Islam as a total way of life (Esposito, 1988, pp.164–71).

It is all too easy for the hostile or cynical observer to question the depth of Muslim devotion and the reality of a universal Islamic community, by pointing to the political dimensions of Islamic revival, to instances of conflict between and within predominantly Muslim states, and to the failure of numerous individuals to perform salat, zakat and siyam with due regularity. However, while evidence of this kind cannot be gainsaid, it merely indicates that in practice there are numerous shades and varieties of religious commitment among Muslims, as among the adherents of every other major religion. The ideal of the *umma* has remained a tremendously powerful and emotive vision in spite, or perhaps because, of the extent to which it can often seem rather threadbare in practice. Muslims in Britain can draw on a rich heritage of faith associated with their south Asian origins. They also have a consciousness of being adherents of a religion which by 1990 was standing tall on the world stage as the most formidable ideological alternative to both Western Christianity and secularity. Although, as we shall see, the difficulties facing Muslims in maintaining their observance and convictions in the British situation have been considerable, this wider context has provided powerful inspiration to persevere.

2 The development of Muslim communities in Britain

In this section a brief survey of the early history and post-war expansion of Islam in Britain will be followed by an examination of the development of religious observance among Muslims. The emphasis of this section will be on the internal development of Islam; whereas the next section will consider the interaction of Muslims with British society as a whole.

Although large numbers of Muslims did not arrive in Britain until after the Second World War, smaller-scale migration occurred from the nineteenth century onwards as a result of political, cultural and commercial activities. In particular seamen from the Middle East and India came to British ports, and became more settled when they took jobs on shore and married local women. In this way permanent Muslim communities formed in ports, notably Cardiff, Liverpool, South Shields, and the East End of London. Other Muslims came to Britain, mainly from India, to study, and some stayed in the country in professional occupations. There were some converts among the indigenous population, particularly among women who had married Muslims. Prominent converts included William Henry Quillian, a Liverpool lawyer who embraced Islam in 1887, and the 5th Baron Headley, who was converted in 1913 (Ally, 1979, pp.1–2 and 1981, p.47; Tibawi, 1981, p.194). In 1915 the Muslim population was estimated to be around 10,000. A number of *zawiyas* (small mosques in the Sufi tradition) were set up around the turn of the century. Some ceased to function after the First World War as a result of bombing of their premises and the lack of leaders after the first generation. However during the inter-war period, Sufis such as Sheikh Abdullah Ali al-Hakimi in Cardiff and Sheikh Ahmad on Tyneside kept Islamic observance alive and even gained some recognition of Muslim needs from local authorities. The communities grew further as a result of continued settlement by seamen and others during the first half of the twentieth century, especially when wartime conditions between 1914–18 and 1939–45 had the effect of stranding them in Britain (Ally, 1979, p.2 and 1981, pp.1, 32–40; Sanneh, n.d., pp.3–4).

During the two decades following the Second World War the earlier trickle of Muslim settlement became a steady and substantial flow. This arose in part from political circumstances, including the partition of India in 1947, civil strife in Cyprus in the 1950s, and in the 1960s and 1970s the hostility of east African governments, notably that of Idi Amin in Uganda, to Asians who had migrated to that region in the nineteenth century. Additionally there was the economic attraction of employment and good wages (by Indian standards) in the British boom of the 1950s. There were also more localized factors such as the construction of the Mangla Dam in southern Kashmir in the early 1960s, which forced a large number of the Mirpuris living in that part of Pakistan to leave their land. The compensation they received enabled them to move to Britain. Particular regions of the subcontinent are thus strongly over-represented:[7] in addition to Mirpur these include the Punjab (Pakistan), Sylhet (Bangladesh) and Gujerat

[7] The term 'over-represented' is of course used here and subsequently in its technical statistical sense, denoting comparison between numbers in Britain and numbers in the Indian subcontinent. No qualitative judgement is implied.

(India). Muslims are similarly over-represented among migrants from regions which remained Indian after 1947, approximately 20 per cent of the ethnically Indian population in Britain, as opposed to 11 per cent in India itself (Ally, 1979, pp.2–3; Wahhab, 1989, pp.6–7). Migration from the sub-continent peaked in the early 1960s as people tried to beat the 1962 Commonwealth Immigrants Act. Since then further growth in Muslim numbers has been a result of natural increase and the arrival of dependents to join bread-winners already in the country.

The enumeration of Muslims presents serious difficulties, mainly because of the absence of any census question on religious affiliation and the lack of any centralized organization of mosques. One is accordingly forced back on calculations based on the numbers born in predominantly Muslim countries. These are an inadequate guide for three reasons. Firstly, not all those born in, say, Pakistan, are Muslims, especially when one remembers that relatively significant numbers of white Christians now living in Britain were born in the Indian subcontinent in colonial days. Secondly, neither converts nor the British-born children of migrants are readily identifiable on this basis. Thirdly, such figures do not indicate what proportion of people from a Muslim background specifically identify with Islam and are fully committed to its practice. The difficulties are illustrated by two estimates of Muslim numbers published in 1969. One gave a figure of 'around a quarter of a million'; the other of one and a half million (Butterworth, 1969, pp.237–8; Nielsen, 1987, p.384). On the basis of this latter figure estimates of up to two million have been extrapolated for the 1980s. More reliable calculations indicate that only in the mid to late 1980s did Muslim numbers approach one million. In view of the continuing discrepancies, even between reputable sources, it would be potentially more misleading than enlightening to offer precise figures. Similarly a breakdown of countries of origin can only be attempted in broad terms: approximately three-quarters of all Muslims in Britain originated in the Indian subcontinent; of the remainder, the largest two groups, in the region of 50,000 each, are Arabs and Turkish Cypriots. Communities in the range of 15,000 to 45,000 apiece originate from Malaysia, east Africa, Iran and Nigeria; and there are a few thousand from other north African countries and from mainland Turkey. Additionally there are an unknown number of converts among ethnic Britons and the Afro-Caribbean population (Joly, 1988, p.34; Nielsen, 1989, p.227; Wahhab, 1989, p.8). Much of the sub-sequent discussion will relate primarily to Muslims from the Indian sub-continent. This is not because other groups have been forgotten, but is a result of constraints of space and a reflection of the emphasis of the available evidence and research.

Just as Muslims originated in certain quite well-defined regions, their settlement in Britain was concentrated in particular districts. The vast majority went to the major conurbations – particularly Greater London,

Greater Manchester, West Yorkshire, the West Midlands and the East Midlands – and within these to particular well-defined inner city districts. One calculation estimates Muslims to be 1.7 per cent of the population overall, but 2.79 per cent in Greater London and 2.96 per cent in West Yorkshire. Overall only 0.3 per cent of the inhabitants of Scotland and Wales are Muslims, although there are substantial concentrations in Glasgow and Cardiff. The different ethnic groups have also shown distinctive patterns of settlement: those from outside the Indian subcontinent are concentrated in the south east, apart from the early Yemeni settlers in the north of England and Cardiff. Bangladeshis are also mainly to be found in London, although there are significant pockets elsewhere, notably of Sylhetis in Bradford. Indians and Pakistanis are generally more evenly dispersed, but regional ties still operate: for example Punjabis predominate in Birmingham, Mirpuris in Bradford and Gujeratis in Leicester (Ally, 1979, p.5; Barton, 1986; Nielsen, 1989, p.228; Wahhab, 1989, pp.7–11).

The process of settlement had significant implications for the development of Islamic observance. Initially communities consisted primarily of men who saw themselves as short-term labour migrants, sending money back to their families in the Indian subcontinent and envisaging that they would in due course return permanently themselves. Accordingly there was a strong incentive to work long hours and little reason to invest in mosques and other religious facilities in Britain. The effect was an almost complete lapse in outward evidence of religious observance. However when women and children also came to Britain, Muslim communities began to make more effort to create the structures to permit the full observance of their religion, even though emotional and spiritual ties with their original homelands still remained strong. The process of developing a religious superstructure naturally relates to the patterns and chronology of settlement: thus by the 1980s it was well advanced among Pakistanis who had been in the country for two decades, but the Bangladeshis who were still arriving in substantial numbers in that decade remained much more in a state of transition (Barton, 1986, pp.55–67; Nielsen, 1987, p.386 and 1989, pp.230–1).

A further distinctive feature of the Muslim population has been its relative youth, a natural result of settlement being led by men in the young employed age group who have subsequently been followed by their wives and children. In 1961, 52 per cent of the (predominantly Muslim) Pakistan-born population in the major conurbations was aged between 25 and 44, as opposed to 26 per cent of the British population as a whole. This tendency became, if anything, even more pronounced as children joined their families in substantial numbers in the 1960s and 1970s (Nielsen, 1984, p.5). Accordingly, even in the 1980s there were few elderly people, and the upbringing and education of children were central Muslim concerns. Occupationally and socially the Muslim community has become very diverse: there is an élite of extremely wealthy families, among which Arabs and Ismailis are prominent; a significant successful professional class; and numerous small shopkeepers and businessmen. However the majority of employed men in the 1970s fell into the skilled and semi-skilled manual categories and in 1984 only about 10–15 per cent of Bangladeshi and Pakistani Muslim households were categorized as professional or managerial (Badawi, 1986, pp.13–14; Nielsen, 1984, p.6; Smith, 1976, p.66).

The steady growth in organized Muslim activity in Britain is well illustrated by the following figures for mosque registrations:

1965	13
1966–70	36
1971–75	50
1976–80	104
1981–85	135
Total to 1985	338

(Nielsen, 1987, p.387)

There is evidence that there are also a significant number of mosques operating which have not been registered with local authorities and so these figures should be taken as minima. When further increases in the later 1980s have also been taken into account, estimates of the numbers of mosques operating at the end of our period range from 600 to over 1,000 (Nielsen, 1988, pp.57–8; Raza, 1991, p.49; Wahhab, 1989, p.13).

In 1989 only an estimated twenty-two of the mosques in Britain had been purpose-built. These include central mosques in several major cities. The Regent's Park Mosque, the most visible Islamic presence in London, was completed in 1978 at a cost of £6 million, largely donated by Saudi Arabia and the Gulf states (Tibawi, 1981, p.206). Similarly the Glasgow Central Mosque and the Saddam Hussein Mosque in Perry Barr (Birmingham) are testimony to the importance of overseas funding in realizing such major building projects (Joly, 1988, p.37; Wahhab, 1989, p.14). Although some of these institutions – especially if constructed in city centres away from Muslim residential areas – could seem somewhat removed from the daily life of the community, others, such as the Saddam Hussein Mosque and the Alice Street Mosque in Cardiff, enjoyed considerable support from ordinary Muslims. The acquisition of these prominent and traditionally Islamic buildings promoted a sense of dignity, stability and coherence during the 1970s and 1980s, as well as providing points of symbolic interaction with non-Muslim society (Barton, 1986, p.194; Joly, 1988, pp.44; Nielsen, 1988, p.57).

However, although for some the most compelling image of Islam in Britain is that of golden domes seen through the trees of a London park, the characteristic mosque was to be found rather in the back streets of Bradford or Birmingham, Manchester or Whitechapel, and consisted of one or more converted terraced houses. It was thus an inconspicuous feature of its environment. A mosque used by Bengalis during the 1970s off the Manningham Lane in Bradford may serve as representative of others. It consisted of two adjoining Victorian houses, each with two main floors, an attic and a cellar. The separating wall between the two houses had been retained, but the internal walls in each house removed, thus providing two large rooms on each floor. The cellar had facilities for *wudu* (ritual ablution) and a kitchen; the attic was living accommodation for the imam; the ground floor rooms were classrooms for instructing the children; and the first floor rooms were used for prayers. The main disadvantage was the impossibility of assembling more than thirty or so people in any one room, a particular problem at Friday prayers. The mosque lacked many of the traditional attributes of Muslim worship: the *minbar* (pulpit) and *qibla* (niche to indicate the direction of Mecca) were purely symbolic (Barton, 1986, pp.88–9).

Muslims tended to use such modest premises for three reasons. Firstly, it was because of limited financial resources associated, initially at least, with a reluctance to make substantial investment in a country that might well prove to be only a temporary home. It is significant that by 1985, when the community felt more settled, the Bradford mosque described above had been replaced by a purpose-built mosque (Barton, 1986, p.194). Secondly it stemmed from fragmentation of Muslim communities on both sectarian and ethnic lines. Birmingham is a good example of this. In the mid 1980s the 80,000 Muslims in the city were served by no less than fifty-five mosques and occasionally two were to be found on the same street. This proliferation reflected both the numerous religious tendencies present – Barelwis, Deobandis, the Jamaat-i-Islaami, the Ahl-i-Hadith, Shiahs, and Ahmadiyyas – and the desire of each ethnic group – Punjabis, Mirpuris, Pathans, Campbellpuris, Bangladeshis, Yemenis, east African Asians – to have its own mosques. Thirdly, the proliferation of small mosques also arose from the devotional, cultural and social needs of Muslims. The availability of a place of worship within walking distance is important for men allowed limited time off work to pray, and for children who attend the mosque after school for religious instruction. Less tangibly, but perhaps even more importantly, mosques become key centres of community identity (Joly, 1988, pp.37–8).

Mosques are run by management committees which usually employ at least one imam to lead the prayers, preach, and teach the children. As there is no formal priesthood in Islam and indeed any suitably-qualified man can lead public worship, the status of salaried imams in Britain can be a relatively subordinate one, closely supervised by mosque committees and lacking the moral authority accorded to the office in traditionally Islamic countries. At least until the 1980s it was usual practice to recruit an imam from a community's country of origin: such men have naturally experienced problems arising from their lack of acquaintance with conditions in the West and from language barriers which could limit contact not only with non-Muslims, but also with the younger members of their own communities. More recently there has been a tendency to employ imams already resident in Britain, a symptom, perhaps, of the loosening of ties with original homelands. By the 1980s imams were being trained in Britain (Barton, 1986, pp.109–20; Joly, 1988, p.36).

The mosque, an institution as well as a building, is the basic unit of Muslim organization. Despite the emergence of numerous bodies seeking to unite Muslims in matters of common concern, no coherent overall structure has yet emerged at a national level, and even local attempts at cooperation can be thwarted by disputes and rivalries between mosques. Nevertheless organizations such as the Bradford Council of Mosques and the Muslim Liaison Committee (in Birmingham) were emerging by the 1980s (Joly, 1988, p.49). At a national level sectarian rivalries reflected genuine differences of opinion about how Islam should develop in a British context, related to the historic divergences among Muslims in India and elsewhere discussed in the previous section. Further complications arose from the readiness of Muslim countries, notably Saudi Arabia and Libya, to finance organizations in Britain which were then regarded with suspicion by other Muslims, as well as non-Muslims (Raza, 1991, pp.68–9), and which accordingly failed to achieve much basis of support among ordinary Muslims. There have been several attempts to develop an umbrella organization which could represent all Muslims in Britain, but neither the Union of Muslim Organizations of Great Britain and Eire nor the UK Council of Imams and Mosques has in practice been able to sustain such a role. A further initiative of this kind, the Council of British Muslims or 'Muslim Parliament' was taking shape in the early 1990s under the auspices of Dr Kalim Siddiqui's Muslim Institute. Some saw this as having the potential to become an equivalent of the Board of Deputies of British Jews as a recognized mouthpiece for the community in its relations with government and society. It was widely criticized however, by Muslims as well as non-Muslims, because it was perceived as having an 'extreme' and isolationist[8] agenda. A Muslim correspondent of the *Evening Standard* (31 October 1991) declared that he would 'not blindly follow Siddiqui'.

In any assessment of observance of the five pillars of Islam the first, shahadah, or witness, is essential, but also intangible. On one level, because

[8] For explanation of this term see below pp.161–2.

it is this profession of faith that identifies a Muslim, it is, by definition, universally observed. In practice, too, it appears that all who identify themselves as Muslims recite it. However, behind the outward recitation lie shades of understanding and depth of commitment which are best indicated by consideration of the other four pillars (Barton, 1986, pp.93–4).

The committed Muslim who practises Islam in a British context has overcome significant obstacles. These begin with geography. In the Middle East and India, days are, of course, fairly even in length throughout the year, but in Britain the long summer and short winter days present particular problems for a religion whose observances are scheduled according to the sun. For example, in high summer at the latitude of Preston, which has a significant Muslim community, the earliest salat of the day should be performed around 3 a.m. and the last one is not due until after 11 p.m. (Shepherd and Harrison, n.d., p.31). When Ramadan (which follows a lunar calendar and hence moves through the solar year on a 33-year cycle) falls in the summer, as it did in the late 1970s and early 1980s, this renders the fast particularly gruelling, because the period from dawn to sunset could be up to eighteen hours (Wilkinson, 1988, p.16). The Qur'anic injunction is quite explicit:

> And eat and drink, until the white thread
> shows clearly to you from the black thread
> at the dawn; then complete the Fast
> unto the night...
>
> (II: 183)

Although when Ramadan falls in winter (as during the 1990s) it is correspondingly less demanding, the regular performance of the salat when daylight is short places particular demands on the routines of schools and places of work.

It is difficult to offer other than impressionistic evidence on the observance of prayer times and fasting, as these are matters of widely differing and potentially polemical assessment. While numerous Muslim households do get up in the small hours of summer mornings to perform the first salat, there are also Muslims who readily admit to flexibility and irregularity in performance of their religious obligations (*The Times*, 17, 18 August 1987; Wilkinson, 1988, pp.15–16). It can be inferred that the trend over the period under review here was towards more regular performance, as the influence of mosques became more established and Muslim employees, parents and schoolchildren became more articulate and able to negotiate the requisite prayer rooms and short breaks from work during the day (McDermott and Ahsan, 1980, pp.38–40). However in Britain, in the absence of that universal communal solidarity which is epitomized by the call to prayer with loudspeakers from the minarets of mosques in Islamic countries, the performance of such obligations remains a matter for the individual. Some compromise seemed inescapable. A Muslim police sergeant commented: 'You can hardly get up with a lot of people in the cells and announce you are going to pray' (*The Times*, 18 August 1987). By the same token, those free from such external pressures and with sufficient self-discipline to sustain regular observance were likely to be more generally committed to a rigorous and conscientious observance of the teachings of Islam. An official of the Commission for Racial Equality observed in 1987:

> Those who retain the Islamic faith will only do so by great effort, finding the opportunity to pray five times a day, for example, from their youngest days. They will not easily surrender what has been so hard won.
>
> (*The Times*, 19 August 1987)

The increase in the number of mosques in the 1970s and 1980s indicates that commitment of this kind was growing. Although there is no obligation to perform the salat in a mosque, the existence of a widely cited hadith to the effect that it is more than twenty times more meritorious to do so means that attitudes to the mosque are a good spiritual barometer. Evidence from one Bradford mosque suggest that attendances were rising significantly: the imam reported that in 1978 only two or three people were present at daily prayer and around forty on Fridays; but within two years there were as many as ten present daily and up to sixty on a Friday. During Ramadan there were around a hundred and twenty present at the night prayers (Barton, 1986, pp.90, 93). Mosque attendance similarly increased in Rochdale during the 1980s, and it was thought that widespread unemployment during the early years of the decade was a contributory factor because this meant that more men had time available (Wilkinson, 1988, p.16).

Evidence concerning mosque attendance rates is patchy. A survey of 60 Muslim householders in Handsworth (Birmingham) published in 1981 indicated the following frequencies of attendance:

Frequency	%
At least once a week	45
At least once a month	15
Less than once a month	0
Special occasions only	32
Never	8

(Ratcliffe, 1981, p.86)

One should note the substantially higher participation rate than that of the nominally Christian population,[9] and the small extent of complete non-involvement. Also interesting is the polarization between a large group of fully-committed people and a somewhat smaller, but significant, number who maintained their links only by means of festivals and rites of passage. A more extensive survey published in 1986 yielded lower figures than those for Handsworth with 51 per cent attendance at festivals, but only 16 per cent on Fridays. A substantial part of the discrepancy can be accounted for by presuming that the householders surveyed in Handsworth were predominantly, if not exclusively, adult males, whereas the later sample included women and children who would not normally attend. Other significant indications were that attendance was substantially higher in smaller Muslim communities and that a small but by no means negligible number of men attended prayers at the mosque every day, thus pointing to the existence of a deeply committed core of worshippers (Holway, 1986, p.152).

The format of prayers in mosques in Britain corresponded to that used throughout the Muslim world, although with some essential adaptation to local conditions, particularly in giving the *adhan* (call to prayer) inside the mosque rather than outside, in deference to non-Muslim neighbours and the restrictions imposed by local authorities (Barton, 1986, p.123; Nielsen, 1988, p.58). The atmosphere of Friday prayers at a mosque in Glasgow in 1972 is conveyed in the following description by a sympathetic, if patronizing, outsider:

Though most of those who pray in the Mosque are from Pakistan, the congregation also includes Indians, Arabs, Turks, and other folk such as Nigerians who happen to be in Glasgow from time to time. There are a few Scotsmen who have embraced Islam and live as far away as Ayr and Anniesland…

About two hundred or two hundred and fifty attended at the most. They arrived in small groups, a few of them with their families including wives or mothers. The ladies have a room apart in which to pray and hear the sermon. Some come in their best clothes, being remarkably reminiscent of any European family attending church on a Sunday morning.

Once inside the Mosque however there was a fairly extensive clothes-changing operation, some having – so far as I could judge – performed their ablutions at home, and come rigged out in white Shalwar and tunic beneath their European clothing. Others performed their ablutions on the premises, and changed certain

---

[9] See Essay 8 for comparative figures.

portions of their clothes for the prayers ... The introductory part was spoken in Urdu, the [sic] came the Adhan, the Khutba or Sermon in Arabic ... This was followed by the two Rak'as of the Salat which are to follow the Khutba, and are extra to the four imposed by the Sunna for noon. After this the worshippers began to leave, some to their homes and others to their work. It is perhaps worth noting that a few of the worshippers came to the Mosque dressed in the uniforms of Bus-drivers and Conductors, as though they had come straight from work.

There were one or two small boys in school caps present with their grandfather (as it appeared), being taught the correct actions and forms of the prayers.

(Ritchie, 1972, pp.16–18)

This extract also illustrates the linguistic complications of Muslim worship in Britain. Arabic, the language of prayer and of formal religious discourse, was most unlikely to be fully understood by worshippers whose first language, in this case, was predominantly Urdu. The ethnic diversity among Muslims in Britain could mean that no single language would be comprehensible to an entire congregation, and there was also pressure to learn a third language, English, in order to enhance life opportunities. Accordingly the problems for imams seeking to teach congregations about Islam have been considerable (Barton, 1986, pp.124–6).

Payment of zakat appears to have been uneven and irregular in Britain. This was mainly because it was difficult to identify suitable recipients, in the terms of the Qur'an:

> The free will offerings are for the poor and needy,
> those who work to collect them, those whose hearts are
> brought together, the ransoming of slaves, debtors, in
> God's way, and the traveller;...

(IX: 60)

Among those whose assumptions about what constituted poverty had been formed in the Indian subcontinent there did not appear to be any 'poor and needy' people in Britain where, at least until the 1980s, the welfare state usually prevented total destitution.

Some fulfilled their obligation by sending money to relatives in Pakistan or Bangladesh. Many seemed to feel that contributions to support the local mosque, technically not zakat at all, were sufficient, but the amounts given for this purpose could be considerable. Thus in the 1970s, £30,000 of the £68,000 cost of the Quwwat-ul Islam Mosque in Preston was raised from local sources, much of it from a levy of £25 a head on every working male Muslim (Shepherd and Harrison, n.d., p.13). In Manchester at a similar period the entire £250,000 cost of a mosque was obtained locally, although here large donations from wealthy businessmen were important and provided a means for them to assert their status in the community (Werbner, 1987, p.10).

There is little published evidence regarding performance of the hajj (pilgrimage to Mecca) by Muslims in Britain. The financial means were more readily available than they had been in India and Pakistan, but although there had been a steady flow of pilgrims, the practice did not appear to be anything like universal (Barton, 1986, pp.95–6). It can be inferred that increased resources and the ease of modern travel were counteracted by the difficulty of getting the requisite time off work and the competing desire to visit relatives still in south Asia.

A further important manifestation of Muslim devotion has been celebration of religious festivals. The two most important festivals are *Eid-al-Fitr* and *Eid-al-Adha*. The former, which marks the end of Ramadan, is a joyful family and communal occasion, celebrated with vigour. It has a role in the consciousness of Muslim children parallel to that of Christmas among their Christian counterparts (Nielsen, 1983). Eid-al-Adha, which coincides with the annual pilgrimage to Mecca, commemorates the devotion to God shown by Abraham in his readiness to sacrifice his son and is traditionally marked by the sacrifice of an animal. This custom has been continued by some in Britain but its form has been modified due to pressure from the majority Christian and secular community, and the other practical difficulties associated with its transition from south Asian villages to British cities (Barton, 1986, p.101; Shepherd and Harrison, n.d., p.80; Werbner, 1988, p.88). The figures quoted above indicate that male attendance at prayers at festivals is close to universal. Some Muslim communities hire large halls or even car-parks so that all can gather in one place (Barton, 1986, p.100; Shepherd and Harrison, n.d., p.80). They have pressed for days off work and school in order to participate in the festivals, a matter complicated somewhat by the fact that their exact dates are determined by the visibility of the moon and cannot be known precisely in advance (McDermott and Ahsan, 1980, pp.57–8).

Mawlid, the anniversary of the Prophet, is also widely observed, particularly among Barelwis. The rites then used have been criticized by more austere Muslim groups as implying the divinization of Muhammad. Modified mawlids can also be held on occasions of personal significance, such as a death or the inauguration of a new business venture (Barton, 1986, pp.97–8). Another popular practice is *khatmi-Qur'an*, a communal reading of the whole Qur'an by women in the home, followed by the serving of a meal. This is a thanksgiving, or a means of seeking forgiveness or divine blessing. Religious motives blend here with the fulfilment of social obligations and competition for status in the community. It is interesting that, in Oxford at least, khatmi-Qur'ans became much more frequent than they had been in Pakistan, an example of the manner in which the popular religion of Muslim countries was adapting and changing in the process of transfer to the British situation (Shaw, 1988, pp.117–21, 127–32; Waardenburg, 1978; Werbner, 1988).

The role of Sufi sheikhs in the early development of Islam in Britain was noted above and, during the 1970s and 1980s Sufism continued to have a noticeable role in Muslim life. Sheikhs could enjoy considerable influence not only over their committed followers, but in the wider Muslim community, although this was not always uncontested by the mosques. In the early 1980s a group in Birmingham was attracting about fifty regular attenders to the Saturday night *dhikrs* (collective spiritual exercises). Sufi groups also joined in the celebration of numerous festivals (Draper, 1985).

The attractiveness of Sufi ritual and spiritual discipline undoubtedly contributed to the capacity of Muslims in Britain to make converts, even though they did not generally engage actively in *da'wa*, inviting others to Islam. Despite Muslim hospitality to converts, their lot was not always an easy one, faced with pressure to adapt to an alien culture and occasionally expected to learn the Qur'an alongside children. West Indian converts displayed considerable zeal; native British ones were generally less self-confident and some eventually ceased to be Muslims (Draper, 1985, pp.102–10). Nevertheless others, such as Yusuf Islam, the former pop-singer Cat Stevens, persisted and could become energetic advocates for their adopted faith (*The Times*, 19 August 1987; Wingate, 1988, p.9).

In the mid 1960s Islam in Britain was the religion of a tiny and barely noticed minority with a handful of institutional resources and only a tenuous hold over the greater part of its professed adherents. By the mid 1980s it had become a well-organized, albeit still deeply divided, religious body, with considerable capital assets, a strong basis of deeply committed support, and a rich and varied devotional and spiritual life. The transformation was a remarkable and rapid one, the combined effect of the increasing 'rootedness' of Muslims in Britain and the world-wide resurgence in Islam. Muslims remained a minority, however, and, despite the increasing numbers, resources and stability of their own communities, many of them retained an acute sense of vulnerability and alienation from the mainstream of life in Britain. This feeling was to receive its most powerlessly forceful expression in reaction to the publication of *The Satanic Verses*. In order to understand why this was so, we must in the final main section of this essay move away from explicitly religious activity to consider the wider impact of Islam on the lives of its adherents and to explore the various patterns of interaction with British society and culture.

3 Towards a British Islam?

Islam, it will be recalled, makes no distinction between the sacred and the secular and provides a complete rule of conduct for the believer. One American convert has written:

> Islam is not a mere belief-system, an ideology or a religion in the usual sense in which these words are understood. Rather it is a total way of life, a complete system governing all aspects of man's existence, both individual and collective.
>
> (Haneef, 1979, p.vii)

It follows that for Muslims in Britain the reality of life in a non-Muslim country has presented particular problems. The devout viewed with considerable antipathy that combination of diffuse Christianity and outright secularity which shaped the attitudes of the majority of the population. The issue is thus a broad clash of cultures, but during the 1970s and 1980s it manifested itself particularly in hostility to the perceived promiscuity of sexual mores and in the desire for the education of children in accordance with Islamic principles. Other problems have included Muslim dietary requirements and Islamic needs relating to death and burial. This section will not examine the details of the various controversies that arose during the period, but use them rather to illustrate the overall situation of Islam in Britain. This approach reflects the tendency for specific issues to become a focus for general concerns, as was to be the case above all in the Rushdie affair.

Islamic thought has usually made a clear distinction between *dar al-Islam* (the abode of peace), territories under Muslim rule, and *dar al-harb* (the abode of war), countries ruled by non-Muslims. Muslims living in dar al-harb potentially had two strategies in order to live in accordance with the teachings of Islam: *jihad*, struggle or *hijra*, emigration. Both were sanctioned in the Qur'an:

> O believers, fight the unbelievers who are near to you,
> and let them find in you a harshness; and know that God
> is with the godfearing.
>
> (IX: 125)

> And those that emigrated in God's cause
> after they were wronged – We shall surely
> lodge them in this world in a goodly lodging
> and the wage of the world to come is greater,
> did they but know;...
>
> (XVI: 43–4)

At the extremes this might mean literal war or emigration, but in practice, as we noted in relation to nineteenth-century India, most Muslims were prepared to settle for less drastic means of safeguarding their religious integrity.

For the first generation of Muslims in Britain who treated their settlement as strictly temporary, the concept of hijra gave a religious dimension to their continuing ties with their countries of origin and their hopes of ultimate return. However as the prospect of return became less realistic, the religious duty of struggling for the means to practise Islam fully in Britain correspondingly intensified. In this respect Islamic teaching was reinforced by other factors, notably the need of black and brown Muslims to find a sense of identity and dignity in the face of the racialist and post-colonialist mentalities still widespread among whites (Raza, 1991, pp.104–7).

In the fluid context of migration and settlement it was by no means clear what precisely constituted the non-negotiable precepts of Islam which believers had to follow. Certainly general principles concerning the regulation of sexuality, the upbringing of children, and abstention from alcohol and from pork were obvious enough, but specific application was much more problematic. This was not only a result of the historic disputes between the schools of Islamic law, and the varying systems of authority among the Indian sects, but also stemmed from the inextricable entwining with Islam of beliefs and practices that were culturally rather than religiously derived. Furthermore for some the British situation implied grounds for legitimate reinterpretation of Islam. Such a process was slow to develop because of the initial absence of an intellectual and spiritual leadership with the requisite combination of an understanding of British conditions and a knowledge of Islamic scholarship.

An examination of some aspects of the particularly controversial issues of sexuality and the position of women will serve to illustrate the ambiguities. A passage in the Qur'an provided the apparent point of departure for much Muslim belief and practice in these matters:

> Say to the believers, that they cast down
> their eyes and guard their private parts;
> that is purer for them. God is aware of
> the things they work.
> And say to the believing women, that they
> cast down their eyes and guard their private
> parts, and reveal not their adornment
> save such as is outward; and let them cast
> their veils over their bosoms…
>
> (XXIV: 30)

This is a general injunction to both sexes to observe decency and avoid sexually provocative behaviour, requiring women in particular to dress modestly, widely interpreted as meaning the wearing of a head covering and loose, unrevealing clothing. This interpretation thus goes some way further than general western conventions of decency in that it does imply, for example, that from puberty the sexes should be segregated for swimming and sport; and that medical treatment involving physical examination should be carried out by a doctor of the same sex as the patient.

However this text has also been linked to the institution of *purdah*, the seclusion of women from all men except their husbands and other close relatives. Social activities and living arrangements are segregated and, in traditional Muslim societies, women going into public places would wear the *burqa*, which concealed their features. The unacceptability of social contact between the sexes was associated with the practice of arranged marriage, often contracted with little if any prior contact between the couple concerned.

In Pakistan, purdah and the regulation of marriage by families had considerable social significance. Among the poor, economic necessity and cramped living conditions meant that strict purdah was impossible. It followed conversely that for wealthier people, the extent to which it was observed was an important status symbol. If a woman went out to work, this suggested that her husband was not keeping her properly. This reflected on *izzat*, family honour. Izzat, though, was most seriously compromised by daughters who had any contact with men, even if wholly innocent, and this could ruin the marriage prospects not only of the girl concerned, but also those of her sisters (Jeffery, 1976, pp.26–35).

In Britain among many first-generation Muslim immigrants the tenacious maintenance of such practices was an essential safeguard of dignity, identity and status in a strange land. Relatively improved incomes and living conditions enabled all who wished to maintain a significant degree of purdah to do so, and fear of easy-going western attitudes to sex meant that girls were even more assiduously isolated from male contact (Mirza, 1989, pp.11–12; Saifullah Khan, 1976). Paradoxically, meanwhile, the better off found a new kind of status symbol in their greater assimilation to British customs. For many poorer Muslims, however, the maintenance of their faith came to hinge on matters such as the provision of single-sex secondary education and the treatment of women in the manner just described which, even though it contravened no law, was met with the incomprehension and distaste of the rest of British society (*The Times*, 18, 19 August 1987).

In analysing such practices it is impossible to draw a clear line between religion and custom as these very terms swiftly become tendentious, both theologically and sociologically. What is clear, however, is that there is no generally agreed Muslim view on the matter. Writers of the Maududi school (see pp.141–2 above) encouraged the separation of male and female domains on the grounds of the potentially disruptive effect of sexual temptation. On the other hand in Britain, articulate and educated younger Muslim women became increasingly ready to challenge conventions. One Bradford-born 21-year old, interviewed in the late 1980s, proclaimed her readiness to wear western dress and talk to men while justifying her arguments for greater autonomy for Muslim women within an Islamic framework. She pointed out that the Prophet himself had worked for a woman for fifteen years and that she had eventually proposed marriage to him and was accepted (Mirza, 1989, pp.9, 14, 24). Conversely, some Muslim women followed professional careers while still adhering to Islamic dress and many accompanying social conventions. A further kind of critical voice began to emerge among converts to Islam such as a formerly devoutly Christian woman who wrote to a Muslim newspaper:

> I personally feel that there is something very strange about the Islamic provision for its women … The mosques are crammed full of men, and there is usually only space left for a couple of lines for women … And it seems totally inferior to the Christian prayer where any woman may kneel or stand with dignity, and concentrate on the union between God and humanity that prayer can bring, and usually far outnumber the male worshippers.
>
> (*The Muslim News*, 19 July 1991)

One should not necessarily treat such viewpoints as representative, any more than one should regard certain well-publicized instances of appalling treatment meted out to some Muslim wives by their husbands and their families (Wilson, 1978, pp.123–7) as the characteristic behaviour of men, but rather note the range of opinion and the existence of sharp debate on the issue within the Muslim community itself. In the light of the steryotyping and controversy rampant in this emotive area, this point cannot be too strongly emphasized.

Parallel tensions existed in relation to education. It is true that many Muslims were anxious that schools should provide for the specific spiritual needs of their children and wanted parents to have the right to withdraw them from sex education lessons. The demand for separate schools for girls was also widespread. However, there has been quite sharp disagreement regarding the desirability of entirely separate Muslim schools. It was estimated that by 1991 there were over 500 madrasas (mosque schools) providing Islamic education after secular school hours and at weekends, and also over fifteen[10] private Muslim day schools, such as the Islamia

---

[10]   Dr Jorgen Nielsen informs us that there were over twenty in 1992.

Primary School in Brondesbury, founded by Yusuf Islam (Raza, 1991, p.57; *The Times*, 19 August 1987). However this dual system has been criticized for inadequate standards and also for maintaining potentially traumatic conflicts of identity within children. Dr Zaki Badawi, an Egyptian-born scholar and principal of the Muslim College, alleged in 1988 that Muslim schools 'do not teach children to cope with the realities of life in Britain ... parents are incapable of understanding that they have moved to another world' (Raza, 1991, pp.59–60). By the early 1980s a number of state schools had substantial majorities of Muslim pupils and this led to requests that they should be transferred to Muslim control with voluntary aided status comparable to that of some Christian and Jewish schools. Efforts were also made to obtain public funding for existing Muslim private schools. However such endeavours were frustrated by the opposition of other Muslims who feared that they would prove socially and racially divisive, as well as by the political reservations of local and central government (*News of Muslims in Europe*, 27 July 1983, 30 March 1984, 31 January 1987).

These divergences among Muslims, as illustrated here in relation to women and education, can be explored further by identifying four general kinds of relationship between Islam and British society. These can be conveniently labelled assimilation and isolation, the two extremes, and integration and redefinition, two middle courses. Such categories inevitably oversimplify a very complex situation, but provide a necessary shorthand for our analysis.

By *assimilation* is meant the decline of distinctively Islamic practices and the growing approximation of Muslim behaviour to that of the majority community. As an article in *The Times* put it in 1987:

> The softer scenario has a vision of the great, unseen phalanx of Muslims following the path trodden earlier by Britain's Jews and Roman Catholics – towards virtually complete assimilation for those who do not demand that they be set apart.
>
> (*The Times*, 19 August 1987)

Such a process was most apparent among some wealthier and better educated Muslims who, perhaps in an unconscious development of the nineteenth-century Indian tradition of Saiyid Ahmad Khan (see p.141 above), rapidly adopted secularized western lifestyles and culture. Accordingly they became alienated from working-class Muslims who were more tenacious of their traditions (Modood, 1990, p.155). For some the crowning offence of the Bombay-born, Rugby-educated Salman Rushdie lay precisely in the manner in which he and his work epitomized this tendency (*The Muslim News*, 22 March 1991).

At a much less dramatic level research on the behaviour of Muslim young people has indicated a closer approximation to Western attitudes than that existing among their parents. A survey in 1982 indicated that 25 per cent of young Muslims did not want arranged marriages while 45 per cent of them, as opposed to 36 per cent of their parents, agreed with the sentence: 'I do not see anything wrong with Asian girls wearing Western clothes'. Only 48 per cent of young people as opposed to 60 per cent of parents professed to pray at least once a day. However while these figures reflect a trend towards assimilation, they also show that it was operating slowly. There was no mass rebellion against parental values and, in terms of clothes at least, Muslim young people remained noticeably more conservative than their Hindu and Sikh counterparts (Anwar, 1982, pp.14–19).

Isolation was the inevitable situation of many first-generation Muslim immigrants, separated from the rest of society by language and culture, perceiving themselves as transient settlers with both a past and a future in other lands, and holding firmly to their religion as the cement of their identity. The Barelwi and Deobandi traditions of Indian Islam, with their tendency in different ways to foster an inward-looking devotional life, provided an effective basis for such development. This attitude has also been interpreted as an application of the concept of hijra, as being a kind of *internal* migration (Christie, 1991, p.460). Accordingly from the 1960s to the 1980s many Muslims continued to live in a 'hidden Britain' (*The Times*, 17 August 1987), concentrated geographically in certain well-defined districts, hardly mixing with whites and desiring little from government except to be left alone.

The isolationist position could thus be characterized as essentially a passing phase in the development of the Muslim community, destined to decline as the first generation grow older and their children explore alternative strategies. However in the late 1980s it began to be restated in a more explicit and articulate fashion, notably by Dr Kalim Siddiqui and his Muslim Institute, and presented by its exponents as the only viable strategy for Muslims in Britain. Whereas the isolation of the first generation linked cultural and ethnic factors to religion, in this new interpretation, which attracted a substantial proportion of its support from among younger people, Muslim identity became explicitly confessional (*The Muslim News*, 22 March 1991; *The Times*, 17 August 1987). Siddiqui and his associates argued that isolation was essential to avoid 'subservience and the total disintegration of … identity', and sought

> To consolidate the Muslim population in Britain into an organized community in pursuit of the goals set by Islam …
>
> To develop the Muslim community as an island of peace, harmony and moral excellence, free of promiscuity, sexually transmitted diseases, drinking, gambling, drug-addition, fornication and the related social and moral disorders which plague our age.

> To create and develop institutions capable of serving the Muslim community in such specialized fields as education, health, research, publishing, the arts, trade and investment.
>
> (Muslim Institute, 1990, pp.13–14)

This strategy implied that the Muslim community would form its own institutions and negotiate with the government to become as far as possible a state within a state under the British Crown, with, for example, recognized authority to determine marriage, divorce and inheritance disputes in accordance with Islamic law (Muslim Institute, 1990). At the time of writing it is difficult to assess how far such a strategy will command general support, but it is clear that numerous Muslims have grave reservations.

The assimilationist and isolationist tendencies had in common an implicit or explicit sense that Islamic and British identities are in a conflict which can be resolved only by the ascendancy of one or the other; in other words, that a 'British Islam' is a contradiction in terms and that true Muslims can be 'British' only in a limited technical sense. This assumption, held by some Muslims themselves, was reinforced by the prejudices and stereotypes held by non-Muslims, not least through the bureaucratic insensitivity that diminished religious categories in favour of ethnic and racial ones and thus seemed to deny the very existence of a Muslim community. For example census categories effectively denied the significance of identifying Muslims as such. Nevertheless two kinds of middle way by which Muslims could seek to remain faithful to Islam while identifying fully with Britain were also developing.

By *integration* is meant the adaptation of British structures so as to facilitate the practice of Islam within them. This strategy implied Muslim recognition of the legitimacy of non-Islamic institutions and readiness to work through them; while government and society had to make space for the observance of Islam, not only as a system of worship, but also as a way of life. This in turn implied not only the provision of mosques and flexibility from employers in relation to prayer times and festivals – central though these matters were – but also many other needs. In 1980 the Islamic Foundation published a summary of Muslim requirements, covering toilet facilities, dietary rules, dress, sex education, religious instruction in schools, sport, birth, death and arrangements in hospitals and prisons (McDermott and Ahsan, 1980, pp.71–4). Many of these issues have been touched on above, but two matters merit further discussion here.

Firstly, Muslims, like Jews, are absolutely prohibited from eating pork, but are otherwise permitted to eat meat provided the animal has been slaughtered under certain conditions, designed to maximize the draining of blood from the carcase:

> Forbidden to you are
> carrion, blood, the flesh of swine,
> what has been hallowed to other than God...
>
> (V: 3)

This usually signified the cutting of the animal's throat without pre-stunning while the name of God was pronounced over it, a process periodically criticized as inhumane by animal welfare groups. There was public revulsion when, particularly in the early years of Muslim settlement, it was carried out in public at Eid-al-Adha (McDermott and Ahsan, 1980, p.36; Shepherd and Harrison, n.d., p.80). Compromise on this issue was assisted by the pre-existence of legislation designed to meet Jewish needs, and resulted in the general endorsement of Muslim procedures, provided they were carried out by recognized slaughtermen in proper abattoirs. Nevertheless the subject continued to be periodically contentious, notably in 1985 when Muslim anger was stirred by a proposal from the Farm Animal Welfare Council that pre-stunning should be made mandatory for all (*News of Muslims in Europe*, No. 33, 30 October 1985).

A second example of a general trend towards the integration of Islamic requirements, despite occasional difficulty, has been the policy of local authorities on the burial of Muslims. Islamic law requires that interment should take place as soon as possible after death and that the body should be laid on its side facing Mecca, that is in Britain on a south-west to north-east alignment. These specifications raise practical issues in relation to the management of cemeteries which have generally been resolved satisfactorily. On the other hand local authorities have been less willing to meet Muslim requests for burial in a shroud rather than a coffin, nor have they readily been able to accommodate the expectation that it should take place within twenty-four hours of death. However Muslims demonstrated flexibility on these points: the authors of *The Muslim Guide* denied that there was any requirement for burial within twenty-four hours; and accepted that 'if special circumstances or the law' required the use of a coffin, Muslims would comply (McDermott and Ahsan, 1980, p.63; Nielsen, 1988, pp.64–6).

It is in the sphere of education that strategies for integration have been most difficult to develop, partly because of the intense emotions aroused; partly because of the lack of a united standpoint among Muslims themselves, but mainly because it is here that interaction with British society is at its most complex. It is hard to accommodate Muslim requirements in schools without generating a real or perceived alteration in the treatment of non-Muslim children. Difficulties over school uniform and meals had generally been resolved by the 1980s, but problems over the curriculum and teaching methods continued (Nielsen, 1988, pp.66–71 and 1989, pp.234–5).

Thus despite significant successes there still remained in 1990 a significant agenda for the proponents of integration. The traditional political quietism of the majority of south Asian Muslims had also led to a sense of powerlessness to produce changes in British institutions. Although there were signs at the end of the period that Muslims were becoming more influential in local politics – Mohammed Ajeeb became the first Muslim Lord Mayor of Bradford in 1985–6 and around the same time Birmingham had four Muslim councillors – the community still lacked an MP (Rex, 1988, p.209; *The Times*, 18 August 1987). The consequent frustration and sense of weakness may well have contributed to the resurgence of isolationist feeling at the end of the decade.

In the late 1980s *redefinition* began to offer a prospect that this potential impasse could be resolved. Faced with the difficulty of sustaining all aspects of the traditional practice of Islam in a British setting some Muslims turned again to the foundational principles of their faith with a view to reassessing what elements were culturally-specific and hence could be discarded in the cause of peaceful coexistence, and what convictions had a timeless validity. It is worth quoting at some length the views of Zaki Badawi, a leading advocate of this approach.

> Our adjustment is inevitable. The first sacrifice we shall make is parts of the individual cultures within the faith – Nigerians, Egyptians, Pakistanis all carrying bits of their culture around their necks like a dead weight, slowing down progress. That will be shed, allowing a return to the basics of our religion.
>
> The position of women will become different, more liberalized. We shall lose our suspicion of science and technology, fears which hold back so many Muslim nations. We shall acquire the idea of democracy, the clever balance of responsibility and freedom; we shall learn such skills, the lack of which means most of our world is governed by dictators ... the greater divisions will not be between Britain and the Muslims, but between the two factions within the faith. This will not be entirely generation-defined, yet it will be the younger people who decide. They see their parents besieged, more rigid in their religion than they would have been even in their old homeland, and they will see that they cling to the conservatism for comfort, from fear.
>
> (*The Times*, 19 August 1987)

Evidence indicates that while younger Muslims might lack Badawi's eloquence, many of them shared his ideas on redefining Islam on its own terms, shifting away from the standpoints adopted by their parents not in favour of secularity or westernization but in a turn towards what they saw as a more legitimate articulation of Muslim principles (Mirza, 1989;

Nielsen, 1983, pp.21–2). Converts too began to contribute to this process (Draper, 1985, p.110). For the isolationists this might be viewed as assimilation by another route but for the advocates of a 'British Islam' this new form of an ancient religion seemed to have exciting potential. Yusuf Islam at least had a vision for reinterpreting the emotive sentiments of William Blake's lines:

> I will not cease from Mental Fight,
> Nor shall my Sword sleep in my hand,
> Till we have built Jerusalem
> In England's green & pleasant Land.
>
> (From 'Milton', Blake, 1982 edn, p.144)

He looked forward to a time when 'Jerusalem is built in England's green and pleasant land, with three divinely inspired religions living side by side with each other' (*The Times*, 19 August 1987).

4 Conclusion: resisting Rushdie

Such visions were rudely shaken in early 1989 as Muslim protests against Salman Rushdie's novel *The Satanic Verses* – published in September 1988 – gathered momentum. The book is a complex and lengthy one, tracing the fortunes of Gibreel Farishta, an ageing Indian film star, and Saladin Chamcha, born and bred in Bombay, but now living in England and seemingly thoroughly anglicized. The twosome miraculously survive the explosion of their plane over the English Channel, but Gibreel develops schizophrenic delusions and believes himself to be an angel, while Saladin acquires horns and hooves, the attributes of the devil. The main plot oscillates dizzyingly between London and Bombay, and concludes with Gibreel's suicide and Saladin's reconciliation to his Indian origins. In the meantime there is much powerful evocation of exile and displacement, the experience of Indian settlers in Britain and of life in the subcontinent itself. Within this general framework there are two subplots which are 'dreamt' by Gibreel. One concerns the impact of a young woman, Ayesha, on Titlipur, a Muslim village two hundred miles from Bombay. She is commanded by Gibreel to lead the people on foot on a pilgrimage to Mecca, and assured that when they reach the Arabian Sea it will be parted so that they can continue their journey across the ocean floor. The pilgrims reach Bombay, walk purposefully into the sea, and drown.

It was the other subplot, in which questions of religious authority and motivation are even more explicitly explored, that outraged Muslims. Here

Gibreel dreams of the city of Jahilia (pre-Islamic Mecca) and the life of the prophet 'Mahound', which constitutes a biting caricature of traditional Muslim perceptions of Muhammad. The name 'Mahound' itself evokes medieval abuse of Islam and its Prophet. 'Mahound' is portrayed as a debauchee who is found 'like a drunk in the gutter' (Rushdie, 1988, p.120); and sleeps with so many women that 'they turned his beard half-white in a year.' (p.366). The prostitutes in a brothel assume the names of the prophet's wives (pp.379–90); 'Mahound's' companions are described as 'that bunch of riff-raff' and 'fucking clowns' (p.101); and Islamic practices are ridiculed (pp.104, 363–4). Most devastating of all, it is implied that 'Mahound' is an unreliable vehicle for divine revelation: subconsciously at least he manipulates it to suit himself, believing that he had 'God's own permission to fuck as many women as he liked' (p.386). This issue is explored particularly in relation to the incident of the so-called satanic verses, recorded by two early Islamic authorities, but rejected as a fabrication by other Muslim writers (Ahsan, 1991; Akhtar, 1990, pp.7–9). It was suggested that Satan inspired two verses (originally following surah LIII: 19–20) of the Qu'ran. These sanctioned the veneration of pre-Islamic Meccan deities. Following subsequent revelation these were removed from the text. In Rushdie's version the story is highly dramatized, as 'Mahound' uses the satanic verses to bolster his flagging popularity (Rushdie, 1988, pp.102–28). Attention is drawn to it by the very title of the novel, which appears to make it the hinge of the whole plot.

In justice to Rushdie it is important to view the 'Mahound' passages in the context of the whole book. Set in this framework, the sceptical and jaundiced view of Islam that they represent is not necessarily Rushdie's own but an expression of the spiritual and mental disintegration of Gibreel Farishta. Nevertheless, the very complexity of the novel, with its surrealistic blending of fantasy and reality, also made it hard for Rushdie to refute criticism convincingly. If 'reality' is a fantastic world in which human beings can fall without injury into the English Channel from twenty-nine thousand feet, then conversely, it is difficult to dismiss the offensiveness of the 'dreamt' 'Mahound' passages by claiming that they were never intended to be related to the historic Muhammad. In the eyes of a Hindu commentator, the coarseness of the language goes beyond the artistically justifiable (Parekh, 1989, p.32), while a Christian writer found common ground with Muslims 'in bearing witness to the reality of the sacred, and in protesting when that which is sacred is treated with contempt or ridicule' (Newbigin, 1990, p.17). Two Muslims stated their position as follows:

> it is not freedom of expression or freedom to question or even freedom to criticize or offend that Muslims are objecting to. It is rather the sheer slander, the abuse, the use of obscene and foul language, and the outrageous liberties which Rushdie has taken

with Islam and its Prophet that has distressed and outraged Muslims. That is what has compelled them to take their own desperate steps of protest. It is in the nature of their faith that Muslims must not abuse or injure the feelings of others, nor should they tolerate any provocative and obnoxious attack on the person of the Prophet, his family members and his Companions. The love of the Prophet is not only the main criteria of Iman [faith], it is the *raison d'être* for the existence of every Muslim. The Prophet is not loved superficially by paying lip service; his Sunna [the way of life] is internalized in every Muslim's behaviour.

(Ahsan and Kidwai, 1991, p.36)

There is no space here to chronicle in detail the Muslim protests against the book. It should be noted, however, that these began in the autumn of 1988 with peaceful representations to the publisher and the government. Only after these had proved ineffective did Muslims resort to a carefully stage-managed burning of the book in Bradford on 14 January 1989, in order to publicize their concern. This incident attracted widespread attention in the media, which was almost unanimously hostile to Muslims. The controversy thus rapidly became polarized. On the one hand Muslims were portrayed as obscurantist and repressive, denying free speech and expression, and presenting a dangerous challenge to liberal values and institutions. On the other hand many Muslims themselves saw Rushdie as the spearhead of a racist secular crusade against them, which diminished them as human beings by abusing their most deeply held convictions, and recalled the worst excesses of Western cultural imperialism.[11] Feelings were further inflamed on 14 February when the Ayatollah Khomeini, spiritual leader of Iran's Shiah Muslims, issued a *fatwa* (judgement) proclaiming Rushdie deserving of the death penalty and urging all Muslims to carry out the sentence. The novelist went into hiding. A few weeks later Iran broke off diplomatic relations with the United Kingdom. During subsequent months emotions gradually cooled, but the impressions created and the standpoints adopted were not so readily erased.

---

[11] Bibliographical note: There were of course numerous nuances between these crude positions. It is quite impossible here to cover the full range of perspectives advanced, but the interested reader might like to contrast a vigorously presented non-Muslim view in Malise Ruthven's, *A Satanic Affair: Salman Rushdie and the rage of Islam* (Chatto and Windus, London, 1990) with the cogent Muslim statement in Shabbir Akhtar's *Be Careful with Muhammad!: The Salman Rushdie Affair* (Bellew, London, 1989). A collectively balanced treatment emerges from Dan Cohn-Sherbok (ed.) *The Salman Rushdie Controversy in Inter-religious Perspective* (Edwin Mellen, Lampeter, 1990). For more extensive bibliographical information see Ahsan and Kidwai, 1991, pp.343–75 and Paul Weller (1990) 'Literature Update on the Salman Rushdie Affair', *Discernment*, vol. 4, no 2, pp.35–41.

The Rushdie affair raised many questions for British society in the late 1980s. What limits, if any, should apply to the right of free speech and written publication? How far could a creative writer be held responsible for the thoughts he attributed to his characters? If Rushdie's 'right' to publish the book was upheld, did it follow that there was an equal entitlement on the part of those offended by it to express their views with a forcefulness corresponding to the extent of their outrage? In concluding this essay, however, our concern is rather with what the whole affair revealed about the position of the Muslim community in Britain at the end of our period.[12] Three key points can be made.

Firstly, the reaction of Muslims to the book demonstrated and confirmed the strength of their religious commitment. Granted that some of the demonstrations were orchestrated by a politically motivated minority, yet there was a massive groundswell of genuine repugnance among ordinary Muslims. Most of them, of course, had not read the book, but the substance of the offending passages was widely publicized. The manner in which the believer identifies with Muhammad meant that an attack on the Prophet was personally deeply wounding. In the words of the Qur'an:

> The Prophet is nearer to the believers than their
> selves; his wives are their mothers.
>
> (XXXIII: 6)

This feeling was at its strongest among the normally passive Barelwis who accord a particularly exalted status to Muhammad. The tendency of the media to characterize the protesters as 'fundamentalist' was therefore dangerously misleading (Modood, 1990, p.154).

Secondly, the controversy demonstrated the continuing divisions in the Muslim community. Rushdie himself came from a Muslim background and *The Satanic Verses* reflects his own experience of living in and between two cultures. Accordingly the affair can be viewed in one sense as a confrontation between different Muslim responses to Western culture. Especially after his life came under threat Rushdie found some sympathizers among secularized middle-class Muslims,[13] a trend which one commentator considered a disturbing one:

---

[12] Some of the wider implications are explored in Volume II, Essays 2 and 3.

[13] This raises the question as to whether, in the eyes of other Muslims, Rushdie and those who supported him could in any defensible sense be regarded as Muslims at all, in view of the sacrilege contained in the 'Mahound' passages. Was the book as a whole a radical but legitimate reinterpretation of traditional Islam, or was it a blasphemous repudiation of it? The issue was further complicated by Rushdie's professed embracing of Islam on 24 December 1990.

168

the ease with which the popular stereotypes of Muslims found a home in the minds of Asian intelligentsia reveals a profound division which may well have long-term consequences which Britain may well come to regret. In any case the creation of an Anglicised middle/intellectual class which does not understand or feel responsible for its own ethnic working class is, I believe, the single most worrying trend in the Muslim and other Asian communities.

(Modood, 1990, p.155)

Generally, however, Muslims were united in their antagonism to the book, but too divided in other respects to agitate effectively against it. The connections of various groups with Pakistan, Saudi Arabia and Iran excited the suspicions of their co-religionists as much as those of non-Muslims. If combined action on a matter of such general and overwhelming concern was impossible, the prognosis for sustained co-operation over, say, education, was gloomy.

Thirdly, the affair revealed the depth of the gulf still separating many Muslims in Britain from their adopted country, but by that very revelation stimulated efforts to span it. Many Britons were horrified by the burning of a book in Bradford and by the death sentence passed on a British subject by a foreign theocrat. It was felt strongly that such things should not happen in a 'civilized' and 'democratic' society. Muslims, for their part, were frustrated and alienated by their lack of legal recourse. Blasphemy laws protected Christianity; libel laws protected living public figures; the Obscene Publications Act controlled pornography and the Official Secrets Act could – as in the case of Peter Wright's *Spycatcher* – provide a basis for censorship in 'the national interest'. However for Muslims, demonstrations and book-burnings seemed the only way of making their views known. In this context, although Khomeini's fatwa embarassed many Muslims in Britain, it also strengthened resolve for a firm stand against the book, reflecting a continuing sense of not having an effective voice in Britain, nor on the world stage. The tragedy of the events of 1989 was that the polarized positions left Rushdie a prisoner of Muslim outrage and the Muslim community itself bruised and misunderstood. However the greatly increased public awareness of Islam and the experience gained by Muslims in presenting their position provided a potential basis for more satisfactory future coexistence.

Thus in 1990 the situation of Muslims in Britain was a paradoxical mixture of achievement and frustration, acceptance and alienation. The visions of the mid 1980s of a Muslim community fully integrated into British life without any loss of its essential Islamic characteristics looked more fragile in the face of the stark polarities of assimilation and isolation illustrated in the Rushdie affair. It remained unclear however what trends, if any, would eventually gain the ascendancy and shape the nature of Islam in Britain in the twenty-first century.

Bibliography

AHSAN, M.M. (1991) '*The Satanic Verses* and the Orientalists' in Ahsan and Kidwai (eds).

AHSAN, M.M. and KIDWAI, A.R. (eds) (1991) *Sacrilege Versus Civility: Muslim perspectives on The Satanic Verses Affair*, The Islamic Foundation, Leicester.

AKHTAR, S. (1990) 'Art or Literary Terrorism?' in Cohn-Sherbok, D. (ed.) *The Salman Rushdie Controversy in Interreligious Perspective*, Edwin Mellen Press, Lampeter.

ALLY, M.M. (1979) *The Growth and Organization of the Muslim Community in Britain*, Muslims in Europe Research Papers, 1, Centre for the Study of Islam and Christian–Muslim Relations, Birmingham.
(1981) 'History of Muslims in Britain, 1850–1980', MA thesis, University of Birmingham.

ANWAR, M. (1982) *Young Muslims in a Multi-Cultural Society*, The Islamic Foundation, Leicester.

ARBERRY, A.J. (1964) *The Koran Interpreted*, Oxford University Press, Oxford.

BADAWI, M.A.Z. (1986) 'Islam in Britain' in Commission for Racial Equality, *World Religions in Education*, Shap Working Party, London.

BARTON, S.W. (1986) *The Bengali Muslims of Bradford*, Community Religions Project, Department of Theology and Religious Studies, University of Leeds.

BLAKE, W. (1982 edn) *Selected Poems*, edited by P.H. Butter, Dent, London.

BUTTERWORTH, E. (1969) 'Muslims in Britain' in Martin, D. (ed.) *A Sociological Yearbook of Religion in Britain: 2*, SCM, London.

CHRISTIE, C. (1991) 'The Rope of God: Muslim minorities in the West and Britain', *New Community*, 17, pp.457–66.

CRAGG, K. (1987) *Islam and the Muslim*, The Open University, Milton Keynes.

DRAPER, I.K.B. (1985) 'A Case Study of a Sufi Order in Britain', MA thesis, University of Birmingham.

EL-DROUBIE, R. (1991) 'Islam' in Cole, W. Owen (ed.) *Five World Faiths*, Cassell, London.

ESPOSITO, J.L. (1988) *Islam: the straight path*, Oxford University Press, Oxford.

GERHOLM, T. and LITHMAN, Y.G. (eds) (1988) *The New Islamic Presence in Western Europe*, Mansell, London.

HALLAM, R. (1972) 'The Ismailis in Britain', *New Community*, 1, pp.383–8.

HANEEF, S. (1979) *What Everyone Should Know about Islam and Muslims*, Kazi, Lahore.

HARDY, P. (1972) *The Muslims of British India*, Cambridge University Press, Cambridge.

HEDAYATULLAH, M. (1977) 'Muslim Migrants and Islam', *New Community*, 4, pp.392–6.

HOLWAY, J. (1986) 'Mosque Attendance', in Brierley, P. (ed.) *UK Christian Handbook 1987/88 Edition*, MARC Europe, London.

JEFFERY, P. (1976) *Migrants and Refugees: Muslim and Christian Pakistani families in Bristol*, Cambridge University Press, Cambridge.

JOHNSTONE, P. (1981) 'Christians and Muslims in Britain', *Islamochristiana*, 7, pp.167–99.

MCDERMOTT, M.Y. and AHSAN, M.M. (1980) *The Muslim Guide for teachers, employers, community workers and social administrators in Britain*, The Islamic Foundation, Leicester.

METCALF, B.D. (1982) *Islamic Revival in British India: Deoband, 1860–1900*, Princeton University Press, Princeton.

MIRPURI, M.A. (1987) 'The Ahl-e-Hadith', *News of Muslims in Europe*, no 39.

MIRZA, K. (1989) *The Silent Cry: second generation Bradford women speak*, Muslims in Europe Research Papers, 42, Centre for the Study of Islam and Christian–Muslim Relations, Birmingham.

MODOOD, T. (1990) 'British Asian Muslims and the Rushdie Affair', *Political Quarterly*, 61, pp.143–60.

MUSLIM INSTITUTE (1990) *The Muslim Manifesto: a strategy for survival*, The Muslim Institute, London.

NEWBIGIN, L. (1990) 'Blasphemy and the Free Society', *Discernment*, vol. 4, no 2, pp.12–18.

NIELSEN, J.S. (ed.) (1983) *Muslim Children Present their Faith*, Muslims in Europe Research Papers, 9, Centre for the Study of Islam and Christian–Muslim Relations, Birmingham.

(1984) *Muslim Immigration and Settlement in Britain*, Muslims in Europe Research Papers, 21, Centre for the Study of Islam and Christian–Muslim Relations, Birmingham.

(1987) 'Muslims in Britain: searching for an identity?', *New Community*, 13, pp.384–94.

(1988) 'Muslims in Britain and local authority responses' in Gerholm and Lithman (eds).

(1989) 'Islamic Communities in Britain', in Badham, P. (ed.) *Religion, State, and Society in Modern Britain*, The Edwin Mellen Press, Lampeter.

PAREKH, B. (1989) 'Between holy text and moral void', *New Statesman and Society*, 24 March, pp.29–33.

RATCLIFFE, P. (1981) *Racism and Reaction: a profile of Handsworth*, Routledge and Kegan Paul, London.

RAZA, M.S. (1991) *Islam in Britain: past, present and future*, Volcano Press, Leicester.

REX, J. (1988) 'The urban sociology of religion and Islam in Birmingham' in Gerholm and Lithman (eds).

RITCHIE, J.M. (1972) 'A Survey of the Muslim Community of the City of Glasgow', typescript, Community Religions Project Collection, Department of Theology and Religious Studies, University of Leeds.

ROBINSON, F. (1988) *Varieties of South Asian Islam*, Centre for Research in Ethnic Relations, University of Warwick.

RUSHDIE, S. (1988) *The Satanic Verses*, Viking, London.

SAIFULLAH KHAN, V. (1976) 'Pakistani women in Britain', *New Community*, 5, pp.99–108.

SANNEH, L.O. (n.d.) 'The Muslim Community in Britain: the religious factor in British immigration', typescript, Community Religions Project Collection,

SHAW, A. (1988) *A Pakistani Community in Britain*, Blackwell, Oxford.

SHEPHERD, D. and HARRISON, S.W. (n.d.) *Islam in Preston*, publisher not stated.

SMITH, D.J. (1976) *The Facts of Racial Disadvantage*, PEP, London.

TIBAWI, A.L. (1981) 'History of the London Central Mosque and the Islamic Cultural Centre 1910–1980', *Die Welt des Islams*, 21, pp.193–208.

WAARDENBURG, J. (1978) 'Official and Popular Religion in Islam', *Social Compass*, 15, pp.315–41.

WAHHAB, I. (1989) *Muslims in Britain: profile of a community,* The Runnymede Trust, London.

WATT, W.M. (1988) *Islamic Fundamentalism and Modernity,* Routledge, London.

WELCH, A.T. (1984) 'Islam' in Hinnells, J.R. (ed.) *A Handbook of Living Religions,* Viking, Harmondsworth.

WERBNER, P. (1987) 'The Fiction of Unity in Ethnic Politics: aspects of representation and the State among British Pakistanis', typescript, Community Religions Project Collection, Department of Theology and Religious Studies, University of Leeds.
(1988) '"Sealing" the Koran: Offering and Sacrifice among Pakistani Labour Mirgants', *Cultural Dynamics*, 1, pp.77–97.

WILKINSON, I. (1988) *Muslim Belief and Practices in a Non-Muslim Country: a study of Rochdale,* Muslims in Europe Research Papers, 39, Centre for the Study of Islam and Christian–Muslim Relations, Birmingham.

WILSON, A. (1978) *Finding a Voice,* Virago, London.

WINGATE, A. (1988) *Encounters in the Spirit: Muslim-Christian dialogue in practice,* WCC Publications, Geneva.

4

HINDU DHARMA IN DISPERSION

by Terence Thomas

Aarti ceremony during Divali at Bradford Interfaith Centre. Photograph © Tim Smith.

1 Hinduism, motherland and migration

The religion and people discussed in this essay do not take their name from a founder or leader, such as Christ or Buddha, nor from a dominant principle, such as Islam, but from a geographical region. The region lies east of the river Indus, hence the name Hindustan[1] , given by successive Muslim invaders over many centuries. Later the various religions present in the region were grouped by outsiders under the name Hinduism. But it is only in the last two centuries that Hindus themselves have come to accept this name for their religion.

The fact that the religion and people were named after the region they occupied is important for two reasons. Firstly, Hinduism is not a single coherent religion, but an agglomeration of many different religious forms, loosely bound together by a common tradition of sacred texts, primarily the Vedas, and one or two commonly held views, such as belief in the reincarnation of souls and that society is divinely divided into classes or groupings. In this structure the class and caste of Brahmans play a leading role. Some 'Hindus' refer to this agglomeration of religious forms as 'Hindu *dharma*' (*dharma* here standing loosely for 'religion'), but that is only to enable them to communicate to westerners something of their own religious attitudes. Hinduism, therefore, stands merely for those forms of human behaviour one normally refers to as religious, which originated in a geographical region called India. To quote a recent source: 'Although in popular writing the alleged content of "Hinduism" is rapidly developing a monolithic and stereotyped character, this is no more than a fairly arbitrary abstraction from a random set of facts' (Hardy, 1990, p.145). Buddhism, Jainism and Sikhism originated in the same geographical region and some Hindus claim that these religions are, in fact, still forms of Hinduism.

The second reason that the regional provenance is important is rather more profound. The relationship of a people to a land is often of vital importance – as witnessed in the history of religions – because the life of the individual and the group, and certainly their healthy spiritual lives, is held to be dependent on the land. Bharat is a vital land for Hindus, especially for the twice-born classes and in particular the Brahmans. For such Hindus, Bharat is a sacred universe, the abode of Brahma, the creator divinity. Within the bounds of Bharat the Hindu is ritually safe; beyond its boundaries lie all manner of impurities and pollutions. This is the traditional Hindu view of the world and, though recently it has tended to become less important and less powerful, many Hindus still undergo purification rites on returning to the sacred soil of Bharat from abroad (Desai, 1963, p.93).

---

[1] The old name for the region is *Bharat*, often accompanied by the word *Mata*, *Bharat Mata*, Mother Bharat, hence the English form *Mother India*.

Visitors to India may have encountered an example of the sacredness of Bharat in the city of Jaipur, with its pink palace of winds, a massive outdoor observatory, and the City Palace. In the courtyard of this palace stands the durbar hall, an open-sided area with a raised floor. In two corners of the hall stand two massive silver urns, each about four feet tall and about five feet in diameter. Each holds a few hundred gallons of liquid. They were made to hold sacred Ganges water when Madho Singh, Maharaja of Jaipur, attended the coronation of Edward VII in London in 1902. They were part of what has been described as Madho Singh's 'life-support system', for they held the water for ritual ablutions without which the Hindu ruler's spiritual life would have been in considerable danger (Burghart, 1987, pp.1–2). From this example we gain insight into the problems that migration or travel and separation from the holy mother-land present to devout Hindus, and into the complexity of their religion.

2   The religious beliefs and practices of Hindus

It is one of the unfortunate legacies of western studies of religions that all too often the image of a particular religion is based on its scriptures or the viewpoint of a dominant group within that religion. In both instances the image will be that of the 'ideal' or 'official' form of that religion. Thus the study of the Christian religion has been, until fairly recently, a systematic study of the Bible and the history of the major ecclesiastical and political movements of the religion. The same has been true of the study of Judaism, Islam and Buddhism. It has also been true for what is collected under the term 'Hinduism'. The living religious traditions of millions of inhabitants of India and other locations worldwide have had a defining process imposed on them by outsiders who guided India's destiny for two to three centuries (Vertovec, 1992, pp.2–8).

In nineteenth-century Britain, a series of books on the major world religions was published. The series, 'Non-Christian Religious Systems', caricaturized these religions, treating 'Hinduism', for instance, as the religion of a series of ancient texts and the 'triumph' of one 'school' of interpretation, namely Vedantism, and its modern development, Neo-Vedantism, a school that became coterminous with Hinduism during the first half of the twentieth century in the West. Thus Hinduism was seen purely in terms of a refined (and obscure) philosophy. This view was reinforced by certain Indian intellectuals, most prominently by Sarvepalli Radhakrishnan, a professor of Oriental studies in Oxford and later a President of the Republic of India, in his often reprinted book, *The Hindu View of Life*. According to Radhakrishnan, 'The differences among the sects of the Hindus are more or less on the surface, and the Hindus as such remain a distinct cultural unit, with a common history, a common literature and a common civilization' (Radhakrishnan, 1961, p.13). While accepting that some Hindus worship 'the personal aspect of the supreme', Radhakrishnan continues, 'The worshippers of the Absolute are the highest in rank; second to them are the worshippers of the personal God, then come the worshippers of the incarnations like Rama, Krsna, Buddha; below them are those who worship ancestors, deities and sages, and lowest of all are the worshippers of the petty forces and spirits.' Furthermore he proclaims the supremacy of 'the sage' and refers to those who use images as 'feeble-minded'. But these people amount to hundreds of millions of Indians, far outnumbering the few élite, intellectual Neo-Vedantists.

This caricature has been so firmly embedded in the western intellect that a scholar writing recently of the religion of Indian migrants to Britain has felt it necessary to point out that 'the process of transplantation that is in operation here is one of popular Hinduism, not its intellectual counterpart' (Knott, 1987a, p.160). What Knott describes is a variation of what the majority of Hindus do, hence, in a sense, what is popular. Knott is aware of this as she has pointed out elsewhere (Knott, 1989, p.244). But what she describes is just Hinduism, no more and no less.

Under pressure from western ideas of religion, some Hindu apologists, including those in dispersion, now refer to their religion as essentially based on a concept of an eternal religion, *sanatana dharma* (Knott, 1986a, pp.77–9; Law, 1991; Pancholi, 1991, p.13; Vertovec, 1992, p.7). The use of the term 'sanatana dharma' is an attempt to give some coherent shape to an essentially free-wheeling approach to beliefs and practices which are held to give significance to life. Only a very small minority of ordinary Hindus in India today, however, would recognize this concept as having any relevance to their own religious behaviour.

As you can see, it is exceedingly difficult to define Hinduism accurately. In Hinduism that is packaged for western consumption, so-called popular Hinduism is often marginalized to the study of the sociology of religion or of anthropology, whereas it rightly belongs to the study of religion, and should be understood as the mainstream of Hinduism. Hinduism as defined here is an extremely diverse agglomeration of phenomena. Unfortunately it has frequently been described as 'pagan', 'polytheistic', 'idolatrous' or 'debased' – terms that contain negative and pejorative judgements. So it is not surprising that some Hindus may be sensitive to how their religious expressions are viewed by others. Thus Hindus often stress that though there may appear to be many gods in their pantheon (330 millions of deities according to Hindu mythology), in fact they worship only one god, though in many forms. There is some justification for this claim for there are among the most ancient Hindu texts clear statements that though God may be found in many forms, God is one. This single supreme being existed alongside the recognition of deities which manifested themselves in the powers of nature, in fire, the sky, wind, thunder and lightning, among others. One of the most ancient forms of sacrifice was that of fire to the god Agni. The ritual itself goes under different names, *homa* or *havan* being the most common. The ritual of the fire sacrifice, in which certain offerings such as ghee (a form of clarified butter) are poured onto the sanctuary fire which is kept perpetually burning, was completely in the control of the Brahman priesthood, so much so that this form of religion has often been referred to as Brahmanism rather than Hinduism. In this form of religion the gods worshipped are remote and rather abstract (see Knott, 1986a, p.117). Gradually this form of religion lost its hold on the people of India and was replaced by more personal forms of worship which were not controlled by the Brahman priesthood. These forms of religion had as their foci more accessible gods, gods with superhuman powers, but powers that were easily recognizable to humans. These gods were placed in temples and in homes.

It may well be that at least some, and possibly many, Hindus do worship more than one deity. Certainly Hindus acknowledge a collection of gods or divine beings. It could be argued that the terms polytheistic or monotheistic are inappropriate in any discussion of Hinduism. An inspection of a Hindu temple, with its multiplicity of shrines and dedications to the divine in its manifold 'forms', should convince anyone of the wisdom of reticence in the use of such terminology. Beyond the temple walls the Hindu 'world' is populated with spirits, benevolent and malevolent. In a world so densely populated with the divine, it is better to observe the phenomenon, describe it, and abstain from any attempt to systematize it along western lines.

Consideration of the use of images is similarly complex. In Hinduism an image is a ritual object occupying ritual space, which may be in a temple, a corner of the home, or at the foot of a tree. As the Hindu 'world' is populated with divine powers or spirits, so too is it filled with ritual objects inhabiting ritual space. Images serve the same purpose as ritual objects in other religions, tangible vehicles believed to access hidden, divine power. Spirit is intangible, but humans find it difficult to exist in a world of intangible spirit. An object, person or space provides the material route into the world of spirit. The religious thinking behind this approach is that the object, person or space cease to be ordinary, of course, when they are used in an iconic way. That is, they become imbued with power, and are to be treated circumspectly, not casually. They usually require to be kept in a ritually purified state.

Some modern Hindu apologists argue that the image itself is not worshipped, that it is not 'idolized' (Pancholi, 1991, p.21). While wishing to respect the views of a Hindu who holds this belief, it is, nevertheless, obvious in the Hindu context (as in the contexts of other world religions including Christianity and Islam, claimed by their apologists to be particularly aniconic) that the way in which the medium of access to the divine is sometimes treated tends to undermine such a view. While it may be 'the duty of the devotees to take the meaning of [the images] in the spirit of righteousness' (Pancholi, 1991, p.25), observation demonstrates that this is not always verified. There are innumerable examples of the objectification or the reifying of the 'spiritual' or the divine in the material object. One of the problems western students face is the use of the terms 'idolize' and 'idolatry'.

> Worshipping as God those 'things' which are not God has been despised in the Western traditions as 'idolatry', a mere bowing down to 'sticks and stones'. The difficulty with such a view of idolatry, however, is that anyone who bows down to such things clearly does not understand them to be sticks and stones. No people would identify themselves as 'idolators', by faith. Thus, idolatry can be only an outsider's term for the symbols and visual images of some other culture. Theodore Roszack, writing in *Where the Wasteland Ends*, locates the 'sin of idolatry' precisely where it belongs: in the eye of the beholder.
>
> (Eck, 1981, p.16)

Some scholars of Hinduism demonstrate that sometimes the image is believed to be the very divine presence. Images that are representative, that is, which portray the divine in the guise of a person or an animal, are made and installed in such a way that the divine is believed to be physically present in the image. The process of making and installing images in these instances culminates not only in rituals that are held to bring divine breath into the image but also, through applying or revealing the eyes of the image, it is believed that the divinity can see the devotee while the devotee 'sees' the divinity itself. The term for such an experience is *darshan* (seeing in a significant way), and it applies to images of wood, stone or metal, and also to humans who are believed to be the presence of the divine in the world. In such instances the image is not only a focus for concentration and meditation but also 'the real embodiment of the deity' (Eck, 1981, p.34). Before the installation ceremonies the images are 'lifeless'. After installation 'the image *is* the deity, *not* merely a symbol of it' (Preston, 1985, p.9).

By contrast, 'aniconic' images are not representative, but abstract or symbolic through some form of association with a divinity. They are seen as tokens or signs of the divinity and not the visible presence of the divinity. Thus one of the most popular aniconic images, the *linga*, often referred to as a phallic symbol, is associated with one of the three most popular divinities. 'The word *linga* means "mark" or "sign" as well as "phallus", and it is in the former sense, as the sign of Shiva, Mahadeva, the "Great Lord", that the *linga* is honored in the *sancta* of the many temples and shrines of India' (Eck, 1981, p.27).

Hindu images are of infinite variety. They may be anthropomorphic (in human guise), theriomorphic (in bestial guise), or therioanthropic (half-human, half bestial); they may be unrepresentational, abstract, like the *lingam* and *yoni*, the male and female generative symbols, as used in the worship of the god Shiva. Representations and images of feet, or a pair of slippers associated with a god or guru, may be iconic. A particularly shaped stone under a tree may become a ritual object. On the bank of a moat around a fort in the city of Nasik is a cannon which commemorates the capture of the fort by the young Arthur Wellesley, later Duke of Wellington. When I visited the site in 1964 the cannon was being used as a shrine. Was this a relic of the nineteenth-century practice of 'ritualizing' the British Raj? (Burghart, 1987, pp.4–5). Inside the fort, Pandit Nehru and other Indian nationalists were imprisoned during their fight for independence, so the fort itself is a shrine of iconic importance of a very different kind.

The more familiar gods and goddesses also have their individual iconography (for example, each figure has so many arms, so many legs, particular objects in its hands, and so on). One of the most popular images in western India is Ganesha or Ganapati, a figure with a chubby human body and an elephant head. The divine can be represented and used by Hindus for whatever reasons in order to express their devotion and in order to acquire merit or a boon from contact with their gods.

Finally, we should be aware that Hindu images enjoy various periods of existence. Many Indian temples contain images of metal and stone which have been installed sometimes for centuries. In the Jagannath temple complex in Puri, Orissa, the main images are made of wood and are replaced by newly carved images every twelve years (Preston, 1985, pp.12ff). But most images have a short existence, often only a day or two for as long as a particular festival associated with a divinity lasts. Images for these occasions are made in their thousands, from mass-produced plastic images to carefully crafted images in bamboo, balsa wood, paper and mud. These images are designed to be 'seen' for a short period and then immersed in the nearest stretch of water and allowed to revert to the natural state of the materials.

Preston sums up the impermanence and the notion of images as follows:

> The principle of *impermanence* ensures the dynamism of Hinduism; the infinite takes form then vanishes. The invisible is made visible in stone, wood, or clay, then withdraws with decay,

or is buried. Thus, spirit in matter never becomes completely crystallized. The immensity of divinity becomes manifest anew for each occasion, and the mystery is retained despite its brief partial revelation.

No rational analysis can totally solve the mystery of the icon. Our *rationalism* has not penetrated to the heart of that deep impulse in the human spirit which must create images of the sacred other. Nor do we understand why such images are destroyed, transformed and re-worked to re-emerge generations later as reminders of primal experiences that will not be set aside. This process of creation and destruction of sacred images, this powerful act of imagination, challenges us to ask why humans must insist over and again that the invisible should be, *must* be, made visible.

(Preston, 1985, p.30)

3   The migration of Hindus to Britain

In spite of the polluting consequences for Hindus who leave Mother India, Hindus have migrated for centuries, traditionally to the east and south-east of India, 'as conquerors' (Ray, 1979, pp.41–4). The evidence of this migration can be seen in the culture of areas such as Indonesia. The area that encompasses Burma, Malaysia and Singapore, and beyond to Indonesia and Java, was, centuries ago, predominantly Hindu in its religious orientation. Between 700 and 1450 CE Indonesia experienced two Hindu empires before being superseded by Islam (Ray, 1979, p.41; Thapar, 1966, pp.120–1).

This, according to Ray, was the first 'distinct' phase of Indian emigration. The second phase consisted of migration to countries associated with the former British Empire, as 'a subject race and as instruments of a colonial power' (Ray, 1979, p.41). Hindus of the lower orders were among those recruited as indentured labour to work in Fiji, Guyana and Trinidad. Many of them came from the broad central area of India known today as Uttar Pradesh. The low castes of this area have, because of the endemic poverty of the region, migrated regularly within and outside India. V.S. Naipaul reflects on his family's migration: 'My grandfather had made a difficult and dangerous journey. It must have brought him into collision with startling sights, even like the sea, several hundred miles from his village' (Naipaul, 1968, p.30). Indians have migrated to the African continent and the Arabian peninsula since the beginning of the Common Era (CE) (Michaelson, 1979, p.353). More recently, under the impulse of the

British Empire, which needed labour to build railways, and so on, considerable settlement of Indians took place in east and southern Africa (Bahadur Singh, 1979).

It has been suggested that the migration of Indians to Britain consisted of four phases (King, 1984, p.2). The first consisted of individuals and a few families in the period between 1930 and 1950. The second consisted of men only, seeking employment in the period 1950–60. Women and children followed in the period 1960–73. These three phases consisted of migration directly from India, but the third phase also involved Indians who, having settled in East African states during the British colonial period, were expelled under Africanization policies. It is estimated that 12,000 Hindus migrated from Kenya to Britain between 1967 and 1968 and 18,000 from Uganda between 1972 and 1973. The fourth phase saw a vastly reduced level of immigration severely controlled by legislation (King, 1984, p.3; Knott, 1981, p.16).

In the post-Second World War period, Hindus migrated to Britain mainly from Gujarat, Punjab and East Africa, but also from the West Indies and Guyana, and from Fiji. Direct migration from other areas of India, such as West Bengal, Maharashtra and South India, took place, but in much smaller numbers. By 1987 the estimated numbers of Hindus settled in Britain was 357,000, compared with 269,000 Sikhs and 564,000 Muslims (Knott, 1987b, p.19). However, it could be argued that while British people have been conscious of the arrival of large numbers of Muslims and Sikhs because of their relatively high-profile religious, social and political action, and the visibility of new mosques, gurdwaras, and turbanned males, the presence of larger numbers of Hindus has hardly been noticed. This is partly because Hindus have tended to adopt a low profile legally and socially, especially in matters affecting their community, and because their dress contains no distinguishing features. Only in one or two places have they established recognizably Hindu temples.

As with other groups who arrived in Britain during this period, subgroups settled in certain locations based on common areas of origin in India. Of approximately 307,000 Hindus in Britain in 1977, it is suggested that 70 per cent were of Gujarati origin, 15 per cent of Punjabi origin and the remaining 15 per cent from areas of India such as Tamil Nadu, Maharashtra, Bihar, Uttar Pradesh and Sri Lanka (Knott, 1981, p.6). Apart from a few who came to Britain voluntarily in order to carry out a profession, most came for 'involuntary' reasons, that is either because of enforced alienation from the dominant population in the countries in which they had settled, such as Sri Lanka, the East African countries, and to a certain extent Fiji, or because of economic pressure in the areas of origin such as Punjab.

Hindus who arrived in large groupings settled in cities such as Birmingham, Leicester, Leeds, Loughborough, Southall, Bradford and Coventry, and in Harrow, Brent, Newham and Wembley in London. By 1989 there were sufficient numbers of Hindus in Britain to maintain various organizations in over sixty towns and cities outside London. Estimates of Hindus settled in Britain numbering more than three-quarters of a million must be deemed exaggerated (Virat Hindu Sammelan, 1989). However, at the Virat Hindu Sammelan (Assembly of Hindus) held in 1989 in Milton Keynes, 319 organizations from the United Kingdom were represented. The fact that such organizations exist is a significant comment on Hindu migration, for it demonstrates a pattern of social relationships that is by no means common in India.

4 The Hindu social pattern

No western study of Hinduism ever omits a reference to caste, and nothing is more misrepresented in western work than its description. From at least the early part of the nineteenth century, when interest in Oriental religions began to grow in the West, until fairly recently, the way in which caste has been treated has been consistent: the emphasis has been on divisions within Hindu society, as described in the most ancient texts. According to this view:

> All the Hindu writings recognize only four pure castes ... The most ancient portion of the Vedas alludes to such a division; and in the laws of Manu, the Ramayana, the Mahabharata, and all the other Sanskrit works of the greatest antiquity, we find the system of castes fully developed. The Greeks who visited the country describe its inhabitants as distributed into certain classes.
>
> (*Penny Cyclopedia*, 1836, vol.11–12, p.230)

The article tells us that the term 'caste' is derived from the Portugese word *casta*, meaning 'race' or 'lineage', but that the Sanskrit term is *varna*, that is 'colours'. The four 'pure castes' are listed as Brahman[2], Kshatriya, Vaisya and Sudra, in that order of hierarchy. The first three castes are distinguished from the Sudras as those to whom the study of the Veda is reserved and who undergo rituals that lead to new spiritual birth. These three castes are the so-called 'twice-born', the Sudras are not.

---

[2] Note that the term Brahman is used for the first of the classical varna or classes and for a caste that is composed of Brahmans.

We are then told that caste divisions are based primarily on different occupations, but that rigid inflexibility of occupations associated with caste as portrayed by some writers is not true. Evidence of the 'true situation' is provided by Mr Colebrook (1765–1837), whose opinion, based on his lengthy experience of India, 'is entitled to the greatest respect'. Mr Colebrook relates 'that almost every occupation, though regularly it be the profession of a particular class, is open to most other tribes; and that the limitations, far from being rigorous, reserve only one peculiar profession, that of the Brahmana, which consists in teaching the Veda, and assisting at religious ceremonies'. The article further points out that the lowest caste, Sudras, have been known to rise to 'royal power', and that Brahmans are sometimes obliged to take on menial tasks and 'have even condescended to cook the victuals of persons of inferior class'. (It is a common assumption in the West that all Brahmans are priests and all Sudras are menials.) It then discusses the existence of 'impure' or 'mixed' castes based on misalliances between partners of different castes.

Introducing a discussion of caste based on such an antique publication is deliberate. For one thing this account, within limitations, is surprisingly accurate. It admits that a description of caste is not simple and straightforward. We already see arguments growing about how the caste system operates, and the realization that, at least in the matter of occupations related to caste, things are not always what they are supposed to be. We also see something of the complications in looking at caste, class, varna and tribe.

Facts that must be emphasized in considering caste in Indian society today (applying in varying degrees to Sikhs, Christians and Muslims in India and Pakistan as well as Hindus) are that there are no such entities as 'pure' and 'impure' castes, and that there are far more than four castes in Indian society. In contemporary India there are hundreds of 'scheduled castes' and hundreds of 'scheduled tribes'. The term 'scheduled' refers to the legal standing of groups which belong traditionally outside the four classical varnas, groups once referred to as outcastes and tribals. Within the structure of the four classical varnas there are thousands of castes or, to use the Indian terms, *jati* or *got* or *gotra*. These groupings can be referred to as castes, sub-castes or sometimes as clans: they are often referred to in anthropological or sociological studies as 'kinship groups'. A recent study has described *jati* as follows:

> *Jati* refers to an indefinite number of divisions in South Asian society, characterized by heredity, endogamy, commensality, an actual or attributed common occupation, and actual or attributed peculiarities of diet. Jatis are ranked in a hierarchy, in which superiority of one jati to others is marked by avoidance of contact of various kinds, notably acceptance of food and water. The

patterns of avoidance are so complex, however, that it is not always possible to arrive at an undisputed ranking order.

(Killingley, 1991b, p.9)

There is disagreement over whether these kinship groups are both more real and more significant for the Hindu in the conduct of private and social life than are the four varnas. The four varnas are usually now referred to as classes rather than castes and are considered, on the whole, only significant in the study of classical Hinduism. In India, it is claimed, the varnas are not that important (Basham, 1988, p.245). Knott (1986a, pp.40–1) believes this to be the case among Hindus settled in Britain. However, Kanitkar (1981, p.95) claims that the varnas 'remain relevant' among Indians in Britain and in other parts of the world. There is some evidence to support this view, and to show that caste members in Britain are aware of their varna, and sometimes attempt to raise their status to a higher varna. Influenced by western interest in Hindu castes, Hindus themselves now sometimes refer consciously to the classes. Ritual status may not be as dominant an issue as it was a generation or two ago, but the social status that applies to caste or varna is quite important. Furthermore, economic status can also be important but, as we saw in the article of 1836, this need bear no direct relationship to caste status. Some Brahmans are and always have been quite poor, while Sudras, and these days members of scheduled castes, formerly outcastes, can be extremely wealthy.

Contemporary Hindus in the West tend to play down the importance of caste, or to suggest that caste is disappearing as a social phenomenon, in rural as well as urban areas, in India and in Britain. Michaelson suggests that the denial of the importance of caste refers primarily to the varna divisions rather than caste proper.

> It is indisputably not the case that they will deny that they are members of a particular *gnati* [Gujarati form of *jati*] … indeed they are quite vocal about the distinctions between these. Indeed, differences between the various *gnati* are a favourite topic of conversation of Gujaratis of all ages, and people constantly refer to what they consider to be the strange customs of *gnati* other than their own.

(Michaelson, 1979, p.352)

One suspects that those who wish to play down the existence and importance of caste put forward this view because of the bad press given to caste in the West and their desire to put a different face on a social system of which they feel they should be ashamed. The truth is, however, that although caste as a ritual social feature involving matters of purity and pollution has changed, the situation is still far from what modernized

Hindus would have it be. One still reads in the Indian press of lower castes being victimized in various ways by higher castes. In 1991 a newspaper reported the fate of a young couple who were considered to have broken caste rules concerning male/female relationships: the couple were hanged by their parents, the executions being forced on the parents by the rest of the adult males in the village. An event as horrific as this is rare, which is why it hit international as well as local headlines. Unfortunately, however, less vicious caste events are not at all rare. Commensality, the rules governing eating between restricted kin groups, are more relaxed than they used to be, but the rules governing relationships based on purity and pollution have not been eliminated, and the rules governing endogamy or marriage alliances are as strongly in force as ever. This is as true of Hindus in Britain as it is of those in India.

5 Caste and other Hindu groups in Britain

In India, Hindus comprise about 80 per cent of the population. Being a large majority affects a group's view, but while Hindus are conscious of caste affiliation, they are not very conscious of their Hinduism. When Hindus who have grown up in India say that Hinduism is not a religion but a way of life they are, generally, not trying to make some ideological point. In India being Hindu usually means just being Indian, just as in Britain there has been a cultural assumption that if one is British then one is a Christian. There is a contemporary religio-political movement, consisting of political and cultural organizations, which is trying to turn India into a Hindu theocratic state, with limited success so far, but with a great deal of communal unrest since its adherents demolished a mosque in Ayodhya in December 1992. The majority of Hindus, however, have shown an anxiety to retain the secular basis of the Indian Constitution while observing their Hindu practices unselfconsciously.

When Hindus migrate and settle in other countries, becoming a minority religious group, they frequently retain their caste affiliation, but change how they profess their religion (Knott, 1987a, pp.160–1). There is evidence that this change happened only gradually in Britain. For example, Desai, writing in 1963, claimed:

> Hindus do not have temples here. The elaborate rituals which are required in a temple are forbidden by custom on foreign soil ... Much of the religion practised by the immigrant has a basis in village or caste in India; the village-kin group rather than the whole community is concerned with religious activities. This group is so small that it could not bear the cost of maintaining a temple ... Hindu immigrants usually delegate their ritual duties

to other members of their families who are still in India. This is true even to the extent that marriage and funeral rites may be carried out by delegation in India, with nothing but a token ceremony in the United Kingdom.

(Desai, 1963, p.93)

Observers have noted that this situation possibly changed by the late 1960s as a result of Hindus migrating from Africa (Knott, 1986a, p.9). These 'Africans', it was argued, had established temples in East Africa and it was natural for them to continue the practice in Britain (Tambs-Lyche, 1975, p.351).

Thus, it is argued, we have a pattern among Hindus in Britain of caste affiliation being carried on sometimes in a more organized way than in India, together with a new religious affiliation developing. The minority status of Hindus in Britain may have forced them into self-awareness and into strategies for the protection and preservation of their self-identity. In addition we find the establishment of certain sectarian movements, some of them originating in India and well established there, others that are usually called 'new religious movements' which, while owing their inspiration to Hindu ideas or personages, are essentially western in origin. The development of religious awareness through the organization of temples will be looked at separately. Here we will concentrate on caste and sectarian affiliation.

Castes and caste organizations

As we have seen, the majority of Hindus who came to Britain in our period had their origins in Punjab or Gujarat, with Gujaratis far out-numbering Punjabis. While the two groups are 'defined religiously as Hindus', they differ greatly in language, cultural habits and in the ways in which they practise their religion (Knott, 1986a, p.36). We have seen that the two groups had largely different migratory patterns, and this has resulted in differences in the ways in which they have expressed themselves as groups.

In a study of East African Gujaratis in London and Leicester it was reported that the group included representatives of twenty-seven different castes (Michaelson, 1979, p.351). Of these, three castes stood out by their large numbers: the Visa Halari Oshwal, Lohana and Patidar.[3] The Visa Halari Oshwals were originally agriculturalists and traders. They are a sub-group of the Baniya, noted in western India as moneylenders and as

---

[3] There were also a few thousand Kanbis in 'various distinct sub-castes'. The Kanbis were originally agricultural labourers and peasant farmers.

such often despised even by those who are not in their debt. The Lohana were and largely continue to be traders, while the Patidars were originally farmers and landowners, often owning substantial holdings, many of whom have now become traders. Many Patidars bear the name Patel, meaning 'village headman', a title given them when in the days of British India they acted as local administrators.

These three caste groupings have different marriage alliances. The Patidars have 'no unified single caste association' and therefore cannot operate nationally in Britain, unlike the Lohanas who have a strong network of caste associations. However, the Patidars do have a strong organization of marriage alliances. In India, Patidar villages are organized into 'marriage circles' and these are replicated in Britain, and often co-ordinated with the Indian lists. Thus by 1979 the Patidars remained the only caste among those Gujaratis who migrated from East Africa to Britain who continued to 'arrange marriages with caste-mates in the Indian villages' (Michaelson, 1979, p.355).

Michaelson's study shows that there were also some differences concerning marriage with spouses living abroad or brought to Britain from India. The preference among Patidars was for their sons to marry girls 'brought up in the [Indian] villages'. The Lohanas, because of their relative wealth, did not arrange such alliances, and the Oshwals gradually moved to this position. The three castes, after some years of living in East Africa, 'became reluctant to send their daughters back to the [Indian] villages in marriage' (Michaelson, 1979, p.358) for practical reasons to do with disparities in wealth, education and social position between the migrants and their caste-mates in India.

Other castes mentioned in this study were Suthar (carpenters), Mistry (carpenters), Mochi (shoemakers), Soni (goldsmiths) and Lohars (blacksmiths). While the three dominant castes mentioned above are prominent among Gujaratis in London and Leicester, in Leeds the most prominent caste among Gujaratis is the Mochi (Knott, 1986a, p.45), followed by the Patidar/Patel, who outnumber the Lohana, Suthar and Brahman put together.

If we look at these groupings from the point of view of the classical varnas, we will see that they are divided almost equally between the Vaishya and Sudra: there are very few from among the two higher varnas, the Brahman and the Kshatriya. However, at least one group of Sudra, the Mochis of Leeds, regard themselves as Kshatriya, because they bear the names of some of the Kshatriya clans from Rajputana, where the warrior clans have always been prominent. In Leeds, Mochi groups often refer to themselves formally as Kshatriya Mandal (Kshatriya Association) (Knott, 1986a, p.44).

The other main group of Hindu settlers, the Punjabis, consists mainly of two castes, the Khatri and the Brahman. The larger group, the Khatri, are known as a trading caste, though as with all caste descriptions one must be aware that not all Khatri are traders. The founder of the Sikh religion was a Khatri, but before his enlightenment he was employed as a minor state official. In Leeds the Khatri have tended to go into business, as have the Gujarati Patidar, Kanbi and Patel (Knott, 1986a, p.47). Many caste members have attempted to find work that accords with their caste tradition. For instance, some Gujarati Mochi in Leeds have been employed by a firm of surgical footwear makers (Knott, 1986a, p.445). Others wishing to elevate their traditional status have found alternative employment, often trading. In Coventry there is a wide diversity of castes, the two predominant being the Mistry (carpenters) with about 125 families, and the Lohana (black-smiths) with about 90 families (Jackson, 1981, p.64).

The Brahman, in spite of their elevated status traditionally, have also taken to trading, or entered professions, while some carry on their traditional priestly duties, as in the Leeds temple studied by Knott between 1977 and 1981 (Knott, 1986a). The West Bengal Cultural Association in Cardiff has used a Brahman who has a professional occupation as their priest for their twice-yearly *puja*, Saraswati Puja in the spring, and Durga Puja in the autumn, performed at a temporary shrine erected in a building owned by the local education authority.

Other Hindu Groups

Swaminarayan Sectarian Vaishnavism

Around 1800, a young high-caste Brahman, Sahajananda Swami, was inducted as a Vaishnavite ascetic into a group under the guru Ramananda Swami. When the guru died Sahajananda took over leadership of the group, and was soon accorded divine status and the name Swami Narayan or Swaminarayan, Narayan being the name given to the god Vishnu under certain aspects, and a name closely associated with the avatar Krishna.

Over time the group became an influential sect[4] in Gujarat, and is reckoned today to include about 5 million devotees (Williams, 1882; Wil-

---

[4] There is no universal agreement in the study of religions over the difference in meaning between 'cult' and 'sect'. In this essay the term 'sect' will be used for a well-established, formally organized group within the overall religion, and the term 'cult' for a recently founded group or movement, especially where there is a cult leader still living. This distinction cannot be precise for there may be movements which are on the way to becoming a sect according to this definition. This could be the case with ISKCON. Sikhism is a clear case in which a cult centred on Guru Nanak was followed by a stage as a sect within Hinduism, eventually developing into a separate, autonomous religion. Although there is a tendency in the popular press to invest the term 'cult' with pejorative meanings, there is no such intention here. I avoid the term 'denomination' because it is customarily applied to Christian churches.

liams, 1984, and 1988, pp.152–85). In the hagiography of the sect and in its doctrines there is a belief that the *acharyas*, or teacher/leaders, of the sect are in a succession that traces its authority and power back to Ramanuja, teacher, philosopher and third acharya of the Sri Vaishnava community of Hinduism. Ramanuja flourished in South India probably in the first half of the twelfth century and was the articulator of one of the main forms of Hindu Vedanta philosophy, Visisht-advaita, qualified non-dualism. Thus the doctrine of the Swaminarayan cult is qualified non-dualism, which teaches that while the Supreme Reality and the individual human soul are essentially one, there are permanent internal distinctions between them so that the human person or soul can enter into a relationship of loving devotion towards the Supreme Being.

The sect itself grew out of Swaminarayan's attempts at reform of Vaishnavism in the face of what he considered its laxity and worldliness. He built up a strong following of disciples in the area around Ahmedabad, in what is now Gujarat State, many of them from the lower castes, who were willing to adopt asceticism in varying degrees for the sake of improving their ritual status (Barot, 1987, p.69). Untouchables were formally excluded. There was a strict code of behaviour for the inner core of *sadhu* and a less strict code for the householder members of the cult. Swaminarayan's ethical code and his doctrinal teaching are available in a two-volume work. Another multi-volume work, written by one of his disciples, gives the traditional story of Swaminarayan's life along with more teaching and forms of worship. His disciples are initiated, men by men and women by women, by a simple ritual of pouring water over the right hand and taking vows that relate to eating and drinking, including strict vegetarianism and total abstinence from alcohol, and to human relations, including the sexual. The sadhus take stricter vows than the householders, including complete celibacy. Men and women householders, however, are also strictly controlled in their relationships.

In 1826, Swaminarayan divided the body of followers into two geographical divisions within India, one based in Vadtal, the original seat, covering the south, the other in Ahmedabad covering northern Gujarat. Swaminarayan laid down strict rules governing the two regions and it appears that although there is occasional rivalry between the activities of the two temples and their affiliates in Britain, no permanent split has ever taken place. However, there have been other splits over the intervening years and today there are, besides the main sect covering the two temples, a number of sub-sects. The twin seats have had a parallel succession of acharyas since the early days. In recent years the acharya of the Ahmedabad seat, Tejendraprasad, has been the more vigorous of the two and has made many journeys to Britain and America. In 1984 he was the key person in the organization of the International Swaminarayan Satsang

Organization in the United States, 'an umbrella organization for Swaminarayan Hindus who are loyal to the Ahmedabad and Vadtal dioceses [sic] but who live outside India' (Williams, 1988, p.159).

Among the breakaway sub-sects two are the most important, the Shree Swaminarayan Siddhanta Sajivan Mandal, which broke away from the Ahmedabad seat during the 1940s (see Barot, 1987), and the Shree Akshar Purshottam Sanstha, also known as the Bochasaswani Purushottam Sanstha, which broke away from the Vadtal seat in 1906 and is considered 'one of the fastest growing religious groups in Gujarat and perhaps in all of India' (Williams, 1984, p.44; see also Pocock, 1976 for a study of this group in London). While relations between the Vadtal and Ahmedabad seats have been relatively harmonious throughout their history, the same cannot be said of some of the sub-sects. Barot reports on bitter conflict between rival sub-divisions of the Sajivan Mandal, including physical violence ending in criminal prosecution and prison sentences after an incident in London in 1971. The remarkable thing was that this violence was between members of the same caste, the Leva Kanbi Patel (Barot, 1987, pp.74–6). Under the leadership of Swami Narayanswarupdas, or Pramukh Swami, the Purushottam Sanstha has survived two minor divisions and maintains a rapid development in Britain and the USA.

All these sects and sub-sects are very active in Britain, having by the late 1980s at least twelve temples throughout England and Wales. Membership is exclusively Gujarati, which is not surprising given the sect's geographical origins. Members carry on their old loyalties and traditions in dispersion. Although many religions, and Hinduism in particular, maintain substantial differences between men and women, especially in the area of public worship, none maintain the division more rigidly than the main Swaminarayan sects. For example, the temple in Cardiff, on the upper floor of a converted building, contains the usual images associated with the sect, with Krishna prominent alongside an image of Swaminarayan himself. The most striking feature of the ritual area, however, is the substantial partition which runs along the centre of the room and physically divides the men from the women. In the nineteenth century, Swaminarayan took steps to improve the status of women, including the abolition of widow suicide, which was a feature of Hinduism generally at the time. Women members of the sect enjoy considerable freedom and are able to take up educational opportunities. There are special orders for women ascetics. The separation of the sexes in worship and in other aspects of the life of the sects is seen as a means of 'protecting both men and women from sexual temptation [and] ... to protect women from exploitation by men' (Williams, 1984, p.145). On Pramukh Swami's visit to Britain in 1985, the national press reported that no women were admitted into his sight. 'Pramukh Swami is respected by women of the Akshar Purushottam

Sanstha as the abode of god, and they press as close as they dare for darshan. They do not, however, approach him for advice and instruction as the men do ... women receive what they consider to be the highest spiritual blessings only indirectly' (Williams, 1984, p.145).

Sathya Sai Baba

One of the fastest growing movements with a Hindu base in Britain is that surrounding the charismatic figure, Sathya Sai Baba, who was born in 1926. In 1940 he claimed to be the reincarnation of Sai Baba of Shirdi in Maharashtra, a locally known miracle worker who died in 1918. Shortly after leaving school he began to receive devotees who sang his and other *bhajans*, or devotional hymns. By 1944 a special building had been built for him to receive his devotees, and four years later an *ashram*, Prashanti Nilayam, was founded near Puttaparthi, his home village, in what is now Andhra Pradesh state.

Although Sathya Sai Baba is acknowledged as a guru who teaches his followers traditionally, through discourse and especially devotional homilies, he is more widely known and deeply revered by his followers for what are claimed to be miracles. These acts (*siddhis*) include healing, mind reading, bodily relocation, the materializing of jewellery and souvenir objects for his followers and, most importantly, sacred ash, *vibhuti*, which is used to smear his followers' foreheads in their act of devotion and has, apparently, been used for healing. It is claimed that a blind person had his sight restored after being made to eat the ash. On some occasions the vibhuti is produced in such amounts that it will cover everything in the room (Bowen, 1988, p.379).

More importantly, however, Sathya Sai Baba claims to be an avatar of Siva and of Shakti, the female principle of power. He is also seen as an avatar of Vishnu and Krishna. His activities and teachings, therefore, take on added power from these associations with Hindu divinities. His claim is that 'All names [of God] are mine'.

The cult has grown in a comparatively short time, now claiming 6 million followers in India and 50 million followers in sixty-four countries worldwide. It has a temple built on the site of his original home, a number of educational institutions, and a major conference centre in Bombay. Training camps have been held in India, and a series of four world conferences was held between 1968 and 1985. It also has a magazine and a number of publications setting out his life story and teaching (Bowen, 1988, pp.342–4).

In Britain the number of centres has grown from one in Bradford in 1970 to fifty-one by 1983, although there is evidence that not all centres are permanent, for some depend on strong individuals to maintain them. In January 1975 the Sri Sathya Sai Service Organization was formed, changing by the early 1980s to the Sathya Sai Baba Council of the United Kingdom. In

1983 the organization had thirty-five office bearers of whom fourteen were Gujarati, twelve came from other parts of India, and nine were non-Indian. Although there is a strong representation of Gujaratis among followers in Britain, this does not reflect the following in India, which covers a broad class of people both in caste and wealth. It is claimed that by 1983 the numbers of westerners probably equalled the numbers of Indian origin. Some of these westerners stress that they are not Hindus, that they do not follow a Hindu guru, and do not wish to be known as 'English Hindus'. They claim that their devotion rises above devotion to a particular religion (Bowen, 1988, pp.48–55).

International Society for Krishna Consciousness (ISKCON)

A similar problem of identity applies to the cult known officially as ISKCON and more popularly as the Hare Krishna movement. The cult owes its origins to a former Bengali businessman turned guru, known to his disciples as His Divine Grace A.C. Bhaktivedanta Swami Prabhupada. In 1965, at the age of sixty-nine, he travelled to New York, and started to teach and hold meetings consisting of meditations on Hindu religious themes and the chanting of Hindu mantras. Two years later, after moving to San Francisco, the movement began to grow more rapidly. Many of his early disciples were drawn from the broadly hippie culture (Rochford, 1982, p.403). In 1969 six disciples came to London and established the first temple in England. Later the same year the Swami himself came to London and installed images of Krishna and his consort Radha. Later centres were set up in Letchmore Heath, near Watford, and Worcester. It is difficult to assess the extent of ISKCON activity.

Clearly the Swami based his teaching on Hindu sacred texts. His initiation brought him into the succession of the medieval Bengali bhakti guru Chaitanya, himself a Vaishnavite. One of his most popular works is his translation and commentary on the Bhagavad Gita, *Bhagavad Gita As It is* (1968). His other works contain teaching on yoga, Krishna consciousness and devotion, and include *The Science of Self-realization* (1977), a collection of sermons, interviews and correspondence with journalists and teachers of religion. Despite the emphasis on Hindu texts and Krishna, some early disciples denied that they were Hindus, or following Hindu forms of religion. They drew a distinction between Hindus who may devote themselves to Krishna as avatar of Vishnu, and their worship of Krishna as 'the Supreme Personality of Godhead' (Prabhupada, 1968, p.xxi) or 'Supreme Brahman' (Prabhupada, 1977, p.95), arguing that Krishna is above all the other gods of the Hindus, is the Supreme Lord of the Vedas, preceding Hinduism as such.

Such emphasis on Krishna has also led to academic debate about the nature of ISKCON. Some scholars argue that the Swami was a highly unorthodox Hindu. However, others argue that there are Hindu texts which provide justification for according Krishna such pre-eminence (Carey, 1987, p.84; Dimock, 1968, p.16). Similarly, it would seem that most Hindus are able to accommodate claims of the kind made by ISKCON for Krishna within the general complexity of Hindu religious experience. This, however, reflects another ambiguity in ISKCON. Although it has had increasing contact with the general Hindu world and Hindu culture, the leadership of the cult remains almost exclusively in the hands of western converts who are inclined to present the claims of ISKCON in a very assertive manner which is not characteristic of other Hindu groups.

The cult in Britain is similarly clearly under the control of western devotees, but also increasingly provides a spiritual home for recently domiciled families that are traditionally Hindu. From the first days of ISKCON's activities in London they set out to attract Hindus, the establishment of the London temple coinciding with the arrival of Hindus forced to leave East Africa in the late 1960s and early 1970s.

The question of Hindu identity is highlighted by the attitude of some members of other Hindu sects who, while appreciating much that goes on in ISKCON temples, object to what they see as fanatical 'un-Hindu' behaviour, 'beyond all reason', and the preaching of 'a sectarian message' that 'other paths are wrong' (Carey, 1983, p.484). Such criticisms may emanate from Hindus who adopt a tolerance not necessarily characteristic of Hinduism before the advent of nineteenth-century reform movements like the Ramakrishna Mission. Nevertheless, what many Hindus object to is probably the unceasing pressure often applied to those considered possible recruits to ISKCON – pressure that must implicitly involve a negative view of the potential recruit's existing religious standpoint. One commentator, on the basis of his observation of such behaviour, concludes that ISKCON is not even 'Indian' in its characteristics (Hardy, 1984, p.16). Whether the increasing numbers of Hindus within ISKCON will transform this situation, only time will tell.[5]

6 Adaptations to the religious life

Temple organization

The migration, dispersion and settlement of any group of people involves many social and cultural disruptions and adaptations. Religious practice and beliefs are an important part of the lives of Hindus, and those who have settled in Britain have faced considerable challenges which call for adaptation. The most thorough study of this is by Kim Knott (1986a), based on her studies of Hinduism in Leeds and concentrating on the activities in and

[5] For a detailed study of ISKCON in Britain, see Knott, 1986b.

around a temple established there in 1970. She detailed all the religious rites carried out in the temple between 1977 and 1980, and concluded:

> ... migrant Hindus continue their practices in a similar way to their ancestors and relatives in India. There is even some conjecture that, in East Africa and Britain, there is an increase in temple activity amongst Hindus. The reasons for this are clear. In social terms the opportunities for meeting, sharing news and reinforcing relationships are curtailed in Britain because of the limitations brought about by the urban situation, the climate and the British working week. In addition to this, there is a growing problem for individuals, particularly those of the younger generation, who are constantly challenged by different ideologies and ways of life, both religious and secular in nature: the English language, British customs and traditions, different leisure activities, and alien moral standards. In India, the beliefs and practices of Hinduism were inextricably related to daily life and social relationships, and they were thus constantly reiterated and reinforced. In Britain, religion, in general, occupies just one compartment of thought and experience, and although Hindus try to live, as far as possible, as they did in India, they cannot but be influenced by this. Temple practice, therefore, has become of crucial importance in the retention of tradition and its transmission from one generation to the next. Attendance at the temple provides an opportunity for the strengthening of social relationships and cultural ties between members of like kin, caste and language groups. The ritual process itself acts as a coded message which reminds participants of and reinforces them in their religious precepts, practices and beliefs. Without temple practice it is unlikely that Hinduism, in any traditional sense, could continue to exist in Leeds. Left to the domestic environment there would be little opportunity to check or reaffirm beliefs and practices, little incentive to pass them on to the children, and still less likelihood of maintaining the ritual hierarchy and the associated concepts of purity and pollution.

(Knott, 1986a, p.115)

Knott seems to regard the establishing of temples in dispersion as almost wholly bound up with the demands of dispersion. Temples, she seems to be saying, fulfil a pragmatic, social and religious need, and the motivations for establishing temples in dispersion create a different perspective from their use in India. This is only partially true.

Any visitor to India will soon become aware of the prevalence of Hindu shrines and temples. In any city visitors will see the *shikhara*, a superstructure representing a sacred mountain, towering above the temple complex and the surrounding dwellings, marking the location of the main temple shrine containing the images of the main divinity of the temple. The area containing the image is a womb-like space where the spiritual power of the temple is concentrated. Sometimes there will also be smaller towers of varying shapes marking the existence of subordinate shrines. Some of the largest temple complexes, certainly in southern Indian cities like Madurai and Kanchipuram, cover several acres of ground. Other shrines can be much smaller, single-storey buildings, some only large enough to hold an image while the devotees carry out their devotions from outside. Sometimes shrines are little more than small piles of stones clustered around the bases of trees identified by smeared colours. Attendance at temple ceremonies is thus vitally important for millions of Hindus at all the shrines in India, and this fact should not be disregarded.

Knott's statement about the importance of the temple in Britain for the 'retention of tradition and its transmission from one generation to another' therefore needs to be put in context. The threat of secular and alien ideas, as seen by the devout Hindu, is just as potent in India as it is for Hindus in dispersion. In her work Knott notes that the Hindu temple in Leeds is closely associated with an organization in India known as the *Vishwa Hindu Parishad*, a name that is incorporated into the official title of the temple. This organization is deeply involved in Hindu communal action in India, and was closely allied to the Bharatiya Janata Party, which was implicated in the demolition of the Babri Mosque in December 1992. Vishwa Hindu Parishad was subsequently proscribed by the Indian government. This Indian-based organization, which has branches among Hindu communities in other countries, originated in India in 1966, one of its aims being 'to protect "Hindu society from the insidiously spreading clutches of alien ideologies"' (Knott, 1986a, p.61). It can be argued that the militant rhetoric of such organizations in India and elsewhere (what the press frequently refers to incorrectly as 'fundamentalism') is an extreme reaction to forces in the modern world that are perceived as threatening traditional values. In India VHP do not meet this perceived threat by building temples, but one can easily see that in dispersion this would be a way of preserving and transmitting traditional values.

Given that temples are an important, integral and popular feature of Hinduism in India, it is thus not surprising that Hindus in dispersion establish them, even building them in traditional Hindu style complete with a highly visible shikhara, as in some temples in the Midlands. Temples are part of Hinduism, whether in Europe or North America, or for those who migrated centuries ago to south-east Asia, where remnants of temples remain today.

There are other motivations for building temples. Being a well-defined sect the Swaminarayan groups can be expected to establish temples for the installation of their sect images and the regular performance of their associated rituals. In a sense this means the constant retention and transmission of their traditions, but not in any special way associated with being in Britain, for their ritual activities have traditionally been centred on temples.

Finally, for certain groups of Indians who lie outside the hierarchy of class and caste, the outcastes, such as the Valmikis or Ravidasis, establishing temples is a positive affirmation of their identity against the negative attitudes of caste Hindus and Sikhs towards them. This motivation is to be found in India and is only replicated in dispersion. Again the retention and transmission of traditions, though in this case traditions only fairly recently conceived, are part of the whole process, but not a determining factor.

It is normal practice for the rituals in Hindu temples traditionally associated with the three 'twice-born' classes to be performed by a Brahman priest, or *pujari*. A different tradition of pujaris pertains among low or outcaste groups and tribes. The majority of Hindus settled in Britain are ranking-caste Hindus and for these it is usual for the ministrations to be in the hands of a Brahman pujari. 'Temples throughout the country have access to part-time Brahmans with some knowledge of the relevant procedure for daily practices and life-cycle rites (*samskaras*) but not all have their own *Pandit* or full-time temple priest' (Knott, 1986a, p.63). The case of the West Bengal Cultural Association in South Wales has already been noted. The same was true of the Leeds temple Knott studied, except that there a Gujarati priest was employed full-time. Although the worshippers in Leeds consisted of members of a number of castes, including Sudras, the temple was normally served by a Brahman. However, when the Brahman was not available to perform his ritual duties, they were performed by Sudras, members of the lowest of the varna (Knott, 1986a, p.142). It is also reported that the priest's wife 'who knew the traditional ritual best of all, took over all the temple duties' while the pandit was away. 'Some orthodox Hindu students who had come from India to Leeds and saw this were quite surprised and even shocked at this pragmatic solution, because the traditional rites going back to the Vedas are not normally conducted by a woman' (King, 1984, p.8). That low class/caste persons and women, who are considered to be potentially extremely polluting, are accepted in a role that demands utmost purity is completely at odds with normal practice and is an example of adaptation of the purity/pollution factor forced on a community in dispersion, and of a flexible attitude towards caste, again forced on the community by local circumstances.

There have been a number of studies of temple practice among Hindus in Britain. Two of them (Jackson, 1981; Knott, 1986a, chs 3, 4) describe the rituals that take place daily and on festive occasions in two temples, one in Leeds and the other in Coventry. They note the differences between the way the rituals are performed in Britain and in India, and rituals that are not normally part of temple worship in India. Factors that cause adaptation in the pursuit of worship practice in Britain include the daily and weekly routines of an industrialized society and the personnel available to perform the rituals. There is also an indirect factor in that the pattern of religious participation already existing in Britain, wherein religion and the rest of life exist side by side rather than intertwined, seems to have some effect on the way in which Hindus approach religious practice following settlement. There is a tendency to act in a more 'congregational' way, for service times to be determined by regular patterns of time and date, rather than depending on the natural structure of a rurally-based life. Jackson's description of the celebration of Holi in Coventry, which in India can be fairly riotous and anarchic, shows how the structure of living, the desire not to be seen as indulging in 'unacceptable' behaviour by one's neighbours, along with climatic factors, regulate and change the festivities (Jackson, 1976, pp.206–8).

Life-cycle rites

Life-cycle rites (*samskaras*) are important for Hindus, as for other religious groups. There is no agreement as to how many samskaras there are in Hinduism, estimates ranging from sixteen to forty. Among them, marriage and death rituals are the 'extremes of auspiciousness and inauspiciousness', the latter being, potentially, an occasion for severe pollution (Killingley, 1991a, p.2). There is some dispute as to whether the funeral rite should be included in the list of samskaras, for they 'affirm and attempt to enhance life on earth' (Shinn, 1981, p.651). Alternatively it is claimed that 'The *samskaras* circumscribe the entire life cycle, extending from prenatal ceremonies to post-mortem rituals' and 'aim at perfecting each individual so that he or she may achieve full civilized humanity' (Kinsley, 1982, p.107). These samskaras are held to 'prepare the person over a period of rebirths for the ultimate goal of release from the cycle of rebirths and the union of the embodied soul with god' (McDonald, 1987, pp.51–2). Most samskaras are restricted to the twice-born castes, that is, the top three varnas. Samskaras help to ensure purity for the individual Hindu and avoid pollution.

Some scholars claim that Bhrahminical literature counts sixteen samskaras, eight of them concerning pregnancy and birth. The rituals relating to pregnancy are designed to protect the foetus and to ensure the birth of a male child; those relating to the period after birth are designed to protect the infant. For instance, the sixth ritual consists of 'prayers repenting the misdeeds of the parents to ensure that the child is born with no impure thoughts or deeds from the parents' (McDonald, 1987, p.52). Although the birth of a child is an auspicious occasion, it is not without its perils resulting from the ritual impurity of the mother. 'The period of pollution following childbirth is said to last for six weeks, during which time the woman should remain indoors and refrain from cooking or lighting candles at the household shrine. With each successive postnatal ritual, the degree of pollution appears to lessen as the mother is gradually reincorporated into the household and begins to resume her normal duties' (McDonald, 1987, p.63).

In devout families, samskaras begin with conception and proceed through birth, puberty and marriage, to death. (For a study of marriage in Britain see Menski, 1991.) Being in dispersion does not pose too many problems for most of these rites. However, in the case of death and mourning, the matter is more problematic. The problems arise for a number of reasons, the most difficult having to do with the delay between death and cremation in Britain – the result of bureaucratic procedures and sometimes pressure on local crematoria.

Firth has studied one Hindu community in Southampton, and much of our information on dying and death rituals and their associated problems comes from this study (Firth, 1991; see also Firth, 1993a and 1993b). According to Firth, Hindu death rituals ideally cover a considerable period of time and include nine stages.

> Stage I is preparation for death, which may be seen as part of a life-long process, or simply the last days, hours or minutes before death. Stage II involves rituals at the moment of death, and Stage III, which may overlap with it, is the preparation of the body. Stage IV is the journey to the cremation ground. Stage V is the disposal of the body, which for adults is normally cremation; Stage VI is the collection of bones (or 'ashes') on the third or fourth day; these may be deposited in the holy river immediately if possible, or await an opportunity for the chief mourner or his representative to go to the Ganges or Yamuna. Stage VII (*shraddha*) involves the rites of the deceased's spirit (*preta*), covering the period up to the twelfth or thirteenth day, when various ceremonies enable it to take on a new spiritual body and become a *pitr* (ancestor). The first ten days of this period after death are a time of extreme impurity (*sutaka*) which reflects also the family's isolation and grief (*soka*). Stage VIII includes ceremonies marking the end of this state. In the final Stage IX, the deceased, as an ancestor, receives daily, monthly and annual oblations.
>
> (Firth, 1993a, pp.52–3)

Problems can begin with the very moment of death. Ideally a Hindu should die while lying on the floor. This might be possible at home but those dying in hospital are often denied this important concession. It is also important for relatives to be present to perform certain rites immediately after death, but often relatives are discouraged from remaining overnight in hospitals and are informed of death a few hours later, causing considerable distress. However, this problem can occur in urbanized India as well as in Britain.

In India the performance of the nine stages, or eight if we begin with the point of death, will cover sixteen days, with the disposal of the body taking place very soon after death, if possible within twenty-four hours. Thus stages two to five will be completed in this initial period. In Britain, however, these stages can cover as many as ten days. Thus while in India the corpse will be prepared for cremation within hours of death, the same preparation rituals can only be carried out in Britain after the corpse has lain in a chapel of rest between death and the day of the cremation. The problems of dealing with a corpse after such a long period are obvious and can be very traumatic for the mourners, especially the chief mourner, the eldest son or nearest elder male relative of the same blood line.

Because of the delay in disposing of the corpse in Britain families have adapted the stages so that stage seven – the period lasting about ten days of intense mourning and of ritual impurity for the family – is observed before cremation, while the body is at the funeral home. Also, because of the need to carry on with daily work, the mourners may not observe strict separation during this period.

The journey to the crematorium, with hearse and limousine, is very different from the walk to the ghat in India, with minor rituals along the route and at the entrance to the ghat. The cremation itself can be problematic, especially for the chief mourner. 'After the prayers the chief mourner presses the button for the coffin to disappear, and then goes down below to ignite the cremator or to push the coffin in, an experience which some find very traumatic' (Firth, 1991, p.77). Finally purificatory rituals, remembering that contact with a corpse is considered highly polluting, pose a problem in Britain. Some mourners have begun the practice of going to a friend's house to bathe and put on fresh clothes before returning to the family home.

Disposing of the ashes again demands a different approach in Britain. In India they would be collected from the ghat after two or three days. In Britain they will be collected in a container from the crematorium and will not be subjected to the rituals common in India. The family may arrange for the ashes to be immersed in a river or the sea, possibly accompanied by a pandit who will chant mantras. Otherwise they may be taken to India, or posted to relatives there, for immersion in one of the holy rivers.

It must be remembered that the rituals surrounding death for a Hindu are crucial for the good resting of the departed soul (*atman*) and for the good conscience of the family. The changes forced upon Hindus in Britain can be traumatic and induce feelings of guilt.

While many Hindus experience some anxiety about the appropriate performance of death rituals, others are pragmatic about what is possible, believing that as long as they have done their best, there will be no negative results ... The biggest problem seems to centre on the death itself: the failure to be with someone at death is a disaster for any community, but for Hindus there are long-term repercussions both for the atman [soul] and for the survivors ... this also creates problems for hospitals unless there are facilities for enabling the patient to be in a room alone with his family, with minimum disruption for other patients. This needs a high level of understanding, both at the administrative level and on the part of doctors and nurses caring for the patients.

(Firth, 1991, pp.80–1)

One conclusion that Firth suggests is that Hindu funerals in Britain may be moving 'towards the consolation of the mourners in this world, rather then being concerned solely with the welfare of the dead in the unseen world, although this may not be recognized' (Firth, 1991, p.82). Rituals are being discarded or adapted, and pandits are engaged in designing rituals appropriate for Hindus in dispersion, but without any standardization of ritual. This is not surprising since the approaches to death and dying in different communities outlined by Firth already contain considerable variations and interpretations.

7 Conclusion

This essay began by looking at the inherent perils for a Hindu travelling outside Bharat Mata: the need to preserve ritual purity and to avoid pollution. It is difficult to avoid this issue in any study of Hinduism. As we have seen, it applies to travel outside India, to social relations in the caste systems, and to life-cycle occasions, especially to birth and death.

Much of what is said about purity and pollution is taken from the traditional scriptural texts and is based on ideal situations. But it is clear that the ideal situation scarcely, if ever, pertains. While purity and pollution have been, and in many cases remain, important issues in the life of Hindus, it is also true to say that Hindus do, even in India, adopt pragmatic approaches to the matter.

While it may be true that traditional ritual demands are not easy for the Hindu in dispersion and there may be occasions when feelings of guilt have to be dealt with, nevertheless most Hindus in Britain appear to be able to carry on a reasonably normal life. Adjustments have been made in the practice of public worship. Even sensitive problems of caste relationships can be overcome. Sometimes approaches to purity and pollution are adapted in order to worship by, for example, lowering caste barriers. In other instances, especially in the case of a sect like the Swaminarayan, caste distinctions, and distinctions of gender, as traditionally understood, are strictly maintained.

It is interesting to note, however, that caste divisions are fairly strictly maintained universally when they apply to the choice of marital partners. Here it would appear that social boundaries are fairly strictly maintained, though it could be argued that these social boundaries also reflect a residue of ritual necessity in ensuring the family line.

In the matter of life-cycle rites, where the issue of purity and pollution is always involved, it would seem from a number of studies that adjustments can and have been made, adjustments enabling the family and the wider community to carry on reasonably trouble-free lives.

Bibliography

BAHADUR SINGH, I.J. (ed.) (1979) *The Other India*, Arnold-Heinemann, New Delhi.

BAROT, R. (1987) 'Caste and sect in the Swaminarayan movement' in Burghart, R. (ed.).

BASHAM, A.L. (1988) 'Hinduism' in Zaehner, R.C. (ed.) *Hutchinson Encyclopedia of Living Faiths*, Hutchinson, London.

BHARATIYA VIDYA BHAVAN (1992) *Brochure*, London.

BOWEN, D.G. (ed.) (1981) *Hinduism in England*, Bradford College, Bradford.

(1988) *The Sathya Sai Baba Community in Bradford*, Community Religions Project, University of Leeds.

BURGHART, R. (ed.) (1987) *Hinduism in Great Britain*, Tavistock Publications, London.

CAREY, S. (1983) 'The Hare Krishna movement and Hindus in Britain', *New Community*, vol.x, no.3, Spring, pp.477–86.

(1987) 'The Indianization of the Hare Krishna movement in Britain' in Burghart, R. (ed.).

DESAI, R.H. (1963) *Indian Immigrants in Britain*, Oxford University Press, London.

DIMOCK, E. (1968) *In Praise of Krishna*, Jonathan Cape, London.

ECK, D.L. (1981) *Darsan: seeing the Divine Image in India*, Anima Books, Chambersburg, Pennsylvania.

FIRTH, S. (1991) 'Changing patterns in Hindu death rituals in Britain' in Killingley, D., Menski, W. and Firth, S. (eds).

(1993a) 'Cross-cultural perspectives on bereavement' in Dickenson, D. and Johnson, M. (eds) *Death, Dying and Bereavement*, Sage, London.

(1993b) 'Approaches to death in Hindu and Sikh communities in Britain' in Dickenson, D. and Johnson, M. (eds) *Death, Dying and Bereavement*, Sage, London.

HARDY, F. (1984) 'How "Indian" are the new Indian religions in the West?', *Religion Today*, 1, (2/3), pp.15–18.

(1990) 'Hinduism' in King, U. (ed.).

JACKSON, R. (1976) 'Holi in North India and in an English city: some adaptation and anomalies', *New Community*, 5 (3), pp.203–9.

(1981) 'The Shree Krishna Temple and the Gujarati community in Coventry' in Bowen, D.G. (ed.).

KANITKAR, H.A. (1981) 'Caste in contemporary Hinduism' in Bowen, D.G. (ed.).

KILLINGLEY, D. (1991a) 'Introduction' in Killingley, D., Menski, W. and Firth, S. (eds).

(1991b) 'Varna and caste in Hindu Apologetic' in Killingley, D., Menski, W. and Firth, S. (eds).

KILLINGLEY, D., MENSKI, W. AND FIRTH, S. (eds) (1991) *Hindu Ritual and Society*, S.Y. Killingley, Newcastle-upon-Tyne.

KING, U. (1984) *A Report on Hinduism in Britain*, Community Religions Project Research Papers (New Series), no.2, The University of Leeds.

(ed.) (1990) *Turning Points in Religious Studies*, T. & T. Clarke, Edinburgh.

KINSLEY, D.R. (1982) *Hinduism*, Prentice-Hall Inc., Englewood Cliffs, New Jersey.

KNOTT, K. (1981) *Statistical Analysis of South Asians in the U.K. by Religion and Ethnicity*, Community Project Research Papers (New Series) no.8, The University of Leeds.

(1986a) *Hinduism in Leeds: a study of religious practice in the Indian Hindu community and in Hindu-related groups*, Monograph Series, Community Religions Project, University of Leeds.

(1986b) *My Sweet Lord: the Hare Krishna movement*, Aquarian Press, Wellingborough.

(1987a) 'Hindu temple rituals in Britain: the interpretation of tradition' in Burghart, R. (ed.).

(1987b) 'Calculating Sikh population statistics', *Sikh Bulletin*, no.4, Cole, W. Owen and Nesbitt, E. (eds) West Sussex Institute of Higher Education, Chichester.

(1989) 'Hindu communities in Britain' in Badham, P. (ed.) *Religion, State, and Society in Britain*, The Edwin Mellen Press, Lewiston/Queenston/Lampeter.

LAW, J. (1991) *The Religious Beliefs and Practices of Hindus in Derby*, Community Religions Project Research Papers (New Series), The University of Leeds.

MCDONALD, M. (1987) 'Rituals of motherhood among Gujarati women in East London' in Burghart, R. (ed.).

MENSKI, W. (1991) 'Change and continuity in Hindu marriage rituals' in Killingley, D., Menski, W. and Firth, S. (eds).

MICHAELSON, M. (1979) 'The relevance of caste among East African Gujaratis in Britain', *New Community*, 7 (3), pp.350–60.

NAIPAUL, V.S. (1968) *An Area of Darkness*, Penguin, Harmondsworth.

PANCHOLI, N. (1991) 'Hinduism' in Cole, W. Owen (ed.) *Five World Faiths*, Cassell, London.

POCOCK, D.F. (1976) 'Preservation of the religious life: Hindu immigrants in England' in *Contributions to Indian Sociology* (New Series) vol.10, no.2, pp.341–65.

PRABHUPADA, A.C. BHAKTIVEDANTA SWAMI (1968) *Bhagavad-Gita As It Is*, Bhaktivedanta Book Trust, New York, Los Angeles, London, Bombay.

(1977) *The Science of Self-realization*, Bhaktivedanta Book Trust, New York, Los Angeles, London, Bombay.

PRESTON, J. J. (1985) 'Creation of the Sacred Image: apotheosis and destruction in Hinduism' in Waghorne, J.P. and Cutler, N. (eds) in assoc. with Narayanan, V. *Gods of Flesh, Gods of Stone: the embodiment of divinity in India*, Anima Publications, Chambersburg, Pennsylvania.

RADHAKRISHNAN, S. (1927, second impression 1961) *The Hindu View of Life*, Allen and Unwin, London.

RAY, N. (1979) 'A cultural history of overseas Indians' in Bahadur Singh, I.J. (ed.).

ROCHFORD Jr, E. BURKE, (1982) 'Recruitment strategies, ideology, and organization in the Hare Krishna Movement', *Social Problems*, vol.29, no.4, April.

SHINN, L.D. (1981) 'Samskara', *Abingdon Dictionary of Living Religions*, Crim, K. (Gen. Ed.), Bullard, R.A. and Shinn, L.D. (assoc. eds) Abingdon Press, Nashville, p.651.

TAMBS-LYCHE, H. (1975) 'A comparison of Gujarati communities in London and the Midlands', *New Community*, 4, pp.349–55.

THAPAR, R. (1966) *A History of India 1*, Penguin, Harmondsworth.

THOMAS, M.M. (1970) *The Acknowledged Christ of the Indian Renaissance*, Christian Institute for the Study of Religion and Society, Bangalore, India.

VERTOVEC, S. (1992) 'On the reproduction and representation of "Hinduism" in Britain', unpublished paper, Oxford.

VIRAT HINDU SAMMELAN (1989) *Souvenir*, Milton Keynes.

VIVEKANANDA, SWAMI (1931) *The Complete Works of the Swami Vivekananda*, fifth edn, seven vols., Almora.

WILLIAMS, M. (1882) 'The Vaisnava Religion, with special reference to the Sikshapatri of the modern sect called Svami-Narayana', *Journal of the Royal Asiatic Society*, 14, pp.289–316.

WILLIAMS, R.B. (1984) *A New Face of Hinduism: the Swaminarayan religion*, Cambridge University Press, Cambridge.

(1988) *Religions of immigrants from Indian and Pakistan: new threads in the American tapestry*, Cambridge University Press, Cambridge.

5

OLD ALLIES, NEW NEIGHBOURS: SIKHS IN BRITAIN

by Terence Thomas

Bowing to the Guru Granth Sahib on entering the Gurdwara, Bradford. Photograph © Tim Smith.

Among the incomers into Great Britain of the post-war period none are more visible than the Sikhs, at least the male sector of the group. They are very visible through wearing turbans which cover uncut hair, and maintaining full beards, two practices bound up with their profession of faith as Sikhs that have caused them no little grief since they first settled in their new homeland. The women's dress is similar to that of other communities, both Muslim and Hindu, who have their origins in north-west India, the *salwar* (baggy trousers) and *kamiz* (loose long shirt).

The Sikhs are Indian in origin, the members of a minority Indian religion that began as a Hindu sect, part of a religious movement that flourished in the middle ages. It is now counted as one of the youngest of the world religions. There are still Hindus who regard the Sikhs as sectarian Hindus, not unlike certain other Hindu sects with similar origins. The Sikhs have been migrants for the best part of two centuries, first within India and then further afield. Among those who have settled in Great Britain are those who have come directly from India and those who, like many Hindus, have come here via certain countries of the Commonwealth or the former British Empire, especially via East Africa.

In the early years of migration to Britain in the 1950s and 1960s Sikhs were involved in many controversial events to do with matters that are central to their religious profession, usually related to the wearing of turbans. There have also been other occasions when the community has been prominent in the news, such as in 1984 over the assassination of the Indian Prime Minister, Indira Gandhi. The Sikh community in Britain has, for a variety of reasons, thus been quite prominent, religiously and politically, since settling in considerable numbers in Britain.

Although, as I shall show, many of the earlier settlers took steps to adapt themselves to their new environment by putting aside the visible signs of their religion, as pressure on, and discrimination against, Sikhs increased in many cities, the community returned to its roots and many traditional expressions of its origins reappeared and, with their reappearance, confidence in the strength of the community also grew. This confidence has resulted in the assertion of the Sikh view of the world within the Sikh community and this has had its impact on the wider British community.

In the rest of this essay I shall consider this development in more detail but begin by looking at the origins, early history and institutions of Sikhism, which is essential for an understanding of more recent developments.

1 The nature of Sikhism

The origins of Sikhism lie in a particular religious movement which flourished in North India in the Middle Ages.[1] It was a movement to simplify and to democratize religion. The movement undermined the monopoly of the Brahman priesthood, who alone knew the sacred language, Sanskrit, and the sacred formulae or *mantra*. The language of this movement, in contrast, was the language of the ordinary people of each region, Hindi, Marathi, Bengali or Punjabi.

The form of religion manifested in the movement was personal devotion to a personal God. Sacrifices, sacred formulae and sacred rituals were abjured. Devotion to God was expressed through hymns and the repetition of the Name of God. Liberation from the cycle of rebirths, from *karma/samsara*, was to be achieved by following the path of utter devotion, *bhakti marga*.[2] Furthermore, liberation from the cycle of rebirths was open to all classes of people, irrespective of caste or sex. Among the devotional leaders, the *gurus*, of this movement, were members of the lower and outcastes such as *Kabir*, the weaver and *Ravidas*, the leather-worker, and also women, such as Mira Bai in Rajasthan and Lal Ded in Kashmir. This role for women was a very important feature of the movement, considering the lack of status of women in priestly forms of Hinduism. These medieval devotional leaders still have their followers and cults in India today.

It is out of this movement that Guru Nanak (1469–1539) came. His followers and successors formed the Sikh religion. He claimed to have had an intense religious experience of being carried up to the courts of God at about the age of thirty. According to the collections of hagiographic 'lives' of Guru Nanak, he carried his message of devotion to God from his home in Punjab[3] to Sri Lanka in the south, east to Patna and Bengal, north into the Himalayas, and west as far as Mecca. He, like the other gurus, built up a following of disciples. This discipleship gives us the name for the group that grew into a religious sect and then into a religion: *Sikh*, meaning disciple. One of the key elements of Sikhism is its devotion to the teaching of a Guru, who spoke the Word (*shabad*) of God; whose words *are* the Word of God. The scriptures are given the name *Guru Granth Sahib*, roughly translated as the Revered Book Guru. The Word was spoken also by five of the nine Gurus who succeeded Guru Nanak. The Guru Granth Sahib also

---

[1]   See Essay 4, 'Hindu Dharma in dispersion', in this volume.

[2]   '*Bhakti*' means devotion, '*marga*' means path.

[3]   'Punjab' is to be pronounced as in the English word 'pun', southern English pronunciation not northern English, and 'jaab'.

contains the hymns and poems of devotional leaders who were not Sikh, thereby demonstrating the connection between Guru Nanak and the general devotional movement.

In the religious tradition to which Nanak belonged God was referred to as *Adi Guru* (Primary Guru) or *Sat Guru* (True Guru) or just Guru. In the Indian religious traditions the term 'guru' can mean simply a religious teacher or mentor, or the founder of a religious cult or monastery, a person to be 'worshipped' as if an incarnation of the divine, or the Divinity itself. So when, in the Guru Granth Sahib, there is a reference to 'the Guru', it is not always clear to whom the term refers. Where the reference is to the Guru speaking then it should probably follow that the reference is to the Divinity. However, devout Sikhs more often than not take the reference to be to Guru Nanak, thereby raising the knotty question: 'Is Guru Nanak, therefore, an incarnation of the Divine?' The official answer is always 'No', but popular piety and official doctrine do not always coincide. Even the 'official' doctrine of the Guru is such that it scarcely avoids making Nanak into a divine/human figure.

Why did this particular cult develop into a separate religion when the cults that grew up around other devotional leaders remained within the Hindu domain? A number of answers are given but none can claim to be definitive. The devout Sikh will claim that the emergence of Sikhism as a separate religion happened as the result of a direct and unique revelation. One scholar has suggested that the separate development was due to the concise and systematic way in which Guru Nanak expressed his beliefs (McLeod, 1975, p.296). On the other hand, a historian of the Sikhs has linked the development to the political situation in Punjab during the formative years of the cult. 'The story of the Sikhs is the story of the rise, fulfilment, and collapse of Punjabi nationalism' (Khushwant Singh, 1991, vol. 1, p.vii). If one considers the evidence dispassionately there is much to suggest that the political answer is the most likely to be true.

The homeland of the Sikhs is the area known as Punjab, meaning the five rivers. The area was the focus of conflict from late antiquity, that is the last few centuries before the Common Era, at least. There were regular incursions from Greece, Persia and Afghanistan. A warrior-based culture developed but the people of the region were never able to defend themselves adequately. Certain sections of the population in the region obviously saw the cult that grew around the name of Nanak as a focal point for the successful organization of a hegemony and the successful defence of the region. A number of the Sikh Gurus were faced with persecution and conflict in defence of their faith, hence the rise of a military culture as part of the developing religion. The movement reached its political apogee with the accession to power of Maharajah Ranjit Singh in 1801 (Khushwant Singh, 1991, vol. 1, pp.200ff). The border between Pakistan and India now divides the ancient Punjab and thousands of Sikhs were forced to migrate at the time of the partition of imperial India in 1947.

Many western scholars have said and continue to say that Sikhism is a deliberate attempt at a synthesis of Hinduism and Islam. Guru Nanak was born and raised in an area of India which was roughly equally divided between Hindu and Muslim influence. Sikhs themselves, however, deny the charge of syncretism and with some justification. According to the traditional stories of the life of Guru Nanak, after his enlightenment he said: 'There is neither Hindu nor Mussulman [Muslim] so whose path shall I follow? I shall follow God's path. God is neither Hindu nor Mussulman and the path which I follow is God's' (Cole and Sambhi, 1978, p.9). He believed, according to this tradition, that his faith was not derived from Hinduism or Islam but directly from God. This was also the belief of the other devotional leaders of his time. Their message was an attempt to break away from the institutionalized religions. Of course, they had their antecedents and Guru Nanak was born a Hindu and derived much of his belief from Hinduism.

When all the evidence has been considered it is strongly argued that while there may be some Islamic influence at work on Guru Nanak, especially in the vocabulary he uses, 'in no case can we accord this influence a fundamental significance' (McLeod, 1968, p.160). McLeod goes on to say that

> a common interpretation of the religion of Guru Nanak must be rejected. It is not correct to interpret it as a conscious effort to reconcile Hindu belief and Islam by means of a synthesis of the two. The intention to reconcile was there, but not by the path of syncretism. Conventional Hindu belief and Islam were not regarded as fundamentally right but as fundamentally wrong. Neither the *Veda* nor the *Kateb* know the mystery.[4]
>
> The two are rejected, not harmonized in a synthesis of their finer elements.
>
> (McLeod, 1968, p.161)

The argument, therefore, is that the religion of Guru Nanak is distinct from both Hinduism and Islam and that fact has motivated Sikh behaviour from the earliest days of the sect. The distinction has been maintained ever since although there was a blurring of the distinction between Hinduism and Sikhism for a period in the nineteenth century which led to a reform movement and the legal restoration of *gurdwaras* (Sikh centres of worship)

---

[4] '*Veda*' refers to the most ancient Hindu texts. '*Kateb*' is another name for the Qur'an, the sacred text of Islam.

to Sikh control. Thus the Sikhs see themselves as a totally separate religion, with the destiny of the religion in their own hands.

While all this is true one can recognize, nevertheless, that in its development and established structure the Sikh religion bears marks of both its Hindu background and its contacts with Islam. Some of these marks are to be seen in the gurdwaras. The worship that takes place there bears the marks of the devotional worship going back to the middle ages in *bhakti*, or devotional Hinduism.[5] However, the particular Sikh development is that the worship is centred on the Guru Granth Sahib. Sikhs treat their scripture with the same intensity as that shown towards the Qur'an in Islam. The scripture is accorded the same mystical power as the Qur'an. In both religions the divine speaks directly through the printed word. However, the actual use of the Guru Granth Sahib in the gurdwara differs radically from the use of the Qur'an in the mosque. The Qur'an is not made the focal point of worship as the Guru Granth Sahib is in Sikhism. Indeed the actual reverence shown towards the Guru Granth Sahib is more reminiscent of the devotion shown towards a divine image in a Hindu temple. In addition to the prostration before the Guru Granth Sahib, it is removed from its place of honour at night, put to rest in a side room and then reinstalled at the start of a new day, just as is done symbolically with a Hindu deity. The consequence is that, whereas the gurdwara retains elements of the Hindu *dharmasala*,[6] it also manifests elements of the Hindu temple, a place for the installation of images of the divine. Thus, although Sikhism is not a syncretism of Hinduism and Islam in its outward symbolism, it borrows elements from both.

An important feature of Sikhism is the place of caste within it. The abjuring of caste was a feature common to the devotional leaders of the movement to which Guru Nanak belonged. Many Sikhs, commenting on Sikhism, will speak as if the Sikh community is free of caste. Some Sikhs will acknowledge the continued existence of caste as an example of social divisions but claim that caste as a social phenomenon based on notions of purity and pollution has been overcome among the followers of Guru Nanak. The *guru-ka-langar*, the common meal, it is often claimed, is not merely a symbol of the overcoming of discrimination on the ground of ritual purity but also a reality. It is certainly true that caste as a form of social division is perpetuated in Sikhism. In fact it is probably as strong as ever, even among Sikhs who are modern in their attitudes and among Sikhs who have had to make other kinds of social adjustment as a result of migration.

---

[5] See Essay 4, 'Hindu Dharma in dispersion', in this volume.

[6] Literally a room or hall of dharma, a space without an image such as one would find in a temple; a place where devotees can participate in devotional songs or listen to devotional homilies.

Marriages are almost invariably arranged between members of the prescribed kinship groups. Some Sikhs are quite open about the persistence of caste in marriage (Bhachu, 1985; Kalsi, 1992, pp.151–6). The persistence of caste is seen also in the organization of gurdwaras. This is the case both in Punjabi villages and in British cities. These divisions explain certain aspects of the development of Sikhism and of its transition to countries such as Britain. However, there is strong evidence that ideas of ritual purity and pollution also persist among Sikhs, in spite of the efforts of some to eliminate such tendencies and the efforts of others to deny that such tendencies exist (Kalsi, 1992, p.23; pp.129–30).

Finally attention must be paid to the important developments which took place over the period between the first and the tenth Guru, that is between 1539 and 1708. While Nanak was against the paraphernalia of religion, such as pilgrimages, ritual ablution and even scriptures, his successors gradually built up an institution which included most, if not all of the things that Nanak had objected to. The final stage of this process (though there were later developments) arrived with the last living Guru according to the major tradition, Gobind Singh (1666–1708). He decreed, towards the end of his life, that there should be no more living Gurus, that authority in future would lie with the community and the scripture. During his lifetime, in 1699, he founded a fellowship of committed believers called the *Khalsa*. After his death the scripture became increasingly the norm of authority and the authority of the congregation was eroded.

The Khalsa (the name means 'the Pure Ones') is the fellowship which demonstrates its commitment by adopting certain visible signs relating to the person. These signs are adopted by the initiate at the time of the initiation ceremony which involves the taking of vows and being sprinkled with *amrit* (nectar), a sweet mixture of water and sugar crystals stirred with a steel sword in a steel bowl (Cole and Sambhi, 1978, pp.122–9). Amritsar, the spiritual capital city of the Sikhs, which houses the Golden Temple built around a large tank of water, takes its name from this 'pool of nectar'. It is held that by leading the Sikhs to adopt the visible signs of their faith Guru Gobind Singh quite deliberately ensured that Sikhs would never shirk their responsibilities and be untrue to their beliefs. The most visible sign of the Sikh is the turban, in the case of the male. However, this is not one of the signs traditionally associated with the fellowship founded by Gobind Singh. The basic signs which relate to women as well as men are: uncut hair and (in the case of men) beard (*kes*), a comb to keep the hair clean (*kanga*), a steel wrist bracelet (*kara*), a short dagger (*kirpan*), and knee-length pants, usually worn under normal clothing (*kaccha*). The signs are popularly referred to as 'the five Ks'. Sikh piety interprets these signs in a doctrinal or ethical way: for instance, the circular bracelet is sometimes interpreted as a symbol of the completeness of the faith, the pants symbolize chastity. Viewed phenomenologically, it is fairly clear that apart from the uncut hair and beard, the signs reflect the military aspect of the Sikh faith, the bracelet being the remnant of the swordsman's wrist protector, the knee-length pants the dress of the infantryman. Vows associated with a person's hair are common in the history of religions. In some cases the vow is accompanied by shaving the head completely, in other cases by refraining from cutting the hair. The comb is used by the Khalsa member to clean but also to secure the hair so that it does not fall to the shoulders and thereby become a hindrance in battle. The turban has become a sacred symbol by protecting the purity of the uncut hair.

The Khalsa has been a strength of Sikhism but also a source of aggravation. Those who belong to the Khalsa regard the fellowship as being synonymous with Sikhism, thereby denying membership of the Sikh religion to those who have not taken the Khalsa vows. However, there are thousands of people, possibly millions, who believe themselves to be Sikh, but who have never taken Khalsa vows or adopted the symbols of the Khalsa. Some of them deliberately refuse the Khalsa symbols on the grounds that they were not sanctioned by Nanak. Such Sikhs are often referred to as *sahajdharis* (those who are connected) or *Nanakpanthis* (Nanak sectarians). There are also thousands who belong to certain sects such as the Nirankaris and Namdharis, who consider themselves Sikhs. The Khalsa regards members of these sects as heretics. There is no question that the Khalsa Sikhs have taken power in much of Sikhism and orthodoxy is defined by them in Khalsa terms. Their slogan is *'raj karega khalsa'*, 'the khalsa shall rule'. At certain points in Sikh worship someone will call out the words uttered in the Khalsa initiation ritual, *'Wahe guru ji ka khalsa'* ('The Khalsa is dedicated to God'), to which the rest of the congregation will reply, *'Wahe guru ji ki fateh'* ('Victory ever is of the Almighty God') (Cole, 1991, p.235). In Britain the impression is given, and many British accept, that Sikhism is synonymous with the Khalsa, so strong is Khalsa propaganda. In trying to answer the question: 'Who is a Sikh?', Hew McLeod says: 'It would be most convenient if there were to be an acknowledged authority, some individual or assembly to whom we might appeal for a clear and certain answer to our question ... Definitions are readily available and willingly dispensed, yet basic disagreements persist and the indisputable answer still seems to elude us' (McLeod, 1989, p.99).

2 The migration of Sikhs to Britain

Punjabis are one of three large groups which constitute the bulk of migration during the second half of the twentieth century from the Indian subcontinent. The other two groups are Gujaratis from western India and

Muslims from Pakistan and Bangladesh. The history of the migration of these groups goes back much further, however, and it is interesting to speculate why Sikhs, especially, have been so ready to migrate. There are the general factors of migration which apply to the Sikhs as to any other group of migrants, arising from economic necessity and consisting of pressure to move out of economically deprived areas into areas which are economically attractive, the so-called 'push-pull' factors. These are certainly evident in the history of Sikh migration but it still does not answer the question: 'Why did Sikhs in particular migrate?'

Although the migration of Sikhs to Britain in significant numbers is a fairly recent phenomenon, dating roughly from the 1950s, Sikh migration within India and within the former British Empire (and more recently the Commonwealth) has been considerable. The history of the Sikhs shows that while the strength of Sikhism lay in the Punjab there were other centres of importance for Sikhs in India. This meant that Sikhs moved between their homeland and such areas of India as Bihar and Maharashtra. The history of the Punjab, which was a key factor in the rise of Sikhism, also contributed to the movement of Sikhs, in that the passage of different peoples through their territory increased their awareness of the world beyond their boundaries. There were, however, two quite distinct historical reasons which were motivating factors for migration.

Following the defeat of the Sikh armies by the British in 1849, Britain annexed the Punjab and from being a valiant enemy the Sikhs became fiercely loyal to the British crown. The Sikhs remained loyal to the British crown at the time of the Indian Mutiny or First War of Indian Independence (1857). They became a significant part of the British Indian Army and fought in countries outside India, especially in World War I and World War II. Those who served abroad sometimes settled down in the countries in which they had served. Even those who returned home had an incentive to migrate when conditions forced them to.

British agricultural reforms within the Punjab led to a large migratory movement from east to west Punjab. Between 1860 and the first decade of the twentieth century, railway lines opened up western Punjab and irrigation canals that drew water from the five rivers recovered millions of acres of desert and transformed the region into the granary of India. To make the overall plan work, Punjabis, at least 50 per cent of them Sikhs, were offered land, some of it free, the rest of it for nominal payment. The Sikhs were apportioned a tract irrigated by the Chenab Canal in 1892. As a result, 'The Punjabis became the most prosperous peasantry of India; and of the Punjabis, the Sikhs became the most prosperous of all' (Khushwant Singh, 1991, vol. 2, pp.116–9).

This colonization is considered to have contributed also to the Sikhs' tendency to migrate. By this time, however, the 'push' factor was already operating in east Punjab. Even before the British created the colonies of small landowners, a culture of small landowner-cultivators was already established in the Punjab. The laws of inheritance meant that during the nineteenth century, land holdings were continually reduced in size. Since alternatives to agriculture were not yet available, as they would be increasingly during the twentieth century, there was pressure to migrate. Small landowners borrowed money to enable them to migrate. 'It is the marginal landholder, who in mortal fear of becoming a *kami* (menial servant) gambles his last to gain it another day' (Aurora, 1967, p.26). Although the pressures were eased slightly by migration to the canal colonies in the late nineteenth century there were still many who were unsuccessful in obtaining new lands and decided to migrate to more favourable locations, such as Australia, Fiji and east Africa. About 25,000 Punjabis, mostly Sikhs, went as indentured labourers to build the railways in east Africa. Many of the others chose Canada and by 1905 there were a few thousands settled there. Some of them gradually moved on to California (Aurora, 1967, pp.28–9).

A significant factor in the propensity of Sikhs to migrate is their general level of education and literacy in English. According to Aurora the Sikhs are reckoned to be the fourth most westernized group in India, ranking below only the Parsis and Jews who migrated to India, and Indians who were converted to Christianity, a westernized religion. Sikhs display an astonishingly high level of English literacy for a rural community. Some of the reasons for this high level of literacy are the influence of close contact with the British army in previous generations, the relative affluence of Punjabis and easy access to large urban centres such as Lahore (pre-1947), Amritsar and Jullundhar and a generally high regard for education (Aurora, 1967, pp.30–1).

In spite of this considerable level of migration of Sikhs from India, relatively few had migrated to Great Britain before the 1950s. An organization of Sikhs was formed in London in 1908, and by 1913 had acquired premises which they used as a gurdwara. But still Sikh migration cannot really be traced back to this period. Such migration began to take more shape in the 1920s when groups of male Sikhs came to Britain, settling particularly in east London and Glasgow, and pursued trade as door-to-door clothes vendors. A significant number of these vendors belonged to the Bhatra caste, and in pursuing this trade they were merely carrying on the trade that they had traditionally pursued in the Punjab along with the profession of astrology. When news of their success got back to the Punjab, other groups, including Muslims, followed them, and by the 1930 the Bhatras had become a minority immigrant group.

Researchers have identified this early migration as the first of four phases of Sikh settlement in Britain (Ballard and Ballard, 1977, pp.21–56). In the 1950s Britain was looking for workers to operate its expanding economy. Many industries in areas such as Southall, Middlesex and Gravesend, Kent (Helweg, 1979) turned to the Punjab for workers knowing of the qualities of hard work of the Sikhs from contacts made with them in World War II. This has been identified as the second phase.

Most of these Sikhs were Jats, members of the land-holding class who had been facing economic pressure for some decades by this time, and they migrated directly from India. They were not skilled workers but they were hard working. Other Jats were highly educated. If they were lucky they were able to continue in their professions but some Sikhs with degree level education from India ended up working in cloth mills in such cities as Leeds. Although this phase of migration involved mainly male members of families the small communities began to organize themselves and to create gurdwaras. Between 1955 and 1959 seven gurdwaras were opened. Of these, five were founded or controlled by Bhatras who, as a caste, pride themselves in their religious devotion and have tried to manifest it by such activities as founding gurdwaras. Between 1955 and 1975 more than fifty gurdwaras were opened by various groups of Sikhs in most major cities in England, Wales and Scotland (Janjua, 1976). By 1989 the number had reportedly grown to 149.

The third phase of settlement came in the 1960s, partly a natural development as wives and children joined the men who were already settled but also, and perhaps more decisively, because of the threat and actual implementation of immigration legislation in 1962 and 1968. There was a period of time before the 1962 legislation could be implemented and this pause saw an enormous influx of family members. It also saw a significant influx of totally new migrants, many of them from east Africa, the descendants of those who had gone there to help build the railways. Most of them had gone from the Punjab to east Africa as craftsmen of different kinds. Collectively they are known as Ramgarhia, and their background is mainly in the carpenter caste, but also the blacksmith, mason and barber castes. In east Africa they became skilled engineers with small firms or else they built up trading businesses. A number of gurdwaras in Britain which bear the name Ramgarhia date back to the late 1960s and early 1970s.

The fourth phase of Sikh settlement, according to Ballard and Ballard, began around 1970. It was identified as a period when many Sikh families moved out of the ghetto circumstances which had originally prevailed and moved into more pleasant suburban housing. It is also identified by the emergence of a younger generation of British-educated Sikhs. Into this situation came also another wave of migrant Sikhs following their expulsion from the Uganda of Idi Amin and other east African states. These new arrivals were, on the whole, better educated and enjoyed higher social status than the earlier settlers. Most of these new settlers were Ramgarhias.

By the 1990s the social picture was of two main groups, the Jats and Ramgarhias, and a sizeable third group, the Bhatras. There were a number of smaller caste groups. In addition to the three groups just named, Kalsi reports that there were in Leeds in the early 1980s Sikhs from the following castes: Jhir (water carriers), Julaha (weavers), Khatri (urban mercantile group), Chamar (leather workers), and Nai (barbers) (Kalsi, 1992, p.86). Although the names of the castes often represent a trade or profession, not all Sikhs carry on their traditional callings in Britain.

3   The Sikh social pattern

While caste identity is of paramount importance, even for Sikhs there are other forms of grouping which give an additional or parallel identity. Thus in looking further at the social pattern of Sikhs in Britain we have to pay attention to these other groupings as well. In addition to the caste divisions giving rise to separate gurdwaras in most large cities where Sikhs are to be found, there are also sectarian divisions, divisions which Khalsa Sikhs are often not prepared to acknowledge.

Britain in many ways presents a picture based on that found in Punjab. There, a village of, say, three thousand souls, may be completely Sikh in composition, but be clearly divided along caste lines. The village of Khodalisher, a few miles outside the city of Chandighar, has virtually a solid boundary drawn through the centre of the village. The village has two wells, one for the Jats and one for the Mazhabis, the Mazhabis being those Sikhs whose origins lie in the sweeper or latrine-cleaning caste, once known as outcasts or untouchables and, in Hindu society, the most pollution-bearing of the castes. The Mazhabis have largely given up latrine-cleaning with the advent of modern urban means of sewage disposal. They also hope that in discarding their old calling they can improve their caste status. It is hard not to conclude, however, that in Khodalisher, with separate sources of water, a commodity which, according to Hindu views of caste, can be easily ritually polluted, there is still some element of the 'purity-pollution factor' of caste division present. The same factor is probably present in the fact that there are also two gurdwaras, one for the Jats and one for the Mazhabis.

In Britain the divisions are not so clearly drawn but they are still there. Not only are they there in the separate gurdwaras, sometimes identifiable by the name of the gurdwara, but also in the social attitudes which appear often to be motivated by notions of purity and pollution. Ramgarhia Sikhs, in conversation, will speak pejoratively of Bhatras and Ravidasis whom they consider beneath them in social status. Ramgarhias often think of Jats, .

theoretically above them in caste ranking, as uncouth and uncultured. Jats adopt supercilious attitudes towards the other groups and those looked down upon work very hard to demonstrate their Sikh credentials, mainly through their organization of gurdwaras, thereby claiming equality and even superiority. There is no doubt that such sentiments do reflect every-day social attitudes such as exist between British classes. But often the tinge of caste discrimination is not far away.[7]

Bhatras

The Bhatras are an interesting group. No one seems to know quite where they belong in the caste hierarchy. The Bhatras themselves have a folk history which is traced back to Sri Lanka where, it is claimed, their forebears were converted by Nanak himself. As part of this folk history they claim that the Gurus entrusted the guardianship of gurdwaras to them. The Bhatras in Britain stem from those who had their homeland in what is now Pakistan. At partition in 1947 they had to migrate. There was already a tradition of Bhatras coming to Britain to follow their profession as itinerant vendors. In pre-partition India they had also been astrologers and undertook ear and nose-piercing. In the 1930s a few Bhatras were to be found in Cardiff and in Manchester (Nyrmla Singh, 1985–6, p.14). In 1976 there were sixty Bhatra households in Cardiff (Thomas and Ghuman, 1976, p.26). In 1985 Bhatras made up 47 per cent of the Sikhs in Manchester (Nyrmla Singh, 1985–6, p.16). Studies have shown the Bhatras to be very traditionalist although the community has changed in some ways, especially in the adoption of new trades and occupations. In 1976 in Cardiff the older generation of males still carried on their vending trade. The younger generation, however, worked in foundries, on the buses, a few had small shops and one or two young males had gone on to further education. Education is not valued for the social advance it might give young people and there is a tendency to mistrust institutions outside the immediate community (Thomas and Ghuman, 1976, pp.89, 92).

The Bhatras show their conservatism most in respect of the place of women in the community. While boys, generally, are not encouraged to succeed educationally, girls tended to disappear completely from school at or soon after puberty (Thomas and Ghuman, 1976, p.77). They believe that girls of fifteen should be at home with their mothers learning homecraft and how to be wives and mothers. At this age they are betrothed in gurdwara ceremonies and are married as soon as they reach the legal age of sexual consent. 'We like our girls to be married off when they are young.

[7] This was claimed, for example, by lower caste people in a BBC Open Space TV programme, *Untouchables in Britain*, broadcast on 4 November 1991.

Mostly they are withdrawn from school at the age of sixteen. They help running family shops or work at home' (Kalsi, 1992, p.94). The majority of Bhatra marriages, 86 per cent in one survey, are arranged and, according to Nyrmla Singh, single women on the whole prefer things to remain that way. Bhatras are also more conservative in respect of marrying within the kinship group (Nyrmla Singh, 1985–6, pp.20–1). While female emancipation is relatively high among Sikhs in Britain generally the same is not true of the Bhatras. Women are kept secluded from contact with males not of the community and in the streets of Cardiff they wear their head coverings in such a way that their faces are covered in a fashion that is reminiscent of *purdah* among Muslims (Thomas and Ghuman, 1976, p.65). 'Some *Bhatra* Sikh women observe *purdah* when they are in the company of male elders from their husband's family' (Kalsi, 1992, p.94).

Ramgarhias

The Ramgarhias take their name from one of the divisions of the Sikh military organization of the eighteenth century. Ramgarhias themselves have a folk history that takes them back to one of the Sikh heroes of the eighteenth century, Jassa Singh Ramgarhia (Khushwant Singh, 1991, vol. 2, pp.178–84). The group is made up mainly of *tarkhan* (carpenters), but also of blacksmith, mason and barber castes. Like most other caste groupings Ramgarhias do not now necessarily follow the occupations of their caste origins. Many of the Ramgarhias who have settled in Britain have come via east Africa where they were well established in skilled occupations or businesses. They have continued to be successful in this country.

As a group they are less conservative than the Bhatras although they do claim to uphold the Khalsa faith more rigorously than anyone. In the Manchester survey (Nyrmala Singh, 1985–6) they stand between the Bhatras and the Jats in terms of their adherence to traditional values. The survey showed that Ramgarhias still had a high percentage of marriages arranged in the traditional fashion (75 per cent), but among the single persons a much higher proportion of them would prefer their marriage to be 'semi-arranged', that is for the partners to be given an opportunity to approve of their parents' choice (Nyrmla Singh, 1985–6, pp.21, 23). This is the pattern which appears increasingly among urbanized, middle-class Indians, in Britain as well as in India.

It is claimed that the awareness of caste divisions among Sikhs in Britain became more prominent after the Ramgarhias migrated in large numbers from east Africa in the late 1960s. Up until the arrival of the Ramgarhias in this influx, Sikhs of different castes had very often collaborated happily in the foundation of gurdwaras which had been managed by inter-caste groups. The Ramgarhias carried over their caste associations and caste ambitions with them from east Africa. Bhachu claims that it was in Britain that Ramgarhias 'first came into contact with other Sikhs, predominantly Jats, who had migrated directly from India and Malaysia, and who formed the majority Sikh population'. Bhachu also claims that the Ramgarhias were in the forefront in restoring male Sikh marks of identity, the turban, mainly white in the case of east Africans, and the full beard (Bhachu, 1985, p.50–1).

Kalsi reports an example of the way in which Ramgarhias asserted themselves among the Sikhs of one of the Leeds gurdwaras during the 1960s. Although they collaborated with Sikhs of other caste groups in running the gurdwara during the 1950s gradually they took over the management and the style of the gurdwara, insisting, for instance, through the adoption of rules for the management of the gurdwara, that no shaven Sikhs should be allowed to conduct any public worship in the gurdwara. The Jats resented these moves as they seemed obviously discriminatory against their caste of largely clean-shaven men. The Jats were forced to organize themselves in order to regain control of the gurdwara management. Subsequently the Ramgarhias, who, as disciples of a Ramgarhia holy man who had migrated with them from east Africa, Sant Baba Puran Singh of Karichowale, had already formed themselves into a group within the gurdwara called the Nishkam Sevak Jatha, seceded from the gurdwara to form their own establishment (Kalsi, 1992, pp.88–9, 112, 120–2).

There is some debate about the ways in which Ramgarhias have built up their identity. As carpenters and practitioners of other crafts they would have experienced treatment as rather low caste people. There are those who would claim that they have used their religion over the centuries to raise their caste status and that being seen as pukka Sikhs is as much a social motivation as a religious one. Kalsi looks at the evidence for this view of Ramgarhia socialization and concludes that it is baseless. His argument is not convincing in that he does not direct it at the very earliest days of Ramgarhia identity, although it is true that those whose views he is criticizing are based on certain assumptions which are deduced rather than demonstrated by hard evidence (Kalsi, 1992, pp.103, 106, 109–12). It can be reasonably argued that low status groups do often employ religion as a strategic force to enhance their self-image and their image in the sight of others. The Ravidasis (see pp.226–7 below) are a case in point. The same has been true of various low castes who have been converted to Christianity in India. That this has happened among Ramgarhias is powerfully argued by a number of scholars (Ballard and Ballard, 1977, p.38; McLeod, 1976, p.102; quoted by Kalsi, 1992, p.103).

Namdharis

The tradition of piety among Ramgarhias is one of the reasons why a significant number of them belong to the Namdhari sect. Namdharis are those who are devoted to the *nam* (*Name*), that is, the Name of the Divine, the Name being a synonym for the Divine. They are commonly known as Kukas, from the cries of ecstasy which sometimes enter their worship. The sect arose in the Punjab as a reform movement within Sikhism during the time of the Sikh Maharaja Ranjit Singh (1780–1839). The founder of the sect, Balak Singh of Hazro, considered that the Sikh religion of his time had deteriorated and that only a return to the purity of Nanak's religion would save it. The sect remained within the main body of Sikhism but eventually it was condemned by Khalsa Sikhs as heretical. One of the reasons for this condemnation is the fact that Namdharis claim to have a living Guru, tracing his lineage from the ten acknowledged Gurus. The Namdharis' twelfth Guru, Ram Singh, the successor appointed by Balak Singh, was responsible for important reforms. 'He strongly rejected the custom of *purdah* (veil), female infanticide, child marriage and supported the right of widows to remarry. He encouraged the use of a white woollen *mala* (rosary) at the time of meditation' (Kalsi, 1992, p.66). The Namdharis became involved in the politics of the Punjab while it was under British rule. There is disagreement over whether this involvement was accidental or deliberate. Cole and Sambhi argue that the 'political characteristic' of the movement was acquired 'by accident rather than design' (Cole and Sambhi, 1978, p.157). Kalsi relies on other evidence and concludes that 'By making freedom from foreign rule an essential part of his *dharm* (true religion), Ram Singh was not only giving a new form to the message of Guru Gobind Singh, but he was also acting as a forerunner of other patriots of India who thought that patriotism was no less a religion (Ahluwalia, 1965, p.136; Kalsi, 1992, pp.66–7). Whatever the true story, the Namdharis ended up in clashes with the British authorities. 'In 1872, a batch of one hundred and twenty-five *Namdhari* Sikhs attacked a slaughter house at the town of Malerkotla in the Punjab. Most of them were arrested for taking part in the incident and sixty-five *Namdharis* were blown to pieces by being tied to the mouth of cannons ... Ram Singh was deported to Rangoon in 1872 where according to the records of the British government, he died in 1885. But *Namdhari* Sikhs believe that Ram Singh is alive and one day he will reappear' (Kalsi, 1992, p.67).

The Namdharis, like the Khalsa Ramgarhias, are now a materially successful group. Although 'officially' proscribed, they attend the gurdwaras of other Sikhs, and family ties and friendships across sect boundaries are maintained. Indeed the Namdharis are admired by other Sikhs for the quality of their religious life and their 'reforming heritage' (Cole and Sambhi, 1978, p.158). They do have their own organization in Britain, the

Namdhari Sangat U.K., and places of worship in Birmingham and London. Their Guru, Jagatjit Singh, visited Birmingham from India for a major festival in 1984 (Kalsi, 1992, p.69). They call their places of worship *dharamsalas*, rather than gurdwaras, in keeping with their intention to return to the purity of Nanak's religion and the period when Sikhism was still emerging from Hinduism (see footnote 6 on p.211 above).

Nirankaris

Like the Namdharis, the original Nirankaris arose out of a movement initiated by an individual who was concerned about the state of the Sikh religion in the early part of the nineteenth century. The originator was Baba Dayal Das, a shopkeeper of the same Khatri caste as the Gurus of Sikhism. His concern was with the growing ritualization of the religion and so he advocated a return to a devotion to the *nirankar* (formless) Divine. According to Baba Dayal, the use of external visible symbols was no help to liberation. The only way was a return to internal devotion along the lines advocated by Nanak. Like the Namdharis, the Nirankaris believe in the existence of a continuing line of living Gurus. It is claimed that the Anand Marriage Act passed in India in 1909, which now regulates all Sikh marriages, was enacted largely through Nirankari influence as the Nirankaris had been practising Anand marriage for many years previously. The Sikh form of wedding ceremony, *anand karaj*, replaced ceremonies which were still based on Hindu rituals. These rituals, including the circumambulation of the *havan* (sacred fire) were excluded, the fire was replaced with the Guru Granth Sahib and the singing of a chain of hymns, the *lavan*, composed by Guru Ram Das was added (Khushwant Singh, 1991, vol. 2, p.124n; Wylam, n.d., p.1). According to Cole and Sambhi the Nirankaris, having lost their headquarters near Peshawar, now in Pakistan, in 1947, 'have now almost disappeared, being reabsorbed into the Sikh [sic] fold' (Cole and Sambhi, 1978, p.156).

The story does not, however, end there. References to the Nirankaris are often confused by the presence of a group bearing the name Sant Niranakari Mandal, also known as Universal Brotherhood, who, far from being 'reabsorbed into the Sikh fold', have come into violent conflict with Khalsa Sikhs, and whose leader, Gurbachan Singh, was assassinated in Delhi in 1980; a demonstration, according to Nesbitt, of 'the explosive blend of politics and religious conviction'. This organization has been 'boycotted' by Sikhs since 1978, 'in accordance with a *hukamnama* [directive or order] issued from the Akal Takht [one of the main seats of Sikh authority located in Amritsar]' (Nesbitt, 1988, p.431–2).

The Sant Nirankari Mandal U.K. was established in 1969, two years after a visit from their Guru. In the 1970s he made two further visits to

Britain and worship services were held in different places including in Leeds Town Hall (Kalsi, 1992, p.83). The organization recognizes Baba Dayal (1783–1857) as the founder of their movement as do other remaining Nirankaris who are not of the Mandal. Members of the Mandal, however, look to a more recent Guru, Avtar Singh, as the inspiration for their faith. It was this Guru's son who was assassinated in 1980. Avtar Singh's hymns are sung in their public worship alongside those of the Guru Granth Sahib. The main cause of tension between the Mandal and Khalsa Sikhs, according to Kalsi, is that they do not regard the Guru Granth Sahib as their Guru (Kalsi, 1992, p.81). Kalsi records a Mandal member's interpretation of this key issue: 'We pay respect to the *Granth Sahib* and follow the teachings of the Sikh *Gurus*, but we do not regard *Granth Sahib* as our guru – it contains the *bani* (compositions) of our *Gurus*. We used to install the *Granth Sahib* in our *sangats* [congregations], but the *Akalis* [Khalsa Sikhs] objected to this practice. Our *satguru Baba* Avtar Singh stopped the practice of installing *Granth Sahib* in the *Nirankari sangats*, because we do not believe in hurting the feelings of other Sikhs' (Kalsi, 1992, p.81).

Nesbitt points to other, rather more moral reasons, for the tension. She relates that the Mandal does not enjoin the 'taboos', in particular the taboo relating to smoking, maintained by Khalsa Sikhs (Nesbitt, 1988, p.432). Kalsi also makes the point that Nirankaris are allowed to eat meat and drink alcohol and do not preach vegetarianism. Although there are Khalsa Sikhs, especially members of the Nishkam Sevak Jatha, who maintain strict vegetarianism, it is not a taboo which is traditional among Sikhs. Indeed Punjabi Hindus are often non-vegetarians. The *Rehat Maryada*, which encapsulates Sikh norms of conduct does forbid 'alcohol, tobacco, drugs or other intoxicants' (Kanwaljit Kaur and Indarjit Singh, 1971, p.9). However, from my own experience, Sikh social occasions, including weddings, would not be the same without large amounts of alcohol.

Nirankaris of the Mandal are strongly against practices which hint at idolatry or ritual. This would account for the fact that the Guru Granth Sahib is not installed in their gurdwaras. They are also very strongly opposed to caste divisions. While marriages are arranged by them along caste endogamous lines they have adopted a certain form of greeting that involves touching each other's feet as a symbol of 'equality within the group'. Touching someone's feet in this manner is a sign of respect by an inferior to a superior person within Hinduism. For instance, a disciple will always kneel and touch the feet of his guru when he approaches him. 'In our movement', a Nirankari claims, 'the touching of each other's feet helps break the hold of the caste system' (Kalsi, 1992, p.82). There is some evidence of the real effect of the Nirankari practice regarding caste in that many Ravidasis, members of the leather-working caste, have joined the Nirankari group in Bradford. A Ravidasi is reported to have led Nirankari worship in Bradford and 'all *Nirankaris* perform the *matha-takna* [kneeling] ceremony in front of this person who is regarded as the representative of the *Nirankari guru* at that time' (Kalsi, 1992, p.82).

Jats

By far the largest group of Sikh settlers in Britain are the Jats. They also constitute the largest group within the Sikh community worldwide. Although they were originally a peasant landowning group, over the past century and more they have diversified and now, apart from still being the largest landowning and farming group in Punjab, they are to be found in all the professions, in India's armed forces as well as occupying unskilled jobs in Punjab and in Britain. They were not among Nanak's earliest disciples. They became Sikhs in large numbers under Guru Arjan (1563–1606) and their entrance into Sikhism radically changed the character of the cult. There are Hindu and Muslim Jats as well as Sikh. Their strength of character and military might, especially during the Anglo-Sikh wars (1845–9) brought them to the attention of the British military authorities and they were recruited in large numbers into the British Indian army. They travelled abroad and it was this experience that led many to migrate and to settle down, first in south-east Asia and then further afield. Although they represent the largest group in Britain they do not show their presence in the names of gurdwaras in the way that the Ramgarhias and Bhatras sometimes do.

This does not mean that Jats are averse to taking control of gurdwaras when it suits them. Reference has already been made to the way in which Ramgarhias took control over the Leeds gurdwara and changed the nature of the gurdwara management. The running of the gurdwara revolved around the issue of the bearded versus the clean-shaven. Jats, who had been prominent in the establishment of the gurdwara although clean-shaven, were offended when they were effectively disenfranchised by a change in the constitution of the gurdwara through the exercise of power by the Ramgarhias. The Jat view of the situation was summed up thus: 'That amendment to the constitution of the *gurudwara* was a clever move to keep the *Jats* out of the management structure. *Tarkhans* (*Ramgarhia Sikhs*) know that our people are mostly *monein* (clean-shaven) who will not be eligible to become members of the management committee' (Kalsi, 1992, p.88). Although the Jats tried to resist these moves by the Ramgarhias they failed through lack of political power. In 1978 the decision was made to organize their *baraderi* (brotherhood or clan organization). Eventually the Indian Farmers Welfare Society, Leeds, was formed. The formation of the Society, according to Kalsi, 'was an important indicator of the polarisation of the Sikh community on caste lines. Caste divisions within the Sikh community now came into the open – *biradari izzat* (honour) became more important than the egalitarian concept of the brotherhood of the Khalsa' (Kalsi, 1992, p.90). Kalsi does not explain why an urbanized group of Sikhs far from their homeland as well as their farmlands should call themselves farmers, but one of the clauses in the constitution of the Society states that membership is restricted to those 'who have a farming background' (Kalsi, 1992, p.90). This is undoubtedly a way of defining membership according to caste group. But could there be a more subtle factor at work. The context of the establishment of the Society, of in effect a caste organization, was a confrontation with Ramgarhias who had gained control of the most precious asset locally, the gurdwara. Part of the history of Jat–Ramgarhia confrontation goes back to the Punjab of 1900. In that year the British regime tried to deal with agricultural problems by passing the Land Alienation Act (Khushwant Singh, 1963, vol.1, pp.154–6). It safeguarded farmers against the depredations of moneylenders. It also defined who would be a landowner and who not. The Jats were given landholding status; the Ramgarhias, among others, were denied landholding status. This meant not only disadvantaged status in a territory where agriculture was the most likely form of financial success but also that the Ramgarhias, and others, would be bound into a social system that bore many of the marks of European medieval feudalism. The system was known as *jajmani*, whereby the lesser served the greater in a system of dependency in terms of employment opportunities and financial reward, or more often reward in kind for services rendered. The Ramgarhias held their first conference as a group in 1901 to try to overturn the terms of the Act (Kalsi, 1992, p.109). They countered this political move by growing strong in vocations other than farming, including the trades, industry and the professions, over the next half century. By the 1970s in Leeds they were strong enough to exercise control thereby denying the Jats their traditional position. To reverse roles the Jats introduced a Society which traced its motivations back to the pre-eminence they were accorded by the British. Declaring themselves a Farmers Welfare Society was a signal to the Ramgarhias that they were intending to restore the correct hierarchy once again. And this they did in Leeds.

Jats did not merely organize themselves politically but they used their new cohesion to enforce standards of Sikhism on their baraderi. One Jat described the change as follows: 'The formation of the Indian Farmers Welfare society has put new *josh* (vigour) into our people. We feel organised and strong ... We began to take part in the affairs of the *gurudwara* as a solid force. Most *Jat* Sikhs were clean-shaven, so we gave them the call "*Sikh bano*" (Let us become *keshdharis*). The response was unbelievable – the political situation in the Punjab also helped our cause' (Kalsi, 1992, p.90). By 1982 there were six Jats on the gurdwara committee out of a total of 27. Still the Ramgarhias, according to the Jats, conducted the affairs of the gurdwara 'as if they owned the place'. By 1983 the Jats had gained complete control of the gurdwara management (Kalsi, 1992, p.90).

Reference above to the political situation in the Punjab points to a further aspect of Sikh Jat culture. Kalsi maintains that Jat dominance in the Leeds gurdwara is seen in the activities of an organization with a very low profile name, the International Sikh Youth Federation. This organization, in fact, has played, and continues to play an important, militant and possibly irregular military role in the independence movement in Indian Punjab. Kalsi reports that a 'large picture of their leader, *Sant* Jarnail Singh Bhinderanwale (the former leader of militant Sikhs who was killed in army action in the Golden Temple [in Amritsar] in 1984, is still hanging in the main entrance of the gurudwara' (Kalsi, 1992, p.91). Members of the Federation staff bookstalls at the gurdwara selling literature that promotes the Khalistan movement. 'They wear saffron turbans and keep their beards flowing' (Kalsi, 1992, p.91). The significance of the saffron-coloured turban is that the wearer is showing his readiness to be a martyr for the cause of Khalistan independence.

The Jats as a caste group in Punjab, taking all religions, are classed fairly low down the caste hierarchy. In the traditional fourfold Hindu classification they belong in the third class, the Vaisyas, below the ruling and military caste and above the menial, service class, although there is one writer who maintains that before they entered into Sikhism they belonged in the fourth, menial class (Marenco, 1976 p.296). However, so strong is the social and economic power of the Jats in Punjab that they sometimes claim for themselves membership of the second, Kshatriya, class, and certainly occupy the highest caste position in many Punjab villages, rating above the Brahmans, who traditionally belong to the highest, priestly, Hindu class.

Ravidasis

Including the Ravidasis in an essay on Sikhism is problematic. The problem is that many Sikhs, possibly most Sikhs, would exclude Ravidasis from the community of Sikhs. There are also Ravidasis who would exclude themselves from the Sikh community. But there are Ravidasis who would claim that they are Sikhs (Nesbitt, 1990). The problem centres on the persistent caste system and the desire of certain groups to enhance their own social standing by adopting the social, and in this case religious, behaviour of a superior exemplar group or groups. Kalsi certainly includes them within the Sikh domain and devotes a whole chapter to the Ravidasi caste group in Bradford (Kalsi, 1992, ch.6).

The Ravidasis originate in the Chamar outcast grouping in the Punjabi caste system. Chamars are a leather-working caste, untouchable because they traditionally handled the skins of dead animals. Over the past two centuries the caste has diversified into agriculture and in Britain into trading.

Ravidasis are to be distinguished from Ramdasias who also belonged to the Chamar caste in Punjab but who were converted to the Sikh community, according to tradition, during the guruship of Ram Das (1574–81). Ravidasis became a distinct group of Chamars outside Hinduism much later. The group did not really begin to develop until after 1947. Ravidasis claim that before they founded their own religious sect they were excluded from Hindu temples and Sikh gurdwaras in the Punjab, and that when they migrated to Britain the same discrimination was exercised against them. I have visited a village in the Punjab where there was a sizeable community of Ravidasis but without their own gurdwara. Members of the community told me that they would not normally attend worship in the Sikh gurdwara but that they usually went along at the time of major festivals and were admitted. Because of the general discrimination against them and in order to enhance their own status, they founded their own bhakti sect.[8] As Chamars they found their inspiration in Ravidas, himself a Chamar who was a devotional leader in fifteenth-century India. The Guru Granth Sahib of the Sikhs is the only repository of Ravidasi's *bani,* or collection of devotional hymns; thus the Guru Granth Sahib is the holy book of the Ravidasis also. Their form of worship is almost identical to the worship pattern of Khalsa Sikhs. Kalsi describes the worship he witnessed in Bradford as if it is identical with Khalsa worship, except for the addition of the name of Guru Ravidas in the main concluding prayer, the *ardas* (Kalsi, 1992, pp.134–5). In the Open University television programme *Caste and Sect: Ravidasis in Birmingham* (see footnote 8) the worship service recorded includes aspects that derive from Hinduism: the blowing of the conch shell and the offering of fire (*ardas*) before the Guru Granth Sahib.

As the Ravidasi community grows in economic strength so their presence in Britain and in Punjab grows. In the town of Phagwada which lies on the Grand Trunk Road from Delhi to Amritsar, a town which is an important centre for Ramgarhia educational institutions, the Ravidasis are gradually building a huge religious, medical and social centre which they hope will rival the Golden Temple of Amritsar in religious importance.

There is Ravidasi testimony that they are quite separate from Sikhs, and indeed they are in terms of organization. But it is not so clear that they lie outside the Sikh religious domain. Kalsi would definitely include them within, but another writer has summed up their status thus: 'not Sikh but ... within the Sikh Universe' (Leivesley, 1986, p.35)!

---

[8]   This information derives from *Caste and Sect: Ravidasis in Birmingham* (1976) Open University/BBC TV programme, AD208 (*Man's Religious Quest*).

4 Religion and settlement in Britain

One of the problems of discussing the religion of a group such as the Sikhs after their migration and settlement is that all too often religious, cultural and social aspects of the community merge and it is not always easy to distinguish what is specifically religious and what is specifically social. Nevertheless, it is possible to distinguish between some religious and social aspects of Sikh life and it is useful to do so in assessing the religious response that has taken place following settlement in Britain.

Sikh behaviour and practice is related to the need to be gainfully employed, whether as part of the ordinary British workforce or in the establishment of businesses. They needed places to pray in which leadership might develop, whether formal or charismatic. They also needed to find means of communicating between themselves and with the outside communities.

Religious and social response in an alien environment

If there is any one aspect of Sikh religion that has seen change, it is in respect of the visible Sikh Khalsa symbols: the beard, uncut hair and related turban. When the early male migrants arrived in the 1950s and even the 1960s, the majority of them discarded their turbans, cut their hair and shaved their beards because of discrimination in employment. 'More than one Sikh, when told a job was taken, has returned home, shaved, and successfully re-applied for the same job' (Brown, 1969, p.155). By these actions they discarded two symbols, one directly Khalsa, the uncut hair, the other Khalsa by association, the turban. They also discarded the *kirpan*, largely because they feared the British laws against the carrying of arms, and probably also discarded the knee breeches usually worn as an undergarment. They thus effectively broke their Khalsa vows. Of the five symbols, they usually kept the steel bracelet, unless they worked with machinery when it could be considered dangerous. The discarding of the Khalsa symbols, especially the turban and long hair and beards, was done in order to demonstrate a degree of desire to assimilate to British norms of dress and behaviour.

Many male Sikhs found it no problem to make such adjustments but for others such actions did not come easily. The first wave of migrants undertook these acts of assimilation fairly quickly and universally but there is evidence that those who followed were more reluctant to do so. A Sikh from Leeds who told how he was virtually forced by his brother to discard the symbols of his faith, on the grounds that he would not find employment, also testified to the pain the action caused him (*Sikhs in Britain*, 1976, Open University/BBC television programme, A228, *The*

Religious Quest). He was not merely reluctant to cut his hair; he found that he just could not do it to himself and only conceded to his brother on condition that his brother took the scissors and the razor to him. Some years later this person grew his hair again and kept a full beard. He looked like a Khalsa Sikh again, but he had not fully internalized the change back to the faith. He still regarded himself as *patit*, fallen or lapsed. That could not be put right until he had undergone the initiation ceremony, *amrit pahul*, taking his vows again, and being sprinkled with amrit, the nectar administered in a properly constituted ceremony. He thought himself still to be unfit to undergo that ceremony but hoped that at some future time he would feel pure enough to accept *amrit* again (see pp.212–3 above). Another Sikh spoke of his anguish when his uncle forced him to cut his hair after coming to Britain in 1961: 'Before I got it cut, I asked my uncle, "I must get my photograph taken" ... I saved my hair ... I'm still keeping it. I was crying all day on that day I got my hair cut' (Bowker, 1983, p.35). Such evidence points to the agonies that many Sikhs underwent in Britain and sometimes still do when their religious behaviour is questioned or ridiculed.

Despite denying this important part of their faith, discrimination against Sikhs continued on the grounds of colour: they found that discarding the turban and cutting their hair had, basically, no significant or enduring effect on the native population, and particularly not on prospective employers. Gradually, Sikhs began to revert to their religious traditions. Later Sikh migrants such as the east African Ramgarhias were horrified at the number of lapsed Sikhs in Britain and they exerted their influence in maintaining the traditions. Gradually, too, some employers began to realize the potential of these hard-working people and began to employ Sikhs despite earlier reactions. 'Recently I heard a story of a Sikh who some years back was deeply distressed when forced to shave in order to gain employment. His work qualities so impressed his employers that not only did they make no objection when he began to grow his hair again, but they took on ten or a dozen more "turban men". The story may be apocryphal' (Brown, 1969, p.155). For others, however, the right to practise their traditions was not won so easily.

In 1964 a London Transport guard decided to revert to being a Khalsa Sikh and was suspended for forty days by his employers. Prayers were said in the gurdwara and there were three days of celebration after his reinstatement (Rose, 1969, p.456). In the late 1960s a dispute arose between male Sikh bus employees and Wolverhampton Council over the right to wear turbans rather than the usual peaked caps. In April 1969, after a two-year dispute the Sikh busmen won the right to be allowed to wear their turbans on duty. In December of that year the Race Relations Board found Wolverhampton Council guilty of racial discrimination. But another dispute was in the offing.

In July 1971 the British Government announced that the wearing of crash helmets for motorcyclists was to become compulsory. Sikhs viewed such a law as an assault on their religious right to wear turbans and not to wear anything on their head that would defile their uncut hair. They organized themselves for protest and soon television news was showing Sikhs in cities such as Birmingham engaging in a well-tried form of Indian protest, the 'courting of arrest'. Sikhs publicized organized scooter and motorcycle protests in which Sikhs rode without crash helmets in open defiance of the law. Many were arrested and fined for contravention of the law. They employed a well-tried argument, namely, that if it was acceptable for Sikhs to fight in numerous wars for the British Empire, including two World Wars, without being required to wear steel helmets as a recognition of their religious observance, then why could they not be allowed not to wear crash helmets? Their protests met with results and in 1976 the law regarding the wearing of motorcycle crash helmets was relaxed for Sikhs. This victory encouraged an editorial in the *Sikh Messenger* (Winter 1986/Spring 1987) to call for the same opposition to the enforcement of hard hats for Sikhs on building sites.

There have been many incidents involving the Sikhs' right to wear turbans and not to be subject to rules and legislation that would involve the defiling of their turbans. One particularly important legal battle came in 1979 when the Commission for Racial Equality took out an injunction against a Birmingham night club for refusing admission to a Sikh wearing a turban. On 25 November 1979, the *Observer* newspaper reported that 'The company's managing director, Mr Weston Edwards, said it was a club rule that all hats must be left in the cloakroom and he was not prepared to make an exception in the case of turbans'.

In the same report a solicitor for the Commission for Racial Equality stated that the Commission had begun proceedings against the head-master of a private school which had turned away a Sikh boy because his turban 'did not comply with the rules of school uniform'. The school was a Christian private school in Birmingham. The grounds on which the turban was rejected was that it was an 'outward manifestation of a non-Christian faith and a challenge to the Christian faith' (*Sikh Messenger*, Spring 1984, p.24). The boy's father, Sewa Singh Mandla, backed by the CRE, sought the support of the courts to enforce his son's right to wear the turban. The high court upheld the boy's right, but the Court of Appeal overturned the judgement on the grounds that the headmaster's ruling did not constitute racial discrimination within the meaning of the Race Relations Act of 1976. The discrimination was, strictly speaking, on religious grounds, and the act did not cover such discrimination. In March 1983, the House of Lords reversed the judgement of the Court of Appeal and created legal history by, in effect, defining the Sikh *religion* as a separate *ethnic community*, a highly debatable judgement.

Although there were many Sikhs who reverted to the traditional Khalsa symbols after living for some time in Britain, reinforced by many of the later incomers, it would be wrong to deduce that the matter has been easily resolved. Many Sikhs in Britain, of all ages, have insisted on their right not to conform to the Khalsa norm while maintaining that they are truly Sikh. There are often tensions between the two sections of the community. On the one hand those who uphold the Khalsa tradition think of the others as having abandoned the Sikh faith altogether in the face of external pressures amounting to what many of them consider religious persecution. Conversely those who have not maintained the Khalsa traditions often think of their fellow Sikhs as importers of the cultural trappings of 'village India'. I have been present at a conference of the Sikh Student Federation when the students have argued vigorously over what can only be termed 'fundamentalist' or 'anti-modernist' and 'liberal' expressions of their religion. The 'fundamentalists' argue that everything must be done according to *gurbani*, the strict 'Word' of the scriptures, and the old established traditions. The 'liberals' argue that *gurbani* and the traditions must be interpreted in the light of modern social and intellectual developments. When Khalsa Sikhs gain domination of a gurdwara, as we saw in the Leeds case, they try to ensure that non-Khalsa Sikhs are not elected, or else pressurize them to conform to the Khalsa norm. Some of those who don't conform argue the liberal, progressive point of view; others argue the Nanak-panthi point of view, namely that Nanak eschewed such outward forms of religion.

The issues of turban-wearing and conformity to Khalsa norms show some of the debatable responses that have arisen in the course of Sikh settlement in Britain. Of a more positive nature, and less controversial, has been the establishment of gurdwaras in Britain.

Establishing gurdwaras

In the early days of settlement the local communities soon began to organize themselves for cultural and religious reasons. Often, a group would hire a space in which to hold a celebration, the birthday of a Guru, or the feast of *Baisakhi*, the spring festival that marks the birth of the Khalsa. Generally speaking these Sikhs had no problem in conducting these celebrations in spaces not otherwise considered holy or set apart. It was very unusual for the Guru Granth Sahib to be installed on such occasions. However, the installation of the Guru Granth Sahib soon became an urgent necessity and for that, space, purposely set aside, was needed.

A variety of buildings were at first acquired. Gurdwaras were set up in terraced houses, in redundant church buildings, in any building that would give enough space for a worship hall, a kitchen and dining room and, if possible, a committee room or classroom. The acquisition of former Free Church buildings was particularly desirable since the layout was suitable for the installation of the Guru Granth Sahib. Symbolically these buildings underwent a change of religion in which the Bible as centre-piece was replaced by the Guru Granth Sahib as centre-piece. Examples include the gurdwaras in Chapeltown, Leeds and Pearl Street, Cardiff. After the first wave of adapted gurdwaras some purpose-built gurdwaras began to appear. Among the earliest was a building of modern design in Prospect Street, Huddersfield (1973–4). A more recent one is the Bhatra gurdwara in Ninian Park Road, Cardiff (1988).

We have already seen something of the nature of the Guru Granth Sahib and the intense reverence that it attracts from devout Sikhs. So intense is the quality of sanctity that applies to it, however, that it is an unusual occurrence for it to be present in an ordinary home. Its presence in the home would demand an appropriate resting place and available time for the regular daily rituals associated with the scripture. Sikhs usually carry out their daily devotions using a book which contains selections of the scriptures and other devotional literature. In large centres of Sikh population in India, or at certain historical gurdwaras such as the Golden Temple in Amritsar or Guru ka Tal near Agra, devotions are carried on all day from the time the Guru Granth Sahib is installed at daybreak until nightfall when it is laid aside with considerable ritual. In most gurdwaras, however, there may be devotions in the morning and in the evening. The Sikh religion does not demand that a special weekly day be set apart for worship such as the Sabbath or Sunday. However, in India, and now in Britain, Sikhs tend to gather at the gurdwara for congregational worship on the weekly rest day which is Sunday in both cases.

Such congregational gathering is a mixture of social, cultural and religious event. Since the *diwan*, the name for the main service, derived from the name of a royal audience, is accompanied by certain ritual and communal acts the occasion lends itself very easily to social gathering. An important aspect of the activities which take place in the gurdwara is the *guru ka langar*, a meal symbolic of the rejection of caste divisions. The meal is very simple: a chapatti, some curried vegetables, lentils or *dahl*, and some fruit followed by a cup of tea. The ingredients are all donated by members of the gurdwara. Sometimes a single family will donate the whole meal to celebrate a family event. The preparation and serving is undertaken by volunteers without distinction of age or sex. In Britain, this is an occasion for Sikh families from a wide area to gather, for gurdwaras serve communities of various sizes depending on the local Sikh population. For instance one of the Cardiff gurdwaras serves as a centre for Sikhs from the whole of South Wales.

One of the distinctive features of the gurdwara culture in Britain is that Sikhs take out membership of their local gurdwara in a way that they would not in Punjab. In the homeland, the gurdwara would be that of the local community, and support for the gurdwara would be naturally forthcoming from that community. In Britain people 'join' the gurdwara of their choice, if possible a gurdwara of their own caste but if not, as is the case in one of the two Cardiff gurdwaras, a 'mixed' gurdwara. Gurdwaras in Britain have adopted a model which is similar to Christian religious establishments by having membership rolls. In one of the Cardiff gurdwaras membership is restricted to members of the Bhatra caste. Hence the support of the gurdwara, lacking the existence of a 'natural' community, or any endowment as it might have in India, is relatively assured by the collection of regular 'dues'.

Another important feature of gurdwara culture in Britain, very often, is the existence of a Punjabi language class. As with all migrant groups there is always a danger of the group losing something of its identity through losing its language, and very few state schools provide facilities for ethnic minorities to learn mother languages. In addition the scriptures are written in Punjabi, though in an archaic form of the language, and the language of worship is Punjabi and most Sikhs in Britain today cannot conceive of worship being conducted in anything but that language. Although there are translations of the Guru Granth Sahib, and in this respect Sikhs are less sensitive than Muslims about the translation of their scripture, nevertheless Sikhs are like Muslims and most Jews in that worship can take place only in the original language of the scriptures. In the modern version of *Rehat Maryada*, the Sikh code of discipline, it says: 'Every Sikh should learn *Gurmukhi* and read the Adi Granth' (*Rehat Maryada*, 1971, p.6). Gurmukhi is the name given to the form of Punjabi in which the Guru Granth Sahib, sometimes referred to as Adi Granth, is written. According to tradition the Gurmukhi script was devised by Guru Angad, Guru Nanak's immediate successor, although it is closely related to the common Devanagari script of other north Indian languages such as Hindi. Hence there are two main reasons for the teaching of Punjabi in the gurdwara: the maintenance of Sikh culture and identity and the provision of future leaders of Sikh worship.

Leadership in the Sikh community

The provision of leaders has given the Sikh community some problems since their settlement in Britain. Sikhism does not have a formal priesthood or ministry like some other religions such as Islam or Christianity. There are a number of different functionaries who maintain the worship of the community and the nurture of younger members of the community. As in many other religions, of course, the primary unit of nurture is the family and within the family the mother plays an important role. In Britain, however, others outside the immediate family also play an important part in nurture.

There is, for instance, the teacher of Punjabi, whether male or female. Within the gurdwara community these teachers play a vital though largely informal role. While many children and young people grow up speaking Punjabi, including second generation British Sikhs (that is, those born in Britain), their ability to read Punjabi is often poor. Thus the main aim of the Punjabi gurdwara school is to teach people to read Punjabi, specifically to read the Gurmukhi script. Implicit in the process of learning to read Gurmukhi is the process of learning to read the scripture. To read the scripture publicly in the act of worship, however, demands further training.

The person who can and does read the scripture publicly is known as a *granthi* (from the word *granth* meaning volume or text), and does not hold any formal office or formal qualification. Rather, men and women are often trained to read the Guru Granth Sahib by parents or someone already proficient in the art. During a period of worship a number of granthis may take part in succession. This is the case especially on the occasion of a reading of the whole Guru Granth Sahib, which lasts for about forty-eight hours, as, for instance, during the celebration of a Guru's birthday or other festival, or when organized privately, with public participation, by someone wishing to celebrate a special family event.

There is another functionary whose duties consist not only of reading the Guru Granth Sahib but also of interpreting the message of this text and other Sikh texts such as the *Dasam Granth*, the text of the tenth Guru, Gobind Singh, or the *janam sakhi*, the narratives of the life of Nanak, which contain cautionary and morality tales and speak of the wisdom of Nanak. The title given to the person who can read and interpret is *gyani*, a word which has its roots in the Sanskrit word for 'wisdom'. A gyani also sings *kirtan*, devotional songs which again impart religious and moral teaching. A gyani is not a priest but a teacher; will usually be married, and may earn a livelihood solely by carrying on the office of a gyani. There are not many gyanis among those who have settled in Britain, therefore individual gurdwaras have had to hire gyanis from India and getting permission from the immigration authorities for gyanis to come to Britain to serve a gurdwara is not always easy. Occasionally one hears of settled Sikhs studying to be gyanis and going to India to Sikh institutions to gain qualifications. Building up the life of the community in Britain will require gyanis from among British Sikhs able to interpret the culture to outsiders. Most of the gyanis who have come to serve in Britain from India have little or no English. Although in theory women may conduct worship as gyanis, in practice few if any are ever appointed to the office.

As one might expect, a religion such as Sikhism does from time to time throw up its holy men and women. Although the religion is formally organized on a very non-sacerdotal and democratic basis, and in its dominant form does not recognize the existence of living Gurus, there have been individuals, who by their charisma or mystical qualities have drawn to themselves disciples. Such a one was Sant Baba Puran Singh (referred to on p.220 above). He was featured in the Open University TV programme *Sikhs in Britain* when he visited some of his followers in Leeds in the summer of 1976. He was greeted with great pomp by the gurdwara committee with the president of the gurdwara garlanding him and bowing low to kiss his feet. When the final draft of the film was shown to the gurdwara committee they insisted on the feet-kissing action being cut out as it was contrary to Sikh custom and doctrine, such actions being reserved in Hinduism for gurus. I relate the incident here to show the reverence for such persons, reverence of a kind which is deep seated in the Indian character, but also to show how Sikh orthodoxy in the British context is determined to maintain a regime which it would be hard put to maintain in India.

It is said that Sant Puran Singh had mystical gifts of an extraordinary kind. He emphasized the importance of initiation into the Khalsa. In 1977 over two hundred of his disciples received amrit in the Leeds gurdwara. His followers undertake not to eat meat nor to drink alcohol, and generally to follow a puritanical way of life. The story is told of a night-long meditation in a Birmingham gurdwara led by Puran Singh. The congregation gathered with him experienced intense spiritual devotion and it was reported afterwards that just before dawn they witnessed the Sant elevating in the meditative posture at least six inches off the floor. When he died in 1983, well over ten thousand followers attended his funeral in Birmingham. His followers who form the Nishkam Sevak Jatha, have gurdwaras in Birmingham, Hounslow and Coventry as well as the one in Leeds already referred to.

Kalsi lists six groups of Sikhs in Leeds who are followers of holy men or sants, apart from the Namdhari, Nirankari, Ravidasi and the Nishkam Seva Jatha. These holy men, including among them a retired bank manager, visit their followers in Britain regularly and are financially supported and revered for the depth of their spiritual teaching or for gifts of divining (Kalsi, 1992, ch.8). Some of them take on an ascetic life and dress in traditional clothes. The retired bank manager, Baba Ajit Singh, a Ramgarhia, dresses in western clothes and tells the fortune of his followers on Saturdays only, since that is the day that he is visited by the spirit of his ancestors who are the source of his power (Kalsi, 1992, p.181). Kalsi's overall study which is largely about the persistence of caste among Sikhs claims that caste plays an important role in the cults of these holy men also.

> It is also evident that the caste identity of holy men is one of the determining factors for attracting *shardhalus* within the Sikh community. A *Ramgarhia* Sikh holy man is usually more popular

among the *Ramgarhias*. The overwhelming majority of the followers of *Baba* Puran Singh Karichowale are members of the *Ramgarhia biraderi* while *Baba* Sarwan Das, who was a *Chamar*, is revered by the *Chamars* only. A few holy men attract followers from all caste groups, such as the *Radhasoami guru* and the *Nirankari guru*, but both these holy men belong to high caste groups and their higher status enables them to transcend traditional caste barriers more easily than holy men from low caste groups would be able to do.

(Kalsi, 1992, pp.183–4)

The presidents and committee members of gurdwaras and other organizations can wield considerable power locally and sometimes in the community nationally. Throughout the '60s and '70s a number of leaders emerged who took responsibility for interpreting the Sikh community to the wider community. Many of these were self-styled 'leaders', often enjoying such status only because of their command of the English language rather than any natural or given claim to leadership (Ballard and Ballard, 1977, p.40). Other forms of leadership have emerged through personal initiative and the publishing of works dealing with Sikhism which have been accepted by the community at large. Piara Singh Sambhi of Leeds, joint author with W. Owen Cole of a standard work on Sikhism, was such a person. In addition, organizations have been formed which are designed to maintain Sikh culture in Britain or to promote Sikh culture in the wider community. In one or two instances an organization has served both purposes. Examples are the Sikh Missionary Society, formed in 1970 and based in Gravesend, and the Sikh Cultural Society of Great Britain, formed in 1960 and based in Edgware, Middlesex. Out of the latter organization emerged Indarjit Singh who, for a time, edited the Cultural Society's journal the *Sikh Courier*. Later he became editor of the *Sikh Messenger* and, at the time of writing, regularly occupies a spot in the Radio 4 programme *Today* as a contributor to the daily 'Thought for the Day', giving a Sikh perspective on current affairs. Also active in the Cultural Society's publishing work has been Manjeet Kaur McCormack, the former Pamela Wylam, a British convert to the Sikh faith, who was Editor of the *Sikh Courier* for a period.

The propagation of Sikhism

The output of the two organizations just mentioned has been prolific, consisting mainly of dozens of pamphlet-size publications. The topics covered have included the stories of the lives of the most significant Gurus, homily-type material on Sikh doctrine and ethics, and translations of documents such as the *Rehat Maryada*, the *Ardas* (the short congregational liturgy with which the main act of weekly worship ends), and the Sikh marriage ceremony. All this material has enabled the Sikh community to adapt somewhat to their English language environment, especially for the sake of young people, and has served as a doorway into the Sikh religion for interested persons in the wider British community.

In addition, the two main English language journals, the *Sikh Courier* and more recently the *Sikh Messenger*, have put before an English readership matters relating to Sikh teaching for personal and communal living and have been a platform for the expression of Sikh comments on contemporary issues in Britain. The *Sikh Messenger*, in particular, has also addressed events which have taken place in India since 1984. In that year events flared up in Punjab, with the incursion of the Indian Army into the Golden Temple and the death of Sant Jarnail Singh Bhinderanwale. He had occupied one of the most important buildings in the Temple complex, the *Akal Takht*, and made it his personal residence, at the same time placing a small army on the battlements of the Golden Temple and turning it into an armed camp. In recovering the Temple from the armed militants, many of Bhinderanwale's armed supporters were also killed, as were Indian Army personnel and many innocent Sikhs and others. Later that year Indira Gandhi, India's Prime Minister, was assassinated by her Sikh bodyguards and many hundreds of Sikhs were killed in the capital, New Delhi, as Hindus took their revenge for the assassination. Terrorist and reprisal killings still go on in the Punjab and in other parts of India organized by Sikh militants who want an exclusively Sikh homeland in the Punjab, and the creation of Khalistan, the Pure Land.

Most Sikh comment in the *Sikh Messenger* concentrated on the alleged atrocities of the Indian army and other security forces, the vindictiveness of the Nehru/Gandhi dynasty and the general alleged persecution of the Sikhs in India. In its Autumn/Winter 1991 edition, the journal reported on a debate in the House of Commons which took place on 29 November 1991 in which the actions of the Indian government were criticized by a Labour MP. In his reply a Government minister pointed out the difficulties of interfering in the affairs of a sovereign state, but said that H.M. Government had, in their regular contacts with the Indian Government, 'encouraged them to exercise the greatest restraint in dealing with the problems facing them, and have emphasized the need to respect human rights'. He went on to list certain actions taken by the Indian Government to deal with abuses of human rights. A section of the minister's speech was also taken up with listing the number of people, civilians and members of the security forces, who had been killed 'in terrorist incidents'. The journal article was entitled 'Persecution of Sikhs in India'. The editorial highlighted certain parts of the debate including the Government minister's references to the problems of relationships with other states within the context of the maintenance of human rights, including the statement:

'If we had dealings only with countries with impeccable human rights records, our influence in the world would be significantly reduced and there would almost certainly be a consequent loss of jobs in this country'. The editorial described this statement as honest but amoral and claimed that it weighed 'human rights in terms of jobs and dubious friendships' (*Sikh Messenger*, Autumn/Winter 1991, pp.5, 21–34). The editorial made no reference to the Minister's remarks about Sikh atrocities and there was no attempt made to suggest means of reconciling the communities in India. The *Sikh Messenger* does not openly preach Sikh or Khalistan nationalism but the editorial policy of the journal seemed here to present an apology for Sikh attitudes towards political independence and to blame the Indian Union Government for all the ills that had befallen Sikhs in India.

5 Attitudes towards Sikhs in Britain

It is not easy to assess the general attitudes towards Sikhs in Britain. Sikhs suffer from the general racial discrimination which is part of British life. On the other hand many Sikhs are well accepted in different sectors of British life, in the professions and in business. However, the scenes of jubilation on the streets of Southall at the news of the assassination of Indira Gandhi filmed by British TV news cameras did cause a sense of revulsion in many British minds. Many Sikhs themselves were offended, too, by the behaviour of their co-religionists. These same Sikhs find themselves neutral or in opposition to Sikh independence action in India or in Britain, but few of them will dare speak out for fear of violent reprisal from Sikh militants. At least one Sikh has been murdered in Britain for expressing opposition to Sikh militancy. In 1991 three Sikhs were found guilty of conspiracy to commit the murder of Sikh moderates in Britain and sentenced to prison terms of between ten and fifteen years. There are Sikhs in Britain who are active in wanting to set up Khalistan. In June 1984 it was reported that the republic of Khalistan was 'officially proclaimed' in a house in West London by Dr Jagjit Singh. Dr Jagjit Singh was reported as saying that 'Some young man will come forward and take off the head of Indian Prime Minister Mrs Gandhi and all those responsible for the desecration of the Holy Temple' (*Western Mail*, 14 June, 1984). Three and a half months later his prediction was more or less fulfilled.

Again it is difficult to assess what the British response to such situations really is. One senses that there is a feeling that involvement by minorities living in Britain in the affairs of their homelands should not be allowed to disrupt the life of Britain. This feeling is heightened when individuals among these minorities threaten violence of any kind, whether against their own community members in this country or against legitimate government in their own homeland. At that point much depends on whether legitimate governments are seen as democratic and non-repressive or otherwise. Among those in Britain who pay any regard to the actions of Indian governments of different political persuasion since Indira Gandhi's assassination, it would appear that the jury is still out.

6 Conclusion

The Sikh community exists as a significant part of the British community. In an interview given in 1981, Khushwant Singh, the Sikh author and journalist said, 'I look forward to the day when a Sikh can say with great pride, "I'm a Sikh. I'm an Englishman"' (*Punjab to Britain*, 1981, Open University/BBC television programme, E354, *Ethnic Minorities and Community Relations*). The English, and the British people generally, have not given too much encouragement for such an expression to be heard very often. There are those, including important British politicians, who would judge members of ethnic minority communities, including the Sikhs, to be disloyal to the land of their adoption merely for expressing support for the Indian cricket team. However, even if Khushwant Singh has not yet heard a Sikh utter such an expression, it is clear that the commitment of most Sikhs living in Britain to participation in the life of Britain is equal to that of any other community. Their contribution to the plural cultures of Britain is not only valuable but an essential contribution to the creation of a state within which diversity is something to be cherished, and not regretted as a loss of some supposed previous uniformity – a uniformity which never existed anyway, especially if viewed from the Celtic periphery of Great Britain.

The Sikh religion is looked upon by its adherents as a progressive, reformed religion, and they have good grounds for maintaining such a view. Unlike some other religions, or divisions of some religions, in which ancient traditions must be maintained, Sikhism, because of its reformed characteristics, has not experienced any great difficulties in being transplanted into alien soil. It will never be a world religion numerically, although it is beginning to be classed among the world religions in academic studies. Its origins in the Punjab and its adherence to the Punjabi language in worship will ensure for the foreseeable future that it remains the religion of a particular linguistic and cultural grouping. There are also many external pressures which give rise to a determination that the religion will remain that way.

In so far as religions have a contribution to make to contemporary life in predominantly secular states, Sikhism can make a contribution equal to that of any other religion. Events in the Indian Punjab cast their shadow over the community in Britain and do cause stresses within the British Sikh community. At the time of writing there is no clear resolution of the conflict in Punjab, and while it lasts British Sikhs will be concerned for the fate of their co-religionists there. However, it is apparent that alongside that concern, the community in Britain is pursuing a vigorous life of its own. It works very hard at making itself accessible to the wider British community, making valuable contributions to civic life and community relations. The history of Britain and of British India has determined much of the course of the religion for the past century and more but within that historical process the religion itself has shown an inner strength and persistence and has to a large extent contributed to its own destiny and it looks like continuing to do so in its new domicile.

Bibliography

AHLUWALIA, M.M. (1965) *Kukas: the freedom fighters of Punjab*, Allied Publishers, New Delhi.

AURORA, G.S. (1967) *The New Frontiersmen: a sociological study of Indian immigrants in the United Kingdom*, Popular Prakashan, Bombay.

BALLARD, R. AND BALLARD, C. (1977) 'The Sikhs: the development of South Asian settlements in Britain' in Watson, J.L. (ed.) *Between Two Cultures: migrants and minorities in Britain*, Basil Blackwell, Oxford.

BHACHU, P. (1985) *Twice Migrants: East African Sikh settlers in Britain*, Tavistock Publications, London.

BOWKER, J. (1983) *Worlds of Faith*, BBC Ariel Books, London.

BROWN, J. (1969) *The Unmelting Pot*, Macmillan, London.

COLE, W. OWEN (ed.) (1991) *Five World Religions*, Cassell, London.

COLE, W. OWEN and SAMBHI, P.S. (1978) *The Sikhs: their religious beliefs and practices*, Routledge and Kegan Paul, London.

HELWEG, A.W. (1979) *Sikhs in England: the development of a migrant community*, Oxford University Press, Delhi.

JANJUA, H.S. (1976) *Sikh Temples in the UK*, Jan Publications, London.

KALSI, S.S. (1992) *The Evolution of a Sikh Community in Britain*, Monograph Series, Community Religions Project Collection, Department of Theology and Religious Studies, University of Leeds.

KANWALJIT KAUR and INDARJIT SINGH (1971) *Rehat Maryada*, Sikh Cultural Society, Edgware.

KHUSHWANT SINGH (1963) *A History of the Sikhs*, 2 vols, Princeton University Press, Princeton.

LEIVESLEY, A.D.W. (1986) 'Ravidasis of the West Midlands', *Sikh Bulletin*, III, pp.35–8.

MCLEOD, W.H. (1968) *Nanak and the Sikh Religion*, Oxford University Press, Oxford.

(1975) 'Sikhism' in Basham, A.L. (ed.) *A Cultural History of India*, Oxford University Press, Oxford. Reprinted in Foy, W. (ed.) (1978) *Man's Religious Quest*, Croom Helm, London.

(1989) *Who is a Sikh?*, Oxford University Press, Oxford.

MARENCO, E. (1976) *Transformations of Sikh Society*, Heritage Publishing, New Delhi.

NESBITT, E.M. (1988) 'Sikhism', in Zaehner, R.C. (ed.) *The Hutchinson Encyclopedia of Living Faiths*, Hutchinson, London.

(1990) 'Pitfalls in Religious Taxonomy: Hindus and Sikhs, Valmikis and Ravidasis', *Religion Today*, vol. 6, no 1, pp.9–12. Reprinted in Wolffe, J. (1993) *Survival, Renewal and Adaptation: a reader on religion in Britain 1945–92*, Hodder and Stoughton, Sevenoaks.

NYRMLA SINGH (1985/86) 'The Sikh Community in Manchester', *Sikh Bulletin*, III, pp.13–26.

ROSE, E.J.B. (1969) *Colour and Citizenship: a report on British race relations*, Oxford University Press, London.

THOMAS, D.A.T. and GHUMAN, P.S. (1976) *A Survey of Social and Religious Attitudes among Sikhs in Cardiff*, Open University, Cardiff.

WYLAM, P.M. (n.d.) *The Sikh Marriage Ceremony* (no publisher; presumably Sikh Cultural Society of Great Britain).

6

FILLING A VOID?
AFRO-CARIBBEAN IDENTITY
AND RELIGION

by Gerald Parsons

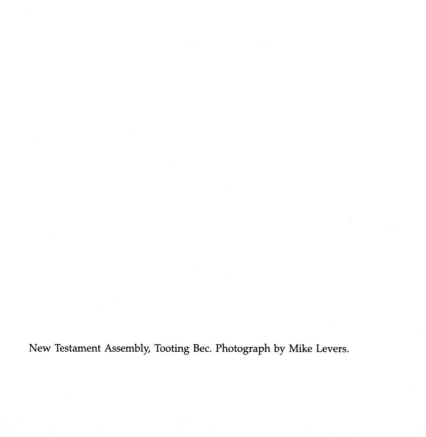

New Testament Assembly, Tooting Bec. Photograph by Mike Levers.

During the Second World War, confronted by the need for more personnel to sustain the war effort, the British War Office and service chiefs found themselves obliged, reluctantly, to accept volunteers from the Caribbean. Their reluctance stemmed from what the service chiefs perceived to be the troublesome and difficult nature of the Caribbean troops who had served Britain in the previous world war. (There had been a mutiny among Caribbean troops who were left neglected in southern Italy at the end of the 1914–18 war. Something of the broader context of this mutiny may be gleaned from the fact that, of twelve battalions of the British West Indies Regiment who served in the First World War, only two saw substantial active service. This was in Palestine, where they were deployed against the Turks, the authorities having explained that it was 'against British tradition to deploy aboriginal [sic] troops against a European enemy'.)

Faced with the need to overcome their prejudices, Second World War service chiefs proposed a propaganda campaign to precede the recruitment of Caribbean military personnel. The Ministry of Information was duly briefed on the 'characteristics of the West Indian'. The characterization included a notable, if also predictable, number of stereotypes. West Indians, it asserted, were temperamentally easily stirred, liked music, display and bright colours, and were congenitally lazy. It also included the observation that: 'Having lost his indigenous African culture, he has not found anything substantial to put in its place (though Christianity has to some extent filled the void). The result is an absence of ethical standards, of any sense of community and of social responsibility' (quoted in West, 1990, p.7).

Even when allowance is made for the still imperial and colonial context of the quotation, both the presumed superiority and the sweeping dismissal of the Afro-Caribbean character retain the power to shock. However, the quotation also provides an excellent and ironic starting point for an examination of the relationship between religion, community and identity within the Afro-Caribbean community in Britain since the end of the Second World War.

We will address this theme in five stages. In the first and second sections, we will examine the emergence and development of Black-led churches and denominations in Britain since 1945. In the third, we will examine briefly the development of black initiatives and presence within the traditional Christian churches and denominations of Britain. Fourthly, we will consider the development and significance of Rastafarianism in the British context. Finally, we will return to the quotation with which we began and re-consider its significance in the light of the intervening material.

1 The emergence of the Black-led churches

One of the most striking developments in the religious life of Britain from the early 1950s to the early 1990s is the foundation, development and remarkable growth of a whole community of flourishing Black-led Christian churches.[1] From modest beginnings in the early 1950s, by 1962 it was estimated that there were at least 77 separate congregations representing at least 13 different groups of West Indian Pentecostal or Holiness churches (Calley, 1965, p.38). By 1966, the number of congregations had risen to at least 390 (Hill, 1971d, p.4), and by the mid 1980s, the estimate stood at over 2,500 congregations, representing over 160 black denominational groups and involving some 100,000 members. This membership, in turn, was estimated to constitute approximately 13 per cent of the total Afro-Caribbean population of Britain, and some 66 per cent of the actively churchgoing part of that community, thus making such churches a significant expression of black communal organization within late twentieth-century British life (Howard, 1987, pp.10 and 13).[2]

The final third of the churchgoing portion of the Afro-Caribbean community in Britain were members of the 'traditional' or 'historic' churches – principally the Anglican, Roman Catholic, Methodist and

---

[1] 'Black-led' rather than simply 'Black' because, although the churches in question had a predominantly black membership, they also included a small minority of white members. There is also a certain ambiguity because several of the denominations which in Britain are 'Black-led' churches are also part of larger international denominations in which the overall leadership is white, including, for example, the New Testament Church of God, the largest of the Black-led churches in Britain. In a British context, however, the designation 'Black-led' remains accurate, although the case of the Seventh Day Adventist Church provides a partial exception even to this general rule. In the early 1950s the Seventh Day Adventist Church in Britain was small, white and mainly middle class. As a result of the emigration of Adventists from the Caribbean to Britain and of the welcome initially extended to black worshippers in British Adventist churches, the denomination had, by the 1980s, become a mainly black and working-class church, although the leadership of the church remained, in this case, disproportionately white. For the Adventist experience see, Howard, 1987, pp.37-8 and Theobald, 1981. It should also be noted that, although the term 'Black-led churches' is widely accepted and commonly intended to carry positive implications, there are also those who object to the term as unsatisfactory or even degrading and lacking in respect. The use of the term in the present context reflects its widely accepted positive implications and implies no disrespect; indeed quite the opposite.

[2] It is difficult to obtain reliable figures in these matters. Those quoted here probably represent a conservative estimate of the numerical strength of the Black-led churches, other commentators suggesting, for example, that membership of the Black-led churches alone may represent as much as 20 per cent of the Afro-Caribbean population in Britain (Gerloff, 1982, p.6; Hollenweger, 1987, p.343). If the higher figure is correct, it renders the argument of the present essay even more pertinent.

Baptist denominations. This balance of membership between Black-led and 'historic' churches was in striking contrast to that which prevailed in the Caribbean. In the Caribbean – where it was estimated in the 1950s that as many as 80 to 90 per cent of the population were members of either the 'historic' churches or one of the Pentecostalist or Holiness churches – the balance between the two denominational groupings was reversed: approximately two-thirds of churchgoers attended one or other of the 'historic' churches, and a third were members of the Pentecostalist, Holiness or Adventist traditions.

These figures clearly represent a major shift in the religious allegiances of many Afro-Caribbean migrants to Britain. Clearly there was a major overall decline in the religious practice of such emigrants. From an estimated 80 to 90 per cent membership of one or other of the churches in the Caribbean, church membership in Britain dropped to only approximately 20 per cent of the Afro-Caribbean population. Such an overall decline in religious allegiance and participation may easily be accounted for. For some, perhaps many, the process of migration itself may well have resulted in a dislocation of religious practice formerly associated with a society more tightly integrated than that to which they had come – a transition made the more striking by the markedly more secular ethos of Britain and, in particular, of the British cities to which the majority of Afro-Caribbean immigrants came. Moreover, even if the secularity of recent and contemporary Britain is sometimes exaggerated or too easily taken for granted, it remains the case that since the 1950s there has been a further increase in the secularization of British life and a further decline in the level and intensity of churchgoing in general. And to all this may be added the frequently cold or even overtly hostile reaction of many of the historic churches to their Afro-Caribbean co-religionists when the latter first contacted them upon arrival in Britain – an issue to which we shall return in more detail later.

To focus principally upon the marked drop in church membership and religious practice following migration, however, would be to miss several much more significant aspects of the changes that have occurred in Afro-Caribbean religious life in Britain since the 1950s. At least three broad trends should be noted. First, there is the sheer fact of the shift, already noted, away from the historic churches and towards the Black-led churches and denominations. The implications of this shift – both in terms of its significance for understanding the relationship between religion and identity within the Afro-Caribbean community in Britain, and in terms of its impact upon and significance for the changing 'shape' of Christianity in modern Britain – will be important themes in this essay. Secondly, however, it should be noted that, although there has been an overall drop in religious practice among the Afro-Caribbean community in Britain compared with that before migration, when located within the British context, the religious practice and active church membership of the Afro-Caribbean community in Britain is notable for its intensity rather than its decline. Thus, the figure of 20 per cent active church membership for the community as a whole compares favourably with the level of active church membership in Britain in general, and is significantly ahead of the figures for England in particular.[3] Even more pointedly, the Black-led churches were significant throughout the period from the 1950s precisely because of their sustained growth. Whilst all of the historic churches experienced more or less serious decline in their numbers, the Black-led churches grew steadily at a rate estimated by some observers in the late 1970s and mid 1980s to be as high as 5 or 6 per cent a year (Charman, 1979, p.44; Jackson, 1985, pp.xv). Membership of the Black-led churches was, moreover, characteristically intense and highly committed, in marked contrast to the often much 'cooler' and more nominal style of membership and participation characteristic of many congregations within the historic churches.

Thirdly, it is significant that the most common locations for such steadily growing Black-led churches were precisely the urban and inner-city areas in which the historic churches faced steadily increasing difficulties, particularly acute decline and a gathering sense of crisis in their own ministries and organizations. Indeed, by the late 1980s and early 1990s, the Black-led churches had often begun to rival and frequently had actually replaced the historic churches as the most thriving, or even as the predominant Christian presence in many of Britain's urban and inner-city areas (Hastings, 1991, pp.559–60). How, then, were such thriving Black-led churches grouped together and organized? What were their principal characteristics? And what might explain their steady growth against some of the otherwise most stubbornly prevailing trends in the life of British Christianity in the four decades from the 1950s to the 1990s?

The community of Black-led churches that had developed in Britain by the 1980s was both large and complex, including over 160 different denominations. Some of these, such as the New Testament Church of God, the Calvary Church of God in Christ, the Church of God of Prophecy, the Apostolic Church of Jesus Christ, the Wesleyan Holiness Church, the African Methodist Episcopal Church and the the African Methodist Episcopal Zion Church, were British branches of larger international denominations. These denominations varied considerably in size but included the largest of the denominational groupings among the Black-led churches of Britain. Smaller denominations, indigenous to the Afro-Caribbean community in Britain, had been founded by particular individuals or groups and had subsequently established additional congregations. Others were

---

[3] For a brief discussion of the relevant figures for Britain in general and England in particular, see essay 1 in this volume, pp.xx-xx.

limited to a single independent church, more or less closely associated with other Black-led churches but not formally linked into a denominational structure.

In matters of theology and worship, it has been observed, it is all too possible to fall into the trap either of failing to distinguish sufficiently between the various Black-led churches – a tendency that at its worst leads to them simply being lumped together indiscriminately as 'holy-rollers' or 'Pentecostalists' – or of making so much of the often intricate differences between them that the substantial common ground is obscured (Howard, 1987, p.13). Most of the Black-led churches are Pentecostal – thus emphasizing the role and significance of the Holy Spirit in Christian life and faith, according a prominent place to speaking in tongues and other 'gifts of the spirit' such as healing and prophecy, and regarding the manifestation of such 'gifts' as evidence that the believer has been 'baptized in the spirit', an experience that is understood to be additional to conversion and water baptism. Estimates of the extent to which Pentecostalism predominates within the overall community of Black-led churches vary, but it is clear that they constitute the majority tradition among the Black-led churches and at least one informed observer has suggested that they may account for over 80 per cent of the membership and attendance at Black-led churches in Britain (MacRobert, 1989, p.120).

The Pentecostalism of the Black-led churches is itself divided into two main strands, however, known respectively as 'Trinitarian' Pentecostalism and 'Oneness' or 'Jesus-Name' Pentecostalism. The Trinitarian strand holds a traditional Christian understanding of the doctrine of the Trinity and uses the traditional Trinitarian formula ('in the Name of the Father, the Son and the Holy Spirit') in the act of baptism. Churches in this tradition commonly use the formula 'Church of God' in their title, as for example in the case of the New Testament Church of God or the Church of God of Prophecy. The Oneness or Jesus-Name Pentecostalists, by contrast, claim to follow the earliest recorded practice of the Apostles in the New Testament and baptize simply 'in the Name of Jesus'. This in turn reflects a different interpretation of the doctrine of the Trinity. Thus, Oneness Pentecostalists teach that the doctrine of the Trinity does not imply that God is to be understood as three persons (as in more 'orthodox' Christian doctrine) but rather that God has been revealed in three forms at different times, that his name is Jesus and that his present form is the Holy Spirit. Most churches in this tradition include the word 'Apostolic' in their title.

The differences between these groups are important. And it should not be overlooked that there has been a tendency among the Black-led churches in Britain for disputes over detailed points of doctrine and practice to lead to divisions and schisms between and within congregations – although, viewed positively, this process has often led to the founding of further new and subsequently thriving congregations and has thus contributed to the spectacular growth in the Black-led churches as a whole (Worrall, 1987, p.6). The common ground and shared characteristics of the various Black Pentecostal churches are, however, in the end more striking and significant than their differences and divisions.

All of the Black-led Pentecostal churches share a conservative evangelical – even 'fundamentalist' – understanding of the Bible. The biblical text is regarded as inerrent and is applied directly to the present circumstances of the congregation and the believer, biblical stories and teaching being woven into a powerful pattern of exhortation and example. The Authorized Version is the most commonly used translation of the Bible, the congregation following the text of the readings and references used in services. The language and ethos of the Authorized Version strongly influence and colour the style of both prayers and preaching. The principal themes of preaching are apt to be the wickedness of the world and the sufferings of God's people, but also the greatness and power of God in delivering his people, the imminence of the Second Coming of Christ, and the certainty of their final vindication as well as the judgement and punishment of evildoers. The power of God to deliver his people in the present will also be emphasized in terms of thanksgiving for salvation itself, for divine assistance in overcoming some specific failing or difficulty, or for spiritual or physical healing – all of which are in turn understood as manifestations of the work and gifts of the Holy Spirit.

Worship, although not conducted according to a set liturgy or order of service, follows a regular but informal pattern of hymn and chorus singing, prayers, readings from the Bible, testimony, preaching and healing. Congregational participation is high with frequent responses, opportunities for personal testimony, and scope for individual contributions in prayer, reading, prophecy, singing and dancing. Music is central to the worship, with choirs and a variety of instruments assisting the congregation in singing an equally varied range of traditional hymns, spirituals, choruses and modern worship songs. The service may well include an 'altar-call', when those who wish to may come forward for the laying on of hands – usually with a request for healing or for the gift of the Holy Spirit. The resulting worship is at once spontaneous and participatory, varying in detail from week to week and calling positively for individual involvement and contribution. Yet it is also ordered and ritualized, the expressions used characteristically conforming to standard biblical formulae and phrases, and the overall pattern of the service reflecting a regular combination of elements. More specifically ritual elements of worship include baptism (by total immersion), communion which is open to all believers and understood as a memorial of the Last Supper, and the washing of the feet of the saints – the latter being a distinctive feature of Black-led Pentecostal worship, men and women performing the rite in separate groups in accordance with the text of chapter 13 of John's Gospel.

The Black-led Pentecostal churches also strongly emphasize the appropriateness of a sharp separation between the Christian 'saint' and the sinful 'world' and hence expect adherence to a strict moral code governing personal morality and lifestyle. Alcohol, tobacco, strong drugs, swearing and extra-marital sexual relationships are all strictly rejected; dress and hairstyles are expected to be plain; cosmetics and jewellery are required to be used minimally; and a variety of 'worldly' entertainments are deemed inappropriate, including cinemas, nightclubs, public houses, dances and exuberant parties. The rejection of 'worldly' values and the insistence upon a distinctive Christian lifestyle is part of a self-conscious sense within Black Pentecostalism that to be a Christian is to be on one side of a clearly marked boundary between belief and unbelief, Christian and non-Christian. Conversion marks the crossing from one state to the other, and maintenance of a distinctive Christian lifestyle is an essential part of the actual content of being a Christian. For the individual that distinctive lifestyle is sustained and nourished by a whole network of religious and church-related activities, such as services, prayer meetings and choir practices, which take up the majority of leisure-time available.

Leadership in the Black-led Pentecostal Churches is at once dispersed and wide ranging, yet also hierarchical and potentially authoritarian. There is a variety of offices and roles which members may fulfil. Different denominations have different structures and specific categories of office, but the general plethora of roles such as deacon, elder, exhorter, Sunday school teacher or choir leader allows for a relatively large number of people to exercise a measure of leadership. But the ordained ministry, although also likely to be exercised by a definitely local leader, is apt to be accorded considerable hierarchical status and authority. And although women constitute a majority of the membership of the Black-led churches, perform crucial roles in maintaining and sustaining their day-to-day life, and are prominent in the organization and leadership of particular aspects of church life (such as Sunday schools, youth work, choirs and fund-raising), the overall leadership of the churches and their hierarchies remains firmly in the hands of men. Thus, whilst women fulfil a wide, demanding and influential range of roles within their churches, the over-arching structures and assumptions concerning questions of gender remain firmly patriarchal – a state of affairs commonly justified by appeal to the Bible and its perceived emphases upon the appropriateness and correctness of male leadership, the susceptibility of women to sexual sin, and the priority given to their role as mothers and hence protectors and sustainers of the family.

Dissent within the congregation – either in matters of theology and belief or in questions of morality and behaviour – is generally unacceptable and has been the cause of a significant number of schisms and divisions within Black-led churches. Ministers, however, have been very much 'of the people', sharing the social, educational and economic backgrounds of their congregations, frequently working full-time in a secular job and exercising their ministry outside working hours. In general they have not received formal training, but exercise a ministry based upon a perceived call and vocation, and characterized by a detailed knowledge of their local community and congregation. Moreover, in emphasizing such local knowledge and perceived 'call' rather than formal training, the ministry of the Black Pentecostal churches reflects a more pervasive characteristic of these churches as a whole. The essential ethos, character and theology of Britain's Black Pentecostal churches, it has been argued, is to be found not in formal statements of belief, written texts and official statements, but in what is said, sung and done in their continuing worship and congregational life.[4]

A third major strand among the Black-led churches of modern Britain derives from the 'Holiness' tradition within West Indian Christianity. The main Holiness churches in Britain are the Wesleyan Holiness Church and the African Methodist Episcopal Church. Much that has been said of the ethos of the Black Pentecostal churches is true of the Holiness churches too, including the intensity of commitment expected of members, the vitality of their worship and the centrality of the Bible and of biblical themes in preaching. Baptism in the Holy Spirit and the practice of 'spiritual gifts' are also part of the Holiness tradition, but tend to be exercised more privately than in the Pentecostal churches. Generally the public worship of Holiness churches will be more like that of the older Nonconformist churches, following a pattern of hymns, choruses, prayers, Bible readings and sermon.

Finally, to the Pentecostal and Holiness strands within the overall community of Black-led churches in Britain must also be added a fourth group of churches, namely those, such as the Church of the Cherubim and Seraphim, of specifically African origin. Mainly comprised of West Africans – and especially Ghanaians and Nigerians – these churches often include a large proportion of students among their members and tend to be predominantly middle class. Their membership is inclined to fluctuate more than that of other Afro-Caribbean churches because many of their members return home on completion of their studies. Their worship is

[4] This summary of the principal characteristics of Black Pentecostal beliefs, worship, ethics and organization is derived mainly from the much fuller summaries provided in Foster, 1990 and 1992; Hill, 1971d; Howard, 1987; MacRobert, 1989; Root, 1979; Worrall, 1987. These collectively provide a compelling sense of the ethos of Black-led Pentecostalism in recent and contemporary Britain.

more formally ceremonial than that of the other Black-led churches, including the wearing of robes, use of incense, and drumming which accompanies congregational dancing and singing of hymns and choruses. Whilst the Bible is of central importance and is interpreted in a very literal manner, in at least three respects these churches differ significantly from the Black-led Pentecostal and Holiness churches. Firstly, there is the prominence, even centrality, given to dreams, visions and prophecies. A vital element in their worship, such phenomena are interpreted for the congregation, the Bible being used extensively in such interpretation. Secondly, prayer and testimony will characteristically be more concerned with the achievement of wordly success than is usual in the Pentecostal and Holiness churches. And thirdly, there is less emphasis upon sin, salvation and the need for a distinctively strict and ascetic lifestyle (Gerloff, 1983, pp.9–10; Hill, 1971d, pp.10–12; Root, 1979, pp.7–8).

2   Developments in the Black-led churches

How, then, may the sheer scale of the growth of these various Black-led churches in Britain between the early 1950s and the early 1990s best be accounted for? And in particular, how may one account for the striking predominance of such Black-led churches within the church-going part of the Afro-Caribbean community in Britain when, as noted earlier, the traditional denominational balance in the Caribbean itself favoured the historic churches?

One interpretation of the remarkable growth of Black-led churches in Britain appeals directly and straightforwardly to the experience of rejection and racism which initially confronted many – probably most – Afro-Caribbean immigrants to Britain during the 1950s and 60s, and which then continued during the 1970s and 80s to confront both them and their children. This view explains the rapid initial growth of the Black-led churches principally as a reaction to the coldness and frequent hostility within the historic churches towards their Black co-religionists when Afro-Caribbean Anglicans, Methodists, Catholics, Baptists and so forth presented themselves at British churches in the 1950s and 60s. Similarly it explains their continued expansion as a response to the general hardening of racial attitudes in Britain from the early 1960s.

The coldness, insensitivity and sometimes overt rejection suffered by Afro-Caribbean Anglicans, Methodists, Catholics and others when they first attended British churches is increasingly well documented. Recognized by some commentators even in the early 1960s (Calley, 1965; Hill, 1963), and subsequently steadily acknowledged during the 1970s and 80s both by ecumenical groups such as the British Council of Churches and by individual denominations[5], the predominant patterns in encounters between black and white members of the historic churches were painful. Often arriving with letters of introduction or evidence of membership and active participation in their churches in the Caribbean, Afro-Caribbean Christians frequently found themselves ignored, patronized or, at worst, asked not to return (Hill, 1971b, p.117; Howard, 1987, p.9; Jackson, 1985, pp. xii–xiii, 7–8 and 36; Smith, 1989, pp.40–2; J. Wilkinson, 1985, pp.13 and 15). Even where rejection was not overt, it was frequently difficult to feel genuinely and fully accepted by the predominantly white congregations – and when in some local churches ministers and lay-members set out to welcome black co-denominationalists, it was by no means unknown for others among the white congregation and membership to leave (Hill, 1971d, p.15). Not all Afro-Caribbean members of the historic churches confronted by such attitudes left: some were determined to stay within 'their' denominations. But it is clear that a significant number of Afro-Caribbean Christians from the historic churches chose to leave their previous denominations – the shock at their hostile reception in what they had long been taught to regard as 'the mother country' painfully increased by the particular coldness and rejection at the hands of their churches.[6] In some cases they moved directly to a Black-led church. In other – and perhaps rather more – cases they may well have lapsed from previously active Christian participation. Significantly, it has been noted that in the 1970s and 80s the Black-led churches appeared to have made major gains in membership among such 'lapsed' former members of the historic churches (Howard, 1987, p.22; Root, 1979, p.7).

In addition to such negative experiences in specifically religious contexts, however, it has been argued that the growth of the Black-led churches in Britain can be related directly to the hardening of racial attitudes and the worsening of race relations in Britain from the early 1960s – and especially from 1964 – onwards (Hill, 1971a; 1971b, pp.117 and 121–3; 1971c; and 1971d, pp.16–19). In this view, the Black-led churches provided a focus for black identity, a sense of community and an affirmation of personal and communal worth within a white-dominated society which in general undervalued or refused to value its black citizens, and which frequently exhibited an active and potent prejudice against black people. In

[5] A number of the key texts in this process are discussed in the next section of this essay.

[6] For specific and compelling personal accounts of various types of prejudice experienced by Afro-Caribbean Christians in British churches see, for example, Jackson, 1985, chs 1–3 and Phoenix, 1991. Surveys of the situation in Methodism (Walton, Ward and Johnson, 1985) and in the Church of England (Moore, 1984) suggest that such experiences were fairly typical and provide further personal examples.

such a context, it is argued, Black-led churches offered a sub-culture in which black communities and individual black people might freely express and assert their communal worth, assume personal leadership and responsibility, and mutually affirm and support each other. Thus Black-led churches provided a striking example of a 'religion of the dispossessed', and their growth could substantially be accounted for by the fact that they provided a sense of worth and stature to people otherwise deprived of significant status by the society in which they lived.

That the growth of the Black-led churches in Britain owes something – and probably a good deal – to both the initial coldness of the historic churches and to the hardening of race relations in Britain from the mid 1960s is clear: hence, for example, the characteristic prominence in their preaching and prayer of themes such as the endurance of present suffering and the certainty of God's eventual deliverance of his people. As more recent studies have suggested, however, there is a risk of attributing too much significance to such essentially 'negative' factors in the growth of the Black-led churches, thus under-estimating and neglecting more positive aspects in their appeal. In addition to the provision of a sub-culture offering the opportunity for personal and communal affirmation in conscious opposition and contrast to the predominantly negative black experience in Britain, it has been argued that the Black-led churches also presented a version of the Christian faith itself deeply and positively rooted in Afro-Caribbean history, consciousness and experience.

It was not only the personal coldness and overt hostility of the historic churches in Britain which alienated many Afro-Caribbean Christians. It was also surprise at the overall ethos and 'tone' of Christianity in Britain. Coming from churches and communities in the Caribbean in which Christian worship and belief (in the historic churches as well as the Pentecostal and Holiness churches) were characteristically extremely lively and spontaneous, the Christianity of the historic churches in Britain seemed to many Afro-Caribbean Christians to be curiously low-key, 'cool' and undemanding, or even, indeed, apparently lax and 'nominal'. The intensity of both worship and commitment and the clear distinction between Christian and non-Christian appeared oddly lacking (Root, 1979, pp.14 and 20; Worrall, 1987, p.13). This however – as we have seen – is precisely what characterized the worship, belief and life of the Black-led churches in Britain.

The Black-led churches not only offered a positive welcome but also provided a lively, inclusive and committed style of worship. Such worship possessed what one commentator has called 'a sense of "weight" – crowded services, hearty singing, conviction' (Root, 1979, p.20). The sheer exuberance and enthusiasm of such worship offered a sense and experience of spiritual 'warmth', 'fullness' and spontaneity in marked contrast to the perceived 'coldness', 'emptiness' and stiff formality of the historic churches. For many Afro-Caribbean Christians who had been members of the historic churches in the Caribbean, therefore, it was the Black-led churches in Britain that offered the most familiar ethos and 'feel' in their worship, even if the form of service and theology was different – and it is likely that it was often this as much as overt hostility within the historic churches that lay behind the spectacular reversal in Britain of the traditional Caribbean balance between membership of, respectively, the Pentecostal and historic churches.[7]

Once viewed as the expression in a British context of a style of Christian spirituality common in the Caribbean churches, the appeal of the Black-led churches as a focus of identity and community may also be seen in much more positive terms. It was not merely that these churches provided a context in which Afro-Caribbean people might celebrate their worth, mutually affirm each other and exercise responsibility and leadership. This they undoubtedly did; but they did so, additionally, precisely in terms of a spirituality which was itself characteristically Afro-Caribbean, which encompassed a specifically religious response to vital elements of the historical experience of Afro-Caribbean people – most notably the experiences of slavery, colonization and white domination – and in which Afro-Caribbean Christians felt instinctively 'at home' (Foster, 1990, p.65 and 1992, p.52; Moore, 1990, pp.18–19).

If such considerations contribute to a more positive and rounded explanation of the rise and growth of the Black-led churches, what may most appropriately be said of their more recent development? It is, arguably, possible to identify three particularly significant trends in the development of the Black-led churches during the 1970s and 80s.

First, there is the steady development of social and political engagement within and among the Black-led churches. The Black-led churches

---

[7] It is important here to maintain the distinction between specifically racial insensitivity or hostility – whether based on overt racism or the persistence of 'colonial' attitudes and assumptions – and the separate fact that much of the 'spirituality' characteristic of the 'historic' churches in Britain was different from that characteristic of Afro-Caribbean Christianity. What to many Afro-Caribbean Christians appeared 'cold', 'empty' or merely 'nominal' Christianity in the 'historic' churches was in fact a different but no less deeply held variety of faith and spirituality. Thus it is also possible to mount an apology for a 'cool', quiet and reflective style of Christian faith and worship no less deeply valued and sincerely lived by those who hold it than is the exuberant, and self-evidently vital enthusiasm of the Pentecostalist. In the present context, the point is to recognize the implications and consequences, historically, of the contrast between the two styles of faith, not to judge between them. It should also be noted, however, that not *all* Afro-Caribbean Christians shared a preference for an overtly evangelical or Pentecostal style of faith. Some Afro-Caribbean Christians themselves preferred a 'cooler' style of Christianity, for an example of which see the remarks of the Antiguan born Anglo-Catholic Ron Farley, in Jackson, 1985, ch.3.

had always, from their very foundation in Britain, displayed a striking concern for the mutual support and well-being – physical as well as spiritual – of their own members. They did not, however, generally display much sign of developing a distinctive style of political involvement. In the later 1970s and 80s this began to change markedly. Many of the leaders of the Black-led churches increasingly came to see their ministry as including a role in leadership within the black community as a whole in a given area. Pastors, ministers and lay leaders from the Black-led churches participated more frequently in local pressure groups and organizations such as parent–teacher associations and police committees. They also took a more prominent role in liaison between local black communities and the police during times of social and racial tension, especially after the inner-city riots of 1981.

Similarly, Black-led churches increasingly organized and ran local community projects, such as workshops for the disabled, nurseries, advice centres, and skill centres for the unemployed, provided educational facilities to supplement state provision, and helped to set-up credit unions and building societies. Such initiatives frequently made a significant contribution to schemes of urban and inner-city renewal and often involved working with government organizations such as the Manpower Services Commission (Arnold, 1992; Foster, 1990, p.68; Howard, 1987, p.22–3; Jackson, 1985, pp.xiv–xx, 16, 25–6, 49 and 55–7; Johnson, 1988b, p.98; Smith, 1989, ch.16; Worrall, 1987, p.12). In so doing, the Black-led churches indicated clearly that their insistence upon a sharp distinction between the 'Christian' and the 'worldly', and their emphasis upon the sufferings of this world and the certainty of future deliverance, did *not* mean that they were simply apolitical or uninterested in issues of social justice. Indeed, the practical and communal engagement of the Black-led churches of Britain in the 1980s points to the emergence of a social theology and a 'social gospel' alongside and within their traditional evangelical and Pentecostal theology.[8]

The second important development during the 1970s and 80s was the emergence of increasing co-operation between different Black-led

---

[8] The development of social and political concern and engagement within the Black-led churches has been particularly well documented in the case of the New Testament Church of God, both at the overall institutional level (Arnold, 1992) and within the work of individual ministers (Jackson, 1985, ch.1; Smith, 1989, ch.16). It should also be noted, however, that some of the social initiatives in which Black-led churches have co-operated with government schemes and agencies have caused other black Christians to voice the concern that such schemes have been used by government to provide short-term palliatives whilst avoiding underlying and long-term needs in the inner cities (Grant, 1990, pp.51–3; Nelson, 1990, p.9). For the wider context of this particular debate, see Volume II, Essay 4.

churches. The first such initiative began in 1968 when a number of the smaller Black-led churches formed the International Ministerial Council of Great Britain. An even more decisive step occurred in 1976 with the foundation of the Afro-Westindian United Council of Churches (AWUCOC). The organization publishes its own handbook and church directory, the 1984 edition of which defined the Council as 'a federation of Black-led churches established to promote a sense of unity without conformity among various church groups', and noted that members 'work together on tackling social and educational issues; doctrine remains a matter for the individual member churches' (AWUCOC *Handbook*, 1984, p.9). Other subsequent organizations for co-operation among Black-led churches include the Council of African and Afro-Caribbean Churches and the West Indian Evangelical Alliance.

Thirdly and finally, it is striking that in the 1970s and 80s the Black-led churches began to assume a place significantly closer to the 'mainstream' of the overall Christian community in Britain. One notable manifestation of this trend was the increasing recognition that they received in areas such as religious broadcasting. An edition of *Songs of Praise* from Southwark Cathedral in 1987, for example, was contributed entirely by black congregations and gospel choirs. In 1990 Channel 4 presented a series of three hour-long documentaries on the Black-led churches in Britain.[9] And in 1991, at the special *Songs of Praise* service from Westminster Abbey at the beginning of the Gulf War, the participants from the various religious traditions included a representative of the Black-led churches – a moment of considerable symbolic significance in terms of the general recognition of their collective stature and role within contemporary British religious life.

Similarly, the Black-led churches also moved towards the ecumenical 'mainstream' of British Christianity. Before the 1970s the Black-led churches had tended to remain somewhat detached from the emerging 'ecumenical establishment' of late twentieth-century Britain – not least because invitations to participate in local councils of churches and similar initiatives were frequently perceived either to be afterthoughts on the part of the historic churches already participating, or to assume that involvement by the Black-led churches would simply mean *their* participation in existing projects rather than the addition of new perspectives contributed by the Black-led churches themselves (Howard, 1987, p.26; Palmer, 1990, p.29). From the mid 1970s onwards, however, this situation began to change.

---

[9] These were *Black Faith: a mighty voice*, *Black Faith: the blood of Jesus* and *Black Faith: last boat to salvation* (Mirus Production for Channel 4, 1990).

In 1975 the Zebra Project in north-west London set out to explore ways in which black and white Christians from, respectively, the new Black-led churches and the established white churches might work successfully together. It developed into a successful and ongoing ecumenical initiative (Charman, 1979; Howard, 1987, p.40; Smith and Holden, 1983). In 1976 a joint working party of representatives of the Black-led churches and of the British Council of Churches was set up to look into ways of deepening contacts between black and white Christians. Three reports were published – *Coming together in Christ*, *Building together in Christ* and *Learning in Partnership* – and in 1981 a new group, 'The Conference For Christian Partnership', was formed to attempt to provide national co-ordination of initiatives between black and white churches (British Council of Churches, 1978 and 1979; Gerloff and Simmonds, 1980; Howard, 1987, p.39). The theme of 'partnership' was also embodied in the foundation of 'The Centre for Black and White Christian Partnership' at Selly Oak Colleges, Birmingham in 1978. The Centre seeks to foster 'leadership in partnership' between black and white led churches, especially through education, and provides courses that combine the insights of 'traditional' and 'written' theology with the 'oral' theology characteristic of the life of the Black-led churches (Gerloff, 1982; Gerloff and Simmonds, 1980; Hollenweger, 1987).

In the 1980s the process of ecumenical engagement moved markedly further. In 1984 the West Indian Evangelical Alliance was founded and included among its aims working with the existing (white-led) Evangelical Alliance and building bridges between West Indian and other British churches (Howard, 1987, p.25; Nelson, 1990, p.8). Perhaps the most significant move of all, however, came in the mid 1980s when the British churches began the 'Inter-Church Process: Not Strangers but Pilgrims' to seek a more effective ecumenical structure to replace the British Council of Churches. One of the key reasons for so doing was the perceived failure of the existing ecumenical establishment to include the Black-led churches (Palmer, 1990, p.24). Both the ensuing discussions and the new ecumenical structures which were eventually established in 1990 were notable, among other things, for the inclusion of representatives of the Black-led churches.

In the early 1990s, it remained to be seen how such participation by the Black-led churches in the ecumenical mainstream of British Christianity would develop. It similarly remained to be seen whether the avowedly evangelical and Pentecostal character of these churches would lead them to become part of a more broadly based evangelical and charismatic orientation and alliance within British Christianity as the twentieth century drew to a close. What was not in doubt, however, was that the Black-led churches now constituted a significant strand within both the British

Christian community in particular and British religious life in general –
and this in turn represented one of the more notable changes in the
religious situation in Britain in the 1990s when compared with that which
had prevailed only four decades earlier in the late 1940s and early 1950s.

3   The black presence in the traditional churches

As we have already noted, the general response of the historic churches to
the arrival in Britain of significant numbers of their Afro-Caribbean co-
denominationalists was undistinguished. Although there were no doubt
numerous local and individual exceptions to the rule, it is clear in retrospect that there was a general failure to make welcome the majority of Afro-
Caribbean Anglicans, Methodists, Roman Catholics, and so forth, who
arrived in Britain in the 1950s and 60s. The hopes and expectations engen-
dered by the baptismal and church membership certificates and letters of
commendation brought by many Afro-Caribbean Christians from their
'home' churches were dashed by the reception (or lack of it) that 'their'
church offered them in Britain. Despite this, however, many Afro-Caribbean Christians from the historic churches determined to stay within
denominations which they regarded as 'theirs' and to which they wished to
remain loyal. The experience of one such Anglican is worth quoting:

> You know that place was strange. We goes there for three years
> every Sunday … you know that every Sunday we end up sitting
> by ourselves. Nobody talks to us, they don't even smile, some-
> times they nod. Anyway I say to my wife, we going to keep going,
> because they is so unfriendly, they not going to stop us from
> praying to God in His house … You know it hurt me so much.
> Back home we all one … we come here and find we aren't one, we
> are different. Man it hurt, it really hurt. Still I says to my children
> you don't go to no clap hand church. You're Church of England
> … you staying in … it's your church too.
>
> (Quoted in Moore, 1984, and Howard, 1987, p.28)

As a result of such determination, as many as 30 per cent of Afro-Caribbean
churchgoers in contemporary Britain still attend one of the historic
churches. It was only in the 1970s and 80s, however, that their churches
began to look in detail and with realism at the position they occupied and
the role they played within their denominations. Research into this area

remains limited and conclusions must therefore be tentative. There is sufficient evidence, however, particularly from a group of five studies and reports from the Methodist, Anglican and Roman Catholic churches published in 1985–86, to identify a number of similar and significant trends.[10]

It is clear that most local congregations of the historic churches in Britain have few, if any, Afro-Caribbean members – although it is also likely that the number of multi-racial congregations is increasing. On the other hand, however, there are also local congregations in all of these churches in which Afro-Caribbean members constitute a substantial part of the local church – and sometimes the majority. The latter is particularly apt to be the case in inner-city areas and in some housing estates. In Methodism, for example, whilst only 1.2 per cent of the total of church members are black, in inner-city churches 35 per cent of regular attenders and in council estate churches 19 per cent of regular attenders, are black. In inner London, the figure rises to 41.4 per cent. Many inner-city churches thus depend on their black members for their very survival (Walton, Ward and Johnson, 1985). Unfortunately, similarly detailed figures are not available for other denominations, but it seems plausible to expect that broadly similar circumstances would be revealed elsewhere, an expectation encouraged by the results of more local research in the Church of England in the diocese of Birmingham (R. Wilkinson, 1985).

Despite the vital role thus played by black members in keeping alive their churches' presence and witness in particular areas and localities, there remained, however, a general absence of black Anglicans, Methodists and Roman Catholics in positions of authority and leadership in their churches. At both national and local levels and among both clergy and laity there was a notable absence of black and Afro-Caribbean representation and participation in the leadership of the historic churches in Britain. As at least two studies of the Church of England insisted, the black and Afro-Caribbean members of the church were likely to seem 'invisible' (Evans, 1985; Moore, 1984). In the 1980s there began to be exceptions to this general pattern: the appointment of Wilfred Wood as Bishop of Croydon and the prominent role of Leon Murray in the Methodist Conference being two examples. The very notability of such appointments, however, in itself drew attention to a

---

[10]   The five reports from these years are: from Methodism, *A Tree God Planted: black people in British Methodism* (Walton, Ward and Johnson, 1985) and *Members One of Another* (Methodist Church Division of Social Responsibility, 1986); from the Church of England, *Inheritors Together: black people in the Church of England* (Wilkinson, Wilkinson and Evans, 1985) and *Anglicans and Racism*, (Board for Social Responsibility, 1986); and from the Roman Catholic Church, *With You in Spirit*? (Report of Cardinal Hume's Advisory Group on the Catholic Church's Commitment to the Black Community, 1986). For useful summaries, comparisons and discussions of these texts, see Howard, 1987, ch.3 and Johnson, 1988a.

deeper ongoing problem. Only when such events as the appointment of a black vicar to the Standing Committee of the Church of England's General Synod *ceased* to be newsworthy, it has been observed, would there be grounds for thinking that substantial progress had been made (Johnson, 1988b, p.99).

In the meantime, the historic churches could at least claim that they had begun to recognize the need to facilitate and promote such leadership from within the ranks of their black and Afro-Caribbean members. Signs of such recognition included proposals in the Church of England's report *Faith in the City* for 'the removal of barriers to the effective participation and leadership of black people at all levels of Church life, particularly in relation to the ordained ministry'. Practical proposals included the appointment of staff with special responsibility for fostering black Anglican vocations to the priesthood, and for the training and deployment of black clergy and the establishment of a Standing Committee on Black Anglican Concerns (*Faith in the City*, 1985, pp.95–100). The Roman Catholic report, *With You in Spirit*, similarly called for the implementation of a variety of practical measures, including the provision of more black priests, whilst Methodist concern that theological colleges should do more to prepare students for work in a multi-cultural society found practical expression in 1991 in the decision to appoint a full-time Tutor in Black Theology at the ecumenical Queen's College, Birmingham. The enduring challenge posed to the historic churches by their attitudes to their black members was, however, reiterated in 1991 by the Church of England Report, *Seeds of Hope: report of a survey on combating racism in the dioceses of the Church of England*. Itself the work of the Committee on Black Anglican Concerns established after the *Faith in the City* report, this document reaffirmed the need to combat racism in the church and to ensure that its black membership was properly reflected in decision-making bodies (General Synod, 1991, pp.5–7).

Such official initiatives were, however, only one aspect of the development of black and Afro-Caribbean Christianity in the historic churches during the 1980s. Whilst the churches began, as institutions, to seek to address the racial inequalities within their structures, black and Afro-Caribbean Christians within these denominations also began, increasingly insistently, to develop and articulate a specifically black or Afro-Caribbean expression of their faith. In part this process was a matter of black and Afro-Caribbean Anglicans, Methodists and Roman Catholics simply – but crucially – making their voices more widely heard, and thus ensuring that their stories were properly told. Notable examples of such testimony to black and Afro-Caribbean Christian experience within the historic churches included contributions to the important and innovatory volumes *Catching Both Sides of the Wind* (Jackson, ed., 1985) and *A Time to Speak:*

perspectives of black Christians in Britain (Grant and Patel, eds, 1990). But it was by no means only a question of exploiting opportunities to speak. It was also a matter of articulating, from within the historic churches, a distinctively black and Afro-Caribbean understanding and experience of Christian faith.

During the 1980s, it was increasingly acknowledged that there was a need for such distinctive self-expression among black and Afro-Caribbean Christians within the historic churches.[11] It was recognized, for example, that beneath the denominational labels under which many Afro-Caribbean Christians came to Britain there existed a distinctively black Christianity, fashioned by several generations of Afro-Caribbean experience and needs. Such Christianity was 'a living stream of faith', characterized especially by an unfettered spirituality in which the twin themes of survival in the face of oppression and of liberation were central, and in which 'longing for the future gave hope to the present' – but it was also a living Christianity which white Christians generally failed to recognize or value (J. Wilkinson, 1985, p.10).

Such failure, moreover, was increasingly perceived not simply as a matter of racial discrimination within the church or of a lack of opportunities for leadership on the part of black Christians, important as these were. More profoundly, the failure was seen to involve a rejection of the distinctive cultural and spiritual heritage and experience of black Christians and, worse still, a requirement that black Christians themselves abandon their own traditions in conforming to white Christian norms (Moore, 1990; Nathan, 1990). As one black Christian put it, describing such experience in a local mixed black and white church: 'You have to leave parts of yourself at the church door. Things like the way you speak, the ways you relate to each other ... they are regarded as just not meaningful ... by the white leadership. Our experiences have not been given any value at all' (quoted in Hobbs, 1991, p.7).

Experiences of this kind in turn prompted the emergence of groups and projects – both formal and informal, national and local – in which these neglected and rejected aspects of black Christian experience could be both nurtured and celebrated. Thus, in the local church that prompted the remark just quoted, black members of the congregation organized meet-

[11]   It should be noted that there was, similarly, a growing recognition that Asian Christians in Britain also possessed a distinctive Christian experience which was apt to be ignored or devalued by the white majority and leadership within the 'historic' churches. For students of religion in general and Christianity in particular in modern and contemporary Britain, the relationship between the black Christianity of Afro-Caribbean tradition and the black Christianity of Asian tradition as each develops within a British context – the extent of their similarities and differences, their common ground and, perhaps also, their points of tension – is likely to be a fascinating theme.

ings to explore and affirm 'black history, black culture and black contributions to Christianity'. Although open to all, the meetings aroused suspicion and hostility from white members of the church. For the black Christians involved, however, 'The atmosphere, of black people being together, enabled a lot of people to feel good about themselves as people and as Christians … It was being able to relax, to feel free and open' (Hobbs, 1991, p.7).

Such local initiatives were examples of the 'black base worshipping communities' which one black American observer of the Church of England in the mid 1980s saw as an essential need of black Christians in the historic churches in Britain (Evans, 1985, p.69). Behind them – or perhaps more accurately within them – there also lay a model of pastoral care significantly different from that of traditional British Christianity. This alternative pastoral model focused, especially, upon communal responsibility, congregational participation, a theological emphasis on liberation and justice (often personalized in terms of the sheer sense of worth implied by salvation and holiness), social commitment against injustice and racism, the presence of black leaders in all church activities and the celebration of the triumphs as well as the pain of black Christian history (Hobbs, 1991, p.4). Similarly, the 1980s also saw increasing discussion and exploration of the concept of a specifically Black Theology in a British context (Board for Social Responsibility, 1986, pp.38–43; Moore, 1980; Pityana, 1989). Such exploration drew upon traditions of black theology elsewhere (especially in North America and in African Christianity) and also upon themes prominent in the politically radical tradition of Liberation Theology, but sought to articulate a 'black theology of liberation' which expressed 'the deepest yearnings of the black people of faith in Britain', affirming black personality and nourishing the hope of black British Christians (Pityana, 1989, p.108).

In the present context, it is not merely the fact that such themes have emerged within the historic churches that is significant. What is equally significant is the striking similarity between such themes in the historic churches and the characteristic emphases and developing concerns of the Black-led churches in Britain. The importance of black Christians being able to express and celebrate their Christian experience freely and authentically; of a dynamic, participatory, and joyful style of worship; of the local Christian community; of social commitment both to confront racism and to address the needs of individuals and communities through self-help schemes; of black Christian experience in developing and affirming a positive sense of identity within a predominantly white society which continues to undervalue black people, thus reinforcing a long history of oppression of blacks by whites: all of these themes – not surprisingly – occur in the recent history of both the Black-led churches and of black Christians within the historic churches in Britain.

'Black religious practice in Britain', it has been observed, 'has a common thread that runs through all denominations' (Pityana, 1989, p.108). That 'common thread' was expressed both informally – for example, by combining both attendance at an historic church and attendance at a Black-led Pentecostal church (Howard, 1987, p.28) – and by more formal means such as the emergence of 'Black Christian Communities' consisting of both Black-led churches and 'those black Christians sojourning in mainstream denominations' (Hobbs, 1991, p.4). How such developing links between black Christians in Britain will in turn relate to the increasing participation of the Black-led churches within the ecumenical mainstream of British Christianity remains to be seen – but it seems likely that the relationship, whatever it turns out to be, will be of considerable significance for the overall 'shape' of the Christian community as a whole in Britain as the twentieth century draws to a close.

4   Babylon and Brixton: Rastafarianism in Britain

Whilst Afro-Caribbean Christians in Britain in the 1960s, 70s and 80s increasingly explored and developed the possibilities and implications of a distinctively black theology and Christian experience, Rastafarianism presented a markedly alternative expression of specifically black religious commitment and identity. The origins of Rastafarianism are associated primarily with the ideas and influence of the early twentieth-century Jamaican evangelical preacher and black nationalist, Marcus Garvey.[12] But in Britain Rastafarianism is probably best known through the music of Bob Marley, the wearing of dreadlocks and woollen tams (headgear in the green, yellow, red and black colours of Ethiopia) and, more disturbingly, through the persistence of negative images and a generally 'bad press' emphasizing Rastafarian use of marijuana, poor relationships between Rastafarians and the police, and the perceived role of Rastafarians in the inner-city riots of 1981.

Rastafarianism first appeared in Britain in the late 1950s (Cashmore, 1987, p.427). After about a decade during which it made little impact, in the late 1960s and 1970s it began to enjoy considerable growth among young Afro-Caribbeans in Britain. The growth of Rastafarianism at this particular

---

[12] For discussion of Marcus Garvey and the roots of Rastafarianism in Jamaica and in the nineteenth-century 'Back-to-Africa' movement, see Cashmore, 1983, ch.2, and 1987, pp.423–6; Clarke, 1986, chs 1–4; Hall, 1985.

historical point may broadly be explained by the conjunction of the emergence of a body of young second- and third-generation Afro-Caribbeans in
Britain who were profoundly alienated from the white society and culture
in which they lived, and the availability of a determinedly alternative
system of beliefs and symbols which combined celebration of their own
black identity with explanation of their oppression by that white culture
and society. For young Afro-Caribbeans increasingly alienated by experiences of unemployment, discrimination and harassment, Rastafarianism
presented a language, set of symbols and lifestyle which offered an affirmation of black traditions, identity and history. At the same time it sharply
rejected the traditions and lifestyles of the white society that had historically oppressed and alienated their ancestors and parents and which now
continued to alienate them. It has also been suggested that the growth of
Rastafarianism in Britain was assisted by disillusionment and dissatisfaction with Black Pentecostalism among Afro-Caribbean youth. For many
second- and third-generation Afro-Caribbean young people in Britain, it is
argued, the lifestyle and values of Black Pentecostalism represented an
evasion of the real challenges presented by white society by a passive
acceptance of an obsolete and compromised set of 'respectable' and essentially 'white' values (Cashmore, 1983, pp.38–41 and 93; Clarke, 1986,
pp.54–5; Howard, 1987, p.24).

Whatever the balance between general alienation with white British
society and specific rejection of the Black Pentecostalist response, by the
1980s Rastafarianism had become a significantly established presence
within virtually every major British city (Cashmore, 1987, p.429). Estimates
of Rastafarian numbers in Britain vary, but it seems likely that there are at
least 5,000 fully committed members of the movement (Clarke, 1986, p.14).
In addition, Rastafarian ideas and images undoubtedly exercise a much
wider and more diffused influence among the Afro-Caribbean youth of
Britain's inner cities than that bare figure would suggest – the diffused but
extremely widespread influence of Bob Marley's music being perhaps the
outstanding example of this phenomenon (Bones, 1985, pp.42–3; Cashmore, 1987, pp.426–7). The development of a specifically British version of
Rastafarianism, it has been observed, has involved 'a diffusion of Rasta
ideas, symbols and motifs in the ghetto culture of British cities and the
emergence of a specifically British reggae and Afro-Caribbean musical
culture' as part of the much wider process of the emergence of 'a black
counter-culture of resistance' among young Afro-Caribbeans (Hall, 1985,
p.292).

What then, are the principal themes of the Rastafarian contribution to
this counter-culture? Rastafarianism does not possess an authoritative or
formalized body of doctrine or a centralized organization and hierarchy. It
is, on the contrary, highly decentralized and individualized in ethos and

structure. This in turn reflects the conviction that the spirit of Jah (God) resides equally in each individual and leads to the insistence that, even linguistically, no one should be dominated by another – hence instead of saying 'you and me', a Rastafarian will refer to 'I and I'. Interpreting the Bible by means of a complex and ingenious process of inference referred to as 'reasoning', Rastafarians identify above all with Africa, and also believe themselves to be the true Israel. Having suffered enslavement at the hands of the white Babylon, they look forward to redemption from slavery and return to the promised land in Africa, symbolized above all by Ethiopia, the seat of an ancient African civilization and symbol of a free and uncolonized African identity.

The Rastafarian perceives the world in terms of a series of radical dichotomies between black and white, good and bad, Zion and Babylon. The experience of oppression, suffering and 'endless pressure' is Babylon. Historically, Babylon encompasses the whole black experience of slavery, colonization and white domination of the African. In late twentieth-century Britain, social inequality and deprivation, unemployment, racial discrimination and harassment at the hands of white-dominated society are all also Babylon. Babylon, moreover, for the Rastafarian, uses both overt repression and more subtle means to undermine the Rastafarian's potential and thus maintain the existing power structure: so even the African identity has been 'colonized' in a process of 'mental slavery'. The Rastafarian, however, looks forward to the coming of a new age in which Babylon will be destroyed and Rastafarians restored to their Zion, a process in which both physical and mental oppression will be overcome.

In terms of lifestyle, Rastafarianism emphasizes the need to avoid contact with Babylon and seeks to assert clear boundaries between the Rastafarian and white society. Rastafarians avoid cutting their hair (seeing this as demanded by the Bible); adopt the green, yellow, red and black colours of Ethiopia; are strongly patriarchal in their attitude to the respective roles and status of men and women; for the most part are vegetarian; use both music and marijuana in their rituals of prayer and meditation to facilitate withdrawal into the world of the spirit and the discovery of Jah in one's inner depth; and are bound together by a strong emphasis on brotherhood.[13]

The growth of Rastafarianism in Britain from the late 1960s onwards was both influenced by and itself a contributory influence in the rise of a more assertive and militant stance on the part of many young Afro-Caribbeans against white society. As a result (and also because of their general use of marijuana and the overtly aggressive position of some

---

[13] For extended accounts of Rastafarian beliefs and lifestyle, see Bones, 1985; Cashmore, 1983; Clarke, 1986, chs 4–7; Hall, 1985.

Rastafarians and their participation in inner-city disturbances) there was, and probably remains, substantial antipathy and outright hostility towards the movement at both official and popular levels, including resistance to the recognition of Rastafarianism as a genuinely religious movement. To some extent such antipathy is a predictable consequence of the overtly oppositional stance characteristically taken by Rastafarians towards white society: they do deliberately and determinedly reject the predominant norms of British society and they do not seek or invite a sympathetic response (Clarke, 1986, pp.96–8).

On the other hand, during the 1980s there were also signs that Rastafarianism was gaining greater recognition as a serious Afro-Caribbean religious option within British society, and within British Rastafarianism itself there were signs of change and development. Two important landmarks were the Scarman Report on the Brixton riots of 10th–12th April 1981 and the 1982 Report of the Catholic Commission for Racial Justice on *Rastafarians in Jamaica and Britain*. The Scarman Report included the important statements that: 'The Rastafarians, their faith and their aspirations, deserve more understanding and more sympathy than they get from the British people', and that 'the true Rastafarian accepts the law of the land'. The Catholic Commission for Racial Justice, meanwhile, recognized Rastafarianism as a 'valid religion' and called for dialogue to facilitate 'mutual learning and sharing' (Clarke, 1986, pp.57–8 and 96).

Within Rastafarianism itself the 1980s produced some developments. It has been suggested that the number of committed Rastafarians may have declined during the 1980s, even if the diffused influence of Rastafarian ideas may have continued to increase (Clarke, 1986, p.59). Among the Rastafarian community, meanwhile, two strands appeared to emerge. Thus, whilst some remained resolutely and implacably critical of white society, others began to explore the possibilities for co-operation with at least some aspects of the dominant society, not least in assisting 'those who are down and out' (Clarke, 1986, pp.61–2). Similarly, a number of Rastafarians moved away from an ideal of total separation from white society and return to Africa and towards an ideal of integration in which their own Rastafarian identity would be respected. For such Rastafarians, it has been observed, 'Ethiopia' came to symbolize not a return to Africa itself, but 'any situation or place in which the constraints of Babylon have been removed, thereby allowing Rastas the freedom to live naturally in the African way' (Clarke, 1986, p.99). Which of these strands predominates within British Rastafarianism will probably depend not only on developments within Rastafarianism itself but also upon the ongoing attitudes of the white majority in British society towards both Rastafarianism in particular and young Afro-Caribbeans in general.

5 Conclusion: identities and communities

We began, we may recall, with a wartime quotation suggesting that Afro-Caribbeans, having lost their indigenous African culture, had subsequently found nothing substantial to put in its place – although 'Christianity had to some extent filled the void' – and, therefore, that they lacked ethical standards and any sense of community or social responsibility. We may profitably return to that quotation once more. Leaving aside the intrinsic offensiveness of its tone, to say nothing of its actual content, we may yet enjoy the ironies that are revealed by considering the quotation in the context of the history of Afro-Caribbean religion in Britain since the 1950s.

To begin with there is the alleged loss of 'his indigenous African culture'. Whatever else may separate them, it is a common theme of both Afro-Caribbean Christianity in Britain (in both the Black-led and the historic churches) and Rastafarianism that the religious experience and spirituality involved are distinctively rooted in black experience, history and culture, which include not only the experience of uprooting and slavery, but also the recollection and retention of an African past and its traditions. Rastafarianism asserts this most obviously. But so also, insistently if less overtly, does Afro-Caribbean Christianity. The evidence of Afro-Caribbean religion in recent and contemporary Britain is such as to suggest that 'his [sic] indigenous culture' was by no means as lost as the writer of the wartime briefing document supposed.

Secondly, we may consider the suggestion that 'Christianity has to some extent filled the void'. Leaving aside the fact that the 'void' referred to was undoubtedly in many respects more supposed than real, the phrase is richly ironic in the context of the recent history of religion in Britain. For many of the Afro-Caribbean population of Britain, Christianity did indeed fill a void – but the void was not one somehow inherent in the Afro-Caribbean character, but the result of the shock of rejection and alienation in a Britain which generations of Afro-Caribbeans had been taught to think of as 'the mother-country'. Moreover, as we have seen, it was the Black-led churches that predominantly filled this void by providing a Christianity rooted in a distinctively Afro-Caribbean version of Christian faith and experience. And when, in the 1970s and 80s, Afro-Caribbean Christians within the historic churches began more assertively to explore their experiences as black Christians, so they too were filling a void of rejection by a rediscovery and reassertion of their own distinctively black experience of the meaning of Christian faith.

This alone would constitute a richly ironic comment upon the quotation with which we began. But in fact there is yet more irony, for Afro-Caribbean Christianity has filled – or at least been a major element in filling

– another notable void which appeared increasingly in the religious life of Britain between the end of the Second World War and the early 1990s. It is well-known that for the historic churches of Britain the inner cities had become an area of increasing pastoral crisis and continuing congregational decline. Yet it was precisely in the inner cities that Afro-Caribbean Christianity most flourished, whether in Black-led churches (not infrequently occupying church buildings originally built for one of the historic churches and now surplus to requirements) or in local congregations of the historic denominations in which a substantial part, and sometimes a majority, of the membership was Afro-Caribbean. 'Some churches', it has been observed, 'might be withdrawing from Handsworth but Christianity was not' (Hastings, 1991, p.560), and what was true of Handsworth was true of a great many other inner-city areas of late twentieth-century Britain as well.

Finally, we may note too the ironic inaccuracy of the last would-be dismissal in the wartime quotation with which we began. Far from an absence of ethical standards, sense of community or social responsibility, the religious history of the Afro-Caribbean community in Britain since the 1950s includes the development of traditions of ethical rigour, communal solidarity and social responsibility which were both substantial and dynamic. Far from being 'absent', the ethical standards of the Black-led churches were, as we have seen, apt to be strenuously strict when compared with the prevailing norms of modern British society. At the same time the Black-led churches provided a sustaining, nurturing and affirming community in the midst of a society which was predominantly negative and not infrequently hostile towards its black members. As for social responsibility, in the 1970s and 80s, Afro-Caribbean Christianity in Britain, as we have seen, steadily developed a tradition of social action and engagement alongside its characteristically evangelical and Pentecostal theology and spirituality. Indeed, far from lacking social responsibility, Afro-Caribbean Christianity had begun, by the 1990s, to perform a prominent role in the leadership and representation of Britain's Afro-Caribbean communities in general. Rastafarianism, meanwhile, provided an alternative set of values and ethics and an alternative sense of community – based upon pride in their history and identity as blacks – for many profoundly alienated young second- and third-generation Afro-Caribbeans for whom it was white Britain itself that lacked genuine ethical standards, a sense of community or social responsibility.

As for the future, it will be particularly interesting to observe the development of both the Black-led churches and Rastafarianism in relation to the class structure within the British Afro-Caribbean community. Within the Black-led churches, it has been noted that working-class young people are more likely to leave than are middle-class young people, and that most of the young people who remain are at college or in white-collar jobs. For students of Nonconformist history it is a familiar pattern: religious commitment and a work-ethic combine to lift the once working-class convert up the social and economic scale (Howard, 1987, p.24). Perhaps the developing social engagement within British Afro-Caribbean Christianity will result in a continuing and substantial interaction between the Black-led churches and the black working class. But if such contact should diminish whilst the social and economic alienation of black working-class youth continues, then Rastafarianism will surely continue to offer a widely diffused alternative. In the meantime we may reflect that when examined in the light of the wartime Ministry of Information's views on the 'characteristics of the West Indian', the religious history of the Afro-Caribbean community in Britain since the 1950s represents a compelling example of the triumph of reality over stereotype.

Bibliography

A HANDBOOK OF THE AFRO-WESTINDIAN UNITED COUNCIL OF CHURCHES (1984) Centre for Caribbean Studies, London.

ARNOLD, S. (1992) *From Scepticism to Hope: one Black-led church's response to social responsibility,* Grove Books, Nottingham.

BOARD FOR SOCIAL RESPONSIBILITY (1986) *Anglicans and Racism,* Church House Publishing, London.

BONES, J. (1985) *One Love: Rastafari: history, doctrine and livity,* Voice of Rasta Publishing House, London.

BRITISH COUNCIL OF CHURCHES (1978) *Coming Together in Christ,* BCC, London.

BRITISH COUNCIL OF CHURCHES (1979) *Building Together in Christ,* BCC, London.

CALLEY, M. (1965) *God's People: West Indian Pentecostal sects in England,* Oxford University Press, London.

CASHMORE, E. (1983) *Rastaman: the Rastafarian movement in England,* Counterpoint, London.

(1987) '"Get Up, Stand Up": the rastafarian movement' in Obelkevich, J., Roper, L. and Samuel, R. (eds) *Disciplines of Faith: studies in religion, politics and patriarchy,* Routledge and Kegan Paul, London.

CATHOLIC COMMISSION FOR RACIAL JUSTICE (1982) 'Rastafarians in Jamaica and Britain', Notes and Reports no.10.

CHARMAN, P. (1979) *Reflections: black and white Christians in the city,* Zebra Project, London.

CLARKE, P. (1986) *Black Paradise: the Rastafarian Movement,* Aquarian Press, Wellingborough.

EVANS, J. (1985) 'The struggle for identity: black people in the Church of England' in Wilkinson, J., Wilkinson, R. and Evans, J. (eds).

FOSTER, E. (1990) 'Out of this world: a consideration of the development and nature of the Black-led churches in Britain' in Grant, P. and Patel, R. (eds).

(1992) 'Women and the inverted pyramid of the Black Churches in Britain' in Sahgal, G. and Yuval-Davies, N. (eds) *Refusing Holy Orders: women and fundamentalism in Britain*, Virago, London.

GENERAL SYNOD (1985) *Faith in the City*, Church House Publishing, London.

(1991) *Seeds of Hope: report of a survey on combating racism in the dioceses of the Church of England*, Church House Publishing, London.

GERLOFF, R. (ed.) (1982) 'British Union: the centre for black and white Christian partnership', *Christian Action Journal* (an edition of the journal devoted entirely to this theme).

(1983) 'The development of Black Churches in Britain since 1952', paper delivered at the 'Development and impact of New Religious Movements' conference, King's College, London.

GERLOFF, R. and SIMMONDS, M. (eds) (1980) *Learning in Partnership*, BCC, London.

GRANT, P. (1990) 'If it happened to you, tell me, what would you do?' in Grant, P. and Patel, R. (eds).

GRANT, P. and PATEL, R. (eds) (1990) *A Time to Speak: perspectives of black Christians in Britain*, Joint Publication of Racial Justice and the Black Theology Working Group, Birmingham.

HALL, S. (1985) 'Religious ideologies and social movements in Jamaica' in Bocock, R. and Thompson, K. (eds) *Religion and Ideology*, Manchester University Press, Manchester.

HASTINGS, A. (1991) *A History of English Christianity 1920–1990*, Collins, London.

HILL, C. (1963) *West Indian Migrants and the London Churches*, Oxford University Press, London.

(1971a) 'From church to sect: West Indian religious sect development in Britain', *Journal for the Scientific Study of Religion*, 10, pp.114–23.

(1971b) 'Immigrant sect development in Britain: a case of status deprivation', *Social Compass*, 18, pp.231–6.

(1971c) 'Pentecostalist growth – result of racialism?', *Race Today*, 3, pp.187–90.

(1971d) *Black Churches: West Indian and African sects in Britain*, Community and Race Relations Unit of The British Council of Churches, London.

HOBBS, M. (1991) *Better Will Come: a pastoral response to institutional racism in British churches*, Grove Books, Nottingham.

HOLLENWEGER, W. (1987) 'Interaction between black and white in theological education', *Theology*, 90, pp.341–50.

HOWARD, V. (1987) 'A report on Afro-Caribbean Christianity in Britain', *Community Religions Project Research Papers*, new series, 4.

JACKSON, A. (ed.) (1985) *Catching Both Sides of the Wind: conversations with five black pastors*, British Council of Churches, London.

JOHNSON, M. (1988a) 'The Spirit still moves in the inner city: the churches and race', *Ethnic and Racial Studies*, 11, pp.366–73.

(1988b) 'Resurrecting the inner city: a new role for the Christian Churches', *New Community*, 15, pp.91–101.

MACROBERT, I. (1989) 'The new Black-led Churches in Britain' in Badham, P. (ed.) *Religion, State and Society in Modern Britain*, The Edwin Mellen Press, Lampeter.

METHODIST CHURCH DIVISION OF SOCIAL RESPONSIBILITY (1986) *Members One of Another*, London.

MOORE, D. (1980) 'Black theology: a tentative exploration', *The Modern Churchman* (New Series) 23, pp.172–9.

(1984) 'Invisible people – black people in the Church of England', unpublished paper.

(1990) 'Through a black lens: telling our history and understanding its significance' in Grant, P. and Patel, R. (eds).

NATHAN, R. (1990) 'Issues for the black minister' in Grant, P. and Patel, R. (eds).

NELSON, C. (1990) 'The churches, racism and the inner cities' in Grant, P. and Patel, R. (eds).

PALMER, D. (1990) *Strangers No More*, Hodder and Stoughton, London.

PHOENIX, S. (1991) 'Land of Hope and Glory' in Hooker, R. and Sargant, J. (eds) *Belonging to Britain: Christian perspectives on a plural society*, CCBI Publications, London.

PITYANA, B. (1989) 'Towards a black theology for Britain' in Harvey, A. (ed.) *Theology in the City: a theological response to 'Faith in the City'*, SPCK, London.

ROOT, J. (1979) *Encountering West Indian Pentecostalism: its ministry and worship*, Grove Booklets, Nottingham.

SCARMAN, LORD (1981) *The Brixton Disorders 10–12 April 1981: report of an Inquiry by the Rt. Hon. The Lord Scarman*, HMSO, Cmnd. 8427.

SMITH, I. (1989) *An Ebony Cross: being a black Christian in Britain today*, Marshall Pickering, London.

SMITH, I. and HOLDEN, T. (1983) *Dialogue Between Black and White Christians: two papers*, Zebra Project, London.

THEOBALD, R. (1981) 'The politicization of a religious movement: British Adventism under the impact of West Indian immigration', *British Journal of Sociology*, 32, pp.202–23.

WALTON, H., WARD, R. and JOHNSON, M. (1985) *A Tree God Planted: black people in British Methodism*, Methodist Church Division of Social Responsibility, London.

WEST, P. (1990) 'Rank Outsiders', *The Listener*, 8 November, pp.6–8.

WILKINSON, J. (1985) 'Inheritors together' in Wilkinson, J., Wilkinson, R. and Evans, J. (eds).

WILKINSON, R. (1985) 'A chance to change' in Wilkinson, J., Wilkinson, R. and Evans, J. (eds).

WILKINSON, J., WILKINSON, R. and EVANS, J. (eds) (1985) *Inheritors Together: black people in the Church of England*, Race, Pluralism and Community Group, Board for Social Responsibility, London.

WITH YOU IN SPIRIT (1986) Cardinal Hume's Advisory Group on the Catholic Church's Commitment to the Black Community, London.

WORRALL, B. (1987) 'Some reflections on Black-led churches in England', *Theology*, 90, pp.3–14.

7

EXPANDING THE RELIGIOUS SPECTRUM: NEW RELIGIOUS MOVEMENTS IN MODERN BRITAIN

by Gerald Parsons

Followers of Hare Krishna in London, September 1976. Reproduced by permission of *The Guardian*. Photograph by Peter Johns.

It is often assumed that recent decades have seen a general decline in the interest in religion in British society and a consequent reduction in the range and extent of religious activity. In fact, however, the period since the end of the Second World War has been marked by a significant expansion in the number and range of religious groups and movements actively present within British society. Thus, this period has seen the emergence not only of flourishing Muslim, Sikh and Hindu communities in Britain – alongside the longer-established Christian and Jewish groups – but also of a remarkably wide variety of New Religious Movements. Indeed, as a result of the coverage by the popular press of such groups from time to time – often in the form of highly sensational and hostile stories about new 'cults' and their alleged 'brainwashing' of young converts – it is likely that most people will have heard of at least some of these new groups. The Unification Church (popularly known as the 'Moonies'), Scientology, Rajneeshism, the Divine Light Mission, Transcendental Meditation (TM), and the International Society for Krishna Consciousness (also known as the Hare Krishna Movement or ISKCON) are probably the most well known.

In fact, however, such groups are only the most prominent examples of an immense, indeed often bewildering, variety of New Religious Movements which have appeared within the British religious landscape since 1945. It has been estimated that as many as 500 such movements were established, more or less securely, in Britain in the period between 1945 and 1990 – although estimates of this kind themselves turn in part upon the complicated question of how, exactly, a 'New Religious Movement' is to be defined (Barker, 1989a, pp.145–9). Such problems of definition, together with aspects of the phenomenon such as the nature of recruitment and organization within the various groups, their relationship to the surrounding culture, the characteristics of their belief-systems and the reactions of society to them, have provided sociologists with ample scope for study and debate. Indeed, so intriguing a phenomenon have New Religious Movements proved for sociologists of religion that, in recent years, the study of such groups has produced what amounts to a sub-discipline within the sociology of religion. The bibliography of published studies of New Religious Movements is now reliably reckoned to run into several thousands of items (Barker, 1989a, p.149).

Here, however, we at once confront a paradox. Because of the detailed attention that sociologists of religion have given to New Religious Movements, both individually and collectively as an overall phenomenon, we know a remarkable amount about a great many of these groups. By contrast, we know much less about the detailed patterns of belief of even active and committed churchgoers in the principal Christian churches of Britain, and less still about the religious outlooks and beliefs of the 'silent majority' of the British population who, according to surveys, continue to believe in God but are happily unspecific about the nature and implications of such belief (Davie, 1990a, p.396; Hornsby-Smith, 1989, pp.20, 210; Wallis and Bruce, 1989, pp.502–4, 511).[1] The paradox lies in the relative numbers of people involved in these different categories. Although the actively committed membership of the traditional Christian churches declined significantly between 1945 and 1990, at the end of the period it still measured its numbers in millions and accounted for something like 15 per cent of the overall population of Britain. Similarly, even if the 'religions of the silent majority' were notoriously difficult to quantify and interpret, yet it is clear that they indeed represented the majority religious outlook of modern Britain and thus embraced what were no doubt the ambiguous and diverse beliefs of many millions of Britons (Davie, 1990a, p.396). Most New Religious Movements, by contrast, measured their numbers of fully committed members in hundreds at most. The Unification Church, for example, was estimated, in 1989, to have about 350 'core' members working full time for the movement in Britain and another 100 or so 'practising' members who regularly attended meetings and donated money. ISKCON was similarly estimated as having only about 300 full-time devotees and TM as having perhaps 400 living in an 'ideal village' in Skelmersdale (Barker, 1989a, pp.150–2).[2]

Such groups also claimed much larger numbers of peripheral adherents and people who had shown some interest in their teachings or participated in their activities. Thus the Unification Church claimed that about 8000 people had become 'associate members', although perhaps only one in ten of those continued to have any contact with the movement. TM, meanwhile, claimed that as many as 150,000 people had taken a four-day course and that 6000 more do so each year, whilst ISKCON could claim several thousand followers within the Hindu section of the Asian community in Britain. Indeed, if we focus not on the 'committed' or 'full-time' membership of New Religious Movements – and if in addition we include as New Religious Movements the vast range of New Age 'self-religions', spiritualities and psychotherapies – then, it has been estimated, it is likely that well over a million people have at least 'dabbled' or 'flirted' with some kind of New Religious Movement in the last quarter of a century or so. And if those with a more or less serious interest in astrology, the occult or notions of alternative or psychic healing are added in, then the figure is even higher. Such a figure is by no means insignificant – a point to which we shall return in the concluding section of this essay. It remains, however, an estimated figure for involvement with *all* of the various New Religious

---

[1]   For an assessment and interpretation of what we do know about the 'religions of the silent majority' see Essay 8 in this volume.

[2]   For estimated figures for more than 20 of the larger New Religious Movements in Britain in 1987, see Clarke, 1987, p.11.

Movements of post-war Britain and a figure, it must be reiterated, that includes even highly peripheral and subsequently discontinued involvement (Barker, 1989a, pp.150–4).

The extremely small committed membership and the relatively minor position of any particular New Religious Movement within the overall structure of the religious life of post-war Britain does not, however, mean that such movements, taken as a whole, are unimportant. On the contrary, the New Religious Movements of post-war Britain, despite their small size, constitute an important element in the religious history of the period, not least because of a number of significant questions and issues which are raised by their existence. Precisely because there are so many of them and because they are so dissimilar in nature, it is impossible within a single short essay to present a survey of the individual New Religious Movements of modern Britain. It is also similarly inappropriate to single out only two or three for special treatment.[3] This essay will therefore address the New Religious Movements of modern Britain as an overall phenomenon, examining in particular four aspects of their nature and significance.

First, the essay will examine the sheer range and variety of New Religious Movements in modern Britain, noting the difficulties inherent in attempts to classify and categorize such diverse groups. Second, it will consider the appropriateness of the term 'New Religious Movement' as a general description of the groups commonly included under the heading. Third, the essay will ask how far and in what ways these movements raise important questions about the position and status of religion in modern Britain and, in particular, how far attitudes towards them reveal the practical limits of religious tolerance and pluralism in modern Britain. And fourth, it will consider the significance of the emergence of New Religious Movements for assessments of the predominant trends and themes in the history of religion in Britain since the end of the Second World War.

1 Characterizing the phenomenon

The sheer range and variety of the New Religious Movements present in modern Britain is one of the most perplexing aspects of any attempt to characterize or categorize this phenomenon as a whole. As Eileen Barker has insisted, because they differ from each other in such numerous and

[3] For brief descriptions of many of the New Religious Movements of post-war Britain, including most of those mentioned in the present essay, see Barker, 1989a, pp.165–216. For an earlier collection of self-definitions by a wide variety of such groups, see Annett, 1976.

important respects, New Religious Movements cannot simply all be lumped together. The term covers such an enormously disparate number of movements that 'almost any generalization about NRMs is bound to be untrue if applied to all the movements' (Barker, 1989a, p.10). Such caution, moreover, is applicable even when attempts are made to classify New Religious Movements within very broad and wide-ranging categories.

It is generally agreed that one of the more comprehensive and useful approaches for interpreting New Religious Movements is the proposal of Roy Wallis to divide them into three broad categories or ideal-types, namely, world-affirming, world-rejecting and world-accommodating (Wallis, 1984). According to Wallis, world-affirming New Religious Movements are essentially individualistic, locating the source of the suffering which they seek to overcome within oneself, not in society. Such groups may lack collective ritual or conventional religious structure. They would include, for example, Transcendental Meditation (TM), Scientology, and many of the psychotherapeutically-based groups often bracketed together under the heading of 'Human Potential Movements'. The world-rejecting category, according to Wallis, includes most of the more recognizably religious groups such as ISKCON, the Unification Church and the Children of God. Finally, the world-accommodating category includes groups allegedly content with or indifferent to the present world order, focusing instead on providing either solace or fulfilment in the interior, personal life. In this group Wallis included groups such as Subud (a mystical movement of Indonesian origin) and the charismatic movement within Christianity, as well as some more esoteric groups (Wallis, 1984, ch.2). Even scholars who readily acknowledge the value of Wallis' proposed categorization, however, also recognize its limitations and maintain that it too fails to take account of the actual diversity and variability of New Religious Movements. The various New Religious Movements, it is objected, do not in fact fit into such clear-cut categories, often being internally inconsistent and thus appearing 'world-affirming', 'accommodating' or 'rejecting' at different points or when viewed from different perspectives (Heelas, 1985; Knott, 1988b, pp.170–1). Even when viewed simply from the specific standpoint of their attitude to the present world order, the three-fold category is apt to break down (Barker, 1987).

If generalized definitions and categorizations are thus apparently doomed to prove inadequate in the face of the sheer complexity and diversity of the phenomenon they are designed to address, how then may some sense of order be introduced to the study of New Religious Movements? In the end it may be more profitable not to attempt to classify such movements according to specific types of belief – whether 'world-affirming' or 'world-denying', 'eastern' or 'western', 'ascetic' or 'libertarian' – but rather to group them much more loosely around very broadly similar sorts of origin or interest. Such an approach, although deliberately imprecise, may at least have the virtue of reflecting and respecting the stubbornly diverse nature of the movements under consideration. The present essay proposes three such broad and inclusive groups of New Religious Movements in modern Britain.

First, there are New Religious Movements which are clearly and straightforwardly derived from traditional world religions. Among the New Religious Movements of modern Britain which may fairly be grouped under this heading are movements derived from the Hindu and Buddhist traditions as well as groups derived from Islam and Christianity. Thus, for example, ISKCON, although only founded in 1966, is directly derived from the Hindu tradition, tracing its origins back to a sixteenth-century devotional teacher and taking the Bhagavad Gita as its key text (Knott, 1986). From the Buddhist tradition, the Friends of the Western Buddhist Order represent an attempt to develop a version of Buddhism which is faithful to the Buddhist tradition and its spirituality yet genuinely Western in form.[4] From the Christian tradition, meanwhile, the Jesus Fellowship Church (and its subsequent off-shoot the Jesus Army) and the London and Birmingham Churches of Christ represent fiercely evangelical versions of Christianity, characterized by intense commitment to the communities concerned, strict supervision of members' lives and aggressive evangelism (Barker, 1989a, pp.185–8). Finally within this group of New Religious Movements we may note movements inspired by the Islamic tradition including a number of distinctively western variants of the centuries-old mystical sufi tradition within Islam (Annett, 1976, pp.81–91).

A second group of New Religious Movements, although identifiably related to major religious traditions such as Christianity, Hinduism, Islam or Buddhism are manifestly less directly or conventionally derived from them and remain distinct and distant from the 'mainstreams' of the traditions involved. Indeed, in many cases, whereas the 'mainstream' of the 'parent' tradition might be prepared to recognize New Religious Movements in the first group as unusual or unorthodox representatives of the

---

[4]   Although a major world religion, the development of the Buddhist tradition in Britain, it has been observed, in many ways resembles the development of New Religious Movements rather than the emergence of British communities representing the other major world religions (Knott, 1988a, p.155). The Buddhist presence in modern Britain is distinctive precisely because, although a major world faith of eastern derivation, its British expression is not the result of migration to Britain. British Buddhism, on the contrary, is predominantly the result of Western interest in and conversion to Buddhist principles and beliefs. Moreover, much of the now substantial British interest in Buddhism has arisen in the period since the 1960s. Thus, it was estimated that of 120 Buddhist groups or centres in Britain in 1985, over 70 were established in the period since 1969 (Green, 1989, p.277). Both the predominantly convert character and the chronology of the growth of British Buddhism justify its inclusion, in the present instance, within a discussion of New Religious Movements in modern Britain.

tradition in question (peripheral and perhaps somewhat eccentric, but more or less 'authentic' nonetheless), in the case of the second group, the predominant reaction of the 'parent' tradition is more likely to be a more or less overt hostility. The ambiguities in this area are, however, considerable. For example, whilst ISKCON is accepted within the British Hindu community and involved in the work of the National Council for Hindu Temples in Britain (Barker, 1989a, p.185), the Jesus Fellowship Church, the Jesus Army and the London and Birmingham Churches of Christ are not accepted within the mainstream of British Christianity, or indeed even within the mainstream of the evangelical tradition in modern Britain. Thus the Jesus Fellowship and Jesus Army are not part of the Evangelical Alliance, whilst the Universities and Colleges Christian Fellowship – the avowedly evangelical umbrella organization for student Christian Unions – explicitly disassociated themselves from the activities of the London and Birmingham Churches of Christ (Barker, 1989a, pp.185–8).

In the case of both ISKCON and the Christian groups noted above, the 'family resemblance' to 'mainstream' Hinduism and Christianity is, however, clear, even if the 'mainstream' responses to them are different. In other cases New Religious Movements which are clearly derived – more or less wholly – from a major religious tradition are manifestly so different and distinctive that they are no longer plausibly classifiable as part of the 'parent' tradition. Christian-derived examples of this case include the Children of God, a communal and highly authoritarian blend of hippy and evangelical emphases characterized by both social revolution and sexual promiscuity (Wallis, 1981 and 1982); the Unification Church, the origins of which lie in its founder's dissatisfaction with Korean Presbyterianism and which claims to complete Christianity by its teachings (Barker, 1984a, ch.2); and various claims by some adherents of the Aquarian movement that 'Christ' is their central symbol and that their interpretation of 'Christ' is more authentic than that of the traditional Christian churches (Perry, 1992, pp.108, 121, 150–1; Romarheim, 1988). Hindu-derived examples include both the Divine Light Mission associated with Guru Maharaj Ji and the Transcendental Meditation movement associated with Maharishi Mahesh Yogi (Barker, 1989a, pp.176–8, 213–4); and also the Rajneesh Movement associated with Bhagwan Shree Rajneesh which aroused considerable controversy in the mid and late 1980s (Barker, 1989a, pp.201–5; Thompson and Heelas, 1986). The Baha'i faith (which first emerged in the mid nineteenth century but grew principally in the period after 1960) similarly has roots within Iranian Shiah Islam but subsequently developed as a separate and universalist religion. (Knott, 1988b, pp.162–3). Buddhism also, it might be argued, provides further examples of New Religious Movements clearly derived from a major religious tradition yet significantly distinct from the 'mainstream' in the shape of the Nichiren Shoshu of the United Kingdom and the Scientific Buddhist Association. The former (which is the

British variant of a modern Japanese version of Buddhism) is not only markedly materialistic but also assertive in seeking converts – neither of which are characteristic traits of traditional Buddhism. The latter, meanwhile, presents Buddhism as a science, not a religion, and seeks to equate it with Western scientific and psychotherapeutic criteria and concepts (Green, 1989, pp.285–9; Morgan, 1987).

The third group of New Religious Movements proposed here is both harder to define and even broader in its scope than the two preceding groups. The largest group of New Religious Movements – both in numbers of individual groups within it and in the diffused range of its overall influence within modern British life – is that clustered around the richly varied collection of 'self-religions', psychotherapies and New Age mysticisms and alternative spiritualities. This large group may be broadly divided into two sub-groups, each of which is simply a clustering of often quite diverse movements around a similar overall theme. The first sub-group consists of the 'self-religions' and religiously 'flavoured' psychotherapies which have increasingly flourished in the last twenty or thirty years. The self-religions have been characterized as 'movements which exemplify the conjunction of the exploration of the self and the search for significance' (Heelas, 1982, p.69). At first sight these various groups frequently do not appear to be religious at all, but rather present themselves as means of self-improvement, of improvement in personal relationships, or of achieving personal success in life.[5] Many of them originated, often in California, as attempts to find new, less expensive and less élite varieties of psychotherapy, and frequently (but not always) in the period since the 1960s were tinged with elements and ideas from eastern religions. In due course, however, the essentially 'religious' orientation or character of a group becomes clearer: the movement or technique offers personal growth, transformation of character, personal enlightenment or psychological rebirth, transcendant or mystical experience, and perhaps even the prospect of some form of personal perfection or contribution to the transformation of the world for the better (Barker, 1989a, p.28–9; Clare and Thompson, 1981; Heelas, 1987).

The range of groups, movements and techniques embaced here is very great. It includes, for example, certain kinds of encounter group, co-

[5]   Indeed, a significant number of large companies, including multi-nationals, have sent their personnel on courses run by some of the 'self-religions' in the belief that such courses render their staff more energetic, innovative and hard-working (Barker, 1989a, p.26). For their part, a number of the 'self-religions' have been only too willing to 'market' themselves as potentially advantageous to business training and management efficiency – a characteristic which has prompted the criticism that they are simply capitalism in New Age clothing. For discussion of the ambiguities involved in both the marketing of 'self-religions' and the consequent dismissal of them as mere entrepreneurialism, see Heelas, 1991 and 1992.

counselling and holism, groups such as rebirthing or *est* which emphasize positive thinking, and organizations such as Exegesis and Scientology. What these various groups tend to share, however, is an overwhelming emphasis upon the inward and the subjective. In general – and in broad contrast to the New Age mysticisms and spiritualities which will be considered in a moment – the 'self-religions' are just what the title implies: attempts to find the sources and potential for development and meaning in life simply from within the individual. By contrast, the even more diverse groups which may be clustered under the heading of 'New Age religions', although also characterized by a conviction that the divine is to be found within the self, tend on the whole to look outwards as well as within the individual and to advocate new ways of relating the 'divine within' either to variously conceived transcendent realities or to the environment as a whole.[6]

New Age spiritualities and mysticisms are amazingly varied, eclectic and syncretistic, borrowing and combining elements from such sources as traditional religions, ancient and esoteric lore, alternative medicine, vegetarianism and ecology, environmentalism and feminism. Sometimes elements of drug-culture or of paganism are added to the mix. The range of specific beliefs and combinations can be bewildering, but certain broad strands and characteristics may be identified within the movement as a whole. The New Age phenomenon thus includes those who are principally focused upon an alternative lifestyle emphasizing, characteristically, community, ecological sensitivity and holistic elements; those who believe in alternative medicines and healing techniques, often linking these to concepts of reincarnation or spiritual evolution; those who are inspired by feminist or pacifist spiritualities; and those who focus upon ancient pagan, psychic, astrological or occult traditions, of either Eastern or ancient British origin. The New Age movement tends to be optimistic in outlook, alternative in lifestyle, green in politics and committed to the view that humanity is entering or on the verge of a new age of consciousness and spiritual development – a belief which the turn of the millenium may well foster (Barker, 1989a, pp.188–92; Cole et al., 1990, chs 1–6; Leech, 1976, chs 5 and 6; Luhrmann, 1989; McCrickard, 1991; Perry, 1992, chs 1–10; Romarheim, 1988).[7]

---

[6] Again, however, it must be noted that even these boundaries are far from clear. Thus, for example, holistic ideas might equally appear as part of a 'self-religion' or as part of an environmentally and ecologically oriented but also communitarian New Age spirituality. Similarly, a movement such as TM or Rajneeshism will incorporate psychotherapeutic elements characteristic of the 'self-religions' and blend these with ideas derived from Eastern religious thought.

[7] For an effective introduction to the range and variety of New Age ideas and beliefs from specifically New Age sources see the two anthologies of New Age writings and rituals in Bloom, 1990 and 1991.

The grouping of New Religious Movements in this three-fold way is helpful to the extent that it enables us to apply a degree of order to a potentially chaotic-looking phenomenon, whilst avoiding the pitfalls inherent in any attempt to classify such Movements according to more specific but inevitably theological or sociological categories. Nevertheless, this approach raises certain further questions, even as it clarifies others. There remains the question of just what qualifies as a New Religious Movement in the first place? What must a particular movement or organization have to be a New Religious Movement? And where does the boundary lie between genuinely New Religious Movements and the emergence of variants of or within traditional religions? It is to such questions that we turn in the second section of this essay.

2 What is a 'New' 'Religious' Movement?

When is a New Religious Movement not really a New Religious Movement? The question is not as absurd as it may at first seem. Quite apart from the problems of categorization considered in the preceding section of this essay, there is a further area of debate over whether or not all of the various types of movement commonly described as 'New Religious Movements' are in fact justifiably described in this way. Thus, it is sometimes objected that a number of the so-called New Religious Movements are actually not new at all, but rather variants of much older religious traditions. Similarly, it is also sometimes argued that many of the New Religious Movements are 'not really religious', either because in some cases they actually claim not to be, or because they lack characteristics or qualities thought to be essential to the notion of 'religion'.

We may perhaps grant without difficulty that, for example, movements such as the Children of God, the Unification Church, the Divine Light Mission, Rajneeshism or Nichiren Shoshu are clearly 'New' Religious Movements, rather than modern variants of older religions, because of the strikingly innovative, unorthodox and unconventional ways in which they adapt aspects of the 'parent' traditions from which they are primarily derived. Something very similar may surely be said of those elements of the New Age movement which appeal – in part at least – to ancient or arcane, esoteric and occult lore, knowledge and tradition. In these cases too, although the traditions upon which these New Religious Movements claim to base themselves may be very far from new, yet the forms in which they are now re-expressed are most certainly distinctively modern and contemporary versions of such ancient traditions and, in this sense, are appropriately described as 'New' Religious Movements.

If these examples are unproblematic, however, others are not so straightforward. Consider, for example, whether the Friends of the Western Buddhist Order, ISKCON, or the Jesus Fellowship Church and the London and Birmingham Churches of Christ are most appropriately described as 'New Religious Movements' or as modern variants of, respectively, Buddhism, Hinduism and Christianity? That each is, indeed, a modern variant of one of these religious traditions is undeniable. What is not clear is where the boundary might be drawn between a 'new variant' and a 'New Religious Movement'; nor is it clear on precisely what grounds such a boundary should be established. The examples cited above illustrate the range of possible responses to this question.

In the case of the Friends of the Western Buddhist Order it is clear that the movement, although committed to developing a version of Buddhism suited to a Western society and context, is fully committed to maintaining traditional Buddhist spiritual insights and perspectives. The movement is new, but it is clearly a new form of Buddhism, not a new religion (Green, 1989; Ratnaprabba, 1987). On balance, then, it is probably inappropriate to define the FWBO as a New Religious Movement, although it is clearly a part of the more general emergence of new religious groups in modern Britain. By contrast, however, one might well wish to classify Nichiren Shoshu, with its distinctive and non-traditional interpretation of the Buddhist tradition, as a New Religious Movement rather than a variant of Buddhism.

ISKCON represents a further interesting case. On the one hand, it is firmly rooted in the Hindu tradition and is accepted by British Hindus as an authentic part of the Hindu community in Britain. Indeed, it has even been argued that the most important thing to note about ISKCON is that it is not an Indian equivalent of other New Religious Movements; that it emphasizes traditional and orthodox aspects of Hinduism; that it already provides a significant route into a fuller and more informed practice of Hinduism for numbers of young Hindus in Britain; and that this role may well increase in the future (Carey, 1983 and 1987). On the other hand, however, in the manner of its appearance in Britain in the late 1960s, its association at that time with the world of pop music and alternative lifestyles, and its appeal to young Western converts (and the opposition this aroused), ISKCON was fully part of the overall phenomenon of and the debate over New Religious Movements.

The Jesus Fellowship Church, Jesus Army and London and Birmingham Churches of Christ present a further variation on the theme of 'New' Religious Movements and 'traditional' religions. As we have seen, these groups are outside the mainstream of Christianity and even outside the mainstream of the evangelical tradition which they claim to represent. On these grounds they may well be classified as New Religious Movements. Their position in relation to Christianity in general and evangelical Christianity in particular is not, however, therefore without ambiguity. On the contrary, comparison of these movements with other groups raises complex questions concerning the criteria to be used in defining a given group as within or without the Christian and evangelical traditions. Thus, if the Jesus Fellowship, Jesus Army and London and Birmingham Churches of Christ are compared with the Children of God and their distinctively promiscuous lifestyle and unorthodox beliefs, the former groups then look very much like an extremely conservative version of evangelicalism whilst the latter clearly stand outside the mainstream. Similarly, if the former groups are then compared with the Restorationist or House Church movement, then although there are differences between them it is possible to argue that the Jesus Fellowship, the London and Birmingham Churches of Christ and the Restorationists are all closer in ethos to each other than any of them are to the 'mainstream' evangelicalism which is to be found in the 'traditional' Protestant denominations. Thus, much of the most significant criticism of the Restorationist/House Church movement has come from other charismatics and evangelicals who see it as, variously, divisive, authoritarian, doctrinally deviant or deluded (Walker, 1988, ch.13).

It would be unusual – though not without precedent (Clarke, 1987, p.15; Walker, 1983) – to describe Restorationism as a New Religious Movement: indeed it is customarily included within the boundaries of evangelicalism and linked to the charismatic movement in general (Bebbington, 1989, ch.7). To an outsider, however, the inclusion of the Restorationists but the exclusion of the Jesus Fellowship and other groups from the evangelical spectrum looks more like a process of internal dispute over doctrinal details within a single religious tradition than the basis of a fundamental division between a traditional religion and a New Religious Movement. Indeed, consideration of the sequence 'mainstream evangelicalism → charismatic movement → Restorationists → Jesus Fellowship' raises in acute form the evangelical version of a dilemma which increasingly affected all religious groups in modern Britain; namely, 'how far can you go?', and on what grounds do you decide?[8]

The point here is not to provide a definitive way of identifying these movements – indeed, there is unlikely to be a definitive solution, since the criteria for such definitions are matters of ongoing debate. The significant point is that it would be a mistake to suppose that, in the kaleidoscope of religion in modern Britain, there is a clear and simple division between 'traditional religions' and 'New Religious Movements'. At best, there is a clear distinction between the 'mainstream' of the traditional religions and

---

[8] For the ways in which this dilemma affected the various traditional Christian denominations in the period between 1945 and the early 1990s, see Essay 1 in this volume.

the overall body of New Religious Movements. At the more conventional end of the spectrum of New Religious Movements, however, and at the more unconventional end of the traditional religions, the distinction between the two groups becomes ambiguous to say the least – a point to which we shall return in a moment.

There remains the other question of definition, however; namely, are the so-called 'New Religious Movements' really religious at all? Thus it may be objected that some New Religious Movements – especially those within the psychotherapeutic, human-potential, 'self-religions' area – are not appropriately regarded as religions, but rather as secular and psychological alternatives to religion. 'Religion', on this view, would imply and require the inclusion of some more specifically supernatural or spiritual dimension. Moreover, there is also the intriguing fact that some of the 'New Religious Movements' (such as Transcendental Meditation or Rajneeshism) explicitly *deny* that they are religions, claiming to transcend or supercede religion, despite the fact that their organizations would qualify as religions under most definitions of the term (Barker, 1989a, p.146).

These are, of course, significant questions of definition, and it is important that scholars should debate the meaning and limits of the term 'religion' – indeed, a failure ever to address this would result in the term losing all coherence and genuine significance.[9] In the present context, however, we may usefully adopt the working definition offered by Eileen Barker that movements may be regarded as religious if they either

> offer a religious or philosophical world-view, or they claim to provide the means by which some higher goal such as transcendent knowledge, spiritual enlightenment, self-realisation or 'true' development may be obtained. The term is, thus, used to cover groups that might provide their members with ultimate answers to fundamental questions (such as the meaning of life or one's place in the nature of things).
>
> (Barker, 1989a, p.145)

The virtue of this definition is that it enables us to avoid undue narrowing of our focus whilst also exploring within the space available a rich variety of questions about the wider significance of the enormous range of so-called 'New Religious Movements' present in recent and contemporary Britain.

There is, however, a further dimension to the debate over what genuinely constitutes a New 'Religious' Movement. Just as there are groups which, although themselves denying that they are 'religious',

---

[9]   Thus, for example, there is a brief discussion of this in the final essay in this volume.

would qualify as such under most definitions of the term, so also and conversely there are other groups – perhaps most notoriously ISKCON, the Unification Church and Scientology – that would also qualify as religions by most definitions but are fiercely denied such status by opponents, and even on occasion by the British courts and political establishment. This takes us into one of the most hotly disputed aspects of the entire phenomenon of New Religious Movements.

Outside the ranks of those personally attracted to one or other of the New Religious Movements and of professionally interested observers such as historians and sociologists, the characteristic perception of such movements was, until the later 1980s and perhaps even after that, overwhelmingly negative. New Religious Movements were characteristically viewed as, at best, peculiar, odd and eccentric, and at worst as malign, anti-social or evil. Specific groups were accused – often indiscriminately and without regard for distinctions between individual movements, to say nothing of whether the accusations were true in themselves – of a variety of anti-social activities including 'brainwashing' converts, causing mental ill health and breakdowns among converts, breaking up families and practising a variety of fraudulent or immoral activities, including financial unscrupulousness, blackmail and sexual promiscuity. Similarly, specific movements such as Scientology and TM have been accused of being in reality business organizations pretending to be religions, and the Unification Church has been accused of seeking the privileges of a religion whilst pursuing political ends. Moreover, in addition to such specific examples of negative stereotyping, New Religious Movements (both individually and as a whole) tended to be dismissed pejoratively as 'cults', 'spiritual counterfeits', part of the 'pathology of religion', or mere social phenomena. At all events, according to such views, New Religious Movements were *not* to be regarded as *genuinely* religious (Barker, 1984a, ch.5; 1989a, chs 2 and 5; 1989b; Beckford, 1983a and b; Chryssides, 1987; Knott, 1986, ch.4).

The origins of such opposition were both various and complex in their inter-relationships. Relatives of converts – and especially parents in the case of young converts – frequently complained of the totality of the commitment of the converts after their conversion experience, and were shocked and concerned by the extent to which often securely middle-class converts proved willing to sacrifice time, money and future career prospects. Specifically 'anti-cult' pressure groups were also formed both to lobby publicly against New Religious Movements and to provide help in 'rescuing' converts, sometimes by kidnapping converts and 'deprogramming' them to overcome their 'brainwashing'. Such 'anti-cult' organizations included both specifically evangelical Christian groups such as the Deo Gloria Trust and family- and parent-orientated groups such as FAIR (Family Action Information and Rescue). The press – and especially the tabloid press – were also prominent in attacking New Religious Movements, the relationship between the anti-cult movement and the press often amounting to one of mutual support. (Barker, 1989a, pp.39–42 and 1989b, pp.186–7, 199–200; Beckford, 1983a, pp.56–8; Beckford and Cole, 1988, pp.209–20; Knott, 1986, pp.75–6; Wilson, 1989b, p.178).

The effectiveness of such opposition should not be doubted. Quite apart from the creation of a framework of public opinion in which the predominant popular view of New Religious Movements was that they were not merely odd but probably undesirable in one way or another, there were also notable cases of New Religious Movements being subjected to fierce attacks in Parliament (where Parliamentary privilege prevented legal action against unsubstantiated accusations) and of decisions against them in the courts, sometimes apparently involving distinctly theological criteria within the process of judgement. In Britain the most famous Parliamentary and court cases involved Scientology and the Unification Church (Barker, 1989b, pp.192–202). In 1984, moreover, the Committee on Youth, Culture, Education, Information and Sport of the European Parliament completed a *Report on the activity of certain new religious movements within the European Community*. The initial report had been prompted by complaints to the European Parliament by 'anti-cult' organizations, including British ones. The final resolution adopted by the Parliament called for

a common approach by the Member States of the European Community towards various infringements of the law by *new organizations operating under the protection afforded to religious bodies* [my italics].

(quoted in Chryssides, 1987, p.26)

Although the resolution was not binding on European governments, both its passing and its significantly sceptical wording were, it has been observed, symbolic victories for the active opponents of New Religious Movements (Barker, 1989b, pp.196–7; Chryssides, 1987, p.26; Knott, 1986, p.81). The moral implications of this situation were considerable and form the theme of the next section of this essay.

3 New Religious Movements and the limits of pluralism

As the conclusion of the previous section of this essay demonstrated, the existence and experience of a number of the New Religious Movements present in modern Britain raise significant issues about the nature and limits of religious tolerance and pluralism in modern British society. There are at least three aspects of this situation which we should note in particular.

First, there is the specifically constitutional and legal dimension. As we have seen, prompted by the campaigning of groups actively opposed to particular New Religious Movements, there have been a number of significant interventions in Parliament and decisions in the courts that suggest that New Religious Movements do not enjoy even that degree of official tolerance that is generally afforded to religious groups in modern Britain. The law, it has been argued, although claiming to be neutral in matters of religion, in practice favours (and perhaps given past history and current legislation *must* favour) what is still the established church in particular and still the majority religious tradition, namely Christianity, in general (Wilson, 1989). Beyond this, it has been argued, it is also possible to perceive on the part of the courts a decreasing degree of favour and an increasing degree of discrimination as one moves 'from' Christianity 'via' Judaism with its now long established position in British society, 'through' Sikhism, Islam and Hinduism, and 'out' to New Religious Movements (Barker, 1984 and 1989b). Viewed in this way, the legal debates and controversies over aspects of the behaviour and nature of New Religious Movements appear as but one more element in a much wider set of debates and controversies over such matters as the right of Sikhs to dissent from legislation concerning protective headgear, the claims of religious groups in respect of religious education, the nature and implications of the law on blasphemy and the concept of free speech, and the implications of all these issues for the concept of a plural society.[10]

If New Religious Movements thus focus issues of equality and discrimination in matters of religion in modern Britain, it is nevertheless important to keep matters in perspective. Thus, as Eileen Barker has insisted, despite the adverse decisions of the courts and the clearly generally unfavourable view of New Religious Movements within the British parliamentary and legal establishment, such religious groups nevertheless enjoy, by the standards of history, considerable freedom and protection. If New Religious Movements in Britain are discriminated against, it is in reality a most 'tolerant discrimination'. It is, as Barker has succinctly put it, not even a question of the establishment seeking to uphold a traditional version of British Protestantism as 'the real truth'. Rather, the basic truth of such a religious position is taken for granted and it is assumed

> that it is the sort of religion that any right-thinking citizen would want to guide his spiritual and, if necessary, his secular life. But

---

[10] On Sikh and Islamic perspectives on these issues, see also Essays 5 and 3 in this volume and Essays 2–5 in Volume II. For excellent surveys, from a variety of religious perspectives, of the range of issues raised by the debates over blasphemy, free speech and pluralism see Commission for Racial Equality, 1989a, b and c.

this is not a forcefully held belief, high in the consciousness of any
but a tiny minority of Britons. It is, rather, an absent-mindedly
taken-for-granted acceptance of what is right and proper.

(Barker, 1984b, p.41)

From the point of view of both the British political and social establishment
and the religiously lukewarm yet residually Protestant majority of the
British population, New Religious Movements challenged such absent-
mindedly taken-for-granted rightness and propriety. They did so, moreover, not merely because their beliefs were different from traditional
British Protestantism, but also because of the passionate intensity and
commitment with which converts to New Religious Movements tended to
hold their beliefs. The degree of whole-hearted life-changing commitment
displayed by many of the followers of New Religious Movements was
strikingly at odds with the restrained religiosity characteristic of the
majority of even the religiously active portion of the population in modern
Britain – hence the widespread assumption that converts must have been
in some way coerced, brainwashed, mentally unbalanced, or plain duped.

Such assumptions – together with consequent attempts to
'deprogramme' converts, to dismiss New Religious Movements as simply
'irrational' or 'incomprehensible' and to deny that New Religious Movements were genuinely religious – raised potentially acute questions concerning what has aptly been called 'the right to be religious' (Chryssides,
1987). Among the mainstream Christian churches there were signs in the
1980s that the importance of this issue was recognized. Thus in 1984 when
the Report on the activity of New Religious Movements was presented to
the European Parliament, the British Council of Churches Committee for
Relations with People of Other Faiths opposed the proposals made, perceiving them to constitute a threat to religious liberty. The Committee also
subsequently included New Religious Movements within its overall programme of dialogue with other religious traditions. This prompted fierce
opposition from some other Christians, although there were also examples
of positive responses to such proposals for dialogue (Barker, 1989b,
pp.188–9; Chryssides, 1987, pp.28–31; Hooker and Lamb, 1986, pp.135–42;
Weller, 1990, p.260).

There remains, however, no little irony in the fact that, whilst such
statements of principle came from the official representatives of mainstream Christian dialogue with other faiths, many of those who most
ardently opposed the alleged irrationality and social undesirability of New
Religious Movements were themselves evangelical Christians of an
explicitly conservative kind. The irony of this lies in the fact that, in terms of
the call for whole-hearted and life-changing commitment, in terms of the
intensity of the conversion experience undergone, and in some cases even
in terms of the alleged irrationalism, mental or psychological damage, or

alleged authoritarianism involved, the more conservative and uncompromising versions of evangelical or charismatic Christianity in late twentieth-century Britain often looked remarkably similar to the New Religious Movements to which they were so opposed.

The *theological* differences between evangelical and charismatic Christians on the one hand and devotees of New Religious Movements on the other were, of course, usually decisive (although one must recall that, as we have seen, there was also an ambiguous area occupied by such groups as the Jesus Fellowship where even the theological differences were not so great). But, to the outside observer committed to neither group, the similarities could be as striking as the differences. Thus, to the outsider, it was not necessarily clear that the alleged 'irrationalism' or 'incomprehensibility' of the beliefs of New Religious Movements was any greater or more 'peculiar' than some varieties of evangelical or charismatic belief in, for example, possession by evil spirits and exorcism, speaking in tongues, or claims of miraculous healing. Certainly, the more extreme end of the evangelical and charismatic spectrum was closer in certain specific respects and in general ethos and style to the world of New Religious Movements than it was to the mainstream Christian tradition in modern Britain.[11] Similarly, critics of charismatic Christianity and of the Restorationist and House Church Movements complained of the psychological damage that might be attributed to the influence of these groups and of their excessively divisive, secretive and authoritarian tendencies – a criticism also levelled against the extremely conservative Roman Catholic organization Opus Dei, a movement which has explicitly been compared with New Religious Movements in this respect. (Davis 1985, p.42; McCrickard, 1991; Martin, 1984, pp.61–70; Mullen, 1984; Noakes, 1984; Walker, 1984, ch.13; Walsh, 1989).

---

[11] To make this point is not, of course, to say anything about the actual rationality and comprehensibility or otherwise of the beliefs of either New Religious Movements or evangelical or charismatic Christianity. Just what constitutes a 'rational' or 'irrational' position in such matters is itself open to debate. The point, however, is that phenomenologically speaking the differences between the two broad types of belief are often less striking than their similarities. Specific examples of this include the collection of essays entitled *What is the New Age?* published by four evangelical Christians (Cole et al., 1990) and two further booklets (Seddon, 1990; Watson, 1991) offering evangelical assessments of the New Age phenomenon. For the reader who is neither an advocate of New Age spirituality nor an evangelical Christian, one of the most significant aspects of the essays and booklets is the way in which, even as they fiercely reject New Age spiritualities and claims, the authors nevertheless regard such beliefs as spiritual rivals to Christianity (and not merely as 'absurd') and advocate an evangelical Christian alternative which is no less supernaturalist or more 'rational' than the New Age beliefs with which they engage.

Consideration of recent attitudes to New Religious Movements in British society thus suggests that such movements are not necessarily so sharply and decisively differentiated from other religious groups as one might suppose. The treatment of New Religious Movements in the press, moreover, confirms this view. The British press, as already noted, tends to be generally negative, frequently hostile and characteristically unable to extend beyond a blatently stereotypical view in its approach to such groups. New Religious Movements, however, are not alone among the religious traditions of modern Britain in thus being negatively stereotyped by the press. One of the issues to emerge from the Rushdie affair was precisely the question of press and broadcast coverage of the controversy and the extent to which Islam was portrayed both negatively and stereo-typically (Cottle, 1991; Neilson, 1992, pp.161–2; Parekh, 1989). Although the two cases are of course importantly different, nevertheless the analogy is potentially significant. When confronted with religious commitment which was not only different from the predominant religious ethos of modern Britain but also of manifestly greater intensity, the press was on the whole apparently unable (and perhaps unwilling) to resist both sensationalism and prejudice.

Taken together, the similarities between New Religious Movements and the more extreme ends of the spectrum of British Christianity and the similarities between press treatment of New Religious Movements and of Islam prompt two further questions. First, how exactly should New Religious Movements be located within the development of religion in Britain since 1945? And second, what was their significance within British religious life by the end of our period? These questions form the basis of the final section of this essay.

4 Locating the phenomenon

What, then, may be said about the significance of the emergence and development of New Religious Movements in assessing the place of religion in modern Britain? We may usefully address this overall question from two directions. First, we may profitably consider the basic chronology and apparent stages in the growth of such New Religious Movements and explore the possible relevance of this chronology to broader questions of periodization within the religious history of Britain since the Second World War. Second, we may explore how far and in what ways the emergence of New Religious Movements in Britain since 1945 may be significant for debates over the alleged secularization or continued religiousness of modern British society.

As in secular matters, so also in religion, the upheaval and turmoil of the 1960s did not simply spring from nowhere. The origins of the 1960s can be identified in the 1950s. Thus, for example, whilst the mainstream Christian churches in the 1950s remained predominantly secure and confident in their attitudes, yet in matters such as liturgy, ecumenism and pastoral reorganization they had already begun to explore ideas which were subsequently to leap dramatically to the centre of their life in the next decade.[12] Similarly, the youth and counter-cultures of the 1960s can also be seen to have their origins – or at least precursors – in the teenage and pop cultures, the political radicalism of CND and the Aldermaston marches, and the emerging challenges to conventional sexual morality of the 1950s (Barker, 1983, pp.36–8; Leech, 1976, ch.1). The presence of New Religious Movements may likewise be identified in the 1950s and, indeed, before that (Knott, 1988b, pp.158–9).

On the other hand, however, it is also clear that in the development of New Religious Movements it was the 1960s that proved the crucial watershed and catalyst. For New Religious Movements (as also for the mainstream Christian churches), the 1960s proved to be a decade after which things were never quite the same again. Despite the widespread talk of secularization, 'man come of age' and 'the death of God', the 1960s, it has been observed, witnessed not the final decline of religion in the West but 'the quite unanticipated rise of an exotic new range of new religious and quasi-religious movements' (Wallis, 1978, p.5). The rise to public prominence of New Religious Movements in general was part and parcel of the explosion of new and alternative lifestyles and beliefs which began in the 1960s. The heady mixture of psychedelic experiment, exploration of the self, political and social protest and simultaneous questioning of authority and searching for alternative moralities was fertile ground for the emergence of new religious styles and movements– be they centred on mystical, psychotherapeutic, environmentalist or ancient and esoteric sources. And yet the relationship between the 1960s and the emergence and growth of New Religious Movements is not a simple one.

It is often assumed – not least by critics of the perceived 'permissiveness' and 'moral laxity' of the period – that the social and cultural revolution of the 1960s was *simply* a matter of counter-cultural protest and the overthrow of traditional authority. This, however, is a distortion of the complexity of that decade and its significance. Certainly, the degree of 'permissiveness' increased and *traditional* moral assumptions were radically questioned. But the 1960s also produced their share of reactions against 'permissiveness', especially amongst groups which adopted the intensely communal, affective and emotionally and psychologically

---

[12] For an account of this, see Essay 1 in this volume, sections 2 and 3.

expressive ethos of the 1960s whilst affirming a morally (and often theologically) conservative stance. Thus, for example, the range of attitudes encompassed by New Religious Movements included not only the generally 'permissive' ethos of hippy and 'Aquarian' mysticisms and spiritualities, but also the austere sexual moralities of ISKCON and the Unification Church. Similarly, within the Christian tradition, the 1960s and early 1970s saw not only the questioning of traditional Christian sexual ethics and the upsurge of interest in pop-culture versions of Jesus in musicals like *Jesus Christ Superstar* and *Godspell*, but also the rise of the intensely expressive but morally and theologically conservative charismatic movement and the brief but significant prominence of the Nationwide Festival of Light.[13]

If, instead of a simplistic image of 'a decade of permissiveness', the upheaval of the 1960s is recognized to be a complex breakdown of the predominance of traditional values and their replacement by an increasingly dramatic plurality of available lifestyles, outlooks and moralities, then it is possible to see the rise of *both* New Religious Movements *and* the charismatic movement within Christianity as part of a much broader process of pluralization and protest against apparently staid and static conventionality. It is thus once again significant that New Religious Movements, far from being simply a peripheral oddity within the spectrum of religious life in modern Britain, may be seen as part of a more general challenge to Britain's conventional religious ethos and tradition.

If the enormous proliferation and rise to prominence of New Religious Movements, together with a good deal of charismatic and charismatic-influenced Christianity, was thus very much a legacy of the 1960s, is it also possible to discern distinct stages in their subsequent post-1960s development? Answers to this question must necessarily be more tentative, but certain trends appear to be identifiable. Although it was the 1960s that provided the crucial catalyst in the emergence and proliferation of New Religious Movements, it was probably the 1970s that witnessed the peak of their prominence – at least as far as the more formal and organized groups such as ISKCON, Rajneeshism or the Unification Church were concerned. In the 1980s patterns of growth became more ambiguous. Many of the more prominent New Religious Movements appeared to pass at least a temporary peak in membership and perhaps even to begin to show signs of decline, although it also remained possible to read the complex statistics involved as evidence of a much slower but more steady pattern of growth (Clarke, 1987).

[13] For the view that the charismatic movement and the activities of groups such as the Festival of Light may legitimately be interpreted as part of the 'sixties' phenomenon, see also Barker, 1983, pp.39–40; Bebbington, 1989, pp.232–5 and 240–8; and Leech, 1976, ch.7. See also Essay 1 in this volume and Essay 7 in Volume II.

On the other hand, the 1980s also saw a massive increase in the more diffuse spiritualities and mysticisms at the New Age and environmentalist end of the spectrum of New Religious Movements. In respect of the environmentalist dimension to this question, there is sociological evidence for the possibility that in the late twentieth century a generational shift is in process within British religious attitudes, a major part of which is an increasing tendency among the young to reject even nominal Christian belief whilst simultaneously taking environmentally- and ecologically-coloured questions about the meaning of existence seriously (Davie, 1990b, pp.461–2). As for the New Age phenomenon, one need only examine the shelves of most ordinary bookshops to discover evidence for the degree of interest in such matters: in the course of the 1980s the appearance of whole shelves and sections devoted to 'New Age', 'Astrological and Occult' or 'Aquarian' subjects became the rule rather than the exception. One may reflect, moreover, that in the world of commercial bookselling the presence in the shops of large numbers of books on such subjects points to the fact that they sell well enough to justify their shelf space. Nor should it be overlooked that this upsurge in diffuse and freewheeling New Age religiosity was in many ways rooted in – or perhaps more accurately was a mutation or reincarnation of – the counter-cultural ethos of the 1960s (Perry, 1992, p.14; Walker, 1992, p.51). Even more diverse and eclectic in their combinations of ideas, more self-consciously pagan and occult, now often significantly and distinctively feminist, and most certainly much more 'Green' and ecological in orientation, the New Age spiritualities of the late 1980s and early 1990s were evidence of the enduring nature of the underlying transformation and expansion of religious sensibilities that had occured some twenty to twenty-five years earlier.

What, finally, may be said of the possible significance of the emergence of the various New Religious Movements for debate over the alleged secularization or continued religiousness of modern British society as a whole? We have seen that they have generated a great deal of interest, both from scholars and also from the public, the media, and other religious bodies, as well as from government and the courts. Such interest has included much opposition and hostility. Despite the furore to which New Religious Movements have often given rise, however, they have in fact attracted only very small numbers of fully committed members and have also experienced a high subsequent drop-out rate among converts.[14]

On the other hand, despite the small numbers of fully-committed converts, interest in the various movements has included a substantial

---

[14] It is, incidentally, worth pondering the significance of the high drop-out rate in relation to charges of 'brainwashing': the evidence concerning drop-out rates suggests that any 'brainwashing' techniques that are deployed are not notable for their long-term effectiveness; on which, see Barker, 1983, p.43 and 1989a, pp.17–19.

number of people who have at least 'dabbled' in one (or sometimes several) of the New Religious Movements. Even more significantly, the diffused influence of New Religious Movements in general – and of an eclectic mixture of psychotherapies, esoteric lore and New Age mysticism in particular – has extended even further into contemporary British life. At this outer edge, the penumbra of interest in New Religious Movements and New Age philosophies amounts to a significant – if also immensely confused and unsystematic – contribution to the 'pick and mix' outlook characteristic of a great deal of popular religiosity in modern and contemporary Britain.[15]

What, then, of the debate over the secularization or otherwise of modern British life and society? As with so many aspects of the debate about secularization, the significance of New Religious Movements may be read in strikingly different ways. On the one hand they may be regarded as part of the fragmentation and privatization of belief which, some scholars argue, are clear symptoms of an increasingly secularized society. On the other hand, however, the whole complex, confused and yet increasingly substantial outpouring of New Religious Movements and mysticisms may also be read as an indication that, whatever *has* happened to the traditional religious allegiances of Britain in recent decades, they have not been replaced by a simple secularity. It would, of course, be possible to argue that a genuinely 'religious' society would be one in which religion, public life and social mores were more or less thoroughly integrated, and that, by definition therefore, a fragmented, pluralized and privatized religious milieu was, in comparison, secularized. It is the contention of the present essay, however, that such an argument would both imply an overly narrow definition of 'religion' and underestimate the genuine religiousness of the various New Religious Movements, philosophies and mysticisms present in recent and contemporary Britain.

Certainly in the period since the Second World War British life has become, in official terms, more secular in the sense that religion has tended, on the whole, to occupy a less prominent place in political life, and in the sense that Britain has become increasingly religiously pluralist, thus continuing a long-established trend towards the removal of religion from the public to the private sphere. There are, of course, exceptions even to this generalization. Thus this essay has argued that the treatment of New Religious Movements in the courts suggests that such privatization and pluralism is less complete than might commonly be supposed. Similarly we have noted that in 'establishment' circles, a *de facto* assumption of what

---

[15] The idea of such a 'pick and mix' popular religiosity may usefully be compared with the notion of the emergence of a 'supermarket of faiths' in modern religiously-plural Britain, for which see Volume 2, Essay 2.

is religiously 'proper' continues to exercise considerable influence and that certain issues – such as the law on blasphemy – continue to arouse controversy over the perceived inequality before the law of religions other than Christianity.

Such provisos notwithstanding, however, it was broadly true that by the late 1980s and early 1990s Britain had become, at an official and public level, a significantly less religious and certainly more pluralist society than it had been in 1945. Equally certainly, it had also become much more fragmented and diversified within its continuing, though increasingly privatised, religious life. Such fragmentation and diversification were clearly observable even within what were still the numerically predominant traditional Christian churches and denominations.[16] It was still more evident, however, beyond the traditional churches and among the now only peripherally or residually Christian section of the population which, although not self-consciously secular or committedly atheist, was nonetheless not actively religious either.

There is good evidence, of more than one kind, that even within that 'not actively religious' section of the population the prevalent outlook was not one of simple, let alone systematic, secularity. Thus, not only did surveys continue to reveal ongoing, if (by traditional Christian standards) unorthodox, religious belief, but in addition research also suggested that within British society there continued to be a very widespread, though substantially unexpressed and undisclosed, incidence of actual experience of a religious or transcendent kind (Hay, 1987 and 1990). And, as we have seen, there is evidence of the emergence of an environmentally-coloured religiousness particularly among the young. It is, surely, within this broad context that one must locate and answer the question of the significance of New Religious Movements and New Age spiritualities for the debate about the secularity or continuing religiousness of modern British society.

When thus located, it is surely the case that the whole phenomenon of New Religious Movements– taken in their widest sense and allowing for the collectively diffused influence of their ideas – suggests that British society is very far from being thoroughly secularized. Religiously fragmented, confused and eclectic, yes; simply or straightforwardly secular, no. Arguably, along with the evidence of continuing but largely unexpressed religious experience, the interest in New Religious Movements and alternative spiritualities in Britain in the last two or three decades is symptomatic of a widespread sense of religious search and quest within modern British society. For students of religion in contemporary Britain, it may well be that, as the last decade of the twentieth century heads towards the first decade of the twenty-first, one of the most interesting questions to

---

[16]   For which process, see Essay 1 in this volume.

watch will be how far the traditional Christian denominations of Britain can successfully address such diffuse religious searching and how far they lose ground to the eclectic universe of new religious options and alternatives.[17]

Finally, apart from the various alternative spiritualities and mysticisms of the New Age and environmentalist movements, what of the prospects of the more formally organized New Religious Movements such as the Unification Church, ISKCON, TM and Scientology? Of such groups, all that the historian may appropriately say at this point is that – for the reasons set out in this essay – they have represented a significant, if minority, element within the religious life of Britain in the last quarter of the twentieth century. Beyond that, as other scholars in this field have also pointed out, their future prospects cannot be predicted (Chryssides, 1987, p.31; Knott, 1988b, p.171). In another fifty years or so, they may have vanished from the scene and become little more than a late twentieth-century footnote in the history of religion. Or they may survive to become more prominent religious options in the twenty-first century. Either way, they are not without interest and deserve, at the very least, to be studied as genuine religious phenomena.

[17] And it will be similarly interesting to see how, within the traditional Christian churches, the balance develops between the more conventional strands of these versions of the Christian faith and the more assertively evangelical and charismatic groups within their ranks.

Bibliography

ANNETT, S. (ed.) (1976) *The Many Ways of Being*, Abacus, London.

BADHAM, P. (ed.) (1989) *Religion, State, and Society in Modern Britain*, Edwin Mellen Press, Lampeter.

BARKER, E. (1983) 'New Religious Movements in Britain: the context and the membership', *Social Compass*, 30, pp.33–48.

(1984a) *The Making of a Moonie: choice or brainwashing?*, Blackwell, Oxford.

(1984b) 'The British Right to Discriminate', *New Society*, 21, pp.35–41.

(1987) 'New Religious Movements and Political Orders', Pamphlet Library No 15, Centre for the Study of Religion and Society, University of Kent.

(1989a) *New Religious Movements: a practical introduction*, HMSO, London.

(1989b) 'Tolerant Discrimination: Church, State and the New Religions' in Badham (ed.).

BEBBINGTON, D. (1989) *Evangelicalism in Modern Britain: a history from the 1730s to the 1980s*, Unwin Hyman, London.

BECKFORD, J. (1983a) 'The public response to new religious movements in Britain', *Social Compass*, 30, pp.49–62.

(1983b) '"Brainwashing" and "Deprogramming" in Britain: the social sources of anti-cult sentiment' in Bromley, D. and Richardson, J. (eds) *The Brainwashing/Deprogramming Controversy: sociological, psychological, legal and historical perspectives*, Edwin Mellen Press, New York and Toronto.

BECKFORD, J. and COLE, M. (1988) 'British and American Responses to New Religious Movements', *Bulletin of the John Rylands University Library of Manchester*, 70, pp.209–24 (special edition on Sects and New Religious Movements).

BLOOM, W. (1990) *Sacred Times: a new approach to festivals*, Findhorn.

(ed.) (1991) *The New Age: an anthology of essential writings*, Rider, London.

CAREY, S. (1983) 'The Hare Krishna movement and Hindus in Britain', *New Community*, 10, pp.477–86.

(1987) 'The Indianization of the Hare Krishna movement in Britain' in Burghart, R. (ed.) *Hinduism in Great Britain: the perpetuation of religion in an alien cultural milieu*, Tavistock, London.

CHRYSSIDES, G. (1987) 'The Right to be Religious', *The Modern Churchman*, 29 (New Series), pp.25–33.

CLARE, A. and THOMPSON, S. (1981) *Let's Talk About Me: a critical examination of the new psychotherapies*, BBC, London.

CLARKE, P. (ed.) (1987) *The New Evangelists: recruitment methods and aims of New Religious Movements*, Ethnographica, London.

COLE, M. et al. (1990) *What is the New Age?*, Hodder and Stoughton, London.

COMMISSION FOR RACIAL EQUALITY (1989a) *Law, Blasphemy and the Multi-Faith Society*, The Commission for Racial Equality and the Inter-Faith Network of the United Kingdom.

(1989b) *Free Speech*, The Commission for Racial Equality, United Kingdom.

(1989c) *Britain: A Plural Society*, The Commission for Racial Equality, United Kingdom.

COTTLE, S. (1991) 'Reporting the Rushdie affair: a case study in the orchestration of public opinion', *Race and Class*, 32, pp.45–64.

DAVIE, G. (1990a) '"An ordinary God": the paradox of religion in contemporary Britain', *The British Journal of Sociology*, 41, pp.395–421.

(1990b) 'Believing without Belonging: is this the future of religion in Britain?', *Social Compass*, 37, pp.455–69.

DAVIS, R. (1985) 'Bibliography: New Religious Movements', *The Modern Churchman*, 27 (New Series), pp.41–6.

GREEN, D. (1989) 'Buddhism in Britain: "Skilful Means" or Selling Out?' in Badham (ed.).

HAY, D. (1987) *Exploring Inner Space: scientists and religious experience*, Mowbray, London.

(1990) *Religious Experience Today: studying the facts*, Mowbray, London.

HEELAS, P. (1982) 'Californian Self Religions and Socializing the Subjective' in Barker, E. (ed.) *New Religious Movements: a perspective for understanding society*, Edwin Mellen Press, New York and Toronto.

(1985) 'New Religious Movements in Perspective', *Religion*, 15, pp.81–97.

(1987) 'Exegesis: methods and aims' in Clarke (ed.).

(1991) 'Cults for Capitalism? Self Religions, Magic, and the Empowerment of Business' in Gee, P. and Fulton, J. (eds) *Religion and Power Decline and Growth*, British Sociological Association Sociology of Religion Study Group.

(1992) 'The Sacralization of the Self and New Age Capitalism' in Abercrombie, N. and Warde, A. (eds) *Social Change in Contemporary Britain*, Polity Press, Cambridge.

HOOKER, R. and LAMB, C. (1986) *Love the Stranger: ministry in multi-faith areas*, SPCK, London.

HORNSBY-SMITH, M. (1989) *The Changing Parish: a study of parishes, priests and parishioners after Vatican II*, Routledge, London.

KNOTT, K. (1986) *My Sweet Lord: the Hare Krishna movement*, The Aquarian Press, Wellingborough.

(1988a) 'Other Major Religious Traditions' in Thomas, T. (ed.) *The British: their religious beliefs and practices 1800–1986*, Routledge, London.

(1988b) 'New Religious Movements' in Thomas, T. (ed.) *The British: their religious beliefs and practices 1800–1986*, Routledge, London.

LEECH, K. (1976) *Youthquake: spirituality and the growth of the counter-culture*, Abacus, London.

LUHRMANN, T. (1989) *Persuasions of the Witch's Craft: ritual magic in contemporary England*, Blackwell, Oxford.

MARTIN, D. (1984) 'The Political Oeconomy of the Holy Ghost' in Martin and Mullen (eds).

MARTIN, D. amd MULLEN, P. (eds) (1984) *Strange Gifts? a guide to charismatic renewal*, Blackwell, Oxford.

MCCRICKARD, J. (1991) 'Born-Again Moon: fundamentalism in Christianity and the Feminist Spirituality Movement', *Feminist Review*, 37, pp.59–67.

MORGAN, P. (1987) 'Methods and Aims of Evangelisation and Conversion in Buddhism, with particular reference to Nichiren Shoshu Soku Gakkai' in Clarke (ed.).

MULLEN, P. (1984) 'Confusion Worse Confounded' in Martin and Mullen (eds).

NEILSEN, J.S. (1992) *Muslims in Western Europe*, Edinburgh University Press, Edinburgh.

NOAKES, R. (1984) 'The Instinct of the Herd' in Martin and Mullen (eds).

PAREKH, B. (1989) 'The Rushdie Affair and the British Press: some salutary lessons' in Commission for Racial Equality, 1989b.

PERRY, M. (1992) *Gods Within: a critical guide to the New Age*, SPCK, London.

RATNAPRABBA, D. (1987) 'A Re-emergence of Buddhism: the case of the Friends of the Western Buddhist Order' in Clarke (ed.).

ROMARHEIM, A. (1988) 'The Aquarian Christ', *Bulletin of the John Rylands University Library of Manchester*, 70, pp.197–208 (special edition on Sects and New Religious Movements).

SEDDON, P. (1990) *The New Age: an assessment*, Grove Books, Nottingham.

THOMPSON, J. and HEELAS, P. (1986) *The Way of the Heart: the Rajneesh movement*, The Aquarian Press, Wellingborough.

WALKER, A. (1983) 'Pentecostal Power: the "Charismatic Renewal Movement" and the politics of Pentecostal experience' in Barker, E. (ed.) *Of Gods and Men: New Religious Movements in the West*, Mercer University Press, Macon GA.

(1988) *Restoring the Kingdom: The Radical Christianity of the House Church Movement*, Hodder and Stoughton, London.

(1992) 'Sectarian Reactions: pluralism and the privatization of religion' in Willmer, H. (ed.) *2020 Visions: the futures of Christianity in Britain*, SPCK, London.

WALLIS, R. (1976) *The Road to Total Freedom: a sociological analysis of Scientology*, Heinemann, London.

(1978) 'The Rebirth of the Gods?: Reflections on the New Religions in the West', inaugural lecture, Queen's University of Belfast, Belfast.

(1981) 'Yesterday's Children: cultural and structural change in a New Religious Movement', in Wilson, B. (ed.) *The Social Impact of New Religious Movements*, Rose of Sharon Press, New York.

(1982) 'Charisma, Commitment and Control in a New Religious Movement' in Wallis, R. (ed.) *Millennialism and Charisma*, Queen's University of Belfast, Belfast.

(1984) *The Elementary Forms of the New Religious Life*, Routledge and Kegan Paul, London.

WALLIS, R. and BRUCE, S. (1989) 'Religion: the British contribution', *The British Journal of Sociology*, 40, pp.493–520.

WALSH, M. (1989) *The Secret World of Opus Dei*, Grafton Books, London.

WATSON, J. (1991) *A Guide to the New Age for Confused Christians*, Grove Books, London.

WELLER, P. (1990) 'Freedom and Witness in a Multi-Religious Society: a Baptist perspective (Part 1)', *Baptist Quarterly*, 33, pp.252–64.

WILSON, B. (1989a) 'Old Laws and New Religions', Pamphlet Library No 20, Centre for the Study of Religion and Society, University of Kent.

(1989b) 'Sects and Society in Tension' in Badham (ed.).

Both the above items by Wilson are reprinted, along with other essays relevant to this theme, in:

WILSON, B. (1990) *The Social Dimensions of Sectarianism: sects and New Religious Movements in contemporary society*, Oxford University Press, Oxford.

8

THE RELIGIONS OF THE SILENT MAJORITY

by John Wolffe

Parish priest and two parishioners. Reproduced by permission of *The Observer*. Photograph by Michael Peto.

'Britain', according to a *Times* headline in November 1989, was among the 'most godless nations in the Western World'. In support of this startling assertion the newspaper cited a recent comparative social attitudes survey indicating that 34 per cent of the sample professed to have 'no religion', a figure exceeded only in the Netherlands. The comparative point may of course be valid, but nevertheless the statistic can be viewed as a glass two-thirds full rather than a third empty. The fact that 66 per cent of the sample, even at the end of our period, were prepared to acknowledge at least some kind of religious affiliation might rather be interpreted as a sign of substantial continuing godliness. Certainly, as the article went on to point out, only 20 per cent of the population professed to attend religious worship regularly (at least once a month), but to deny the reality and quality of the religious life of the 46 per cent who apparently acknowledged a religious affiliation without regularly practising it would be to beg a whole host of questions (*The Times*, 6 November 1989).

Most of the essays in this book have been concerned with the activity of that substantial minority who regularly participated in religious observance. The size of that minority is itself a matter of debate. If the criterion of weekly attendance, more stringent than that reported by *The Times*, is applied, then the 1988 figure was only 11.9 per cent (Jowell, Witherspoon and Brook, 1988, p.29). This is a measure that had some consistency across the period under examination: in a 1954 Gallup poll 14 per cent stated that they had been to church on the previous Sunday (Gallup, 1976, pp.403–4). There was a noticeable decline between the 1950s and the 1980s – and it might be argued that the growth in non-Christian religions masked a greater falling off in Christian attendances – but no dramatic change. In the 1954 poll, 91 per cent of the sample professed to have a religion and 78 per cent to believe in some kind of God or life force (Gallup, 1976, pp.404–5). The latter figure had only declined to 73 per cent in 1984 according to a Harris poll (*The Times*, 28 May 1984). Thus, although problematic opinion poll figures must be interpreted cautiously, it seems that throughout the period between a half and two thirds of the British population held some kind of religious belief and identification without being regularly involved in religious organizations. This proportion may have declined slightly by the 1980s but it still remained very substantial. It is with this 'silent majority' that we are now concerned.

The subject-matter of this essay thus constitutes a religious 'tradition' in a significantly different sense from that employed in the earlier essays in this book. It provides an investigation of what has been termed 'general religion' as opposed to the forms of 'particular religion' discussed hitherto. These two categories have been defined in the following way:

> The particular religion has usually been identified with churches, synagogues, missionary movements, denominations, revivals,

and the like. General religion has been discussed under such categories as democratic faith, social religion … generalized religion, common faith … and now 'civil religion'.

(Jones and Richey, 1974, p.3)

The category of 'general religion' has been developed by scholars with particular reference to the United States, but it is also helpful in a British context. It provides a framework in which to develop the common-sense observation that institutional churches, gurdwaras, mosques, synagogues and temples have not by any means had a monopoly of broadly religious belief and 'God-language' since the Second World War. Indeed it might even be argued that at the very time that particular religion became more of a minority interest, general religion continued to influence the lives of a substantial majority of the population.

Before commencing this analysis it is desirable to note some of the difficulties inherent in evaluating non-institutional religion. The problem did not begin to attract serious academic attention until the 1960s and so apart from the 1954 Gallup poll already cited and a Mass Observation survey, *Puzzled People* (1947), there is very little relevant material from the first two decades of the period. In 1963, however, Thomas Luckmann in an influential essay, *The Invisible Religion*, attacked the widespread assumption 'that church and religion are identical' (Luckman, 1967, p.27), and called for much more far-reaching study of the place of religion in society. In the ensuing twenty years both sociologists and religious strategists showed a growing interest in non-institutional religion, itself an interesting trend in intellectual religious consciousness that generated a considerable amount of evidence and commentary in the 1970s and 1980s. However the chronological imbalance of the material makes it more than usually difficult to evaluate the nature and extent of changes.

Even where there is a good quantity of evidence, there are significant difficulties in assessing it. It is a frequent quip that surveys on sexual activity are likely to be distorted by the very fact that readiness to answer such a survey implies a lack of reticence that is not necessarily representative of the population. A similar point could be made in relation to religion, a subject which many appeared to find even more intimate and embarrassing than sex. There are also problems with the context and manner in which a survey is conducted and with the wording of questions, which make it very difficult to compare one set of results with another. For example, a survey commissioned by the Bible Society and conducted in autumn 1982 yielded a figure of only 7 per cent who had no religion compared with 31 per cent in a Social Attitudes survey conducted in spring 1983. The Bible Society survey was concerned entirely with religious matters whereas in the Social Attitudes survey these made up only a small part of a much larger questionnaire (Harrison, 1983, pp.27, 31; Jowell and Airey, 1984, p.195).

A survey conducted in Leeds, also in the autumn of 1982, indicates the effects of the wording of a question: when asked directly if they had a religion, 23 per cent of the sample said 'no', but when asked what they would put on a form which asked for their religion, only 9 per cent said they would write 'none' (Krarup, n.d., pp.25, 37). Some observers, notably David Clark, who lived in Staithes, North Yorkshire between 1975 and 1976, have used the technique of participant observation, but this has its own drawbacks in dependence on personal impressions and the fact that as a participant the observer can hardly avoid influencing in some way the environment being studied (Clark, 1982, pp.35–45). Accordingly it would be unwise to place too much stress on any single survey or investigation.

The apparent inconsistencies in the evidence can, alternatively, be interpreted as indications of subtlety and variety in non-institutional religion. It is inherently probable that considerable variations should exist, given the numbers of people under consideration and the almost infinite permutations of social class, educational achievement, age, geographical location and so on. This is the case even when, as will perforce be the case in this essay, we limit our view primarily to the majority white population. Consideration of ethnic minorities would further substantially increase the variety of the picture: 95 per cent of people of south Asian origin resident in the United Kingdom have identified themselves as Hindus, Muslims or Sikhs, but not all of these are directly associated with a place of worship (Knott and Toon, n.d., pp.5–6). For example, a person could be sincere in recitation of the *shahadah*, professing faith as a Muslim, but never attend public prayers, except perhaps at festivals, nor maintain the other pillars of Islam. Hinduism, relatively lacking in corporate worship, has been particularly subject to such ambivalences. By the 1980s, moreover, the diffusion of New Religious Movements and New Age spiritualities was adding yet further dimensions. Accordingly the reader must study the present essay in conjunction with the various material on the unofficial aspects of institutional religion that has appeared in previous essays of this book.[1]

Given the diversity of the material it is desirable to have some broad categories in mind before commencing more detailed analysis. Scholars have advanced various concepts, notably 'folk religion' and 'implicit religion' for describing the beliefs and practices of those who are not regular participants in public worship. While not necessarily denying the usefulness of these terms, I shall adopt the four categories of *conventional religion, civil religion, common religion* and *invisible religion*. By *conventional religion* is meant involvement with organized formal religious institutions and acceptance of their teachings. For people who are not regular

---

[1]   See particularly Essays 1, 4 and 7.

churchgoers evidence of this will be found both in general attitudes to the churches and in occasional participation in worship, whether at annual festivals such as Christmas and Easter, or in life cycle rituals, particularly christenings, marriages and funerals. *Civil religion* denotes the use of religious forms and language in public life, especially in the ceremonial associated with the monarchy. *Common religion* covers a wide variety of activities and beliefs relating to the supernatural, however people perceive it, but not to institutional religion. Some folk traditions and astrology, for example, come under this heading. Finally, *invisible religion* refers to those aspects of both individual and community life which do not have an explicit visible supernatural reference, but can be seen as broadly 'religious' in that they relate to people's perception of their place in the cosmos or – in a form sometimes known as surrogate religion – are a kind of collective activity that inspires intense commitment; for example, football, pop concerts and some aspects of nationalism. In such circumstances they become highly visible socially.[2]

It may seem difficult to differentiate between these concepts at first, but the distinctions will become clearer in the discussion that follows. At the outset, though, it should be emphasized that there are no rigid boundaries in the diffuse territory of popular religious belief. In particular these categories should not be understood as separating out definable groups of people, but rather as exploring a variety of ways in which a single individual not regularly involved in a religious organization could nevertheless be 'religious'. This whole discussion will raise the question of how widely we can usefully extend the definition of 'religion', and the implications of this for the usual perception of post-war Britain as an increasingly 'secular' society – points that will be further explored in the conclusion of this essay.

1 Conventional religion

The lowest common denominator of conventional religion was suggested by a man on a council estate in Hull who generally expressed secular views. He was asked by a researcher, 'If a hospital or similar institution asked you to write your religion on a form, what would you put down?' and replied, 'Bloody Christian, I suppose!' (Forster, 1989, p.481). Evidently, given a

---

[2] The conceptual framework adopted here broadly follows that advanced by Toon (n.d.). There is no space here to consider conceptual problems in detail: the literature is surveyed in Ahern and Davie (1987) and Bailey (1990b). I use the terms 'conventional religion' and 'civil religion' in preference to, respectively, 'civil religion' and 'civic religion' in order to avoid confusion.

certain bureaucratic or institutional pressure and a residual desire not to appear unconventional, many people will express at least a minimal degree of identification with Christianity. A similar inference can be drawn from the comments of an atheist who complained in *The Times* in 1985 that she did not feel a totally comfortable member of the community. 'In an age which is thought to be increasingly godless', she went on, 'so much of our social structure is still wedded to the Christian church, whether society as a whole is conscious of this or not' (Serena Sutcliffe, *The Times*, 24 May 1985).

There is a distinction between unconscious, unarticulated Christianity and the specific beliefs, expressed in a defined theological framework, of the minority of activist churchgoers. However even those who attend church regularly may often have rather vague reasons for doing so. A young female Catholic schoolteacher said:

> Religion is a private, personal thing: you can get on with it if you like. But I don't like very religious people who push it on you … Religion is a way of life; it gives you standards to live by. Living a Christian way of life I think is more important than regular churchgoing. I go to Church because it means that at least once a week I do something with a religious base. Otherwise I would go along all the time without thinking of religion.
>
> (Hornsby-Smith, Lee and Reilly, 1985, p.248)

A Methodist superintendent minister complained in the early 1970s of the absence of specific commitment among the congregations in Staithes:

> I doubt whether some of them have any faith at all. They're worshipping the building, that's all – the bricks and mortar … It's pathetic really.
>
> (Clark, 1982, p.80)

Weekly churchgoing is most likely to be found in Northern Ireland and, within England, in the north west, a reflection presumably of continuing Catholic allegiance to Sunday duty. Such churchgoers are more likely to be female than male, most frequently live in medium-sized towns outside the major conurbations, and generally come from the older age groups, though not necessarily the very elderly (Forster, 1989; Harrison, 1983). This last point raises the problem of whether churchgoing is an activity which fluctuates during the life cycle of an individual – an early Sunday School allegiance giving way in the face of the distractions and pressures of young adulthood, eventually followed by a return to observance as family commitments become less and consciousness of mortality grows – or whether there has been a genuine generational difference between, broadly speaking, those born before and after the Second World War. Survey evidence remains too sketchy for firm conclusions to be drawn but the latter view appears to command greater support among scholars (Davie, 1990, pp.457–62). It was also the perception of one old person interviewed in Aberdeen:

> Well, the young folk winna bother wi' the kirk. The older folk – well, we were brought up wi' the kirk, and of course, naturally, I suppose, it's … the natural thing for ye tae still stick tae yer own beliefs.
>
> (Williams, 1990, p.62)

There is also evidence that churchgoing is higher among the middle class, and the élite in particular, than among the working class. In Aberdeen in 1980, 39 per cent of the higher social groups in a survey of the elderly claimed to attend church at least once a month, but only 15 per cent of the lowest classes (Williams, 1990, p.285). A 1986 survey of 151 MPs, businessmen, academics, lawyers, civil servants, doctors and others indicated that 55 per cent of them claimed to attend worship at least once a month (Homan, 1989, p.147). On the other hand from a sample of 207 working-class Hull residents only 6.8 per cent claimed to attend monthly or more; while 66.2 per cent said they never attended (Forster, 1989, p.485).

In addition to the 20 per cent or so of the population who claim to attend religious worship at least once a month, about a further 20 per cent go once a year or more, presumably at festivals and special occasions, including Harvest and Remembrance Sunday as well as Christmas and Easter. Such infrequent attendance often appears to be associated with significant identification with a particular church or religious organization: thus in 1976, 800 out of 2000 homes in Winterbourne, near Bristol, were prepared to subscribe forty pence regularly for the parish magazine and in 1986 an Anglican church was observed with a regular congregation of 25 but a flower rota of 50 (Bailey, 1976, p.124; Gimson, 1986, p.24). In the case of Staithes such expressions of residual institutional loyalty were at their most forceful at chapel and Sunday School anniversaries and Harvest, rather than the more traditional Christian festivals. An incident at the Bethel Chapel in Staithes at Harvest, 1975, may well, however, suggest another insight into the essentially conservative and undemanding character of such allegiances. The sermon was preceded by a rousing chorus with the words,

> Follow, follow, I will follow Jesus
> Everywhere, anywhere, I will follow on

and the preacher responded by shouting at the congregation: 'I wonder? Would you?' Several remarked afterwards, 'That's not what we come to the Harvest for!' (Clark, 1982, p.105).

A further dimension of conventional religion is indicated by the proportion of 30 to 40 per cent of the population who only attend services for baptisms, weddings and funerals. Rates of baptism declined substantially during the period; in the Church of England from 441,000 in 1951 to 230,000 in 1977, a drop of 48 per cent during a period when the birth-rate fell by only 18 per cent. Nevertheless in 1968, 49 per cent of English babies were still being baptized in the Church of England (Central Statistical Office, 1980, p.244; Pickering, 1974, p.64). In the 1970s and 1980s the rite continued to appeal to those not otherwise closely associated with the church: at Winterbourne in the early 1970s the incumbent noted that out of 175 requests for baptism over a period of six and a half years, only about half a dozen had come from regular churchgoers (Bailey, 1976, p.129). At Staithes in 1975, christenings still were an important aspect of community life (Clark, 1982, pp.125–6) and in Hull in 1986 only one of 207 respondents claimed to be unbaptized and only 7.6 per cent had not had their children christened (Forster, 1989, p.487). Such continuing allegiance to the rite is all the more striking as it is apparently at its strongest in working-class districts otherwise notable for low levels of regular church attendance. Motivation appears to reflect a sense of tradition rather than any religious commitment of an orthodox kind. Herein lies the basis of considerable tension with those clergy who will only baptize the children of regular churchgoers (Ahern and Davie, 1987, pp.100, 118, 127). Thus around a single practice of a conventional religious kind a wide variety of beliefs and values can be found.

In the case of marriage, the popularity of church services similarly declined somewhat but remained substantial. In 1977 the proportion of Registry Office weddings exceeded 50 per cent for the first time in England and Wales, but in Scotland it was still only 38 per cent and in Northern Ireland 9 per cent. These figures are distorted by second and subsequent marriages in which, irrespective of the wishes of the couple, the reluctance of many clergy to marry divorcees was likely to determine the issue. In 1977, 66 per cent of first marriages were held in church in England and Wales and 72 per cent in Scotland (Central Statistical Office, 1980, p.244). These proportions remained almost stable during the 1980s: in 1988, church marriages were still 52 per cent of the total in England and Wales and 58 per cent in Scotland; and 69 per cent and 71 per cent respectively for first marriages (Central Statistical Office, 1990, p.166). Moreover, motives for choosing a Registry Office wedding did not include, except in a small minority of cases, a specific rejection of a church wedding. Rather couples still regarded a religious ceremony as the ideal, but one they could not attain either for financial reasons or because of embarrassment and the need for speed in cases of pregnancy (Forster, 1989, pp.487–9).

Burials and cremations are perhaps the most universally religious rites of passage, although there is no legal requirement for any ceremony.

In practice, however, in nearly every case, except that of stillborn children, some kind of religious ceremony takes place (Pickering, 1974, pp.68–9). There is some evidence that commitment to this was declining a little by the 1980s especially in working-class neighbourhoods. A woman from Bethnal Green commented: 'I don't care what they do. They can put me in a plastic bag and stick me down the chute, you know what I mean?' (Ahern and Davie, 1987, p.98). In Hull, 22.2 per cent of the sample expressed no positive preference for a Christian funeral, although it was notable that only 4.8 per cent specifically did not want such a ceremony, the rest being in the 'don't care', 'don't know' and 'no answer' categories (Forster, 1989, pp.489–90). Generally younger people were less likely to express a preference for a religious ceremony, but whether this reflects generational changes or merely the fact that they had not yet given the matter much thought remains unclear.

Nevertheless it would be unwise to ascribe extensive religious significance to funeral rituals given the degree to which these are shaped by the routines of those most conventional of professionals, undertakers. A bereaved family has to take a strongly individual initiative if regular practice is to be varied in this respect. Moreover the trend since the war away from burial in favour of cremation may also in some respects be interpreted as a symptom of declining religiosity, especially when there is only a brief ceremony at the crematorium not preceded by any church service. The point here is not so much one about religious beliefs relating to the destiny of the body after death, but rather one about what has been called the 'professionalization of death' in which the role of the clergyman and community religious responses has declined in favour of that of the hospital doctor, the crematorium staff and the ubiquitous undertaker (Clark, 1982, pp.134–5).

Accordingly, although there has been in post-war Britain a widespread continuance of occasional participation in religious ceremonies this does not not necessarily imply explicit personal acceptance of Christianity. It can be seen rather as a reflection of tradition, community loyalties and a desire to mark the key events of both the annual round and the personal life cycle. In order to explore this hypothesis we must now examine some further aspects of residual contact with organized religion, before considering the evidence of opinion polls and other sources for what people actually believed in relation to conventional Christian teaching.

Attendance at Sunday School as a child may well have been an important factor in the continuing significance of conventional religious allegiances. Of the 1986 Hull sample, 81.2 per cent had attended Sunday School themselves and 67.1 per cent of those with children sent or had sent them as well. There was, however, a noticeable difference between older and younger people in this respect: in 1986 only 11.8 per cent of parents under 30 sent their children to Sunday School whereas 76.7 per cent of those over 60 had done so. Even allowing for the fact that the figures may be distorted by the proportion of infants too young for Sunday School among the children of the younger age group, these figures still imply an important shift in attitudes in the generation growing up in the 1960s and 1970s (Forster, 1989, pp.490–2). On the other hand they indicate that even in the 1980s a substantial proportion of the adult population had had contact with organized Christianity in childhood. This is confirmed by the 1982 Leeds sample in which 89 per cent of those who did not currently attend religious worship indicated that they had done so at one time in their lives and 'growing up' was a widespread reason for ceasing to do so (Krarup, n.d., pp.28, 30). In Staithes in 1976 from a total population, including adults, of some 1500, over a hundred children were regularly attending Sunday School. Attendance, however, ceased at twelve or thirteen, but, at least among older people, left a sense of lifelong affiliation to the chapel concerned, expressed in attendance at Sunday School anniversaries, which were 'perhaps the most important annual event in the religious life of the village' (Clark, 1982, pp.75–6, 98).

We should also note the large audiences for religious television programmes. The growth of these *outstripped* the increase in the number of households with televisions between 1960 and 1980. In February 1988 the audience for *Songs of Praise* on BBC1 was 6.9 million people and for *Highway* on ITV 7.8 million as compared with a total of 6.7 million for the non-religious alternatives on BBC2 and Channel 4. During that month 87 per cent of a sample claimed to have seen at least one religious programme. Obviously physically sitting in front of the television set during a religious broadcast does not necessarily imply that one is paying attention to it, but, at the very least, failure to switch off or change channel indicates a lack of hostility. The proportion of those who claim to watch religious programmes attentively was smaller, but was nonetheless substantial: 56 per cent in 1968 and in 1987, 39 per cent in Great Britain and 51 per cent in Northern Ireland (Svennevig et al., 1988, pp.9–17).

Most of the evidence discussed so far in relation to conventional religion has been concerned with *participation*, whether in the form of regular attendance at Christian worship, occasional presence at baptisms, marriages and funerals, or at the extreme of passivity, the mere failure to turn off the television set when *Songs of Praise* comes on. It remains, however, to consider the extent to which conventional Christian beliefs have been held by the 'silent majority' of the population. In this territory the researcher is heavily dependent on the slippery evidence of opinion polls, but on a superficial reading some clear trends can be noted. To take a key indicator of Christian orthodoxy: in 1955, 71 per cent of a sample believed Jesus to be the Son of God; in 1963, 60 per cent; and in 1982 in Leeds, only 43 per cent. Belief in life after death was professed by 54 per cent in 1955, and 40 per cent in 1982 (Gallup, 1976, vol. I, pp.405, 682;

Krarup, n.d., pp.48–9). In 1963, 35 per cent of a sample believed in the existence of the devil; in 1973 only 18 per cent (Gallup, 1976, vol. I, p.682; vol. II, pp.1250–1).

It is tempting to conclude that the period saw a steady decline in conventional Christian belief. However, even if this may be broadly true the point should not be stated in simplistic terms. One indication of the difficulties is given by a 1987 poll in which respondents were asked not to choose between alternative statements of who Jesus is, but to indicate on a scale from 'certainly true' to 'certainly not true' their attitude to the single statement 'Jesus Christ is the Son of God'. In Great Britain 45 per cent said it was 'certainly true' and 29 per cent 'probably true', a total of 74 per cent, higher than the figure for 1955 (Svennevig et al., 1988, p.31). We have of course no way of telling how people in 1955 would have responded had they been given a similar range of options, but even if we suppose that all 71 per cent would have said 'certainly' rather than 'probably', it would seem that the trend has not been from acceptance to rejection, but from confidence to uncertainty. Moreover it is worth noting the much higher figures for Northern Ireland in a 1986 poll where 76 per cent considered the statement 'certainly true'; another 16 per cent 'probably true'; 6 per cent said 'don't know'; and only 2 per cent rejected it (Svennevig et al., 1988, p.31).

A further dimension of conventional Christian religiosity of an individual kind is personal Bible reading and prayer. Evidence on these matters is sketchy before the last decade of the period, but in the 1980s it seems that both practices had a significant degree of support. In 1982, 39 per cent of a sample said that they had read the Bible during the last year and attitudes towards it were generally favourable. 62 per cent of individuals and 81 per cent of households possessed a Bible (Harrison, 1983, pp.17, 18, 26). In Hull in 1986, 47.8 per cent of the sample said they believed the Bible to be inspired or dictated by God (Forster, 1989, p.484).

Prayer attracted notably substantial participation: in Leeds in 1982, 71 per cent of the sample professed to pray at some time and 38 per cent of the total said that they did so at least once a week (Krarup, n.d., pp.64–5). In the Hull sample of 1986 the figure was lower, but still a majority at 52.7 per cent (Forster, 1989, p.485). The *Spectator*'s élite sample were not asked whether they prayed themselves, but 48 per cent of them believed that prayer can alter the events of life on earth (Homan, 1989, p.147).

Evidence of a more qualitative kind has emerged from a study of the attitudes of older people in Aberdeen in the years 1978–80 to issues of illness, death and bereavement. Although there were signs of purely secular views, such as the idea of death as annihilation, in general religion had a discernible influence on people's outlook. Behind the activist desire of old people to 'keep going' lay a moral imperative traceable back to the force of the Protestant work ethic in an earlier Scotland. Also widespread was the expectation of reunion with loved ones after death. Many seemed to adhere to some kind of theistic faith, although they did not readily relate it explicitly even to crises in their lives. Moreover apparently 'secular' innovations had an appeal because they struck a chord within an inherited religious consciousness: cremation corresponded to the Puritan tendency to dispose of the body with minimal ceremony; and the hospice movement appeared to draw on an alternative religious tradition of ritual dying (Williams, 1990).

It would be possible to multiply the evidence of surveys and other sources, but space is limited and it should now be possible to suggest some provisional conclusions. Although only a small but not insignificant minority of people in post-war Britain regularly attended church and held orthodox Christian beliefs, a much larger proportion – possibly as much as three-quarters of the population – professed a belief in God, some degree of acceptance of the divinity of Christ, prayed on occasions, possessed a Bible, felt some kind of identification with a religious organization, and attended worship occasionally. Although the numbers of conventional Christians may have declined somewhat during the period and the degree of their commitment weakened, the extent of the changes between the 1950s and the 1980s should not be exaggerated.

2 Civil religion

The concept of civil religion has been defined, with particular reference to the United States, as

> the widespread acceptance by a people of perceived religio-political traits regarding their nation's history and destiny. It relates their society to the realm of absolute meaning, enables them to look at their political community in a special sense, and provides the vision which ties the nation together as an integrated whole.
>
> (Piérard and Linder, 1988, pp.22–3)

This has been seen as expressed in the 'God-language' of American presidents, notably that of Kennedy and Reagan, and in the various rituals associated with the machinery of state, the flag, the school system, and above all, the regular national holidays of Memorial Day and Thanksgiving. It is pertinent here to consider to what extent a parallel exists in the United Kingdom. We begin by noting some significant differences from the context operative in the United States.

Firstly, in Britain it is the monarch and the royal family, rather than an elected politician, who plays the central role in state ceremonial. An American president has an opportunity to articulate and propagate a civil theology in an explicit manner that is denied to a British monarch. Moreover the rituals associated with a presidency have a regularity which those of a monarchy do not have: inaugurations take place every four years, but there was only one coronation during the whole period surveyed in this book. The ceremonial calendar was filled up rather with something entirely lacking in America – the marriages and life cycle rituals of other members of the royal family. Underlying these differences in practice lay one of ideology. Much of the language of American civil religion has been bound up with the exaltation of the republican ideal, but in Britain the monarchy has not so much been idealized in the abstract as idolized in the individual.

Secondly, while in the United States there has been a constitutional separation of church and state since the early nineteenth century, England and Scotland in the late twentieth century still possessed Established Christian churches retaining formal links with the Crown. Thus there was at least the potential for statements of the civil faith to take a form closer to Christian orthodoxy than was the case in America.

Thirdly, the historical pattern of development of ethnicity and nationality in Britain has been substantially different from that in the United States and this has implications for the articulation of national civil identity in religious language. Although religion in Victorian Britain showed considerable diversity, pluralism in America was even more extensive, albeit, with the exception of the Jews, predominantly under the broad umbrella of Christianity. Only in the twentieth century did Britain acquire an ethnic and religious pluralism comparable to that of the USA. Accordingly the cultural pressure to develop a civil religion distinct from orthodox Christianity came relatively late. On the other hand the United Kingdom, unlike the United States, has long encompassed at least four national groups, apart from the dominant English, who have sought an ideological legitimation for their sense of territorial identity: the Welsh, the Scots, Ulster unionists and Irish nationalists. Herein there was a basis for alternative civil religions.

Such complexities must be borne in mind when considering the main features of civil religion in Britain. It will be helpful here to note Durkheim's definition of a religion as 'a unified system of beliefs and practices relative to sacred things' (Durkheim, 1915, p.47) and to comment first on the relevant *beliefs* articulated by the sovereign and then turn to consider the *practice* as represented in state ceremonial.

The most regular and prominent occasion for public utterances by British monarchs since the Second World War has been the annual Christmas broadcast to the Commonwealth, a tradition initiated by George V and steadily maintained by his son and grand-daughter. The broadcasts began on radio, but from 1957 appeared on television as well. On most occasions the tone was one of general moral reflection and exhortation on themes such as the value of family life, service to the community and the promotion of international understanding. Nevertheless both George VI and Elizabeth II also regularly used specifically religious language. Thus in the first post-war Christmas broadcast the King said:

> With my whole heart I pray to God, by whose grace victory has been won, that this Christmas may bring to my peoples all the world over every joy they have dreamed of in the dark days that are gone.

In 1950 he compared the trials of modern life with those of Bunyan's *Pilgrim's Progress* and stressed the crucial importance of preserving the spiritual inheritance of the Commonwealth, founded on faith in God. Two years later, Elizabeth II, in her first Christmas broadcast, movingly and directly asked her peoples to pray for her at her coronation, seeking from God wisdom, strength and faithfulness in service.

Subsequent Christmas broadcasts by Elizabeth II were characterized more by continuity than by change, indicating an identification with Christianity perceived in terms of moral and spiritual values rather than of dogmatic theology. The linking of the broadcasts to a major Christian festival was also important, contrasting with the tendency of other heads of state to link their utterances to days of national rather then religious significance. The Christmas theme helped to secure the continuance of religious reference, especially as the tone appeared resistant to the secularization and commercialization of the festival. This was balanced by awareness that the audience extended throughout the Commonwealth, which checked not only narrow nationalism but also exclusivist Christianity. Even in 1952 the Queen added the qualifying clause 'whatever your religion may be' to her request for prayers and, in 1982, she spoke of how every country in the Commonwealth had become multi-racial and multi-religious. 'At this time of the year', she continued,

> Christians celebrate the birth of their Saviour, but no longer in an exclusive way. We hope that our greetings at Christmas to all people of religious conviction and goodwill will be received with the same understanding that we try to show in receiving the greetings of all other groups at their special seasons.

It would be straining the evidence to claim to discern any pronounced pattern of change in the religious tone of the Christmas broadcasts. The conclusion 'God bless you all' was becoming rather less automatic by the 1980s, but in 1989 Her Majesty could still suppose that 'Many of you will have heard the story of the Good Samaritan', even if she did implicitly qualify this assumption by then repeating the parable. The continuation of the broadcasts as part of the institution of Christmas appeared to command general public assent and it may well be that the Queen's Christian references struck a residual resonance among many who would never listen to religious professionals. As with the popularity of other religious broadcasts such as *Songs of Praise*, acceptability was probably enhanced by the absence of any strong doctrinal claims.

Leading clergy have readily concurred in the Queen's tendency to propagate a generalized Christianity, but sometimes made more explicit its role in the life of the nation. The first post-war archbishop, Geoffrey Fisher, had a strong sense of the identification of the nation with Christianity even if, particularly when preaching on the death of George VI, he acknowledged that declining moral and spiritual standards implied a certain drift away from the tradition (Carpenter, 1958, pp.225–6). His successors proved noticeably more reticent in claiming any specific divine endorsement for the British nation as it stood. In his broadcast on the death of Sir Winston Churchill, Archbishop Ramsey declared that 'Britons should again thank God for one of the great men of all time', but in his tribute to the deceased in the House of Lords he struck an internationalist note, perceiving Sir Winston as a proponent of the broad idea of Christendom and the law of forgiveness as applied to nations (*The Times*, 26, 27 January 1965). In 1977, preaching on the Silver Jubilee of Elizabeth II, Archbishop Coggan called for 'thanksgiving for the way God has guided us and the leadership which he has given us in our Royal House', but the general burden of the sermon was, with substantially greater emphasis than that shown by Fisher in 1952, a call for penitence, rededication and a refounding of national life on Christian principles (*The Times*, 8 June 1977). Most emphatic of all, Archbishop Runcie at the service in July 1982 which followed the Falklands War maintained that

> those who dare to interpret God's will must never claim him as an asset for one nation or group rather than another. War springs from the love and loyalty which should be offered to God being applied to some God substitute, one of the most dangerous being nationalism.[3]

> (*The Times*, 27 July 1982)

What, then, of the *practice* of civil religion in Britain? How do we evaluate the rituals that seemed to give focus to the links between God, the nation, and the various institutions and communities within it? It is necess-

---

[3] The use of religious language in a political context, notably by Margaret Thatcher in the 1980s, is considered in Volume II, Essay 3.

ary here to bear in mind an important analytical distinction between *religious* and *civic* ritual. Religious ritual is founded on the conviction that direct contact is being made with God, or at least with something transcendent; its symbols represent the supernatural; all those present are expected to participate, not just to watch, and this involvement is expected to have wide implications for the way that they live their lives. Civic ritual, on the other hand, affirms the solidarity of an institution or nation state without any necessary supernatural reference; its symbols, such as a flag or mace, strengthen the identity of that group; at ceremonies there is an audience rather than a congregation; and participation is only significant for the individual as it relates to his or her involvement with the institution concerned (Bocock, 1974, pp.60–6).

These theoretical categories were frequently mixed in practice. In particular there were many occasions when an apparently religious element remained in a primarily civic form of ritual. For example, the singing of 'Abide with me' continues a regular part of the proceedings at the Cup Final, and Oxford MAs still kneel at graduation ceremonies to have a Bible placed on their heads and the words '*In nomine Domini et filii et spiritus sancti*' pronounced. It is true that such signs of residual religiosity reveal much more about the force of tradition than about the beliefs of the participants. Nevertheless, they cannot be dismissed entirely: it is significant that for most of the period they were accepted without apparent unease or resentment even by those with no religious allegiance, a sign that there was little public pressure for self-consciously secular ritual. Pure civic ritual can be found in modern Britain, as for example in the degree ceremonies of some of the newer universities, but it is less common than might be expected.

On the other hand, to categorize all rituals with any signs of religious forms and language as 'civil religion' would be to render this concept dangerously broad and diffuse. Accordingly attention will be concentrated here on those rituals where the religious element was stronger and sustained rather than incidental, but civic functions were also very much in evidence. In other words it is suggested that where it is hard to categorize a ceremony as either 'religious' or 'civic' it becomes meaningful to talk of civil religion. In developing this hypothesis we shall first consider the great rituals of state associated with the royal family, and then briefly examine the development of Remembrance Sunday.

The rituals associated with the death of George VI in February 1952 provided a striking expression of the links between religious consciousness and national life. Church services and broadcasts by religious leaders operated as a focus for national mourning: for example, St Paul's Cathedral was crowded out on the day of the King's funeral. In describing the lying-in-state, attended by over 300,000 people in three days, *The Times* used religious language, referring to the people's 'pilgrimage' to the shrine of their late King and reflecting on human transitoriness and divine transcendence (Cannadine, 1983, pp.152–3; *The Times*, 7–16 February 1952). But was this any more than an analogy of religion? On the day of the King's funeral *The Times* leader writer acknowledged that many did not go to church, but still felt that there was a 'subtle connexion between the Throne and the faith of Englishmen'.

> [T]he sentiments evoked by the death and succession of monarchs have a quality which it is no impiety to call religious. They go beyond and beneath the bare externals of the ancient partnership between Church and State ... Monarchy expresses more vividly than any other element in the constitution that conception of honour founded on service, of obedience freely given and repaid by diligent protection, which is the distinguishing mark of the Christian view of leadership.

Theologians, the writer continued, were right to distinguish between secular emotion and religious faith, but religious truth could still be approached through temporal loyalty (*The Times*, 15 February 1952).

Such judgements are ultimately unverifiable, but they seemed to reflect the public mood, stirred particularly by George VI's personal qualities and the sense of mystery readily associated with death. However when a similar assessment was made of the coronation of Elizabeth II in 1953 it proved, academically at least, to be more controversial. Shils and Young argued that the coronation was a reaffirmation of the fundamental moral and religious values of society, focused on the ceremonial acts of the Queen herself, including the oath to maintain the laws of God, the reception of the Bible as a source of inspiration, the anointing as symbol of the sacred nature of her office, and the benediction as an expression of the obligation of her subjects to their sovereign (Shils and Young, 1953, pp.67–70). This view was criticized for confusing the traditional language of the service with the reality of contemporary public beliefs when only a minority were committed to Christianity and the Bible was irrelevant to the lives of most of Elizabeth II's subjects (Birnbaum, 1955, pp.15–16; Bocock, 1985, pp.215–8). The debate might be characterized as a clash between credulous and sceptical sociologists, but it did point up the potential for a disjunction between official forms and popular attitudes. Nevertheless the evidence that such a tension existed seems limited: other studies of the coronation and surveys of attitudes to the monarchy suggest that, even if the public did not necessarily explicitly identify with the symbolism of the service, their involvement with it was sufficiently intense for at least a link with religion to be appropriate (Blumler, 1971, pp.147–50, 170; Cannadine, 1983, pp.153–4). Moreover, even if many features of the ceremonial are better characterized as 'civic' rather than 'religious' ritual, the central acts of the service in the Abbey had an undeniably spiritual and sacramental character as was recognized in the reverent and discreet nature of the television coverage (Bocock, 1974, pp.102–7; Chaney, 1983, pp.130–3).

After 1953 the most numerous irregular major state occasions by far were royal weddings, and this chance consequence of a family life cycle naturally served to shape the nature of the connections between religion and the monarchy. It is worth noting that the practice of holding royal marriages amidst major ceremonial in Westminster Abbey or St Paul's Cathedral dates only from the reign of George V: Queen Victoria's children and grandchildren had usually had relatively small-scale private or semi-private weddings (Cannadine, 1983, p. 151). Between the 1920s and the 1980s, however, high profile weddings focused idealized images of religion, romance and family life. The image of royal marriage presented was a traditionally Christian one, the implications of which were summed up in the comments of the Archbishop of Canterbury on the wedding of the Prince of Wales in 1981, when he suggested that the ceremony was an 'assertion … of … the deepest convictions of our country' and that the royal couple stood as 'representative figures for the nation'.[4] The continuing high-profile commitment of the royal family to church weddings probably strengthened residual attachment to such ceremonies among the population as a whole. At the end of the period, however, the image weakened. At the marriage of the Duke of York in 1986 the religious elements of the ceremony seemed to become more ancillary than central and *The Times* recorded with amusement but no apparent disapproval the malapropism of an American radio commentator who had said that 'the Archbishop of Canterbury has consummated the marriage'. In the early 1990s the divorce of the Princess Royal and the separations of the Prince and Princess of Wales and the Duke and Duchess of York caused the policy of high-profile royal weddings to backfire seriously on the House of Windsor.

Weddings – with the partial exception of that of the heir apparent in 1981 – served more to present the monarchy as an image of earthly human conduct than to link it to reflection on the transcendent and mystical. The Investiture of the Prince of Wales at Caernarfon Castle in 1969 should be seen in a similar light: although a religious service formed part of the proceedings, it was – in accordance with precedent – the Queen herself rather than a senior member of the clergy who crowned her son. Only in the Silver Jubilee of 1977 did the celebrations centre on an event that appeared

---

[4] When such comments are recalled a decade later they appear unwittingly double-edged. They seem, however, to have rung true at the time, an indication of how rapidly circumstances and attitudes changed in the late 1980s and early 1990s. At time of going to press it is impossible yet to offer a satisfactory perspective on recent events in the royal family, but their implications for the future place of the monarchy and religion are likely to be significant.

to give specific religious significance to the monarchy itself, the service in St Paul's officially entitled 'A form of prayer and thanksgiving to Almighty God commemorating the blessings granted to the Queen's most excellent Majesty during the 25 years of her reign'. The spiritual tone was supported by the biblical derivation of the concept of jubilee itself and by the widespread holding of local church services to mark the occasion (*The Times*, 6, 8 June 1977).

The Jubilee thus serves as a partial check to the impression that the period saw a shift in the image of the monarchy from Christian symbol towards a secularly conceived focus of national identity and unity. Furthermore, long perspectives are essential in assessing such matters and the 1990s provided an inadequate vantage point for evaluating changes since 1953: no monarch had died or been crowned for nearly forty years and the public response to such events was hence very much an unknown quantity. Nevertheless two trends are suggestive. Firstly, mass ownership of televisions brought an abrupt end to the Victorian and early twentieth-century practice of holding local church services *simultaneously* with great state occasions. These had encouraged in a specifically religious context a powerful sense of participation in the unseen event. However in 1953 the novel attraction of the silver screen was severely weakening this tradition, and in 1977, the inevitable was recognized in that local Jubilee church services were held not simultaneously with the St Paul's ceremony, but on the previous Sunday. To apply the distinction made earlier, those watching on television appeared much closer to the audience of civic ritual than the congregation of religious ritual. Secondly, the more critical views of the royal family emerging by the 1990s in the light of their all too human failures and limitations seem to reflect a shift from a spiritual and idealized perception of monarchy to a functional and utilitarian one, weakening the religious significance of the coronation rite and other royal rituals.

A further perspective is provided by consideration of the place of Remembrance Day in post-war British life. Between the two world wars Armistice Day had been observed with great ritual and intensity of involvement. The entire nation stopped in the middle of the working week to observe two minutes' silence at 11 a.m. on 11 November. In 1946, however, the commemorations were moved to the Sunday immediately before 11 November, thus reducing the drama and impact of the two minutes' silence and also raising with greater acuteness the question of how – if at all – the proceedings could be linked with orthodox Christianity (Cannadine, 1983, p.234). In 1950 a Yorkshire clergyman attacked the 'theology of Remembrance Sunday' which he understood as implying that God was the special guardian of the nation, and that the war dead, who were instruments in the divine purpose, had the status of Christian martyrs (Pawley, 1950). Pressure for reform of the services grew in the 1960s and resulted in 1968 in official changes including the withdrawal of overtly patriotic hymns and a shift of emphasis away from remembrance towards penitence and commitment (*The Times*, 28 August 1968). During the 1970s and 1980s discussion continued about the nature and significance of the occasion, now that less than half the population could remember either of the two World Wars (*The Times*, 8 August 1980; 10 November 1984). Nevertheless, especially in the wake of the Falklands War of 1982, it was clear that an appreciable basis of public support remained.

Underlying debate over the future of Remembrance Sunday was the difference in emphasis between the churches on the one hand and the British Legion and the state on the other. Within the tradition associated with a well-established event these pressures were usually obscured, but they came into the open in 1982 in connection with the Falklands service. The form of service, reflecting a somewhat uneasy compromise between churchmen and politicians, contained little thanksgiving and no allusion to 'victory'. In his sermon the Archbishop of Canterbury did acknowledge that the decision to take military action, however unpalatable, had been a right one, but as we have seen, he unequivocally condemned nationalism and the general tone of the service implied a seeking for peace and reconciliation. Sir John Biggs-Davison gave forceful utterance to a view apparently shared by other Conservative MPs: 'It was revolting for cringing clergy to misuse St Paul's to throw doubt upon the sacrifices of our fighting men' (*The Times*, 27 July 1982). Bocock (1985, p.213) presents the row as a tension between the needs of 'religious' and 'civic' ritual. This analysis is helpful up to a point, but needs to be refined by the recognition that those who wanted a more nationalistic thanksgiving for victory were not denying the transcendent religious nature of the proceedings, but rather urging their own understanding of the appropriate way in which to relate to God in the circumstances.

Is it then appropriate to recognize the existence of a British civil religion in this period? Much depends on definitions. Only rarely was language used or were rituals held that explicitly exalted the nation itself or claimed God's favour for it in the characteristic manner of American civil religion. A historical perspective is helpful here: extensive public religiosity linked to a strong sense of national mission can be seen as a feature of societies enjoying great or increasing international influence: for example sixteenth-century Spain, or seventeenth-century Holland. In a period of weakness or decline it is harder to maintain the conviction of divine guidance or blessing. At the time of Britain's zenith as a great power in the late nineteenth and early twentieth centuries, claims to God's especial favour were extensively made. Conversely the ascendancy of the United States in the mid twentieth century is reflected in the tone of its civil religion (Smith, 1986; Wolffe, 1989).

Nevertheless, as indicated above, there was a wide range of contexts in which religious language and rituals continued to have a prominent role in British public life, to the extent that a less specific application of the term 'civil religion' would seem valid. The corner-stones of this continuing public acknowledgement of God have been the central role of the church in state ceremonial and the adherence of the monarchy to Christian belief. In Glasgow in 1968 it was noted that positive veneration for the monarchy was frequently associated with a belief in the reality of divine guidance of the nation (Rose and Kavanagh, 1976, p.566). However, the cultural ascendancy of this very traditional alliance of throne and altar weakened somewhat during the period, and there were signs that great set-piece religious services were ceasing to be a focus of near universal consensus.

A parallel agenda of questions relating to the composite nature of the British state was given a sharper edge by the resurgence of nationalist aspirations in Wales, Scotland and Ireland. Even in 1953, in Northern Ireland the coronation of Elizabeth II had provoked demonstrations of dissent from Roman Catholics of a kind inconceivable in mainland Britain (Farrell, 1976, p.204). In Wales the issues were brought into sharp focus by the Investiture of 1969 which, despite the support of the majority of the people of the principality, stirred a substantial protest from nationalists objecting to the imposition of an Englishman as a symbolic leader of their country. A Welsh academic perceived the matter in religious terms. Sensing a need to explore the problem of British identity he continued,

> Not the least of the failures of the established Church of England has been its almost total inability to identify, define, and submit to critical Christian examination the distinctive character, for good and ill, of English nationalism.
>
> (D. Jenkins, The Times, 28 June 1969)

The frustration of the Welsh, Scots and Irish had, he implied, a spiritual as well as a political dimension. There was no event comparable to the Investiture to bring such tensions into the open in Scotland, but the links between the Church of Scotland and Scotland's aspirations to nationhood suggest that it was only through good will and good luck that the constitutional conundrum whereby the Queen was an Anglican in London and a Presbyterian in Edinburgh was not more rigorously tested.[5]

Moreover the status which civil religion gave to Christianity in general and to Anglicanism in particular raised questions that became increasingly apparent. Even in the early 1950s there had been some protests on behalf of the Church of Scotland that it was not being accorded sufficient prominence, but as late as the Silver Jubilee service of 1977 little recognition had been given to other Christian groups. The Archbishop of Westminster took part in the marriage of the Prince of Wales in 1981, but this was the first time a Roman Catholic clergyman had participated in a royal wedding

---

[5] See also Volume II, Essay 3.

since the Revolution of 1688. Surveys in the 1960s and 1970s suggested that enthusiasm for the monarchy was greatest among Anglicans and weakest among Roman Catholics (Blumler, 1971, p.159; Rose and Kavanagh, 1976, pp.556–7). The slow and limited recognition accorded to non-Anglican Christians in state ceremonial had its corollary in the continuing absence of any official participation by non-Christian religious groups. In that negative sense civil religion continued firmly Christian. It remained to be seen whether the need of the state to maintain such ceremonials as an inclusive symbol of national unity would in due course come into conflict with their equally traditional place within the ministrations of the Established church. In the past British Jews were readily prepared to identify themselves with Christian ceremonies, for example on the death of George VI (*The Times*, 15 February 1952), but it did not follow that in the long term Hindus, Muslims and others would adopt the same course.

As the last decade of the century opened, these issues began to come into sharper focus. The future of the monarchy became a matter of public debate in a way it had not been since the abdication of Edward VIII in 1936. The argument was put forward that the coronation service would now be wholly inappropriate in a 'multicultural and secular society', and that a non-religious alternative should be devised (Martin, 1991). However at the service held in May 1991 to mark the conclusion of the Gulf War, there was experimentation rather with a more inclusive variety of religious ritual. The ceremony was held in Glasgow Cathedral under the auspices of the Church of Scotland, but there was participation by the Archbishops of Canterbury and York, the Roman Catholic Archbishop of Glasgow, and the Moderator of the Free Church Federal Council for Wales. At the end of the service a Jewish, a Christian and a Muslim child each read from their respective holy books and linked hands in a prayer for understanding and peace in the world.

Nevertheless, despite such signs of change at the very end of our period, the post-war decades as a whole were characterized by wide public acceptance of a diffuse but still significant Christian element in the ceremonial life of Britain. Taken alongside the evidence advanced in the first section for the continuance of conventional religion in the lives of ordinary people, there is considerable reason for qualifying the view of Britain as a 'godless nation'. However, were the discussion to conclude at this point it would leave unresolved a number of important questions. Is it valid to judge the religious beliefs of the British people solely by reference to the terms set by official Christianity? Are there beliefs and practices that can properly be termed religious, but not in any meaningful sense Christian? To what extent have the cultural and scientific developments of the period been reflected in people's religious consciousness? It is to these and related issues that we shall turn in the remainder of this essay.

3 Common religion

Common religion was defined earlier as belief and practice that relates to the supernatural without being directly associated with formally religious organizations. It is a broad category which for analytical purposes may usefully be considered under four subdivisions: firstly, the supernatural elements in folk tradition; secondly, more generally diffused elements of superstition and supernatural conviction; thirdly, specific beliefs such as astrology and ghosts; and finally, the evidence for direct religious experience relating to a substantial proportion of the population. These categories will be considered in turn. It should be noted at the outset, however, that this is a field which remains significantly under-researched: accordingly the evidence can only be of a provisional and patchy kind.

The first sub-heading, folk religion, has been seen by some writers as a broader category encompassing all forms of non-institutional supernatural belief (Towler, n.d., pp.5–6). The term is used here, however, in a more specific sense relating to those aspects of common religion in post-war Britain that can readily be regarded as part of a longstanding folk tradition. Historical studies, such as those of Keith Thomas on the early modern period and of James Obelkevich on nineteenth-century Lincolnshire, have indicated the richness and importance of such alternative religious beliefs in the past (Obelkevich, 1976; Thomas, 1973). Although the hold of such 'subterranean theologies' existing outside the influence of educated culture (Martin, 1967, pp.74–6) had weakened by the middle of the twentieth century they still retained an appreciable influence. School children in the 1950s held a variety of beliefs relating to white horses, black cats, four-leafed clovers, horseshoes, stones and lucky charms. They also had developed superstitions relating to less traditional features of their environment such as ambulances, trains and women drivers, the last being held to portend bad luck. There were also a wide range of practices associated with particular days in the calendar. Some of these, such as practical joking on 1 April and 1 May had no discernible religious overtones, but others, such as burning effigies of Judas Iscariot on Good Friday and carolling at Christmas reflected an unofficial response to major Christian festivals. Other days were associated with particular superstitions or supernaturalist reference, such as the belief of girls that the first boy they saw on St Valentine's Day would be the one they eventually were to marry, and, in particular, the references to witches, evil spirits and forms of divination associated with Hallowe'en (Opie and Opie, 1959, pp.206–31).

Obviously such traditions reflected various levels of practice 'just for fun' or from kinds of 'half-belief'. Moreover the fact that the available evidence relates mostly to children, who are more likely to be fanciful than are their elders, should also suggest a note of caution. On the other hand, the prevalence of folklore among the youth of the 1950s suggests that it was still known and remembered, if not necessarily acted upon, by a significant proportion of the adult population of the 1960s, 1970s and beyond. Certainly this was true of Staithes in the mid 1970s, where local fishermen held that bad luck should be avoided by not doing anything important on a Friday; not uttering the word 'pig' and not putting to sea after meeting a woman on the way to the boat. There were also folk beliefs associated with the annual round and the individual life cycle, such as the insistence that houses should be clean before midnight on New Year's Eve when the New Year was ritually introduced by a 'first-footer', always a man. Some more conservative families still adhered to taboos relating to women who had recently given birth and to unbaptized infants (Clark, 1982, pp.91–5, 122–3, 151–6).

Nevertheless, it can be suggested that the general trend during the period was that such folk religion declined in importance. The argument for this is dependent not so much on the scanty hard evidence as on the perception that such forms of belief are dependent for their vitality on closely-knit and relatively stable communities, where they can be transmitted and practised. Such traditional social patterns had already been eroded considerably by 1945, and continued to decline during the subsequent decades, leaving isolated and conservative communities such as Staithes much more the exception than the rule. What forms of common religion, then, can be found in the much more individualistic and anonymous world of modern urban Britain?

The second subdivision is generalized superstition and supernaturalism, such as touching wood or fearing the number thirteen. This can in some respects be regarded as a diffused version of the first category, lacking its variety and community character. A sample in the late 1960s of women who had had six or more children, among whom Roman Catholics were of course substantially over-represented (31 per cent of the total), provides an indication of some of the characteristics of such belief. Many were vague about their denominational allegiances and felt that one did not have to go to church in order to believe. Other views frequently expressed included the association of religion with an ethical code; belief in the efficacy of prayer; and a sense that religion was taken for granted, a product of upbringing or a source of meaning in life. Such themes in common religion lacked much theological content and certainly did not represent an overall interlinked system of ideas (Towler and Chamberlain, 1973, pp.1–28).

Evidence for the prevalence or otherwise of superstition in modern urban Britain is particularly scanty and much of what we do know is derived from a survey in 1968 of 181 people from the London Borough of Islington. On the basis of their answers these were classified as:

Very unsuperstitious	28%
Quite unsuperstitious	30%
Quite superstitious	24%
Very superstitious	18%

(Abercrombie et al., 1970, p.110)

Women were more superstitious than men and manual workers more superstitious than non-manual. The young and the elderly were more superstitious than intermediate age groups.

In Islington by far the most common superstition was touching wood, done by over three-quarters of the sample. Just under half would throw salt over their shoulder if spilt; 22 per cent believed in lucky numbers, 15 per cent in not walking under ladders, and 10 per cent held the number thirteen to be unlucky. However, although the popularity of particular super-stitions varied widely, only about 6 to 8 per cent of the sample appeared to take them really seriously: many of those who touched wood said they were doing so from habit, custom or at most a sense of, 'Well, it can't do any harm...', and only a small minority thought failure to do so would make any difference. On the other hand the majority of the much smaller group of people suspicious of the number thirteen would genuinely feel unhappy if they had any association with it. An exception to the general propensity of women to be more superstitious than men was in beliefs relating to gambling and sport. This impression is reinforced by the readiness of professional footballers to see 'luck' as an explanation for the flukes of the game; an excuse for their failures and a force to be channelled in one's favour by particular rituals, such as Nobby Stiles's re-tying of his bootlaces on the field before kick-off (Gowling, 1973).

An important insight derived from the Islington study is that, although those most prone to superstition were quite likely to be *occasional* church attenders, regular churchgoers, who went at least once a month, were notably unsuperstitious. 58 per cent of weekly attenders were in the 'very unsuperstitious' category, compared with 38 per cent of monthly attenders, and 28 per cent of those who never went. Only 5 per cent of weekly attenders compared with 16 per cent of non-attenders were 'very superstitious'. This implies that there was a genuine distinction in ways of being 'religious' between people committed to the teachings and struc-tures of orthodox Christianity on the one hand, and on the other those for whom nominal Christian affiliation was part of a wider collection of supernaturalist and superstitious belief.

Thirdly, we turn to fortune-telling and the paranormal. These are kinds of belief that can usefully be distinguished from those considered under the first two headings in this section, partly because they are associated with a range of 'professional' practitioners; partly because of the quasi-scientific air acquired by some of their claims. The most significant contrast, however, is that while folk religion and superstition appeared to be declining during the period, those other forms of common religion were stable in their appeal or even gaining in popularity. Two Gallup polls from the mid 1970s imply, if anything, that such beliefs were advancing:

Belief in	1973	1975
Black magic	10%	14%
Horoscopes	22%	27%
Ghosts	18%	18%
Flying saucers	15%	20%

(Gallup, 1976, vol. II, pp.1282–3, 1417–8)

The samples from Islington in 1968 and Leeds in 1982 again provide a basis for some more subtle, but still cautious comparisons. In Islington 60 per cent and in Leeds 75 per cent said that they sometimes looked at their horoscopes in the newspapers and 15 per cent and 14 per cent respectively seemed to take them seriously, a noticeably higher proportion than the 6 to 8 per cent of the Islington sample who genuinely believed in superstitions. The motivation of the more sceptical horoscope readers ranged from the half-belief of a woman who said she did it 'for a bit of fun and hope' to those who merely wanted to 'get a laugh'. 18 per cent in Islington and 35 per cent in Leeds said that they had their fortune told at some time, and 23 per cent of the Leeds sample considered that some forms of fortune telling might have something in them. It seems that belief of this kind is substantially more widespread in the lower social classes (Abercrombie, 1970, pp.100–2; Gorer, 1955, pp.267–9; Krarup, pp.38–43). 30 per cent in Islington and 36 per cent in Leeds believed in ghosts and 15 per cent and 14 per cent respectively claimed to have encountered one personally (Abercrombie, 1970, pp.101–2; Krarup, n.d., pp.56–8). A somewhat differently conceived survey in Nottingham yielded a figure of 13 per cent who were classified as having experienced the presence of the deceased or help from them (Hay and Morisy, 1985, pp.214, 217).

The final form of common religion is that of direct religious experience. There had been quite extensive study of people's personal spiritual experience in the United States in the early decades of the twentieth century, an intellectual fashion which had its legacy in William James's classic work, *Varieties of Religious Experience* (1902). The movement declined, however, in the 1920s and 1930s because of the rise of conflicting schools of thought in psychology. In Britain interest revived in the 1960s as a result particularly of the work of Sir Alister Hardy who in 1969 set up the Religious Experience Research Unit in Oxford. Hardy devised a question to tease out the various kinds of private spiritual experience that could occur quite independently of any conventional religious beliefs:

> Have you ever been aware of or influenced by a presence or power, whether you call it God or not, which is different from your everyday self?
>
> (Hay, 1982, p.113)

In August 1976 Hardy's question was included in an N.O.P. opinion poll and yielded a total of 36 per cent of positive responses, made up of 18 per cent of the total who said they had had this kind of experience once or twice; 10 per cent several times; 6 per cent often, and 2 per cent all the time (Hay, 1982, p.118). This was followed by a more detailed sample of 172 people in Nottingham which yielded the much higher positive response rate of 62 per cent. This difference was explained by the researchers as being a result of a more sensitive interview technique which enabled a larger proportion of respondents to talk about experiences which were often intensely personal and a source of some embarrassment. In a trend reminiscent of some other aspects of common religion the frequency of reported experiences of this kind increased in relation to the age of the respondent. However there was a striking contrast with belief in super-stition and horoscopes in that reports were more frequent from people of greater educational attainment: in the N.O.P. poll only 29 per cent of those who left school at 15 gave positive responses, which compared with 65 per cent of a sample of postgraduate students. An exception to this pattern was reported experience of ghosts which was more frequent among the poorly educated (Hay, 1982, pp.120–2; Hay and Morisy, 1985).

The nature of the experiences reported by the Nottingham sample were classified as follows:

	Number	%
Presence of or help from God	30	28
Assistance via prayer	10	9
Intervention or control by a presence not identified as God	14	13
Presence of or help from the deceased	23	22
Premonitions	11	10
Meaningful patterning of events	11	10
Miscellaneous	8	8

(Hay and Morisy, 1985, p.217)

An example of the first category was the following:

> Something woke me up. There was something or somebody by my bed: I wasn't frightened. Within ten minutes the torment I'd felt, for some strange reason left me. I think I had more peace then than I'd had for a long time … I have enough knowledge to know that there's somebody there, to know that I need never be so alone again … he decided I needed help.

Individuals tended to interpret such experiences according to their pre-existing beliefs: for example conventional Christians were likely to see the presence as God or Jesus; those of a more secular frame of mind advanced materialistic or at least quasi-scientific explanations. For others, conscious of a gap between their experience and their beliefs, the former remained unexplained. Although a substantial majority felt that their lives had been enriched by the experience only a small minority perceived it as a 'conversion' which fundamentally altered the direction of their life and their framework of belief (Hay, 1982, pp.142–3; Hay and Morisy, 1985).

It has not been possible here to cover all aspects of common religion, but the examples discussed should be illustrative of other related forms of belief. Although survey evidence has to be treated tentatively because of the difficulties of sampling, drafting questions and obtaining honest responses, there were extensive indications of supernaturalist but non-institutional religion in post-war Britain. Certainly only small minorities of the population regularly engaged in folk practices, saw superstitions as other than habits or figures of speech, really believed that they have seen a ghost or lived in a constant state of mystical religious experience. Nevertheless these minorities did not necessarily consist of the same people and were cumulatively substantial. Moreover the various levels of half-belief testified to by majorities of the population in some instances indicate that in any overall assessment of the religiosity of the British people, common religion should receive significant attention.

4   Invisible and surrogate religion

The forms of belief and practice discussed in the three earlier sections of this essay range widely in character but all share some kind of reference, however diffuse, to supernatural agency. It remains in this final section to consider forms of 'religion', or in some people's eyes, 'pseudo-religion' or 'quasi-religion', which lack that distinguishing feature, but which are still significant in the spiritual life of people in post-war Britain. We shall return to the fundamental question of whether these categories can properly be labelled 'religious' at all, at the end of the section.

The study of invisible religion in Britain since the 1960s has reflected Luckman's hypothesis (1967) that the process by which individuals establish their own consciousness and identity is inevitably associated with the construction of a 'moral universe of meaning', which Luckmann held to be, by definition, a 'religious' process. Whereas in the past such 'moral universes' had been transmitted by formal religious institutions, in modern society, individuals work out their own schemes of values by which they make sense of the world. According to Luckmann, everybody has an inescapable psychological and anthropological need for such a structure of meaning and hence all possess some kind of 'religion'.

Similar ideas have been developed by Edward Bailey, a clergyman who combines parochial responsibilities with research into what he calls 'the implicit religion of contemporary society'. Bailey has categorized the 'creed' of invisible religion in terms of a substantial range of themes and 'integrating foci' which cannot be discussed in detail here. Two key points should, however, be noted. Firstly, Bailey stresses the extent to which people see their selfhood, their personal identity and autonomy, as a matter of ultimate sacredness. They recognize that the self comes to life in relationships with other people and with institutions, but these interactions, if they are to be acceptable, must be governed by the ethic of leaving the self inviolate. In other words, formal religious structures that impose a creed and structure of belief on the individual trespass into the sacred territory of personal identity and are therefore not only intolerable but 'anti-religious'. Secondly, on the other hand, people do perceive Christianity as a framework of values which leaves the self inviolate, but which also provides the moral imperative to help others and to recognize their value and autonomy. Thus the second commandment of Christ to love one's neighbour as oneself, becomes primary. God himself, Christ and the Church are implicitly regarded as symbols rather than as supernatural forces, and are not the central objects of belief and loyalty, but rather subsidiary parts of an overall fabric of values (Bailey, 1990b).[6] Bailey summarizes this widespread philosophy as follows:

> I believe in Christianity
> I insist on the right of everyone to make up his own mind
> And I affirm the value of values ...
> Everyone has to have a value-system;

[6] For this reason Bailey's 'implicit religion' has here been classified as 'invisible religion' under the terms of the definition above (p.310). It must be reiterated, however, that popular religious ideas do not readily fit into superimposed categories, and others might prefer to see what is described in this paragraph as a further manifestation of 'conventional religion'.

'Christianity' is the best value-system available;
Christ, God and the Church stand for 'Christianity'.

(Bailey, 1986b, pp.178–88)

Invisible religion thus has points of contact with conventional religion in that it stimulates the wish to have children christened and to maintain some kind of residual identification with the Church. For many this is expressed in the affection for church buildings themselves which is a widespread feature of English culture. This is illustrated at one level by the appeal of a great medieval cathedral such as Lincoln, dominating the skyline of a small but bustling city and having an inescapable place in the subconscious of its inhabitants and an attraction for hordes of tourists (Clarke, 1986, p.33). On a different level of community is the affection of villagers for 'their' church, or chapel, a loyalty which may be the more intense among those who never or rarely darken its doors (Bailey, 1976, p.133; Clark, 1982, pp.88–90). Overlaying this has been the sense of the church, particularly the Church of England, as part of the very fabric of national identity. Thus one man who said that he had no religion still justified describing himself on a form as 'Church of England':

> Well, it's part of our tradition, because I am British [sic], I am Church of England. It's part of my upbringing, it's part of our way of life. We are a Christian country.[7]

(Cottrell, 1985, p.177)

A similar sentiment lay behind the wide appeal of the work of John Betjeman, encapsulated in lines such as the following:

> The holly in the windy hedge
> And round the Manor House the yew
> Will soon be stripped to deck the ledge
> The altar, font and arch and pew
> So that the villagers can say
> 'The church looks nice' on Christmas Day.

(From 'Christmas', Betjeman, 1958, p.188)

Invisible religion can also be discerned in a variety of contexts completely removed from the structures of conventional religion. Three examples may illustrate some possible applications of the concept. Firstly, the

---

[7] Such sentiments are of course rich in ambiguity in relation to the position of both non-Christian minority ethnic groups, and also of the non-English parts of Britain, but this does not prevent them from being widely held. See above, pp.326–7 and Volume II, Essay 1.

appeal of the countryside, reflecting a cultural tradition that can be traced back to the poems of Wordsworth and the paintings of Constable and Turner, has been a deep current in English life and one with spiritual overtones in that beauty and solitude are seen as lifting people 'out of themselves' (Russell, 1986, pp.44–5). Secondly, the sea can inspire a similar response in a different way, through the seafarer's awareness of being at the mercy of forces beyond human control, the sense of the ship or boat as a place of sacred security, and the ritual character of the disciplined routine of life on board (Clynes, 1986, pp.47–8). Finally, the public house has also been presented as an institution with a religious dimension: it is a building with sacred space (the bar) and a social organization with a strong sense of shared moral values and a fixed pattern of ritual (Bailey, 1976, pp.84–111; Bailey, 1990).

Whereas 'invisible religion' is categorized as being essentially an expression of individual beliefs and values, even if these may be reflected in shared activities, the related category of 'surrogate religion' denotes specific commitments to organizations and ideologies which, while not making supernatural claims, do provide, or claim to provide, an overall scheme of values or 'moral universe'. An interesting borderline case between invisible and surrogate religion is that of the peace movement, which also incidentally provides a significant point of contact with both conventional and orthodox religion. In part, the values expressed by peace activists in the 1960s, '70s and '80s reflected the sacred individualism of invisible religion and the diffused deposit of 'Christianity' in popular culture. On the other hand the movement generated its own organization and ideology which could inspire the intense commitment to an alternative scheme of values which is characteristic of surrogate religion (Martin, 1983).

Four examples will illustrate the dimensions of surrogate religion: football, politics, business and popular science. The committed *football* fan engages in a variety of rituals and adopts a range of symbols centred on the match that suggest an intensity of allegiance comparable to and often exceeding that of the adherent of a conventional religious group. Given the opportunity, fans follow their team all over Europe, and commit all their financial resources and spare time to activities associated with it. Like forms of sectarian religion, football offers an exciting sense of purpose to those whose lives otherwise may be drab and lacking in hope (Coles, 1975). This is not to say that everyone who ever attends a football match is participating in an act that is religious for them in any defensible sense of the word, but in relation to the hard core of fans whose life and values are focused on their team the term 'surrogate religion' finds one of its most clear-cut applications.

In *politics*, a parallel distinction needs to be made between involvement that is active, but not all-consuming, and the surrogate religion that exists when a movement defines the ultimate values and loyalties of the adherent. Accordingly it would usually be inappropriate to see the mainstream British political parties as surrogate religions, although certain aspects of them would provide the germs of such an argument. These include the ritual singing of 'The Red Flag' at Labour Party conferences and the over-riding commitment of the Thatcherite wing of the Conservative Party to the 'free market' during the 1980s. A much more compelling case can be made for viewing as religious parties of the political extremes, particularly those of the far right, such as the National Front and the British National Party. These use ceremonies and symbols, inspire fanatical devotion to their aims and leaders and uphold a sense of historical mission. The point can also be made in relation to the far left, where the adherence to a perceived absolute set of values associated with the movement is similar although here the ritual aspect is less apparent (King, 1986, p.53).

Some *business* organizations, too, can manifest attributes of surrogate religion, depending on their specific ethos and mode of operation. By the 1980s commercial success was increasingly seen as contingent on having a strong corporate image, the cultivation of the single-minded loyalty of the workforce, and the use of 'evangelizing' sales techniques. The widespread application of psychological techniques in relation to recruitment, personnel management and redeployment suggested the subtle and not so subtle imposition of particular frameworks of values (Ahern, 1986, p.51; Long, 1986, p.49). There was a point of contact here with the 'human potential movement', a range of practices developing and promoted in the 1970s and 1980s, designed to unlock under-utilized capacities in the individual psyche. As time went on these movements, such as Transcendental Meditation, became noticeably more spiritual in their orientation (Wallis and Bruce, 1986, pp.157–87).[8]

Finally, a surrogate religion of a rather different kind, because it is associated with a strongly articulated set of beliefs rather than a dominant institution, can be designated by the term *popular science*. This label is chosen to distinguish it from academic science on the one hand and science fiction on the other. Popular science is unlike the former in that it offers dogmatic general interpretations of the world and the nature of human existence; unlike the latter in that these are presented as 'true'.[9] It is most clearly represented in the writings of authors such as Lyall Watson, John Mitchell and Erich von Daniken. Two main strands have been

---

[8]   See also Essay 7, pp.283–4.

[9]   The claim that science in its academic as well as its popular form can be regarded as a form of religion is considered and rejected in Donald Wiebe (1989) 'Is science really an implicit religion?', *Studies in Religion*, 18, pp.171–83.

distinguished: Danikenism, which postulates that the earth was colonized in prehistoric times by spacemen who will shortly be returning to help set up a truly enlightened world government; and Atlanticism, under which human history is perceived as a process of decay from the ideal society existent at the dawn of time in the Lost Continent of Atlantis when men had an absolute knowledge of reality and so were in effect gods. Both are fundamentally at variance with orthodox religion, Danikenism because it rejects transcendent explanations altogether; Atlanticism because it deifies human beings themselves. The widespread appeal of such ideas was indicated by the extensive sales of books that advance them and by their prominence in the tabloid press (Ashworth, 1980, pp.353–76). Psychologists at Newcastle University were disconcerted in the late 1970s to find that 51.4 per cent of a sample of undergraduates from their own institution believed that alien spacecraft had visited the earth and 30.4 per cent thought this the likely origin of myths about ancient gods (Hammerton and Downing, 1979, pp.433–6). In the mid 1980s a researcher in the East End of London encountered a lift engineer who considered Samson's strength would be explained if he came from a spacecraft (Ahern and Davie, 1987, p.108).

The very facility with which instances of invisible and surrogate religion can be multiplied prompts an objection. Are we not in danger of perceiving 'religion' in so many places that the term loses its meaning, and the distinctiveness of the formalized and institutional traditions discussed in the earlier parts of the book becomes obscured? Understandable as this objection is, however, the desire to impose a clearly defined limit to this field of enquiry is likely to distort a human reality in which boundaries are indistinct. It is not possible to say with confidence where 'religion' ends and other things begin.[10] The point can be illustrated by quoting a description of tea-breaks on board ship which might for some seem incongruous if not blasphemous:

> Wet through and numb with cold, men approach the 'Urn' with the solemnity and reverence of one receiving a sacrament: it is the warm 'chalice' of our fellowship, reflecting our common human need. The comment, 'Jesus! that's good!' is our great thanksgiving.

> (Clynes, 1986, p.48)

---

[10] At first sight it might seem possible to resolve the dilemma by setting out a clear definition of 'religion' and then applying it. The problem here is that such a definition would, inevitably, be itself subjective and controversial, and the ambiguity would simply be translated from the sphere of history and sociology to that of philosophy and theology.

To categorize this activity rigidly as either 'religious' or as 'not religious' would be unsatisfactory. It is 'religious' for the writer and bears some resemblance to the Holy Communion ritual of institutional religion. On the other hand, from a 'non-religious' viewpoint one would question whether the resemblance goes much beyond the fact that both involve communal drinking, and wonder whether the writer is imposing his own private religious symbolism on the behaviour of others. The inescapable ambiguities have led to the use of the term 'quasi-religion' in relation to the more marginal aspects of invisible and surrogate religion. Nevertheless to recognize that a boundary is unclear and subjective is not to say that it does not exist. The section now concluded should be read as an attempt to map out that frontier.

5   A religious or a secular Britain?

The preceding sections of this essay have explored the various ways in which the majority of the population not actively involved in any religious tradition can still be regarded as 'religious'. The evidence mustered may well seem hard to reconcile with the general perception that modern Britain is a 'secular' society. The purpose of this concluding section is to suggest a framework for reconciling these apparent conflicts of evidence and interpretation.

It must first be observed that the distinction between a 'religious' and a 'secular' society is a relative, not an absolute, one. Religion did not determine every aspect of life in the Middle Ages; nor has it been wholly eliminated in communist China. No wholly 'religious' or wholly 'secular' society has ever existed. A change in the balance of the religious and the secular is better regarded as movement through a spectrum rather than radical transformation.

The evidence that a substantial movement of this kind occurred over the century between, say, 1880 and 1980 is on one level undeniable, and we can accordingly say that *secularization* occurred. Regular participation in public worship greatly declined and numerous churches were closed. Non-religious interpretations of the world gained ground in intellectual life. Religion moved from the centre of politics, where it had served in many ways to define the positions of the two major parties, to become an issue which engaged very little parliamentary time. The relative quantity and prominence of religious publications substantially decreased. The development of the welfare state superseded many of the social functions of the churches, while their importance in education was noticeably reduced. Instances of the trend could be multiplied.

'Secularization' is therefore a useful historical label for a number of related changes, but the term becomes more controversial when it is made part of a wider theory of society. Secularization, some historians and sociologists argue,[11] is inherently related to 'modernization' and is the inevitable consequence of the Enlightenment of the eighteenth century and the large-scale industrialization of the nineteenth. Although religion will survive among pockets of committed adherents who defy general cultural and social trends, these will be of marginal significance. Much of the evidence addressed in earlier essays in this volume could indeed be squared with such a hypothesis; for example the weakening position of the Christian churches, and the alarm of Jewish leaders about the future of their faith in Britain. True, the resurgence of evangelical Christianity and the consolidation of immigrant religions might point in a different direction, but these could be presented as essentially small-scale reactions against the general trend, their very vigour a sign that resistance to it requires considerable determination. On this hypothesis, the religions of the silent majority are interpreted as the final retreating eddies of the outgoing tide of faith which will themselves shortly disappear.

The theory is compelling, but too tidy. Historically, there is a problem with the chronology, in that in Britain at least, the immediate sequel to the Enlightenment and industrialization was not religious decline, but a great outpouring of energy by the churches, as expressed in the Evangelical Revival of the eighteenth century and the Anglican revival of the nineteenth, and the growing strength of Roman Catholicism and Nonconformity during much of the Victorian era. In the medium term it seemed that Christianity had proved very adaptable to social and cultural change. This is not to deny the reality of 'decline' in the twentieth century, but rather to set it in a somewhat shorter perspective. It becomes possible to postulate a theory of oscillation rather than of linear decline, whereby the secularization (in the narrower objective sense) of the twentieth century is seen as a long reaction to the religiousness of the nineteenth, triggered particularly by factors such as the intellectual reception of Darwin and biblical criticism, and the political, social and cultural impact of the First World War. The pattern can be traced further back into the past: the religious vigour of the nineteenth century was a reaction against the perceived stagnation of the eighteenth, while that itself reflected exhaustion and repugnance after the religious conflicts of the seventeenth century. This crude pattern would need, of course, to be refined in details: in relation to the specific period under consideration here we might note how a modest resurgence of Christianity in the 1950s was followed by the turmoil of the 1960s, and the ambivalences of the 1970s and 1980s.

---

[11] There is no space to give a full account here. See Gilbert (1980), Kent (1987), Thompson (1988) and Wolffe (forthcoming) for further information.

Oscillation is not the same thing as circularity. The twentieth century no more resembles the eighteenth than the Victorian period recreated the Reformation era. Indeed the very religious vitality and variety of the nineteenth century had been a major factor in forcing an end to the control of religious life by Anglican and Presbyterian state churches. As we have seen, Established churches survived in England and Scotland, but their significance was much reduced. It would be hard to conceive of this development being significantly reversed in any conceivable future Britain.

Nevertheless there is a framework here for suggesting that the future could have in store a resurgence of religion. On this hypothesis what now appear as anomalies in relation to the secularization theory become the signs of things to come. Resurgent evangelical Christianity, contemporary movements in Islam, New Religious Movements and New Age cosmologies can all be seen as indications of the turning of the tide. However while some strands of Christianity may share in this process, it could be that a characteristic feature of twenty-first century religion will be a change in the position of Christianity from the normative expression of religion in Britain to a position of prominence but not necessarily of dominance within a much more varied range of religious options. An analogy can be drawn with the situation of the Church of England and the Church of Scotland in nineteenth-century Britain: they proved sufficiently adaptable to survive in a modified form, but the nature of their role was dramatically changed. The experience of one key variety of Christianity in the nineteenth century perhaps indicates the course to be followed by the religion as a whole during the twenty-first.

If this hypothesis is valid, the religions of the silent majority need to be viewed not only as the eddies of a retreating tide, but also as the rock-pools eventually to be refilled and linked together by an advancing one. Religious institutions may indeed have been marginalized in terms of the day-to-day activities of most of the population, but they still had a limited role to play at times of crisis and of celebration, both personal and national. Diffuse supernatural beliefs persisted and surrogate religions flourished. Indeed, while churchgoing declined somewhat and traditional folk religion became less widespread, other forms of 'fringe' belief, such as astrology and popular science, appeared to be gaining ground. It might be objected that the very variety of such alternative spiritualities was a sign of the weakness of organized religion, but it should be noted that even in the midst of the relative official religious vitality of the Victorian era, non-participation and adherence to unofficial beliefs had been widespread.

Speculation about the future is obviously a hazardous undertaking, which is engaged in here only because in the attempt to discern trends in the past there can be few more dangerous fallacies than assuming that the present is the logical rather than accidental endpoint from which one is working. The reader of this essay during the later 1990s and beyond will be better equipped than is the author to judge whether the dominant trend of the twenty-first century is likely to be continued secularization or resurgence of modified religion. At the time of writing, the secularization hypothesis does, however, seem rather less credible than it did a decade or so ago, and signs of an increasing religious reference in both public and private life give some foundation for the suggestion that the tide is turning. It remains to be seen whether this is a lasting trend or a short-term fluctuation.

Meanwhile the very uncertainty and ambivalence identified here can be held to constitute the characteristic nature of the religious position of the silent majority in late twentieth century Britain. At one pole are the committed minorities with integrated frameworks of belief held within institutional religious contexts; at the other pole is another minority with an explicitly and consistently secular view of the world. In between is a great predominance of various shades of partial, personally-constructed, and alternative belief. While for some this may provide the organizing principle of their lives, for most such 'religions' exist in often unresolved tension with a day-to-day life governed by 'pragmatic secularity' (Cottrell, 1985). As John Habgood, Archbishop of York from 1983, put it, 'religion, including the Christian religion, is a much more complicated phenomenon than any simple distinction between believers and non-believers will allow' (Habgood, 1983, p.91).

The readiness of the British – and above all the English – to adhere to diffuse forms of religion can be seen as a result of an historical experience during the preceding two centuries in which there was no clear-cut confrontation between the religious and the secular, of the kind that occurred in nineteenth-century France or twentieth-century Russia. In Britain 'secular' and 'religious' views were intermingled, and the same people could take different sides in different debates (Williams, 1990, p.329). On the other hand the contrasting experience of Ireland, where religion in an official Christian sense has maintained extensive social and political significance, stemmed from the motivating and polarizing potential of confrontation between two varieties of Christianity, which have been, at the very least, symbolic of much wider conflicts.[12] Other societies in which high support for the churches has been associated with a strong link between religion and national identity include Poland and, in a very different way, the United States.

The ambiguities of attitudes in Britain can be encapsulated in two quotations. The first comes from a Roman Catholic priest who was talking to secularly-minded social scientists about the evidence for widespread

---

[12] For fuller discussion of the situation in Northern Ireland, see Volume II, Essay 3.

supernaturalist beliefs among their students. 'It seems', he said, 'that your ministry is no more effective than mine'(Hammerton and Downing, 1979, p. 436). The last word, however, should be given to a widower, explaining to the local parson why he wanted his wife's funeral held in the parish church he never attended: 'I do believe in … Thingummy, and I've brought my children up to be Church of England' (Coombs, 1986, p.56).

Bibliography

ABERCROMBIE, N. et al. (1970) 'Superstition and Religion: the God of the gaps', *A Sociological Yearbook of Religion in Britain*, 3, pp.93–129.

AHERN, G. (1986) '"Rite de Massage", or Redeployment Consulting in Alien England' in Bailey (ed.).

AHERN, G. and DAVIE, G. (1987) *Inner City God: the nature of belief in the inner city*, Hodder and Stoughton, London.

ASHWORTH, C.E. (1980) 'Flying Saucers, Spoon-bending and Atlantis: a structural analysis of new mythologies', *Sociological Review*, 28, pp.353–76

BAILEY, E. (1976) 'The Religion of a Secular Society', PhD thesis, University of Bristol.

(ed.) (1986a) *A Workbook in Popular Religion*, Partners, Dorchester.

(1986b) 'The Religion of the People', in Moss, T. (ed.) *In Search of Christianity*, Firethorn, London.

(1990a) 'Implicit Religion, a Bibliographical Introduction', *Social Compass*, 37, pp.499–509.

(1990b) 'The Implicit Religion of Contemporary Society: some studies and reflections', *Social Compass*, 37, pp.483–97.

BETJEMAN, J. (1958 edn) *Collected Poems*, edited by the Earl of Birkenhead, John Murray, London.

BIRNBAUM, N. (1955) 'Monarchs and sociologists', *Sociological Review*, 3, pp.5–23.

BLUMLER, J.G. et al. (1971) 'Attitudes to the monarchy', *Political Studies*, 19, pp.149–71.

BOCOCK, R. (1974) *Ritual in Industrial Society: a sociological analysis of ritualism in modern England*, Allen and Unwin, London.

(1985) 'Religion in modern Britain', in Bocock and Thompson (eds).

BOCOCK, R. and THOMPSON, K. (eds) (1985) *Religion and Ideology*, Manchester University Press, Manchester.

CANNADINE, D. (1983) 'The context, performance and meaning of ritual: the British monarchy and the invention of tradition, c.1820–1977', in Hobsbawm, E. and Ranger, T. (eds) *The Invention of Tradition*, Cambridge University Press, Cambridge.

CARPENTER, E. (ed.) (1958) *The Archbishop Speaks: addresses and speeches by the Archbishop of Canterbury, The Most Reverend Geoffrey Francis Fisher, PC, GCVO, DD*, Evans Brothers, London.

CENTRAL STATISTICAL OFFICE (1980) *Social Trends*, 10, edited by E.J. Thompson, HMSO, London.

(1990) *Social Trends*, 20, edited by T. Griffin, HMSO, London.

CHANEY, D. (1983) 'A symbolic mirror of ourselves: civic ritual in mass society', *Media, Culture and Society,* 5, pp.119–35. Reprinted in Bocock and Thompson (eds).

CLARK, D. (1982) *Between pulpit and pew: folk religion in a North Yorkshire fishing village,* Cambridge University Press, Cambridge.

CLARKE, P. (1986) 'Lincoln, a Cathedral City' in Bailey (ed.).

CLYNES, B. (1986) 'Reflections of the Sacred' in Bailey (ed.).

COLES, R.W. (1975) 'Football as a surrogate religion', *A Sociological Yearbook of Religion in Britain,* 8, pp.61–77.

COOMBS, M. (1986) 'Believing in Thingummy' in Bailey (ed.).

COTTRELL, M. (1985) 'Secular Beliefs in Contemporary Society', DPhil thesis, University of Oxford.

DAVIE, G. (1990) 'Believing without Belonging: is this the future of religion in Britain?', *Social Compass,* 37, pp.455–69.

DURKHEIM, E. (1915) *The Elementary Forms of the Religious Life,* translated by J.W. Swain, Allen and Unwin, London.

FARRELL, M. (1976) *Northern Ireland: the Orange State,* Pluto Press, London.

FORSTER, P.G. (1989) 'Residual religiosity on a Hull council estate', *Sociological Review,* 37, pp.474–504.

GALLUP, G.H. (1976) *The Gallup International Public Opinion Polls: Great Britain 1937–1975,* 2 vols, Random House, New York.

GILBERT, A.D. (1980) *The Making of Post-Christian Britain: a history of the secularization of modern society,* Longman, London.

GIMSON, A. (1986) 'What Think They of Christ?', *The Spectator,* 13 December, pp.19–24.

GORER, G. (1955) *Exploring English Character,* Cresset, London.

GOWLING, A. (1973) 'The Place of Luck in the Professional Footballer's Life' in Weir, D. (ed.) *Men and Work in Modern Britain,* Fontana, London.

HABGOOD, J. (1983) *Church and Nation in a Secular Age,* Darton, Longman and Todd, London.

HAMMERTON, M. and DOWNING, A.C. (1979) 'Fringe Beliefs amongst Undergraduates', *Theology,* 82, pp.433–6.

HARRISON, J. (1983) *Attitudes to Bible, God, Church,* Bible Society, London.

HAY, D. (1982) *Exploring Inner Space: scientists and religious experience,* Penguin, Harmondsworth.

HAY, D. and MORISY, A. (1985) 'Secular Society, Religious Meanings: a contemporary paradox', *Review of Religious Research,* 26, pp.213–27.

HOMAN, R. (1989) 'Elite Religiosity in Britain', *Archives des Sciences Sociales des Religions,* 67, pp.145–54.

HORNSBY-SMITH, M.P., LEE, R.M. and REILLY, P.A. (1985) 'Common Religion and Customary Religion: a critique and a proposal', *Review of Religious Research,* 26, pp.244–52.

JONES, D.G. and RICHEY, R.E. (eds) (1974) *American Civil Religion,* Harper and Row, New York.

JOWELL, R.G. and AIREY, C. (eds) (1984) *British Social Attitudes: the 1984 Report,* Gower, Aldershot.

JOWELL, R.G., WITHERSPOON, S. and BROOK, L. (eds) (1988) *British Social Attitudes: the fifth report,* Gower, Aldershot.

KENT, J. (1987) *The Unacceptable Face: the modern church in the eyes of the historian*, SCM, London.

KING, C. (1986) 'Popular Religion and Political Extremism' in Bailey (ed.).

KNOTT, K. and TOON, R. (n.d) 'Muslims, Sikhs and Hindus in the UK: problems in the estimation of religious statistics', Religious Research Papers, 6, Department of Sociology, University of Leeds.

KRARUP, H. (n.d.) 'Conventional religion and common religion in Leeds Interview Schedule: basic frequencies by question', Religious Research Papers, 12, Department of Sociology, University of Leeds.

LONG, J. (1986) 'Implicit Religion and the Business Corporation' in Bailey (ed.).

LUCKMANN, T. (1967) *The Invisible Religion: the problem of religion in modern society*, Macmillan, New York (first published in German, 1963).

MARTIN, B. (1983) 'Invisible Religion, Popular Culture and Anti-nuclear sentiment', in Martin, D. and Mullen, P. (eds) *Unholy Warfare: the Church and the bomb*, Blackwell, Oxford.

MARTIN, D. (1967) *A Sociology of English Religion*, Heinemann, London.

MARTIN, G. (1991) 'Throne on the Scrapheap', *The Times Higher Education Supplement*, 5 April, p.13.

MASS OBSERVATION (1947) *Puzzled People: a study in popular attitudes to religion, ethics, progress and politics in a London Borough*, Victor Gollancz, London.

OBELKEVICH, J. (1976) *Religion and Rural Society*, Clarendon Press, Oxford.

OPIE, I. and OPIE, P. (1959) *The Lore and Language of Schoolchildren*, Clarendon Press, Oxford.

PAWLEY, B.C. (1950) 'The Theology of Remembrance Sunday', *Theology*, 53, pp.178–84.

PICKERING, W.S.F. (1974) 'The persistence of rites of passage: towards an explanation', *British Journal of Sociology*, pp.63–78.

PIÉRARD, R.V. and LINDER, R.D. (1988) *Civil Religion and the Presidency*, Zondervan, Grand Rapids.

ROSE, R. and KAVANAGH, D. (1976) 'The Monarchy in Contemporary British Culture', *Comparative Politics*, 8, pp.548–76.

RUSSELL, A. (1986) 'The Countryside, Nature and Popular Religion' in Bailey (ed.).

SHILS, E. and YOUNG, M. (1953) 'The meaning of the coronation', *Sociological Review*, 1, pp.63–82.

SMITH, P. (1986) 'Anglo-American religion and hegemonic change in the world system, c.1870–1980', *British Journal of Sociology*, 37, pp.88–105.

SVENNEVIG, M. et al. (1988) *Godwatching: viewers, religion and television*, Libbey, London.

THOMAS, K. (1973) *Religion and the Decline of Magic*, Penguin, Harmondsworth.

THOMPSON, K. (1988) 'How Religious are the British?' in Thomas, T. (ed.) *The British: their religious beliefs and practices 1800–1986*, Routledge, London.

TOON, R. (n.d.) 'Methodological Problems in the Study of Implicit Religion', Religious Research Papers, 3, Department of Sociology, University of Leeds.

TOWLER, R. (n.d.) 'Conventional and common religion in Great Britain', Religious Research Papers, 11, Department of Sociology, University of Leeds.

TOWLER, R. and CHAMBERLAIN, A. (1973) 'Common Religion', *A Sociological Yearbook of Religion in Britain*, 6, pp.1–28.

WALLIS, R. and BRUCE, S. (1986) *Sociological Theory, Religion and Collective Action*, Queen's University of Belfast, Belfast.

WILLIAMS, R. (1990) *A Protestant Legacy: attitudes to death and illness among older Aberdonians*, Clarendon Press, Oxford.

WOLFFE, J. (1989) 'Evangelicalism in Mid-Nineteenth Century England', in Samuel, R. (ed.) *Patriotism: the making and unmaking of British national identities, Vol. I: Politics*, Routledge, London.

(forthcoming, 1994) *God and Greater Britain: religion and national life 1850–1950*, Routledge, London.

INDEX

occupational status, of Muslims 147
Opus Dei 293

Pakistan, and Islam 141, 142, 146, 158
paranormal experiences 330–1
Parliament, and New Religious
    Movements 290, 291
Paul VI, Pope 35–6
peace movement 336
Pentecostal churches 246, 247, 249–52, 255,
    256
Piara Singh Sambhi 236
pilgrimages, in modern Britain 7–13
politics
    and Anglo-Jewry 116, 127–8
    and Protestant churches 76
    and religion 339
    as surrogate religion 336–7
popular science 337–8
prayers, personal 316
pregnancy, and Hindu rites 198–9
Protestantism 31, 46–88
    in the 1950s 46–55
    in the 1960s 55–68
    in the 1970s and 1980s 68–81
    charismatic movement 14, 28, 29, 66–7,
        69, 77–8, 83–5
    church membership 68–9
    clergy 49
    and conservative theology 71–2
    conservative trends within 65–7, 75
    decline 67, 68–9
    evangelicalism 69, 73–4, 83–5
    and Judaism 126
    and liberal ethics 75
    and liberal theology 67, 70–1, 72–3, 77
    liturgical revision 77–8
    and social issues 75–6
    urban churches 49–50
public house, and invisible religion 336
Punjabi language, and Sikhism 233, 234,
    239
Punjabis
    and Hinduism 188–9
    and Sikhism 209–10, 213, 215–16, 221,
        225–6, 226–7, 240
purdah, and Islam 158

quasi-religion 333, 339
Quoist, Michel 62

race and racism
    and Afro-Caribbean Christians 253–5
    and the Christian churches 63, 75
    and Judaism 127
Radhakrishnan, Sarvepalli 176–7
Rajneeshism 277, 282, 285, 288, 296

Ram Singh 221
Ramsey, Ian, Bishop of Durham 59
Ramsey, Michael, Bishop of Durham and
    Archbishop of Canterbury 38, 47–8, 320
Rastafarianism 265–8, 269, 270, 271
religious pluralism
    in Christianity 18–20, 80, 87–8
    and Judaism 124
    and New Religious Movements 290–4
Remembrance Day services 324–5
residual religious allegiance 31–2
ritual, religious and civic 321
Riza, Ahmad 140
Robinson, John, Bishop of Woolwich,
    Honest to God 56–8, 59, 72
Roman Catholicism 25, 31–46, 80, 82–3
    and Afro-Caribbean Christians 261, 262
    Catholic Charismatic Movement 42, 83
    and the Catholic press 36, 41
    church attendance 31, 45, 311
    converts to 35
    devotional practices 32, 37
    as distinctive sub-culture 32–3
    and ecumenism 78, 79
    and Judaism 125–6
    lay Catholics 45
    Liberation Theology 75
    and the monarchy 326–7
    'People of God' 39
    priests/clergy 41–2, 43, 44, 45
    Vatican II 35–9, 40, 41, 42, 43, 44, 126
    worship 35, 37–8
royal family, and civil religion 318–20,
    321–4
Runcie, Robert, Archbishop of Canterbury
    320, 325
Rushdie, Salman 18–19, 128, 135, 155, 160,
    165–9, 294

Sacks, Dr Jonathan 125, 128, 129
Sant Baba Puran Singh 235
Sant Jarnail Singh Bhinderanwale 226, 237
Satanic Verses (Rushdie) 128, 135, 155,
    165–9
Sathya Sai Baba 192–3
Scarman Report on the Brixton riots 268
Scientific Buddhist Association 282–3
Scientology 277, 284, 289, 290, 300
Scotland
    and civil religion 318, 326
    and ecumenism 78, 79, 80
    marriages 313
    and Protestantism 31
    see also Church of Scotland
secularization 14, 298–9, 339–40
self-religions 283–4
Seventh Day Adventist Church 246

351